U.S. LATINO ISSUES

U.S. LATINO ISSUES

Second Edition

Rodolfo F. Acuña

An Imprint of ABC-CLIO, LLC
Santa Barbara, California • Denver, Colorado

Library of Congress Cataloging-in-Publication Data

Names: Acuña, Rodolfo, author.
Title: U.S. Latino issues / Rodolfo F. Acuña.
Description: Second edition. | Santa Barbara, CA : Greenwood, an imprint of ABC-CLIO, LLC, [2017] | Includes bibliographical references and index.
Identifiers: LCCN 2016037605 (print) | LCCN 2016038119 (ebook) | ISBN 9781440853227 (hardcopy : alk. paper) | ISBN 9781440853234 (ebook)
Subjects: LCSH: Hispanic Americans—Social conditions. | Hispanic Americans—Ethnic identity. | Hispanic Americans--Statistics. | United States—Ethnic relations. | United States—Population. | United States—Relations—Latin America. | Latin America—Relations—United States.
Classification: LCC E184.S75 A67 2017 (print) | LCC E184.S75 (ebook) | DDC 305.868/073—dc23
LC record available at https://lccn.loc.gov/2016037605

ISBN: 978-1-4408-5322-7
EISBN: 978-1-4408-5323-4

21 20 19 18 17 1 2 3 4 5

This book is also available as an eBook.

Greenwood
An Imprint of ABC-CLIO, LLC

ABC-CLIO, LLC
130 Cremona Drive, P.O. Box 1911
Santa Barbara, California 93116-1911
www.abc-clio.com

This book is printed on acid-free paper ∞

Manufactured in the United States of America

Contents

Preface

A word about *U.S. Latino Issues*. This is not your standard textbook or monograph. Instead, it involves a pedagogy that encourages the use of inquiry, a Socratic question and answer approach. It was in part influenced by the pedagogical reform after the launching of Sputnik in the fall of 1957 and the work of reformers such as Edwin Fenton and Paulo Freire in the 1960s. Mesoamerican societies also developed learning systems that were more praxis centered than our own. The story in these cases was used to encourage students to answer and ask questions. Thus, the narratives in *U.S. Latino Issues* are not all inclusive. For instance, when dealing with gender, sexuality is seemingly left out of the narrative. The presentations are not meant to be depositories of knowledge but epistemological launching pads that allow students to explore. For me it is a return to my roots. My first three textbooks, *The Story of the Mexican American*, 1969, 3rd grade; *A Mexican American Chronicle*, 1969, high school; and *Cultures in Conflict*, 1970, 5th grade; were based on the Inquiry Method. They were influenced by educational reformers Edwin Fenton and Paulo Freire. The most prominent of this genre was written by historians John Caughey, John Hope Franklin, and Ernest May, *Land of the Free: A History of United States*. Hopefully this book will encourage experimentation.

Acknowledgments

I want to acknowledge the support of Dr. Kimberly Kennedy White for her professionalism. She has made this a better book. I would also like to acknowledge Rashmi Malhotra at Westchester Publishing Services for her contribution to the production of the book. So much of the learning about Chicanas/os, Central Americans, and Latin Americans comes from personal contact. I owe a great debt to my Chicana/o, Mexican, and Central American students. Thanks to the many contributors to the book; you are my teachers. To my sons, Frank and Walter, and my granddaughters and grandsons, and especially my grandson Nick, who died this past summer—died of anxiety. I am forever grateful to my wife, Lupita, and my daughter, Angela. My wife is a special person and without her this book would not have been possible. As I have repeatedly said, writing does not come without a price; the writer steals time from those around him. I have stolen a lot of time from my wife and daughter, and I hope this book's contribution is worth some of the lost moments.

Introduction

In the fall of 1957, American education launched an era of intense educational reform. The Soviet Union beat the United States into space by putting Sputnik into orbit, which led to cries for educational reform. Initially, reformers just wanted to go "back to the basics" and convert education into math and science factories. However, many educational reformers wanted to widen educational reform to include languages, the social sciences, and humanities. They believed that the problem was not that the United States did not get to outer space before the Russians, but how and what American students learned.

The sense of urgency produced by the Sputnik launch and the fear that perhaps the United States was not number one made it clear that it was in the national interest to change education, not only for the curricula in mathematics and science, but also for the humanities and social sciences as well as for education. This atmosphere opened the door for reformers such as Edwin Fenton from the Carnegie Institute, who claimed that a key to better learning was the use of an Inquiry Method to sharpen the critical thinking of students. This method was not new; in fact, it dated back to the Greek philosopher Socrates (c. 470 BCE–c. 399 BCE). Indeed, most ancient civilizations have had methods of learning. Learning to resolve conflicts was considered just as important as practical results such as putting someone into space.

Are Hispanics Latinos? Are Latinos Mexican Americans?

U.S. Latino Issues concerns a group of people who the U.S. Census Bureau calls Latinas/os or Hispanics. Although Latinas/os can be of different nationalities, as with Asian Americans, the census lumps them together for the census count; however, in 2010, it allowed them to list mixed ethnicities. When and why the Latina/o identity came about is a more involved story. It is said that originally the term *Latin America* was used by France under Napoleon III when he wanted to put Emperor Maximillian on the Mexican throne. The term implied the cultural kinship with France. The French named the countries Latin America in order to be more compatible. Today, politicians, the media, and marketers find it convenient to deal with the different U.S. Spanish-speaking people under the same umbrella.

Many people with Spanish surnames contest the term *Latino*. They say it is misleading because no Latino or Hispanic nationality exists since no Latino state exists. Therefore, generalizing the term *Latino* slights the various national identities included under the umbrella. Some critics argue that the Latino identity was artificially constructed by the U.S. government. According to critics, the purpose was to erase the collective historical memory of the various Spanish-speaking groups. Critics also accuse the supporters of the term *Latino* of being cheerleaders for a system that celebrates the false impression that Latinos are making it in society, resulting in flag-waving ceremonies that celebrate the notion, "We are number one." Finally, the Latino identity erases the reality that most people under this umbrella are of mixed-race background.

The supporters of the term *Latino* argue times have changed and national identities as we once knew them are outdated. They believe clinging to national identities promotes nationalism, factionalism, and thus, division. They argue that the term *Latino* is more inclusive. This school of belief is divided into two factions, one preferring the term *Hispanic* and the other preferring *Latino*. The popularity of these terms is greater within professional and business groups who live closest to Anglo-Americans and who want to forge a national presence. In turn, government agencies support the trend for statistical reasons and find it more convenient to lump the disparate groups into one.

With this controversy in mind, *U.S. Latino Issues* turns to introducing the different nationalities within the contested Latino identity, taking into account their individual realities without debating the political correctness of the term, the definition of which depends on the person's view of the world.

Why do you think that the term Latina/o is used?

WHO ARE THEY AND HOW MANY SO-CALLED U.S. LATINAS/OS ARE THERE?

The 2000 Census Report listed 35.3 million Latinos in the United States. Latinos made up 12.5 percent of the nation's population, and by the year 2005, Latinos were the largest minority in the United States, outnumbering African Americans and totaling 45.6 million in 2014 (Krogstad and Lopez, 2015). The population of U.S. Latinos grew 60 percent between the 1990 census and 2000 when the Census Bureau counted 22.4 million of them. Mexican Americans were the largest group, making up 58.5 percent of total Latinos, and probably more if the census acknowledged that 17.3 percent of the respondents marked themselves as Latino or Hispanic without designating a nationality. This growth continued over the next decade, and by 2015 Latinos numbering 55 million had become a national minority, with considerable growth in the South. Because of the economic depression, however, the Mexican population declined from 2009 to 2014, with a net loss of 140,000 from 2009 to 2014 ("Latino Population Booms In the South," 2013).

By the turn into the 21st century, there was a significant growth of new immigrants from the Dominican Republic, Central America, and South America. The growth of the new Latino population created tension as the numbers of old Latino groups, such as Cuban Americans, who registered 2 million by 2015, are being challenged for leadership by the newcomers (González-Barrera, 2015). The Pew Research Center estimated 1.8 million Dominican origin people resided in the United States in 2013 (982,000 were foreign-born) and 2 million Salvadorans (1.2 million were foreign-born) (López, "Salvadoran," 2015). Also, the new Latinas/os were growing more rapidly than Puerto Ricans, who are by definition U.S.-born, or Cubans, who are 57 percent foreign-born "compared with 35% of Hispanics" (López, "Dominican," 2015; Krogstad, 2015; López, "Cubans," 2015). Note: There has been a recent heavy migration from Puerto Rico to the mainland (http://www.pewhispanic.org/2014/08/11/puerto-rican-population-declines-on-island-grows-on-u-s-mainland).

U.S. Latinas/os, especially those of Mexican ancestry, are young compared to the rest of the U.S. population. According to the Pew Research Center, the median age of Latinos in 2015 was 29. Although they are younger than most other racial or ethnic groups, they are growing older as a group. "By comparison, the median age for non-Hispanic blacks is 34; it's 43 for non-Hispanic whites and 36 for Asians" (Krogstad & López, 2015). Meanwhile, the median age of Mexicans nationwide is even lower at 26 (López, "Mexican," 2015). (Some 35 percent of Mexican Americans were born in Mexico.) (Table I.1)

Table I.1 2010 U.S. Census Bureau Latino Results

Subject	Number	Percent
Hispanic or Latino origin		
Total population	308,745,536	100.0
Hispanic or Latino (of any race)	50,477,594	12.5
Mexican	31,798,258	63.0
Puerto Rican	4,623,716	9.2
Cuban	1,785,547	3.5
Other Hispanic or Latino	12,270,073	24.3
Dominican (Dominican Republic)	1,414,703	2.8
Central American (excludes Mexican)	3,998,280	7.9
Costa Rican	126,418	0.3
Guatemalan	1,044,209	2.1
Honduran	633,401	1.3
Nicaraguan	348,202	0.7
Panamanian	165,456	0.3
Salvadoran	1,648,968	3.3
Other Central American	31,626	0
South American	2,769,434	5.5
Argentinean	224,952	0.4
Bolivian	99,210	0.2
Chilean	126,810	0.
Colombian	908,734	1.8
Ecuadorian	564,631	1.1
Paraguayan	20,023	—
Peruvian	531,358	1.1
Uruguayan	56,884	0.1
Venezuelan	215,023	0.4
Other South American	21,809	0.2
Spaniard	635,253	1.3
All other Hispanic or Latino	3,452,403	6.8

Source: Bureau of the Census, The Hispanic Population: 2010 Census, May 2011. http://www.census.gov/prod/cen2010/briefs/c2010br-04.pdf

In looking at the table, why would many observers mistake all Latinas/os for Mexicans?

Mexicans have been in the United States longer than any Latino group. That is because the Southwest once belonged to the Mexican nation and it shares a 2,000-mile border with the United States. Ninety percent have indigenous DNA. The second largest Latino group is the Puerto Ricans, who numbered 4,623,716 million, or 9.6 percent of the Latino total. According to a 2012 Pew report, the Puerto Rican community in the United States had a median age of 27, contrasted to the U.S. average of 37. Central Americans had a median age of 29.2. The total U.S. Dominican population is 1,414,703 million. An estimated 2.0 million Latinos of Cuban origin resided in the United States in 2011 (Puerto Ricans in the United States, 2013; Brown and Patten, 2013a–d).

It was reported in 2012 that Latinos accounted for 26.3 percent of the U.S. population younger than age 1. The share for whites was 49.6 percent, African Americans, 13.7 percent, and Asians 4.4 percent. Because U.S. Latinos are young, they have a higher birthrate than white Americans. These figures are even more dramatic considering that Latinos compose half of all infants born in California (Passel, Livingston, and Cohn, 2012).

Are Latinos achieving the American Dream?

Apart from differences in nationality among U.S. Latinos, class and gender differences exist. U.S. Latinos are represented heavily in all classes. Representation in the middle class is generally the measure of whether an individual or a group has achieved the American Dream. That is why so many Latinos are obsessed with obtaining a college education, since it is an indication of upward mobility. Another measure is income. It is reported that 37 percent of Latino families make between $40,000 and $100,000 a year. What is deceiving is that few of these families would qualify to buy a home or even rent one in Los Angeles, San Francisco, or New York (Benson, 2013; Kotkin and Cox, 2015; Second-Generation Americans, 2013).

Some 13.1 million Latinos lived in poverty according to the 2014 poverty rate—23.6 percent. The poverty rate and the number in poverty for children under age 18 was 20.7 percent, 15.0 million. Gender differences, rates for immigrants, and being 65 and older were also factors. Latinos in 2014 cited education as a top issue, ranking with the economy and above health care and immigration (Krogstad, 2015).

What prevents Latinos from achieving the American Dream?

There are forces working against this Dream of a Higher Education. Too many Latinos drop out of high school, and although the school dropout rate fell from 32 percent in 2000 to 14 percent in 2013, Latino students from ages 18 to 24 lagged behind the other groups (Fry, 2014). Over the same period, the U.S. national dropout rate fell from 12 to 7 percent. The Latino dropout rate remained higher than African Americans (8 percent), whites (5 percent), and Asians (4 percent).

Poverty among Latinos became more acute as the government reduced benefits such as food stamps, which hunger forced them to take. In fact, the cause of poverty among Latinos is not that Latinos are not working. In 2000, 80.4 percent of Latino males were working compared with 74.3 percent of non-Latino white males, suggesting that Latinos were poor not because they did not work, but because employers did not pay Latinos sufficiently (Yzaguirre, 2001). Thanks to the Bureau of Labor Statistics, it is clear that the demographic shift with respect to ethnicity was not negative. Sparked by immigration and relatively high fertility rates, the number of Latinos in the civilian workforce more than doubled, from 10.7 million to 25.4 million workers between 1990 and 2014. This 137 percent increase dwarfed the 13 percent increase in the number of non-Latino civilian workers—almost doubling the representation of Latinos among all civilian workers from 8.5 percent to 16.0 percent ("The Increasing Importance of Hispanics in the U.S. Workforce," 2015).

As with class status, gender played a role within each nationality. As late as 1997, 51 percent of black women worked full time compared to 42 percent of white women and 35 percent of Hispanic women who were 16 years and over. By 2014, 51.4 percent of Latinas 16 and over worked in the civilian labor force (Household Data Annual Averages, 2014).

At the bachelor's degree level, the number of degrees conferred to Latino students more than doubled between academic years 2002–03 and 2012–13. In 2002–03 Latinas received 7.3 percent and Latinos 6.4 percent of the total college degrees. By 2012–13 Latinas received 11 percent and Latinos 9.8 percent (http://nces.ed.gov/programs/digest/d16/tables/dt16_322.20.asp?current=yes). Despite the progress, Latinas and Latinos encounter obstacles in higher education. Many are first-generation college students; there are low expectations as well as financial constraints and a lack of English and knowledge skills about how to apply for and graduate from college. Often parents cannot or are reluctant to fill out financial aid or admission papers. They are hesitant in allowing their children, especially their daughters, to leave home. Although parents often emphasize to their daughters that education is key to avoiding working from sunrise to sunset, it is a big step. The progress of Latinos is vital. The Center for American Progress writes that "Latinas are a growing and influential constituency in the United States. The Latina share of the female population in the United States will increase from 16.4 percent today to 25.7 percent in 2050."

As of 2013, according to the Center, "Latinas owned about 1 out of every 10 women-owned businesses." But despite the progress, Latinas earned 55 cents to the dollar when compared to white, non-Hispanic males. They earned 78.1 cents to the dollar in comparison to white women and 88 percent of Latinas/os (Jackson, 2013).

Why is it essential to talk about Latina progress? Is it fair to be paid less for equal work?

For the sake of inclusion from now on we will use the term Latinas/os in order to include Latina females.

WHERE DO LATINAS/OS LIVE? *DOES IT MATTER?*

Where Latinas/os live greatly depends on when they came to the United States and on their economic class. Of the Latino nations, Mexico is the closest in proximity to the United States. Thus, at first Mexicans resided primarily in the border states and on the West Coast, but during the 1990s this changed and Mexicans spread throughout the nation. Most of the new Latinos (close to 1.4 million) lived in New York State and on the U.S. mainland.

According to the Pew Research Center, the Latina/o population is still anchored in traditional settlement areas, although in recent years it has dispersed across the United States. The largest 100 counties where they live have 71 percent of Latinas/os. Los Angeles County has 4.9 million Latinas/os—9 percent of U.S. Latinas/os. The Latina/o share of these counties, however, has fallen from 75 percent in 2000 and 78 percent in 1990 as the population has grown outside of the 100 counties. The same report indicates that 52 percent of the 100 counties are in three states—California, Texas, and Florida. Along with Arizona, New Mexico, New York, New Jersey, and Illinois, eight states have 74 percent of the Latina/o population. Nevertheless, their share too is down from 79 percent in 2000 and 84% in 1990, indicating the dispersal of the U.S. Latina/o population (Brown and Lopez, 2013). However, in 2011, out of the ten states with the most Latinos, Mexicans were the largest group in California, Texas, Illinois, Arizona, Colorado, New Mexico, and Georgia; Puerto Ricans were the largest group in New York and New Jersey and Cubans were the largest in Florida.

According to the 2010 U.S. Census, the Latina/o population increased by 15.2 million between 2000 and 2010. It accounted for over half of the 27.3 million increase in the total U.S. population. Between 2000 and 2010, it grew by 43 percent, "which was four times the growth in the total population at 10 percent" (Ennis, Ríos-Varga, and Albert, 2010). The diversity of Latina/o population varies widely. For example, in metropolitan New York, Puerto Ricans are 28 percent of Latinas/os, followed by Dominicans at 21 percent and Mexicans at 12 percent. Puerto Ricans are 51 percent of Latinas/os in Orlando, 34 percent in Tampa–St Petersburg, 56 percent in Philadelphia, 29 percent in Boston, and 69 percent in Hartford. Puerto Ricans are U.S. citizens and the island of Puerto Rico belongs to the United States, so Puerto Ricans are not considered to be typical immigrants. Cubans are 55 percent in Miami, 21 percent in Fort Lauderdale, and 21 percent in West Palm Beach (21%). Salvadorians are the most numerous at 32 percent in metropolitan Washington, D.C. ("Where do most Hispanics in the USA live?", 2013).

THE HISTORY

Some Americans of Mexican descent were in the Southwest long before Anglo-Americans arrived in what is now the United States. The Southwest became part of the United States because of two wars, the Texas War of 1836 and the Mexican American War that ended in 1848 in which the United States took half of Mexico's land. The Gadsden Purchase of 1853 also contributed to the Southwest becoming part of the United States. The large-scale Mexican immigration throughout the twentieth century augmented their numbers.

Various factors drove Mexican immigration to the United States, including the uprooting of Mexicans in the last quarter of the 19th century as the railroads, financed by foreign capital, advanced the commercialization of agriculture, displacing many small farmers. In addition, industrialization created a demand for Mexican workers in the United States. Labor contractors recruited them to work on the railroads, mines, farms, stockyards, and in other industries. As the need for labor pulled Mexicans into the United States, each wave of Mexican immigration met with intense discrimination as Mexicans established colonies (*colonias*) and enclaves (*barrios*) and their own community, religious, and labor organizations. During the first quarter of the 20th century, the bulk of the Mexican migration to the United States was to Texas and Arizona. However, by the second quarter of that century, California became a favorite destination for Mexicans.

Where do Latinas/os live?

During the 1980s, Mexican immigrants continued overwhelmingly to settle in California. Changes took place, and during the 1990s the trends shifted. Work opportunities in poultry plants, slaughterhouses, and restaurants pulled Mexican immigrants to the South and Midwest. Mexicans also harvested tobacco and other crops there. Besides a large population in California, Mexicans, along with other Latinos, now make up almost one-quarter of the population in some counties of North Carolina, Georgia, Iowa, Arkansas, Minnesota, and Nebraska. This movement has transformed the Mexican American population from a regional minority to a national presence. This migration also paved the way for other Latinos, who in previous decades had primarily moved to large cities.

Puerto Rico became a possession of the United States in 1898 after the Spanish–American War and the signing of the Treaty of Paris. In reality, Puerto Ricans did not have a choice in this annexation. Ever since the annexation, Puerto Ricans have struggled to define themselves. Some wish to become a state within the American republic and others are fighting for the independence of Puerto Rico. Technically, Puerto Ricans became American citizens in 1917 under the Jones Act, but conditions on the island resembled those of some third-world countries. Puerto Ricans began trickling into the United States soon after annexation, and the 1920 census registered 41,094 Latinos in New York City alone. Of these, 21.2 percent were Cuban and West Indian, 17.9 percent Puerto Rican, and 18.9 percent were Central and South American. The rest of the Latino population, almost 36 percent, was from Spain. This number grew to 110,223 ten years later, and the Puerto Rican population grew to 40.7 percent (44,930). The Puerto Rican migration quickened and spread to other parts of the United States around World War II. In the state of New York, the Puerto Rican population rose from 61,463 in 1940 to 811,843 in 1970.[1]

After 1959, with the success of the Cuban Revolution, Cuban political refugees came in larger numbers to the United States. From 1959 to

1963, 215,000 Cubans arrived in the United States. The 1966 Cuban Adjustment Act gave Cubans political asylum and made Cubans eligible for government-sponsored and subsidized programs. Cubans dominated Miami, the closest city to Cuba, and formed a sizable number in New York and New Jersey. The Miami Cuban community grew from 50,000 to 580,000 between 1960 and 1980. The white upper- and middle-class composition of Cubans gave them more power and visibility than other Latinos. Despite economic and social advantages, however, Cubans suffered discrimination. Cubans also have remained culturally cohesive, acculturating rather than assimilating into American society. Cuban Americans are far from homogeneous, however. Although the first wave was mostly whites of Spanish origin (criollo), other waves in the 1980s included working-class Africans as well as white and mixed blood Cubans. Cuban leader Fidel Castro allowed 125,000 Cubans to leave the island for four months during the Mariel boat lift (named after the Port of Mariel) in 1980. Meanwhile, economic conditions on the island worsened as subsidies from the Soviet Union ended and a U.S. embargo isolated the Cuban government economically.

The Dominican Republic shares the large island of Hispaniola with Haiti, once a French possession. By 1960, 13,293 Dominicans lived in New York City; 10 years later, 66,914 resided there. The Dominican migration accelerated in 1960 with the assassination of dictator Rafael Trujillo to the United States. This first wave of migration consisted of many wealthy Dominicans who had benefited from the Trujillo regime. A U.S.-sponsored 1963 coup toppled elected president Juan Bosch of the Dominican Revolutionary Party. After this point the Dominican Republic was in turmoil suffering a civil war. In April 1965, the 3rd Brigade of the 82nd Airborne Division landed at the San Isidro Air Base. These events led to the further intervention of the Organization of American States. The chaos drove many progressives out of the country. According to one observer, the Dominicans "[I]n steadily rising numbers but almost unnoticed . . . have been arriving for almost four decades now. Outside New York City and a few other places in the northeast, not many Americans seemed to have noticed their growing presence" (Castro, 1997). Perhaps the Dominican Republic is best known for its baseball superstars such as Sammy Sosa, Alex Rodríguez and Manny Ramírez. Between 1961 and 1986, some 400,000 Dominicans migrated to the United States, primarily to New York City, with another 44,000 migrating to Puerto Rico. (The 2010 census estimated a population of 68,036 Dominicans in Puerto Rico.) While Census 2000 counted 764,945 Dominicans, other sources estimated that there were 1.5 million

Dominicans by 2000. (The Dominicans have a sizable undocumented population.) While many Dominicans are poor, the population has a sizable middle class who fled the island after the overthrow of Trujillo, and who now operate businesses in the United States. There are now 1,414,703 Dominicans, 2.8 percent of the U.S. population (Castro, 1997).

Central Americans are the newest arrivals, representing 4.8 percent of the U.S. Latino presence. (This probably is a dramatic undercount.) In 20 years, Central Americans have developed many eateries and community organizations. In addition, 1979 was a watershed year for Central America, and larger numbers began arriving in the United States because of the instability back home. The overthrow of dictator Anastacio Somoza in Nicaragua destabilized the region, and rebels launched wars of liberation in Guatemala and El Salvador, where the military killed 200,000 and 50,000, respectively. To a lesser extent, Panamanians, Hondurans, and Costa Ricans also migrated north. Generally, Central Americans as a group are less educated, work at menial employment, and are darker than South Americans and Cubans. Most live in Latino neighborhoods, keeping their first culture intact. The 2010 Census counted 3,998,280 Central Americans, 7.9 percent of U.S. residents.

In Nicaragua, after the overthrow of Somoza, the Sandinista Party assumed control of the government. The Sandinistas sought economic aid, which the Soviet Union volunteered. The United States funded the counterrevolutionaries, whom Americans called Contras, and because of the U.S. economic embargo, the Sandinista government was unable to stabilize. In the 1980s, one-tenth of Nicaraguans left their country, a third of them college-educated, white-collar workers or businesspeople. Many Nicaraguans entered the United States as political refugees and many settled in the Miami area. In 1980, an estimated 25,000 Nicaraguans lived in the United States; in 2000 the census reported the number rose to 177,684 (Shorris, 1992; Suro, 1999). As we shall see, this number has changed dramatically.

The largest group of Central Americans is Salvadoran, who have large populations in Southern California, Houston, Washington, D.C., and New York. Most came to the United States because a bloody civil war ripped through the country from 1980 to 1992. After Puerto Rico, El Salvador is the most densely populated country in Latin America. The Salvadoran civil war had many causes, not the least of which was the monopoly of the country's land by slightly more than a dozen elite families. During the 1980s, the military imposed a dictatorship as the guerrilla forces under the Farabundo Martí National Liberation Front (FMLN) fought to break this control. The 1980 census counted about 30,000

Salvadorans in the United States; the 2000 census counted 655,165 Salvadorans. The 2010 census counted 1,648,968 Salvadorans—3.3 percent; that number is probably closer to 2 million today.

Guatemala has been in political turmoil for much of its existence. The latest civil war came about when the CIA sponsored the overthrow of President Jacob Arbenz in 1954 when he threatened the plantations of the United Fruit Company. The civil war escalated in the 1980s as the United States supported the military government, and the military killed more than 200,000 Guatemalans. The 1980 census showed about 71,000 Guatemalans living in the United States. This number grew from 230,000 in 1990 to 372,487 in 2000 and 1,044,209, 2.1 percent, in 2010. According to some sources, many Guatemalans in the United States are of Mayan origin, for which Spanish is a second language. Many Guatemalans are former villagers whom the military drove off their land. Guatemalans are more dispersed within areas than Salvadorans and live primarily in Los Angeles, San Francisco, Chicago, Houston, and Washington, D.C., where they share space with other Latinos. Many also are farm workers.

Although Honduras did not experience the degree of civil turmoil of El Salvador, Nicaragua, and Guatemala, Honduras was used as a base of operations by both the CIA and the Nicaraguan Contras. The 2000 census recorded 217,569 Hondurans in the United States; in 2010 it grew to 633,401, 1.3 percent. Hondurans settled in California, southern Florida, and New York. The Honduran population is diverse, with a large community of Honduran Garifuna, black English-speaking Hondurans from the Caribbean coast, settling in the Bronx and parts of Brooklyn, New York. Although wealthier Hondurans also have migrated to the United States, a sizable number work as migrant farm workers.

The other Central American nations have sent fewer immigrants to the United States. Costa Rica has enjoyed relative peace and prosperity, and therefore has not sent large numbers of immigrants. The largest concentration of Costa Ricans is in the Miami area because Miami is a major financial and business center for Latin America. However, Costa Ricans are also found in Los Angeles and New York City. The 2010 census counted 126,418, 0.3 percent.

A construct of the United States, Panama came about in the early 1900s when the United States wanted to build a canal. The United States fomented a revolution there, which caused Panama to get its independence from Colombia in 1903. Like most people of the region, many Panamanians are of mixed blood—Indian and Spanish; however, an African admixture (West Indians brought to the canal to work and never taken back) has been significant, along with some population of

Chinese and Hindu ancestry. In 2010, 165,456 Panamanians were counted, 0.3 percent of the U.S. population (Ennis, 2011).

Before the 1980s, most South Americans were either political exiles or were wealthier than the other U.S. Latino groups and lived apart from them. Today, South Americans account for 2,769,434 or 5.5 percent of the Latino total population. The South American bloc is smaller than the rest largely because of distance and the cost of transportation, which until recently was prohibitive for most people. A good number of South American immigrants are political refugees, and as a group, many are better off than the rest of U.S. Latinos. For example, many Argentines came to the United States between 1976 and 1983 during the Dirty War (Benedetti, 2013). In addition, many Argentine Jews fled the country because of anti-Semitism. One in five Argentines who fled settled in the New York City area and another group settled in Miami. Their numbers, however, remain relatively low. Fewer immigrants have entered from Bolivia because the cost and difficulty of travel keep them from migrating in larger numbers. According to the Pew Center, "An estimated 242,000 Hispanics of Argentinean origin resided in the United States in 2011. . . ." Argentines have higher levels of education than the overall population. Forty percent of Argentines ages 25 and older have at least a bachelor of arts compared with 13 percent of all Latinas/os (Brown and Patten, Argentinian, 2013a).

The Colombian migration took place during the 1950s and early 1960s during the civil war, called *La Violencia* (The Violence), in which hundreds of thousands of Colombians were killed. Many middle-class Colombians and merchants migrated to the United States during this period. The growth of the drug cartels created instability during the late 1970s, which encouraged more Colombians to migrate out of the country. The Colombian American population stood at 77,000 in the 1970s and escalated to around 470,000 by the year 2000. Colombians live primarily in New York City, New Jersey, and Miami. An estimated 989,000 Colombian origin residents lived in the United States in 2011 (Brown and Patten, Colombians, 2013b).

An estimated 645,000 Ecuadorians resided in the United States in 2011. Bad governments and the interference of other nations have afflicted Ecuador and have caused hundreds of thousands of Ecuadorians of all classes to migrate to the United States. Cheaper transportation has made emigration easier for Ecuadorians. Miami became a sort of Ellis Island for Ecuadorians and other immigrants from South America. Some 60 percent lived in New York City in 2000 and another 10 percent live in Los Angeles (Brown and Patten, Ecuadorian, 2013d).

The pattern of Peruvians entering the United States was similar to other South Americans, with the wave in the 1950s and 1960s being primarily middle class, followed by a larger wave of 100,000 Peruvians in the second half of the 1980s as political and economic instability gripped the country. An estimated 200,000 Peruvians lived in the New York tristate area by 2000, and another 230,000 are spread out nationally. Educator Félipe Reinoso became the first Peruvian American elected as a Connecticut state senator in 2000. According to the Pew Center, an estimated 628,000 Peruvian origin people lived in the United States in 2013, accounting for 1.2 percent of Latinas/os, About two-thirds of Peruvians are foreign-born (López, Peruvian, 2012).

Venezuelans arrived during the 1980s because of an economic crash. Before this, Venezuela had enjoyed relatively good times and did not have much emigration because of a boom in oil. Today, fewer than 100,000 live mostly in Florida, New York City, and other major East Coast cities. An estimated 248,000 of Venezuelan origin lived in the United States in 2013, accounting for 0.5 percent of Latinas/os, and 69 percent are foreign-born. Like the Cubans, many were tied to conservative rulers. The median age of Venezuelans is 34. Forty-two percent live in Florida; half of Venezuelans ages 25 and older—14 percent of all Latinas/os and 30 percent of the U.S. population—have at least a bachelor's degree (López, 2015).

Many Chileans arrived after the CIA orchestrated the overthrow of Chilean president Salvador Allende in 1973. More than a million Chileans left the country between 1973 and 1990; however, few migrated to the United States. Many Chileans returned to Chile after military dictator Augusto Pinochet left office, leaving about 69,000 Chileans currently living in the United States. According to the 2010 U.S. Census 126,810 Chileans lived in the United States. Chileans are the fourth smallest Latina/o group from South America. There are high concentrations in Queens, New York; northern New Jersey; Miami, Florida; and Nassau County, New York. To this day there is resentment against the United States for its role in the overthrow of Allende in 1973 (Kornbluh, 1973). The other Latin American countries—Bolivia, Paraguay, and Uruguay—have a relatively small presence in the United States.

Some U.S. Latina/o organizations consider immigrants from non-Spanish-speaking Latin American countries such as Brazil and the West Indies as U.S. Latinos. This argument also makes sense for French-speaking Haitians who share the island with the Dominican Republic. The boat people from Haiti should be considered Latinos as much as those of other nations. Haitians are from Latin America, and many U.S.

Latinos can trace back their ancestry to Africa. About 514,000 Haitians and West Indians, natives of the Bahamas, Barbados, Jamaica, Trinidad, and Tobago, live in Florida. That makes Florida the West Indians' second most popular destination, slightly behind the state of New York, which has received Jamaicans and Haitians for decades. Haitians and West Indians also have migrated to Boston. Many of these immigrants speak English or French, as do smaller number of Belizeans. Brazilians are considered Latinos; however, Brazilians speak Portuguese and some do not have a strong national presence in the United States—although they are part of the cultural world of U.S. Latinos.

Who do you think is a Latina/o? What problems do you foresee with this identification?

THE CONTESTED IDENTITY

Identity among Latinos is contested because they are composed of disparate races and nationalities. Roughly 50 percent of Latinas/os were U.S.-born in 2013, with great variations from group to group (Puerto Ricans, for instance, are U.S. citizens). The rate of immigration plays a decisive role in Latino population growth: many native-born Latinos are, in fact, the children of new immigrants who tended to be young and had comparatively high fertility rates. Racially, Latinos are diverse.

As of 2013, Mexican immigrants were the largest source country of foreign born: 28 percent. Mexicans are mostly mestizos, a mixture of Indian and Spanish (and to a lesser extent African and Asian); Puerto Ricans are a mixture of African and Spanish and some Indian; Nicaraguans are a mixture of Indian, Spanish, and African. Latinos are similar to one another in that Latinos were all colonized; Spain conquered and controlled most of them for more than 300 years. Consequently, most U.S. Latinas/os speak Spanish, although with different intonations, something that is often not reflected in contemporary Hollywood movies. Latinos all have a strong sense of connection with their mother countries, bringing with them historical memories and cultural variations. At home, many continue eating foods favored in their mother countries, and these cuisines often differ from the Mexican cuisine, which the Mexican Indian has heavily influenced. Enchiladas, tacos, and mole are all Mexican foods, and other U.S. Latinos do not necessarily eat spicy foods.

So why, if Latinos are different, do people use *Hispanic* or *Latino* as terms to describe their origin? The best and most logical reason is that various federal programs require data on the ethnic makeup of the community for federal affirmative action plans, community reinvestment reports, and public health service requirements. Not everyone has the same needs, however. As mentioned, there is no one Hispanic or Latino nationality. The terms themselves are misleading, since Hispanic technically means Spanish, and Latin American countries fought wars of independence against Spain and formed separate nation–states. In addition, the designation Latino comes from Latin American, which was a designation of the French, supposedly Napoleon III, to imply cultural kinship with France during attempts to impose Maximilian as Emperor of Mexico. Others say that it refers to an Italian language. Both words have political baggage, especially for Mexican Americans who, to avoid discrimination and to differentiate themselves from darker Mexicans, often call themselves Spanish Americans or Latin Americans. Moreover, many Mexican Americans prefer the term *Chicano*, which was adopted during the 1960s as a political term embracing collective responsibility to bring about social change for their community and within the country.

In short, considerable controversy exists within the disparate Spanish-speaking populations about whether *Latino* and/or *Hispanic* are valid terms. Because the same words are used to refer to different notions of their identities, confusion is apt to result when speakers do not realize they are using these words with different senses. When people use notions of race and gender, they understand and use them in different ways. When they use terms such as *Hispanic* and *Latino*, are they referring to ethnicity, caste, or nationality? Being precise is important, because these terms carry with them different meanings and interests. Realistically, are U.S. Latinos ready to surrender their individual histories? This has not been the case with Jewish Americans, Irish Americans, and others.

Using the term *Latino* also raises a concern for African Americans. In the view of some African Americans, the broadness of the term *Latino* has cut ever-shrinking civil rights entitlements. Critics charge that all too often Latinos stretch the notion of the entitlements of the civil rights acts. African Americans argue that entitlements should be limited to identifiable racial and ethnic minorities who have suffered historical discrimination which has resulted in economic, social, and political disadvantages. African Americans point out that Spaniards and Italians do not meet this criterion (Table I.2).

Table I.2 Quo Vadis

Latin America	Population
United States	318,892,103
Brazil	202,656,788
Mexico	120,286,655
Argentina	43,024,374
Colombia	46,245,297
Canada	34,834,841
Peru	30,147,935
Venezuela	28,868,486
Chile	17,363,894
Ecuador	15,654,411
Guatemala	14,647,083
Cuba	11,047,251
Dominican Republic	10,349,741
Honduras	8,598,561
Paraguay	6,703,860
El Salvador	6,125,512
Nicaragua	5,848,641
Costa Rica	4,755,234
Puerto Rico	3,620,897
Uruguay	3,332,972
Jamaica	2,930,050

Sources: CIA Factbook https://www.cia.gov/library/publications/the-world-factbook/rankorder/2119rank.html. http://www.distancefromto.net/distance-from/United+States/to

Based on the Introduction, from where are the most likely sources of immigration to the United States and why?

ABOUT THIS BOOK

The book is divided into 12 chapters, each addressing an important and controversial issue pertinent to Latinos. A background section introduces each chapter about U.S. Latino communities and their history, then frames each issue, after which arguments for and against the issue are presented, followed by a section with questions for students to discuss and debate. At the end of the chapter, there are selected readings for the student who wants further information. Additional Internet sites can be found through Google, America Online, or other search engines.

The first chapter is on race classifications. In the 2000 Census Report, close to half the Latino population classified itself as white. In the 2010 Census Report, 26.7 million Latinos out of 50.5 million identified as white (Ennis, Ríos-Varga, and Albert, 2010). This has led to a debate about the reasons for this, since, for example, 60 percent of Mexicans in Mexico are identified as mestizo and another 30 percent as Indian. Opinions range. Some say that classifying Latinos as white dilutes the identity of white Americans. Others respond that it does not matter. The question here is presented so as to introduce students to the notion of race, which has been one of the most overriding and divisive issues in U.S. history. It is an issue that potentially divides U.S. Latinos, hence the term *contested identity*.

Chapter 2 is on race and cultural identity. It deals with processes such as assimilation and acculturation. Historically, assimilation meant almost complete absorption into American society, leaving only symbolic veneers of their immigrant identity. It explores, among other things, how other groups have fared. What remains of Italian culture among Italian Americans other than pizza and the Godfather movies? In reality, the question of assimilation has wider implications and groups tend to hang on to their culture longer than their racial identity. Are Latinos the same? American conservatives are waging a culture war in America concerning whether minorities should forget the past and melt in. What cultural fusion has occurred? Arguments are presented from both sides.

Chapter 3 deals with cultural and linguistic diversity in education. A manifestation of this is the resistance of the schools to bilingual education. The debate over bilingual education has raged in most parts of the country, with opponents trumpeting that the official language of America is English and that bilingual education dilutes that mission and divides people. Most U.S. Latinos have interpreted this attitude as an attack on them and have responded negatively to ballot initiatives such as California's Proposition 227. The issue has divided many Americans and promises to continue raising questions in the future as U.S. Latino as well as Asian populations grow and seek to retain their original languages and cultures.

How does American society resist diversity? As recently as fifty years ago, many believed that one had to be a White Anglo Protestant American (WASP) to be a real American. Do you believe that this is still the case? Is the "make America great again" concept a return to the WASP ideal?

Chapter 4 deals with Chicana/o studies. It is an area studies intended to help students better adapt to school and improve their skills. A Stanford study suggested that culturally relevant classes could narrow the achievement gap between white and minority students, particularly blacks and Hispanics. Everyone agrees that the gap should be closed. There is evidence that the Tucson Unified School District closed the gap only to have nativists scuttle it for political reasons. Researchers at Stanford's Center for Education Policy Analysis (CEPA) suggest that "culturally relevant teaching may be a powerful way to boost the achievement of minority students, particularly those labeled as 'at-risk.'"

Chapter 5 is about borders. The United States shares about 2,000 miles of borders with Canada and Mexico. Because of the higher standard of living in the United States—Americans consume about 50 percent of the world's resources—it is a desirable place for those wanting to emigrate. Consequently, large waves of both authorized and unauthorized immigrants have entered the United States since the 1970s, touching off nativist reactions from some white Americans worried that people who differ racially and culturally may not assimilate (or will assimilate) into American society.

Chapter 6 addresses the issue of affirmative action, which is again part of an ongoing national debate on how best to achieve equality in our society. Affirmative action is a wedge issue that divides society between liberals and conservatives and between whites and people of color. The debate is part of the culture war in the United States, which raged during the second half of the 1990s and still demands attention.

Chapter 7 involves interracial dating and marriage. With Latinos, the acceptance of interracial dating and marriage depends on housing patterns and regional differences as well as country of origin and the darkness of the individual U.S. Latino's skin. The acceptance of interracial dating also depends on whether the minority partner conforms to the majority culture. For example, interracial dating and marriage is much more problematic in Georgia and Mississippi than it is in Florida. The issue is also a question of different generational responses.

Chapter 8, "Latino Health Issues," explores issues related to a healthy society. Also discussed is public funding for education and health services to undocumented immigrants and their families. The issue of immigration is complex. Some estimates say there are as many as 11 million to 12 million undocumented immigrants in the United States. American-first groups say the U.S. taxpayer should not pay for the education and medical care of people who have broken the law and are in the United States illegally. Others respond that more than 80 percent of the U.S. Latino population work, pay taxes (in comparison to slightly less than 75 percent of white males), and contribute to society, and that everyone has a constitutional right to an education. They argue that the reason that undocumented and other poor Latinos have to seek subsidized medical care is because employers are not paying for the cost of social production. These arguments often are heated, with one side accusing the other of being un-American or racist. Finally, the chapter explores health issues among Latinas/os.

Chapter 9, "Immigration and Losing Fear: DACA–DAPA," combines these two topics to offer a more nuanced view of immigration. What are the major hurdles to a comprehensive immigration bill and the phenomenon of DACA? What is different today from 1986?

Chapter 10 discusses the military and political presence of the United States in Cuba. While the various nationalities under the U.S. Latina/o label are alike, often looking and sounding alike to the majority culture, showing that there are differences is important. Whether the United States is violating the sovereignty of Cuba is discussed with regard to the U.S. base at Guantanamo Bay. Also, what impact will the lifting of the embargo have?

Chapter 11 centers on Puerto Rico, which is part of the United States and has commonwealth status. However, supposedly the island is almost bankrupt. What responsibility does the United States have to the people of Puerto Rico? The chapter presents this question: what rights do the Puerto Rican people have to limit military exercises on the adjoining island of Vieques? The chapter also discusses the impending bankruptcy of Puerto Rico and whether it should remain a commonwealth state or be independent. The answers to these issues are complex, controversial, and involve different points of views, even among Puerto Ricans.

Finally, Chapter 12 is about Central America, which is the fastest growing Latina/o people in the United States. It is the third largest Latino group in the United States. An attempt is made to tie events in the home county to those in the United States. What roles did the CIA play to motivate wars and what role does the War on Drugs play in this migration?

The format of the book is designed to encourage discussion, and the topics are more often controversial than not, which will hopefully open the door to further debate. Scholars keep talking about the search for truth, but we package much of our knowledge in sound bites, and what we know as we reduce truth to acceptable paradigms is that we are free to deduce the answer without going outside the official model to explore other possibilities.

ANOTHER POINT OF VIEW (POV)

Identity: Does It Matter?

José De Paz, Community Organizer, Los Angeles Unified School District

Self-perception plays a significant role in an individual's chances for success in any society. In the United States, that self-perception includes race, ethnicity, and country of origin—RECO for short

Some aspects of RECO are more beneficial than others. For example, social failure indicators (lower levels of educational attainment, employment, income, political influence, cultural visibility, life expectancy and health levels, and higher levels of poverty, crime, incarceration, etc.) are generally associated with communities of people of color. On the other hand, indicators of social success are generally associated with white American communities.

Some people, hoping to eliminate or minimize the stigma of "social failure," identify with a successful example, carefully crafting their identity to fit an "American" stereotype and believing that this "mainstream" self-image will offset or neutralize a negative RECO label. Thus, they reject any racial, ethnic, or country adjective attached to the label "American" in their self-description.

However, this pseudo self-definition or image is the result of a negative self-perception or even self-hatred. It comes from a feeling of inferiority, and the belief that if people leave descriptors such as Mexican out of the equation, then they will be perceived in a different light. This denial is an attempt to erase historical memory. However, the reality is that no one can completely escape his or her past. This cleansed self-identity does not work for the vast majority of people.

Take Ted Williams, arguably the greatest batter of all time. During his career, very few people knew that he was a Mexican American. His mother, May Venzer, was Mexican American, and she moved to San Diego to raise Ted on her own. In 2001, Williams wrote that "if I had had my mother's name, there is no doubt I would have run into problems in those days, [with] the prejudices people had in Southern California." During his playing career, he hid behind his father's name, Williams, forgetting his childhood and his Spanish-speaking cousins and grandmother.

I feel that we should include our country-of-origin nationality in what we call ourselves for various reasons:

We can't hide. United States society will never "melt" 100 percent into one people/race/native-born nationality. There are too many Mexicans and Latinos living to the south of us and in our midst. There is no such thing as a color-blind anything in the United States.

Ted Williams represents the past, a time when white was right. Today, many people are denying the notion of being "American," turning away from the illusion of the Melting Pot and instead acknowledging and embracing their different backgrounds (including their nationality).

Mexicans and Mexican Americans in the United States are different than people from countries south of Mexico. They are different from their white, black, and Asian neighbors. They should embrace their differentness that is enriched by an indigenous past.

A healthy self-identity includes our country of origin in our nationality. It lets others know what I am and I am just fine with it. It provides continuity for our link with the richness of our culture and that of our parents and grandparents, and it enhances the development of self-respect and reflects a positive self-identity. The result is that U.S. society becomes more tolerant and stronger in its diversity.

Our identity enhances our unique historical role and present-day reality in the United States Southwest (I'm more than an immigrant; my roots are here and I belong here). Identity takes us from disappearing into the "Latin American countries' melting pot" to showcasing our different cultural characteristics and cultural contributions to U.S. society. It takes us from disappearing into the "U.S. melting pot" to seeing ourselves as a reflection of U.S. diversity.

Identity does not contradict being 100% "American." Likewise, it does not contradict considering oneself Latino or Hispanic. It is not "nationalistic pride"; it is who we are.

Another Take On the Term Latino

Benjamin Torres, President and CEO of CDTech in South Los Angeles, a community leadership and economic development nonprofit organization.

For most of my activist life, I have adamantly defended the term *Chicano*, and I still do. However, times have changed and there comes a point when we must reassess our words and strategies. We must move on and discuss the term *Latino* in relation to the data in this chapter. In order to do that, we must put the phenomenon into a historical context and discuss how similar groups have identified themselves.

The truth is that groups do not identify themselves. What they are called is for the most part a construct of the majority society. It is determined by government and the media. Only occasionally are people able to describe themselves. This self-identification is critical because it often clashes with a group's political ideology. This disagreement holds up progress, and this is bad because agreement is necessary to create space for discussion, permitting the minority group to develop strategies and organizational methods.

For example, the term *Chicano* came about in the 1960s as a political term. It was a time when Negroes became Black and Black Power rejected "Jim Crow" segregation in the southern region of the United States. Similarly, the term *Chicano* represented a quest for self-determination, power, political awareness, and a movement focused on deconstructing institutional racism. Those using the term resisted assimilating into mainstream American society. They took pride in their defiance of American cultural norms and committed themselves to reform.

However, a lot has happened since those turbulent days. Blacks became African Americans and the Mexican origin community has grown from under 5 million to 35 million. Moreover, in 1970 there were only a million Mexican immigrants—"In 2014, Mexican immigrants accounted for approximately 28 percent of the 42.4 million foreign born in the United States, making them by far the largest immigrant group in the country" (Zong and Batalova, 2016).

It must be remembered that the Chicano movement was driven by youth and students who were, for the most part, first generation and children of Mexican parents. These activists were never able to convince the majority of Mexican Americans that they were Chicano. The population growth within the community further complicated matters. There was a continuous flow of Central Americans as well as Mexicans during the 1980s and 1990s. The word *Chicano* was alien to them. Growth and diversity forced a change in identity.

Working as a community organizer has forced me to re-evaluate my hard stance on Chicano and my aversion to Latino. From the perspective of one who works with diverse Latino groups, I find that the term is not the end of the world. Latino is not all that negative because it allows organizers the opportunity to measure how people who migrated from Latin American countries compare to each other. They are similar but they are different. Too much time is wasted trying to convince

Mexican, Salvadoran, and South American immigrants that they are Chicano.

Admittedly, the U.S. government, media, and the dominant group hijacked the terms *Chicano* and *Mexican American*. They forced an identity on us. They forced Latino and, worse, Hispanic on us. This process was reinforced by the entertainment and music industries where the word *Latin* is used to glamorize our experience. While I don't like it, I cannot only blame corporate America. Chicanos have been complicit in this hijacking. They abandoned the word *Mexican* and have not built a political power base. If we had had power, we could have controlled what we called ourselves.

The late *Los Angeles Times* editor, Frank del Olmo, recognized the threat of the term *Hispanic* in the 1980s and offered Latino as an alternative. I have never used the term *Hispanic* and never will. Both terms, *Hispanic* and *Latino*, fail to recognize native Mesoamerican ancestry. Yet I have to function in a broader community.

As we have discussed, the growth of Latinos as a whole was from 5 million to over 50 million (*Hispanic* is the census term). Within this context, the various Spanish-speaking nationalities are grouped. They are comingled with Mexicans. For the most part, those working in the Census Bureau are white, and to most white people all Latinos look alike. Further, the Chicanos are generally not part of this process, which internally is controlled by Latino national organizations.

Once more, the term *Latino* is not perfect—not even preferable. It was socially constructed by European nations with imperialistic designs. "The term Latin America was introduced by the French Empire of Napoleon III. When Napoleon invaded Mexico the term was coined and used to place France among the countries with influence in America. It was also used to exclude the Anglo-Saxons and to give exclusivity to those European countries with Latin based languages. The term has evolved over time and now to understand it, it is necessary not only to consider language but economic, social, political, ethnic, and cultural characteristics as well" (Latin American History).

Working at a South Los Angeles social service organization, my main concern is to bring about change. The term *Latino* facilitates quantifying government and corporate data. These data give me the tools to map out strategies and convince others that what we are doing is important. In other words, the data help me make my case and bring about change. They give me the ability to take a snapshot of how Latinos compare as a category to other ethnic and race groups nationally or locally.

More importantly, politically the term *Latino* can be used to galvanize different groups and to organize and advocate for a large number of individuals who may be struggling. Where do they stand in health services, economic status, educational attainment, and social mobility? How can we change this for the better?

Once more, this is not the 19th century; it is not 1970. Whether we like it or not, we are no longer a local or regional minority. We are a national minority. Mexicans live throughout the United States, and they interact with different "Latino" groups. A cultural fusion is taking place in other barrios that we cannot ignore. Aside from generational differences, there are also economic divides—not all Mexicans and Latinos are poor. We have different class interests.

Instead of arguing about words, we should concentrate on organizing. We should promote the economic, social, and political interests of the "Latino" population. More and more, our neighbors come from all parts of Latin America. We must be strategic and understand what is to be changed.

The beauty of the term *Chicano* was that it was grounded in the spirit of change and resistance to American racism. However, we are a lot closer to 2042, when Latinos will be the largest ethnic population in the United States, than we are to 1969.

NOTE

1. See Boricua.com http://www.boricua.com, accessed January 16, 2016. It is a valuable tool in accessing contemporary Puerto Rican Websites.

BIBLIOGRAPHY

Acuña, Rodolfo. "Criticism: An Abandoned Process." *counterpunch*, November 22, 2013. http://www.counterpunch.org/2013/11/22/criticism-an-abandoned-process

Acuña, Rodolfo. *Occupied America: A History of Chicanos* 8th ed. New York: Pearson, 2015.

Benedetti, Mario. The Disappeared: The Triumph of Memory. NACLA Report on the Americas. 46, no. 4: 78, 2013.

Benson, John. "Why You Can't Pigeonhole Latinos Into One Social Class." *Huffington Post*, January 22, 2013. http://www.huffingtonpost.com/2014/01/22/latino-social-class_n_4644287.html

Brown, Anna, and Mark Hugo Lopez. "Mapping the Latino Population, By State, County and City." *Pew Research Center*, August 29, 2013. http://www.pewhispanic.org/2013/08/29/mapping-the-latino-population-by-state-county-and-city

Brown, Ana, and Eileen Patten. "Hispanics of Argentinean Origin in the United States, 2011." *Pew Research Center*, June 19, 2013a. http://www.pewhispanic.org/2013/06/19/hispanics-of-argentinean-origin-in-the-united-states-2011

Brown, Ana, and Eileen Patten. "Hispanics of Colombian Origin in the United States, 2011." *Pew Research Center*, June 19, 2013b. http://www.pewhispanic.org/2013/06/19/hispanics-of-colombian-origin-in-the-united-states-2011

Brown, Ana, and Eileen Patten. "Hispanics of Cuban Origin in the United States, 2011." *Pew Research Center*, June 19, 2013c. http://www.pewhispanic.org/2013/06/19/hispanics-of-cuban-origin-in-the-united-states-2011

Brown, Ana, and Eileen Patten. "Hispanics of Ecuadorian Origin in the United States, 2011." *Pew Research Center*, June 19, 2013d. http://www.pewhispanic.org/2013/06/19/hispanics-of-ecuadorian-origin-in-the-united-states-2011

Bureau of the Census. "Why a Question on Hispanic or Latino Origin? Various Federal Programs Require Data on the Ethnic Make-Up of the Community." http://slideplayer.com/slide/7319462

Bureau of the Census. The Hispanic Population: 2010 Census, May 2011. http://www.census.gov/prod/cen2010/briefs/c2010br-04.pdf

Bureau of the Census. The Hispanic Population: 2010 Census, May 2011. http://www.census.gov/prod/cen2010/briefs/c2010br-04.pdf

Castro, Max J. "Making Pan Latino Latino Pan-Ethnicity and the Controversial Case of the Cubans." *Harvard Latino Law Review* 2, Fall (1997): 179. http://www.latcrit.org/media/medialibrary/2013/09/lcimcastro.pdf

CIA Factbook. https://www.cia.gov/library/publications/the-world-factbook/rankorder/2119rank.html

Cisneros, Jose et al. v. Corpus Christi Independent School District et al., Civ. A. No. 68-C-95. United States District Court for the Southern District of Texas, Houston Division 324 F. Supp. 599; 1970 U.S. Dist. LEXIS 11469. June 4,1970.

Dávila, Arlene, and Augustín Laó-Montes. *Mambo Montage: The Latinization of New York*. New York: Columbia University Press, 2001.

del Olmo, Frank, "Latinos by Any Other Name Are Latinos." *Los Angeles Times* (1886–Current File), May 1, 1981, p. D11.

Delgado, Richard, and Jean Stefancic. *Critical Race Theory: An Introduction* 2nd ed. (Critical America). New York: NYU Press, 2012.

Ennis, Sharon R., Merarys Ríos-Varga, and Nora C. Albert. "The Hispanic Population: 2010 Census Briefs." U.S. Department of Commerce Economics and Statistics Administration, U.S. Census Bureau, May 2011. http://www.census.gov/prod/cen2010/briefs/c2010br-04.pdf

Fry, Richard. "U.S. high school dropout rate reaches record low, driven by improvements among Hispanics, blacks." *Pew Research Center*, October 2, 2014. http://www.pewresearch.org/fact-tank/2014/10/02/u-s-high-school-dropout-rate-reaches-record-low-driven-by-improvements-among-hispanics-blacks

Garza, Hedda, and James Cockcroft. *Latinas: Hispanic Women in the United States*. Albuquerque, NM: University of New Mexico Press, 2001.

González, Juan. *Harvest of Empire: A History of Latinos in America*. New York: Penguin, 2000.

González-Barrera, Ana. "More Mexicans Leaving Than Coming to the U.S." *Pew Research Center*, November 19, 2015. http://www.pewhispanic.org/2015/11/19/more-mexicans-leaving-than-coming-to-the-u-s

González-Barrera, Ana, and Mark Hugo Lopez. "Is being Hispanic a matter of race, ethnicity or both?" *Pew Research Center*, June 15, 2015. http://www.pewresearch.org/fact-tank/2015/06/15/is-being-hispanic-a-matter-of-race-ethnicity-or-both

Grenier, Guillermo J., Lisandro Perez, and Nancy Foner. *Legacy of Exile: The Cubans in the United States*. Allyn & Bacon New Immigrants Series. New York: Allyn & Bacon, 2003.

"Hispanic Education Statistics." *Hispanic*, June 29, 2014. http://hispanic.com/blogs/updates/14726913-hispanic-education-statistics

Household Data Annual Averages. 4. Employment status of the Hispanic or Latino population by age and sex. Labor Force Statistics from the Current Population Survey. Bureau of Labor Statistics. Department of Labor, 2014. http://www.bls.gov/cps/cpsaat04.htm

"The increasing importance of Hispanics to the U.S. workforce." *Monthly Labor Review*, U.S. Bureau of Labor Statistics, September 2015. http://www.bls.gov/opub/mlr/2015/article/pdf/the-increasing-importance-of-hispanics-to-the-us-workforce.pdf

Jackson, Mareshah. "Fact Sheet: The State of Latinas in the United States." *Center for American Progress*, November 7, 2013. https://www.americanprogress.org/issues/race/report/2013/11/07/79167/fact-sheet-the-state-of-latinas-in-the-united-states

Kornbluh, Peter. "Chile and the United States: Declassified Documents Relating to the Military Coup, September 11, 1973." http://nsarchive.gwu.edu/NSAEBB/NSAEBB8/nsaebb8i.htm

Kotkin, Joel, and Wendell Cox. "The U.S. Cities Where Hispanics Are Doing The Best Economically." *Forbes*, January 20, 2015. http://www.forbes.com/sites/joelkotkin/2015/01/30/the-u-s-cities-where-hispanics-are-doing-the-best-economically/#2715e4857a0b7faef9384bce

Krogstad, Jens Manuel, and Mark Hugo Lopez. Hispanic population reaches record 55 million, but growth has cooled." *Pew Research Center*, June 25, 2015. http://www.pewresearch.org/fact-tank/2015/06/25/u-s-hispanic-population-growth-surge-cools

Krogstad, Jens Manuel. "Puerto Ricans leave in record numbers for mainland U.S." October 14, 2015. http://www.pewresearch.org/fact-tank/2015/10/14/puerto-ricans-leave-in-record-numbers-for-mainland-u-s

Lao-Montes, Agustín, and Arlene Dávila, eds. *Mambo Montage: The Latinization of New York City*. New York: Columbia University Press, 2001.

"Latino Population Booms In The South: Pew." *Huffington Post*, September 3, 2013. http://www.huffingtonpost.com/2013/09/03/latino-population-growth_n_3860441.html

"Latinas and the Educational Pipeline." City and County of Denver, CO, 2010. https://www.denvergov.org/Portals/713/documents/LatinaUnderrep.pdf

López, Gustavo. "Hispanics of Salvadoran Origin in the United States, 2013." *Pew Research Center*, September 15, 2015. http://www.pewhispanic.org/2015/09/15/hispanics-of-salvadoran-origin-in-the-united-states-2013/

López, Gustavo. "Hispanics of Dominican Origin in the United States, 2013." *Pew Research Center*, September 15, 2015. http://www.pewhispanic.org/2015/09/15/hispanics-of-dominican-origin-in-the-united-states-2013

López, Gustavo. "Hispanics of Cuban Origin in the United States, 2013. Statistical Profile." September 15. 2015. http://www.pewhispanic.org/2015/09/15/hispanics-of-cuban-origin-in-the-united-states-2013

López, Gustavo, "Hispanics of Mexican Origin in the United States, 2013." *Pew Research Center*, September 15, 2015. http://www.pewhispanic.org/2015/09/15/hispanics-of-mexican-origin-in-the-united-states-2013

López, Gustavo. "Hispanics of Peruvian Origin in the United States, 2013." *Pew Research Center*, September 15, 2012. http://www.pewhispanic.org/2015/09/15/hispanics-of-peruvian-origin-in-the-united-states-2013

López, Gustavo. "Hispanics of Venezuelan Origin in the United States, 2013." *Pew Research Center,* September 15, 2015. http://www.pewhispanic.org/2015/09/15/hispanics-of-venezuelan-origin-in-the-united-states-2013

Majfud, Jorge. "Why the name of Latin America?" http://majfud.org/2011/03/02/why-the-name-of-latin-america

Oboler, Suzanne. *Ethnic Labels, Latino Lives: Identity and the Politics of (Re)presentation in the United States*. Minneapolis, MN: University of Minneapolis Press, 1995.

Paley, Grace. *A Dream Compels Us: Voices of Salvadoran Women*. Cambridge, MA: South End Press, 1990.

Pardo, Mary. *Mexican American Women Activists: Identity and Resistance in Two Los Angeles Communities*. Philadelphia, PA: Temple University Press, 1998.

Passel, Jeffrey S., Gretchen Livingston, and D'Vera Cohn. "Explaining Why Minority Births Now Outnumber White Births." *Pew Research Center*, May 17, 2012. http://www.pewsocialtrends.org/2012/05/17/explaining-why-minority-births-now-outnumber-white-births

Pérez, Emma. *The Decolonial Imaginary: Writing Chicanas into History (Theories of Representation and Difference)*. Indianapolis: Indiana University Press, 1999.

"Puerto Ricans in the United States: Research roundup." *Journalist's Resource*, July 2, 2013. http://journalistsresource.org/studies/government/immigration/puerto-ricans-in-the-united-states-research-roundup

Rodríguez, Clara E. *Changing Race: Latinos, the Census, and the History of Ethnicity in the United States*. New York: NYU Press, 2000.

Sándoval, Carlos (Director). "A Class Apart." *American Experience*, PBS, April 21, 2009.

Santa Ana, Otto. *Brown Tide Rising: Metaphors of Latinos in Contemporary American Public*. Austin, TX: University of Texas Press, 2002.

Second-Generation Americans. "A Portrait of the Adult Children of Immigrants." *Pew Research Center*, February 7, 2013. http://www.pewsocialtrends.org/2013/02/07/second-generation-americans

Shorris, Earl. *Latinos Biography of a People*. New York: Norton, 1992.

Suro, Robert. *Strangers among Us: Latinos' Lives in a Changing of America*. New York: Vintage Books, 1999.

"Where do most Hispanics in the USA live?" http://geo-mexico.com/?p=9994. Based on Pew Research, "Mapping the Latino population, by State, County and City," August 29, 2013.

"Why did Napoleon III coin the term "Latin America?" *English Language and Usage*. http://english.stackexchange.com/questions/16003/why-did-napoleon-iii-coin-the-term-latin-america

Yzaguirre, Raúl. "Census Shows Disparity in Education of Latino Children." *Hispanic Online*, Hispanic Magazine.com, April 2001.

Zong, Jie, and Jeanne Batalova, "Frequently Requested Statistics on Immigrants and Immigration in the United States." Migration Policy Institute, April 16, 2016.

SELECTED VIDEOS

BuzzFeedVideo. "Americans Pronounce Latino Names," YouTube video, posted February 27, 2015. https://www.youtube.com/watch?v=7esLY0AQ1cQ

BuzzFeedYellow. "Latino Or Hispanic?" YouTube video, posted September 4, 2015. https://www.youtube.com/watch?v=KBDGwB50YBY

Flama. "People Who Suck at Latin American Geography," YouTube video, posted March 24, 2015. https://www.youtube.com/watch?v=r83AphdYedQ

Flama. "Types of Spanish Accents—Joanna Rants," YouTube video, posted October 1, 2015. https://www.youtube.com/watch?v=VlK-neOypDM:

"Latinos and Identity—Why Labels Don't Fit." ES Video Productions LLC, YouTube video, posted May 10, 2012. https://www.youtube.com/watch?v=tRsIf9ZY5u8

Legend, Frank. "I'm Not MEXICAN, I'm LATINO!" YouTube video, posted April 20, 2013. https://www.youtube.com/watch?v=nMkxEiyxY1k

MexicanInvasionPride. "Shit Latinos and Hispanics Say—Russell Peters—Latino/Brown Pride," YouTube video, posted January 28, 2012. https://www.youtube.com/watch?v=ZXsvcNb1LbE

NicanTlacaWomenWarriors. "Mexica Movement Member Interview- Huitzilyolotl X. Anahuac," YouTube video, posted July 9, 2015. https://www.youtube.com/watch?v=XdkxUcZm0Ow

NicanTlacaWomenWarriors. "Not Hispanic! Not Latino! Truth of Identity from Truth of History, part 1," YouTube video, posted May 27, 2014. https://www.youtube.com/watch?v=WAmj5CDKBJc

Rendón, John Jairo. "Geography of the world Latin America Video part one," YouTube video, posted September 10, 2012. https://www.youtube.com/watch?v=JLLPi4DeI18&list=PLma9H-xhTDH7yzKMXSi2tD2UKZocsTW4b

TheRealOreo1. "Why Mexicans Are Not Latinos or Hispanics," YouTube video, posted March 23, 2012. https://www.youtube.com/watch?v=AwRP_QFoHsg

Wilson, Sebas. "Hispanic/Latin is NOT a race," YouTube video, posted August 17, 2012. https://www.youtube.com/watch?v=DfJUj3ZHTG0

1

Race Classification

BACKGROUND

Race is one of the most pressing, controversial, and potentially the most divisive issue in American society. Like all other constructs, it falls hardest on gender and that is why Chicanas insisted that Chicano be spelled Chicana/o, showing that history involves two genders. This simple act makes Chicanas and Latinas visible. Historically, a person's race and gender have determined the success and failure, acceptance and rejection of that person. They are social constructs—used to keep people in their place. Despite its importance, the definition of race in America has been arbitrary, depending greatly on the dominant society's definition. The United States once applied the simplistic standard deeming that if a person had one drop of African blood, he or she was Negro. In the case of Latinas/os, this standard has varied, largely depending on their class.

In colonial Mexico, the more Spanish one looked the more privileges he or she was entitled to. This same standard applied in the United States in placing the Indian, the African, and the immigrant in visual castes.[1] As in many societies, girls and women were chattel. In New Spain, mixed bloods were denied privileges; for example, a female needed her father's consent to marry. Children from mixed marriages were suspect and could not enter religious communities until her or his blood lineage was verified. If a child was born on the wrong side of the bed, illegitimate, he or she could not become a priest or a nun unless his or her father recognized him or her as his son or daughter. How is this an example of sexism? Race determined station and privileges in life. Western European societies imposed a patriarchic family structure on the Indians in the form of the nuclear family. It was not uncommon to marry 14-year-old Indian girls to men in their twenties, thus reinforcing the father as the head of the family. The Spanish colonies had a well-defined caste system. In descending order, peninsulares, those born in Spain, were at the top, followed by criollos, full-blooded Spaniards born in the colonies. The pecking order was then by mixed bloods: mestizos, mulattos, African slaves, Indians, and several dozen other mixtures.

Many government entities before World War II classified working-class Mexicans as belonging to the Red race, or just simply the Mexican race. For instance, in the 1930 census, the U.S. Bureau of the Census listed them as Mexican.[2] The Census Bureau instructed census takers that "[p]ractically all Mexican laborers are of a racial mixture difficult to classify, though usually well-recognized in the localities where they are found. In order to obtain separate figures for this racial group, it has been decided that all persons born in Mexico, or having parents born in Mexico, who are not definitely white, Negro, Indian, Chinese, or Japanese, should be listed as Mexican ('Mex')" (Acuña, 2005). In the 1940 census, the instructions were, "Mexicans are to be regarded as white unless definitely of Indian or other nonwhite race." The 1950 Census Report required " 'white' (W) for Mexicans unless they are definitely of Indian or other nonwhite race." The importance of race was not lost on Mexican American organizations. Mexicans, aware that being white carried privileges in the United States, pressured the federal government to label Mexicans as Caucasian, which the Census Bureau did in 1948 (Overmeyer-Velázquez, 2013).

Mexican Americans were not the exception. The United States is a country of immigrants, and perceptions have been changing regarding the race of other groups. For example, in 1909 the census listed Armenians as Asiatic. Because of pressure from Armenians, a court held that year that Armenians were white. In 1922, the U.S. Supreme Court ruled that people from India, although technically Caucasian, were not white. Before the 2000 census, Congress held hearings attempting to decide a classification for Middle Eastern Arabs (Clara Rodriguez, 2000b).

In 2010, the Census Bureau allowed the respondent to self-identify: "For the first time in Census 2000, individuals were presented with the option to self-identify with more than one race and this continued with the 2010 Census, as described by Office of Management and Budget (OMB). There are 57 possible multiple race combinations involving the five OMB race categories and Some Other Race." The Bureau explained: "The Summary File provides data on Hispanic origin and race, including information on the population reporting more than one race as well as detailed race combinations (e.g., White and Asian; White and Black or African American and American Indian and Alaska Native). In this report, the multiple-race combination categories are denoted with the conjunction and in bold and italicized print to indicate the specific race groups that comprise the particular combination" (Humes, Jones, and Ramírez, 2011). The changes made by the Bureau have not satisfied everyone, however.

Why will this change be more important as time marches on?

The racial diversity among U.S. Latinos has also formed particular notions of race, making it even more difficult to categorize Latinos and Latinas racially. The 300 to 400 years of Spanish colonialism in Latin America constructed racial categories to benefit those of Spanish blood. The more Spanish blood the Spanish subjects had, the more privileges they acquired. In fact, the Spaniards constructed an elaborate categorization of race mixtures.

These racial classifications were listed on the individual's baptismal records for most of the colonial period. However, because much of the colonial population was mobile and people did not carry their baptismal certificates with them, the colonial subjects identified themselves without records.[3] The standard classification was based on how Spanish or white a person looked. By the end of the 18th century, the race categories had dwindled to Spaniard, mestizo, Spanish-mestizo, Indio-mestizo, African-mestizo, and Negro. People understood the social and political importance of being white or nearly white. The term *mestizo,* for example, was almost synonymous with not being Indio. Vigorous race mixing characterized the Latin American colonies of Spain. The Spaniards and other Europeans brought Africans to the plantations of the New World to replace the millions of native Indians in the West Indies who had died. According to Gonzalo Aguirre Beltrán, in 1810, 10.2 percent of New Spain were reportedly Afro-mestizos and only 0.2 percent African; 11.5 percent were Indio-mestizos but 60 percent were Indian. Since the census was based largely on self-identification, these categories were in all probability higher. The European or white population never rose above 0.8 percent from 1570 to 1810 (Beltran, 1972, p. 233) (Table 1.1).

The Spaniards repeated this scenario throughout Latin America. For example, Mexico had a population of 25 million indigenous people around the year 1580, and 75 years later, hardly more than 1 million were left. In central Mexico, 95 out of every 100 people perished. In western and central Honduras, 95 percent of the native people were exterminated within the span of half of the 16th century. In western Nicaragua, 99 percent died, with the population falling from more than 1 million people to fewer than 10,000 in about 60 years, from 1519 to the 1580s. The causes were the rapid spread of European diseases, overwork, warfare, and often the enslavement of the Native American. Spanish colonialism created a racist regime, which drew its justifications from an appeal to biblical authority. Racial stereotypes were constructed such as the idea that the Indians lacked reason and that Indians were like infants who had to be educated by *gente de razon* (rational people), that is, Christian people who were adults. The Spaniards also rationalized the enslavement of Africans by saying that they did not have a soul or that they were biologically inferior to whites. Racial stereotypes went a long way in justifying a cruel and exploitive system in both Latin America and the United States, where labor systems allowed others to be treated as less than Spanish or as less than American.

The race admixture of the different Latin American countries varied; however, an individual's status and consequent treatment within society depended on race. In Cuba and Puerto Rico, the three major ethnic groups are African, Spanish, and mulatto, whereas Nicaragua has a blend of all three. In Argentina, people are mostly European in the Buenos Aires area, but are mainly mestizos in the Pampa area. The mixture

Table 1.1 Racial Categories in Mexico during the Spanish Colonial Period

Year	Total Percent	Europeans	Africans	Indians	Creoles	Afro-Mestizos	Indio-Mestizos
1570	100.0	0.2	0.6	98.7	0.3	0.1	0.1
1646	100.0	0.8	2.074.6	9.8	6.8	6.0	
1742	100.0	0.4	0.862.2	15.8	10.8	10.0	
1793	100.0	0.2	0.161.0	17.8	9.7	11.2	
1810	100.0	0.2	0.260.0	17.9	10.2	11.5	

Source: Gonzalo Aguirre Beltrán, Población Negra de México (México: Fondo de Cultura Economica, 1972), 233.

in Mexico is characterized as Spanish, Indian, and mestizo; however, growing evidence indicates that African and Asian admixtures are also present.

Supporting the idea of various admixtures in Mexico is anthropologist Eric Wolf, who wrote in his book *Sons of the Shaking Earth*, "The total number of Spaniards who migrated to Middle America has been estimated at 300,000. With the Spaniard came another element of population, the African slave. Approximately 250,000 were imported into Mexico during the three centuries of the slave trade . . . No part of Middle America is without Negro admixture, although the physical evidence of this admixture has probably been submerged." After denunciating the African influence, Wolf states, "Negroes were not the only slaves imported into Middle America. Small numbers of Indians, Burmese, Siamese, Indonesians, and Filipinos were also brought in to serve in similar capacity" (Wolf, 1959, p. 29). Theodore G. Vincent, in a recent book on Mexican President Vicente Guerrero, who had both Indian and African blood, posits that an "estimated 100,000 Asians [were] brought to Mexico in slavery on the Manila-to-Acapulco galleons. The Spaniards labeled the Asians 'African' because the Spanish wanted more slaves, and by law only Africans could be slaves" (Vincent, 2001, p. 1).[4] Little is known about the importation of Asians into colonial Mexico, but it is important to think about it in the context of race.[5] What is known is that racial mixing took place in every corner of the Spanish empire and affected the social construction of race.[6] If Latinos, similar to other colonized people, wanted to move up in racial categories, then white was right.

It is no wonder, then, that almost half of U.S. Latinos (48 percent) would classify themselves "white only" on the 2000 census. In 2000, some 42 percent chose another race, and only 4 percent said they were black or African American alone; approximately 6 percent reported two or more races (Grieco and Cassidy, 2001). In 2010, while Mexico's population ranged from 9 percent to 17 percent European and about 60 percent mestizo and 30 percent Indian, 52.8 percent of Mexican Americans self-identified as white. Among other U.S. Latinos 85.4 percent of Cubans, 65.9 percent of South Americans, 53.1 percent of Puerto Ricans, 40.2 percent of Salvadorans, 38.5 percent of Guatemalans, 29.6 percent of Guatemalans, and 49.4 percent of all others self-identified as white. According to Peter Wade, specialist in race concepts of Latin America, "Racial categories and racial ideologies are not simply those that elaborate social constructions on the basis of phenotypical variation or ideas about innate difference but those that do so using the particular aspects of phenotypical variation that were worked into vital signifiers of difference during European colonial encounters with others" (Wade, 1997).

The truth is that most Mexicans, Salvadorans, and Latinas/os are mestizos, which means they are at least of two races. However, historically in the case of Mexicans they are Indians. Race classification confuses. This confusion has led Jamaican-born Harvard sociologist Orlando Patterson to argue in 2001 that white people were not becoming a minority in the United States because Latinas/os were classified as white. Patterson argued that claiming America is becoming less white fuels the fears of the white majority. Patterson wrote, "The New York Times reported that 71 of the top 100 cities had lost white residents and made clear only in the third paragraph of the article that it is really 'non-Hispanic whites' who are now a minority in these cities" (2001). According to Patterson, what this and other articles fail to take into account is "the fact that nearly half the Hispanic population is white in every social sense of this term; 48 percent of so-called Hispanics classified themselves as solely white, giving only one race to the census taker." Thus, if the Hispanic population is added to "a robust 69.1 percent of the total population of the nation," whites are 75.14 percent of the total population, down by only 5 percent from the 1990 census. According to Patterson, "Recent studies indicate that second-generation Hispanic whites are intermarrying and assimilating mainstream language and cultural patterns at a faster rate than second generation European migrants of the late nineteenth and early twentieth centuries" (Patterson, 2001). While one may not agree with Patterson, his arguments have merit in questioning the Census Bureau's policies of race categorization as well as the education system.

On one hand, the census allows citizens to classify themselves in as many racial ways as they wish, eliminating the notion that races are immutable categories. This action raises the question, however, of whether dismantling of racial constructs in America is a good thing. What other system of identification would take its place? Patterson is correct that Latinos, similar to blacks, have used race to identify inequalities and needs and to justify rights such as affirmative action and voting rights. Many minorities fear that without race as a factor, it will be impossible to assess the needs of Latinos and implement programs to correct inequalities. This notion also raises the following questions: even if Latinos are classified as white, does that make them white? Do most Americans look at them as white? Will their inequality go away if they are classified as white?[7]

The word *ethnic* comes from the Greek *ethnos*, which was from the word *ethnikos*, originally meaning heathen or pagan. Over time ethnic referred to other tribes, and the word gradually took on racial characteristics. Because of the different nationalities that came to the United States, the word *ethnics* became known sometime around World War II as a polite way of referring to non-WASP Americans.[8] In the 1960s, the word became synonymous with minority groups and cultural constructs. However, the discussion of ethnicity has always been important, and Anglo-Americans have blurred the lines between race, ethnicity, and nationality.[9]

Given this discussion, it is not surprising that many Americans are confused about what race they belong to. Given three racial categories—Caucasian, Asian, and Negroid—what test should be used to decide what race a person is? During the 18th century in colonial New Spain (Mexico), the priest would look at the person and say, "*Tiene parecido de Español.*" ["He looks like a Spaniard."] This practice was the standard, and everyone strived to look like Spaniards because looking like one brought substantial privileges. Indians and Africans wanted to look like mestizos because that made them look more like Spaniards, which again moved them up in status. Similarly, in the United States, being an American was being white, so light-skinned African Americans had more privileges than darker-skinned African Americans. Many lighter-skinned African American slaves worked in the big house instead of in the fields. The rape of some slaves by their white owners produced lighter-skinned offspring. Over the years, African Americans who had light skin sometimes chose to pass as white to take advantage of the privileges that accrued to white people. It is not surprising that members of ethnic minorities have also striven to be white and even have changed their last names to English equivalents in the hope of acceptance (e.g., Martínez to Martin).

Determining race or ethnicity is not an easy chore. Which test will be applied—the United States one-drop-of-blood test or the Spanish colonial test where if a person looks like a European, she is white? Why is race important? The consequences of racism still harm a wide body of people. Racial stereotyping is not a relic of the past. In some countries such as the United States, Great Britain, and Australia racism is revealed when governments opt to eliminate the potential for conflict by simply denying or severely limiting entry of non-Europeans.

In 1986, Japanese Prime Minister Yasuhiro Nakasone remarked that the average American intellectual standard is lower than the average Japanese standard because of African Americans and Latinos in the United States. The Japanese prime minister said the source of Japan's strength lies in its "racial homogeneity" (Lewis, 1991). In 1997, University of Texas Law School Professor Lino Graglia remarked that "Blacks and Mexican-Americans are not academically competitive with whites in selective institutions. . . . It is the result primarily of cultural effects. They have a culture that seems not to encourage achievement. Failure is not looked upon with disgrace" ("UT Professor Blasts Efforts for Diversity on Campus," 1997).

A postscript: Although colonial censuses clearly show a considerable African presence in Mexico, this fact is played down despite the fact that there were more Africans than Spaniards in 1800. African was in denial in not counting its African population. By 1646, the census showed 13,780 Europeans and 35,089 Africans—the native population had declined to 1,269,607. According to a study by demographer Robert McCaa, the decline of the African population in Mexico did not take place until the mid-18th century. The decline of the African presence was not the result of any epidemic or increases in the Indian or Spanish populations but the result of self-identification. Births during Mexico's colonial era were recorded by parish priests who would note the race classification of the baptized infant. Increasingly priests would say *"dice que es mestizo o criollo."* [He says he is a mestizo or criollo.] Such record keeping led to the disappearance of Mexico's African ancestry. The Mexican government's acknowledged presence of Afro-Mexicans added a "Third Root" in the 1990s ("Africa's Lost Tribe in Mexico," 2012).

Yielding to the pressure of African Mexicans, in 2015 Mexico counted persons of African heritage in its population survey. It counted 1.38 million people of African heritage, 1.2 percent of its population. They lived in three coastal states and in Guerrero where nearly 7 percent identified as African. The study showed that overall they were poorer and less educated than the national average. Ana Campoy noted, "Like the US, Latin America and the Caribbean have a history of slavery that resulted in a large number of residents of African descent—about 150 million, accounting for about 30% of the region's population, according to the United Nations." Caught up in the illusion that they were mixed race nations, Latin American and the Caribbean's African identity died except in Mexico—except in the faces, DNA, and memory of Afro-Mexicans (Campoy, 2015).

Does it matter what race a person is? Do African Mexicans have a right to be counted?

Some U.S. Latinos argue that the U.S. census historically has listed them as Caucasian. There are only three races to choose from—Caucasian, Asian, and Negroid. U.S. Latinas/os are of Asian, African, and even white ancestry. However, most Latinos are neither Asian nor African and, although most have Indian blood, the only choice they have is to pick Caucasian. In the meantime, the mixed category is not catching on. There is also the problem of wanting to be white: when some Latinos are asked about their race, they will drag in a Spanish or French grandparent. Being white is important to them because of the racist history of this country and also the habit of mind constructed in colonial Mexico. History informs them that in order to become American, Latinos must follow the example of Jews and Italians and become at least hyphenated white. According to this reasoning, this position does not make them anti-African American, but only recognizes the reality in America that lumping Latinos in with African Americans makes them second-class Americans and gives racists reason to discriminate against U.S. Latinos. Therefore, it is refreshing that African Mexicans insist on being counted.

When Orlando Patterson raised the question of whether U.S. Latinos were white, the xenophobe Steve Sailer came out with a series of articles titled "Pondering Patterson: OK, How White Are Hispanics?" (Sailer, 2001). Sailer argued that only 9 percent of the residents of Mexico are white, that 30 percent of Mexicans are predominantly Indian, and that 60 percent are mestizos. While these statistics are correct, they become a pretext and a negative justification for discriminating against U.S. Latinos in the context of U.S. history. Listing Latinos as nonwhite also gives Sailer and others the opportunity to divide Latinos into races, thus weakening the group by setting up a scenario where lighter-skinned Mexicans are accepted as Latinos or Hispanics and darker-skinned Latinos are relegated to an underclass.

Race has been used to distinguish people. For example, race has been included in the census since 1790 when Negroes were listed as "all other persons." The 1940 census helped the government roundup people of Japanese ancestry for the purpose of internment; race justified this confinement. Even during World War II, race was used to exclude nonwhite people, which is why Mexican American organizations fought to be white; to be other than white was to be inferior. The courts also recognized this argument.

It is important to remember this history. For example, in *Hernandez v. State* (1952), the Texas Court of Appeals ruled that Mexicans were "not a separate race but are white people of Spanish descent," and the lawyers for the Mexican American community did not dispute this rationale. The court held that Mexicans were members of and within the classification of the white race, as distinguished from members of the Negro race. The strategy of Mexican American civil rights organizations was to claim the racial identity of the majority of Americans. They argued that the Treaty of Guadalupe Hidalgo (1848) made Mexican Americans citizens and recognized them as white. Mexican American organizations eventually won the legal battle, and most courts declared that Mexicans were white. This ruling was a tremendous victory because in 1930 a Texas state court held that Mexican American public school students could not be segregated from children of other white races because of their ethnicity. Mexican Americans guarded this white status because they knew that in this country being white brought privileges. So when the 1930 census identified Mexican Americans as "other race," Latino civil rights organizations protested, and in 1950, the census reclassified Mexicans as white. Being called white was a right because Mexican Americans fought for the United States during World War II. Today the Census Bureau includes the designations "white, of Hispanic origin" and "white, of non-Hispanic origin." In 2010, it gave the respondent the liberty to mark mixed races.

Many Latinos wrongheadedly believe that the Census Bureau should abolish these classifications, and it should classify all Latinos as white. As mentioned previously, the Treaty of Guadalupe Hidalgo guarantees Mexicans the right of citizenship, and because nonwhites could not be citizens, it was logical that the Treaty recognized Mexicans as white. It was a gimmick: it meant that to accept the label nonwhite or even "other white" was demeaning and a surrender of Treaty rights. Not much had changed from colonial Mexico.

Since 1970, the job of determining race has been left up to the individual. In 1980, the census classified Latinos as an ethnic group. Latinos could choose from 15 race categories. This change raised the issue that Latino identity went beyond race; it was a cultural identity. It is argued that culture unites all Latinos. Race after all is a human construct, and it has little to do with science. Why should Latinos want to identify as nonwhite? African Americans do not consider Latinos nonwhite.

Would Blacks consider Latinos black if they chose to list themselves as black? What is the difference between white and black racism? Because of the distorted construction of race in this country, many blacks such as Professor Patterson are resentful and consider Latinos white; thus Latinos will never be part of their world. African Americans believe whites have decided to let Latinos into their club. Many African Americans also believe that they created the civil rights movement, and it was through their sacrifices that civil rights gains were made. So some Latinos rationalize that economically it makes more sense to try to fit in.

Do racial classifications divide people? How can these racial divisions be overcome?

Many social scientists argue that race is a social construct, and eugenics is an inexact science at best and racist at worst.[10] The reality is that historically, race has been more divisive for Latinas/os than other groups because Latinas/os come in different colors. The Census Bureau has thus given Latinos the option of being white or other, or mixed race; in other words, of being "anything but Mexican" or a Latino nation (Acuña, 1996). Given the choice, Latinas/os will choose white because this designation has more privileges. According to newspaper columnists Patrisia Gonzales and Roberto Rodríguez, this choice has the effect of "whitening" the country via "demographic genocide." They posit that "[a] check of any encyclopedia will show that between 85 percent and 90 percent of all Mexicans and Central Americans are either indigenous or indigenous-based mestizos" (Gonzales and Rodríguez, 2000). The columnists correctly argue that the European population in Latin America was never large enough to be dominant outside of countries such as Argentina and Uruguay.

For over 300 years of Spanish rule and 180 years of U.S. rule, Mexicans and other Latinos have been conditioned to accept that being white is superior to being Indian. The Census Bureau itself has refused to accept admixtures, and it was only in the 2000 census that the reason for this choice became clear. By lumping all Spanish-speaking peoples under the rubric of Hispanic/Latina/o, the Census Bureau confuses identification and encourages a crossover, which some Latinos have come to accept. The exercise of identifying oneself as white is a joke among Latinas/os. In Mexico, for example, a person may call him- or herself white, but others will wink and comment "*y no mas le faltan las pumas!*" [He or she is "only missing his, or her, feathers!"] People should be proud of their heritage and not strive to be white; pride is what adds value to a person.

Give examples of someone trying to pass for another race.

In summary, the census is supposed to clarify the racial landscape; instead it has confused and scrambled it. The policies of the Census Bureau are as much an ideological battle as they are an attempt to count people. The censuses allow social scientists the room to invent and exaggerate differences. They confuse the strategies that the disparate Latino groups should use to bring about equality. For example, some scholars believe that Mexican Americans should follow the route of European ethnics and assimilate and that they should separate themselves from African Americans. If Latinos were to follow the latter strategy, it would lead to divisiveness. Latinos and African Americans live side by side, struggling for the same space, and they share common problems. Labeling Latinas/os white would abandon the mission of many U.S. Latinas/os to bring about equality, a goal that European immigrants largely abandoned as they were accepted as white. They assimilated as individuals, became white, and in the process left the poor behind.

Rather than changing the way a person thinks about race, the designation of U.S. Latinas/os as white further complicates the process. The Census Bureau argues that self-identification gives Latinos more options. However, history shows otherwise. Under the Spanish system, the look-alike test was no better than the one-drop-of-black-blood test.

The history of immigrants to the United States resembles that of Sisyphus, the mythical founder and first king of Corinth who was condemned to a lifetime of pushing a boulder up the hill. Every time Sisyphus made progress, the rock rolled back on him, threatening those below. It is plain that to make progress, others have to help push the boulder up the hill. Group identity contributes to a collective memory that bonds you to others. Second- and third-generation Latinas/os help the newcomers.

Which argument do you agree with and why?

Does identity help you forge a collective memory?

How does everyone benefit from the boulder going up the hill?

How does having a choice contribute to a group disappearing?

Why do we use Latinas/os rather than just Latino?

Lastly, how is this extensive historical context on race a prelude to a discussion on gender and sexual preferences?

ANOTHER POV (POINT OF VIEW)

Should Latinos Be Categorized as White?

Mary Pardo, Professor of the Department of Chicana and Chicano Studies and Marta López-Garza, Professor of the Department of Chicana and Chicano Studies and the Department of Gender and Women's Studies, California State University, Northridge

Should Latinos be categorized as white? When we, Mary Pardo and Marta López-Garza, discussed how best to approach this project we decided to approach it together. We otherwise felt forced into a discussion that was restricted to two opposing positions, limiting the discussion to a binary worldview. We prefer to problematize what we consider to be an assimilationist way of examining the issue of race classification. We believe it is important to be cognizant that it is the history of colonization that has placed us in the position of having to answer questions of racial categorization in a dichotomist, Western way of thinking and seeing the world when, in fact, racial identities are fluid and a result of social constructs.

Racial classifications were created during European conquest and colonization of the Americas and other parts of the Southern Hemisphere, beginning around the 1400s, as a means to control indigenous populations. Racial designations have since been dictated by ruling groups and used to bestow or withhold privileges and promote an ideology of white supremacy. In terms of racism and racialization, there is continuity between that historical time—when European countries (the British, Portuguese, and French along with the Spaniards) invaded and colonized the Americas—and now with our experiences as Latinos in the United States.

With the presence of Latinos in the United States over the past 150 years, racial classification of Latinos has changed throughout this country's history of census taking, confirming the argument that race is a social construct. Recently, the 2000 U.S. Census allowed Latinos to self-identify as white, black, Asian, or Native America, but many Latinos hesitated to choose among these racial classifications because Latino racial identity is complex and the classifications fall short of capturing what it means to be "mestizo," of mixed ethnic/racial heritage. The racialization of Latinos in the United States and the resulting inequalities continue into the 21st century regardless of the shifting census classifications for Latinos. Obviously, therefore, neither restricting racial classifications nor allowing Latinos to classify themselves will ensure equity.

We have been raised and instructed for generations to believe that assimilation will save us. In other words, the "whiter" or "more American" physically, psychologically, and/or culturally we are, the more likely we will succeed. The common notion is that the more one assimilates (i.e., the "modernization theory"), the more likely one is to achieve the "American Dream." The underlying premise of the modernization theory is that people of color should leave behind their culture, traditional languages, practices, and beliefs and assimilate into the European American culture, and in so doing, be considered more rational, civilized, *gente de razon*. This theoretical approach suggests that the cultures of immigrants and people of color are substandard. It further suggests that "white" (European) culture is superior and therefore by assimilating into that culture/identity one can embody that superior status.

Since the era of colonization, what has occurred as a result of Latinos accepting "white" culture as superior and their/our own culture as inferior is the devastating consequence of internalized racism. This Eurocentric ideology has influenced our values as Latinos since our colonization centuries ago. Racial classification is a phenomenon we continue to experience in different but oppressive ways. The underlying message is to appear as assimilated as possible.

We have observed that the way students classify themselves is shaped by what family members believe or tell them, or what they have heard in school, or from the media and society in general. It is context driven. That is why ethnic and Chicana/o studies in schools are crucial. This is where many of us are awakened to our history and can reinscribe our cultural identities.

Some argue that the U.S. Census Bureau's policy of "allowing" people to self-identify will lead to Latinos losing entitlement rights. In our estimation, this argument is spurious. The so-called entitlements or privileges, which in fact are our rights and for which we fought long and hard, are already being taken away, regardless of how we classify ourselves as Latinos and people of color in general. For example, affirmative action continues to be contested in the courts ever since the 1978 California Bakke case. More recently are the two contentious 2013 U.S. Supreme Court rulings. One overturned a key provision of the 1965 Voting Rights Act, allowing states to enact new and stricter voting laws that have resulted in depressed voter turnout, particularly among people of color. The second 2013 ruling was in regard to the University of Michigan undergraduate affirmative action admissions policy where the Court ruled against the affirmative action policy.

What the social movements of the 1960s and 1970s demonstrated is that while racial classification has been used to oppress and segregate, ethnic and racial identity can and has been used to forge political consciousness and activism. We agree that while racial classification is often an individual act of self-identification, when it occurs in a collective consciousness arena, it is a political decision and can be a social justice tool; for example, applying an affirming classroom exercise where students identify their family origins, the continent(s) from where their ancestors came, and their racial origin. The purpose of this pedagogical approach is to help students from every part of the globe reflect on the modernization theory, the assimilationist propaganda with which they have been raised, and affirm their indigenous roots. With this pedagogical approach, the racial classification is applied as an affirmative educational tool to begin the discussion of how "white as superior" is a social construct. This pedagogical approach gives way to a sociopolitical understanding of colonization which led to the racialization of Amerindians as well as of those forced to come to the Americas from African, Asia, and elsewhere. Identifying with their roots allows students to embrace their indigeneity instead of claiming the assimilationist colonial identity that signifies internalized racism.

Question: Will racism be eliminated if racial classification is no longer practiced? The answer is No. Abolishing racial classifications or categories will not ultimately dismantle racism, which is the real problem. So even if we take away all racial classifications, racial domination will still exist if we as a society do not address the underlying cause and origins of racism.

This response leads to a different discussion, which we will not pose in this section, of why racism continues to exist and how it can be eradicated.

Is there a Latino race? Why would someone call themselves a mestizo?

What Race is a Latino? Some Mexican Americans in California Aren't Even Sure (Neither Are We)

Dennis Romero, *LA Weekly*, May 25, 2011*

Have you ever looked at your light-skinned, green-eyed Latino neighbor—or perhaps he's kinky haired and the color of cinnamon—and asked, "What the hell are you?"

* Reprinted with permission.

It's a question Latinos even ask themselves, apparently, especially when filling out a U.S. Census Bureau form, which doesn't give them a race of their own, only an ethnicity or nationality. In other words, Latinos can choose a race from white, black, Asian/Pacific Islander, or Native American/Alaska Native—but not "Latino"—because it's not a race.

It's true. But it's still confusing, and so many Latinos check "some other race" when filling out census forms, or they skip the question altogether. It's all about self-identity, so there's no wrong answer . . . except that most anthropologists would say that most Latinos, unless they're direct descendants of Africans or other immigrants to the Americas, are white . . . except that it doesn't entirely make sense, does it? The prevailing theory about the origin of indigenous Americans is that they came to the continent from Asia thousands of years ago, which would make purely indigenous Latinos . . . Asian. That's a concept that would make some Asians laugh.

And, well, most Latinos are mixed with European blood, though plenty of Jews, Germans, Austrians, and Japanese (none of them races unto themselves) ended up south of the border too, particularly in the past 200 years.

And so, we skip the race box and head on down to ethnicity and nationality.

Mestizo, Chicano, Latino, Hispanic, Mexican, Salvadoran, and Puerto Rican are popular, but they don't identify race, but rather ethnicity, culture, and national heritage.

(We love how some Asian Americans identify themselves as Hawaiian. Really? We're Californian. But it doesn't get to the heart of the matter, now, does it?)

"We don't obsess about race," Cesar Juarez, a 24-year-old community organizer in San Jose, told the *Mercury News*' Joe Rodriguez.

Indeed, we predict a day when that top tier identifier of race is no longer even on the census. In 2020? Who knows.

But anthropology seems to be debunking race as a scientifically justifiable category: There's a much bigger difference between man and woman than black and white.

Where does Caucasian end and Asian begin? Where does Asian end and Arab begin? Where does Arab end and African begin?

And, for the love of God, what's Rosie Perez?

It all seems a little bit . . . racist, don't you think?

A PARTING SHOT

Latin America is not racially homogeneous. According to the *CIA World Factbook*, the following selected countries have the racial admixtures noted below—a word of caution is that these categories are often based on self-identification. Consult the *CIA World Factbook*: https://www.cia.gov/library/publications/resources/the-world-factbook

"Guatemala: mestizo (mixed Amerindian-Spanish—in local Spanish called *Ladino*) and European 59.4%, K'iche 9.1%, Kaqchikel 8.4%, Mam 7.9%, Q'eqchi 6.3%, other Mayan 8.6%, indigenous non-Mayan 0.2%, other 0.1% (2001 Census Report)

Mexico: mestizo (Amerindian-Spanish) 62%, predominantly Amerindian 21%, Amerindian 7%, other 10% (mostly European)

Puerto Rico: white 75.8%, black/African American 12.4%, other 8.5% (includes American Indian, Alaskan Native, Native Hawaiian, other Pacific Islander, and others), mixed 3.3%

Cuba: white 64.1%, mestizo 26.6%, black 9.3% (2012 estimate)

Dominican Republic: mixed 73%, white 16%, black 11%

Honduras: mestizo (mixed Amerindian and European) 90%, Amerindian 7%, black 2%, white 1%

El Salvador: mestizo 86.3%, white 12.7%, Amerindian 0.2% (includes Lenca, Kakawira, Nahua-Pipil), black 0.1%, other 0.6% (2007 estimate)

Argentina: white (mostly Spanish and Italian) 97%, mestizo (mixed white and Amerindian ancestry), Amerindian, or other nonwhite groups 3%

Chile: white and nonindigenous 88.9%, Mapuche 9.1%, Aymara 0.7%, other indigenous groups 1% (includes Rapa Nui, Likan Antai, Quechua, Colla, Diaguita, Kawesqar, Yagan or Yamana), unspecified 0.3% (2012 estimate)"

NOTES

1. Ghettos, barrios, schools, etc.
2. My own birth certificate lists me as belonging to the Mexican race.
3. They often travelled thousands of miles to work in the mines or to evade oppressive conditions. See Rodolfo F. Acuña, *Corridors of Migration: The Odyssey of Mexican Laborers, 1600–1933* (Tucson: University of Arizona Press, 2007).
4. For more information, see links to Laurence Iliff, "Black Mexicans see pride in lost history: Communities starting to discover roots, fight discrimination," *The Dallas Morning News*, April 3, 2002, http://www.latinamericanstudies.org/mexico/black-mexicans.htm; Gonzalo Aguirre Beltrán, *La Poblacion Negra de Mexico: Estudio Etnohistorico* (Xalapa: Universidad Veracruzana, 1992); Vincent Villanueva Mayer Jr., "The Black Slave on New Spain's Northern Frontier: San Jose De Parral 1632–1676" (PhD diss., University of Utah, 1975), 78. Blacks were among the army

assembled at Vera Cruz by Hernando Cortes in his assault on Mexico City. Mayer argues that the importation of African slaves was tied to a die problem of labor and the epidemics that ravaged New Spain in 1531, 1545, 1564, and 1576–1577. From a calculated 25 million, the number of Indians fell to fewer than 2 million in 1595. Later successive epidemics decimated the population. Between 1519 and 1650 the Viceroyalty imported an estimated 120,000 black slaves, which is two-thirds of all slaves imported into the Spanish possessions in the New World.

5. The Manila Galleon sailed between 1570 and 1815 annually, and from 50 to 80 percent of the crew was Filipino. "By one account, some 60,000 Filipinos sailed on the galleons from Manila to Acapulco." These were not slaves, although slaves were probably part of the cargo. "There were also many who belonged to the mestizo class, products of intermarriages between Spanish and native Filipinos who traveled as merchants, technicians or functionaries." Jonathan Best, "Endless War in Mindanao," *Philippine Daily Inquirer*, July 2, 2000. Given what we know about the Spaniards in Mexico and their justification for using war as a pretext for making prisoners slaves, many Filipinos were probably enslaved during these bloody wars. The division of the Philippines into Muslim and Christian as a consequence of Imperialism is harvesting bitter fruits today. See also Howard M. Federspiel, "Islam and Muslims in the Southern Territories of the Philippine Islands during the American Colonial Period," *Journal of Southeast Asian Studies* (September 1, 1998): 1ff.

6. Traders from Asia and Europe, such as the Portuguese and then the Dutch, traded with the islands. (See Kerry Nguyen-Long, "Vietnamese Ceramic Trade to the Philippines in the Seventeenth Century." *Journal of Southeast Asian Studies* 30, no. 1 (March 1, 1999): 1ff.) Slavery was a terrible institution that made huge profits for Europeans and those engaged in it and dispersed people around the globe. (See Jose S. Arcilla, S.J., "Roots: The Philippines in the 1600s." *Business World (Philippines)*, February 21, 2000.) Arcilla writes, "Philippine slavery, for example, was condemned by the first Manila Synod of 1583–86, but it was a dead law. Spaniards and Filipinos continued to have slaves." A 12-year-old boy in 1687 sold for 50 pesos in the Philippines.

7. See also Orlando Patterson, "Race Over." *New Republic Online*, December 30, 1999; Orlando Patterson, *Rituals of Blood: Consequences of Slavery in Two American Centuries* (New York: Basic Books, 1998); Orlando Patterson, "Race by the Numbers," *New York Times*, May 8, 2001.

8. White Anglo-Saxon Protestant Americans.

9. Theodore W. Allen, 2000; this is a 22-page paper. The category reads: " 'White' Persons 'of Spanish culture or origin'—Mexicans, Puerto Ricans, Cubans or Central Americans, and unspecified others, are collectively classed as an 'ethnic group,' regardless of race."

10. Eugenics is the study of human genetics and of methods to improve the inherited characteristics, physical and mental, of the human race. Efforts to improve the human race through bettering housing facilities and other environmental conditions are known as euthenics.

BIBLIOGRAPHY

Acuña, Rodolfo F. "The Illusive Race Question & Class: A Bacteria That Constantly Mutates." Occasional Paper No.59, Julian Samora Research Institute, November 2005. http://www.jsri.msu.edu/upload/occasional-papers/oc59.pdf.

Acuña, Rodolfo F. *Anything but Mexican: Chicanos in Contemporary Los Angeles*. London: Verso, 1996.

Allen, Theodore, W. " 'Race' and 'Ethnicity': History and the 2000 Census." http://clogic.eserver.org/3-1%262/allen.html.

Beltrán, Gonzalo Aguirre. *Poblacion Negra de Mexico*. Mexico: Fondo de Cultura Economica, 1972.

Benitez, Norma. "The Patriarchy Disguises Its Strategies Because It Doesn't Want to Lose Power" (XI EFLAC in MEXICO: Feminist Voices Raised in Chorus). *Women's Health Journal* no. 2 (2009): 34.

Butler, Paul. "A Mix of Colors: Country's Swirling Demographics Put New Twist on Meaning of 'Minority.'" *Dallas Daily News*, June 3, 2001.

Campoy, Ana. "Power in Numbers: Mexico Has Started Counting Its Afro-Mexican Population." *Quartz*, December 10, 2015. http://qz.com/569964/mexico-has-started-counting-its-afro-mexican-population/

Central Intelligence Agency World Factbook, 2010. Xxx https://www.cia.gov/library/publications/the-world-factbook/geos/mx.html#People.

Collier, Melvin J. "African Americans and Mexicans Are Cousins." *Roots Revealed*, June 9, 2013. http://rootsrevealed.blogspot.com/2013/06/african-americans-and-mexicans-are_9.html

Etzioni, Amitai, "Inventing Hispanics: A Diverse Minority Resists Being Labeled." *Brookings Institution* 10, no. 1 (Winter 2002).

Gonzales, Patrisia, and Roberto Rodríguez. "Census Demographic Suicide." *Column of the Americas*, Universal Press Syndicate, week of March 17, 2000.

Grieco, Elizabeth M. and Rachel C. Cassidy. "Overview of Race and Hispanic Origin." U.S. Census Brief, March 2001, p. 10. https://www.census.gov/prod/2001pubs/c2kbr01-1.pdf.

Haney López, Ian F. *Racism on Trial: The Chicano Fight for Justice*. Cambridge, MA: Belknap Press, 2003.

Haney López, Ian F. "Race, Ethnicity, Erasure: The Salience of Race to LatCrit Theory." *LatCrit: Latinas/os and the Law: A Joint Symposium by California Law Review and Berkeley La Raza Law Journal*. *California Law Review* 85, no. 5 (1997): 1143–1211.

Haney López, Ian F. *Racism on Trial: The Chicano Fight for Justice*. Cambridge, Mass.: Belknap Press, 2003.

Humes, Karen R., Nicholas A. Jones, and Roberto R. Ramirez. "Overview of Race and Hispanic Origin: 2010." U.S. Department of Commerce: Economics and Statistics Administration. U.S. Census Bureau, March 2011, p. 2. http://www.census.gov/prod/cen2010/briefs/c2010br-02.pdf

Latindi@frican@. "Columbus, Latinos and the US Census?" *Latino Rebels*. May 9, 2016.

Lewis, Claude. "Minorities Feel Japanese Sting." *Journal of Commerce*, August 26, 1991.

McCaa, Robert, "The Peopling of Mexico from Origins to Revolution," preliminary draft (notes omitted from web version) for Richard Steckel & Michael Haines (eds.), *The Population History of North America* (Cambridge University Press). December 8, 1997. http://www.hist.umn.edu/~rmccaa/mxpoprev/cambridg3.htm.

"New laws create voting barriers." *Los Angeles Times*. 7 May 2016, A5.

Overmeyer-Velázquez, Mark. "Good Neighbors and White Mexicans: Constructing Race and Nation on the Mexico—U.S. Border." *Journal of American Ethnic*

History vol. 33, no. 1 (Fall 2013), pp. 5–34. https://www.jstor.org/stable/10.5406/jamerethnhist.33.1.0005?seq=1#page_scan_tab_contents.

Patterson, Orlando. "Race by the Numbers." *New York Times*, May 8, 2001.

Patterson, Orlando. "Race Over." *New Republic Online*, December 30, 1999.

Patterson, Orlando. *Rituals of Blood: Consequences of Slavery in Two American Centuries*. New York: Basic Books, 1998.

Pew Research Center. "Multiracial in America: Chapter 7: The Many Dimensions of Hispanic Racial Identity," June 11, 2015. http://www.pewsocialtrends.org/2015/06/11/chapter-7-the-many-dimensions-of-hispanic-racial-identity.

Rodríguez, Cindy. "Latinos Give U.S. New View of Race." *Boston Globe*, January 2, 2000a.

Rodríguez, Clara E. *Changing Race: Latinos, the Census and the History of Ethnicity in the United States*. New York: NYU Press, 2000b.

Román, Miriam Jiménez and Tom Mbakwe. "Africa's Lost Tribe in Mexico." *New African Magazine*, October 1, 2012. http://www.newafricanmagazine.com/africas-lost-tribe-in-mexico.

Sailer, Steve. "Pondering Patterson [II]: OK, How White Are Hispanics?" *VDare*, May 25, 2001. http://www.vdare.com/articles/pondering-patterson-ii-ok-how-white-are-hispanics.

Santa Anna, Otto. *Brown Tide Rising: Metaphors of Latinos in Contemporary American Discourse*. Austin: University of Texas Press, 2002.

Skerry, Peter. *Counting on the Census? Race, Group Identity, and the Evasion of Politics*. Washington, DC: Brookings Institute Press, 2000.

Skerry, Peter. "The Black Alienation: African Americans vs. Immigrants." *The New Republic* 30 (January 1995).

Skerry, Peter. *Mexican Americans: The Ambivalent Minority*. New York: Free Press, 1991.

Sued-Badillo, Jalil, "Christopher Columbus and the Enslavement of the Amerindians in the Caribbean; Columbus and the New World Order 1492–1992," *Monthly Review* 44, no. 3 (July 1992): 77ff; "UT Professor Blasts Efforts for Diversity on Campus." *The Houston Chronicle*, September 11, 1997.

Vincent, Theodore G. *The Legacy of Vicente Guerrero, Mexico's First Black Indian President*. Gainesville: University Press of Florida, 2001.

Wade, Peter. *Race and Ethnicity in Latin America*. London: Pluto Press, 1997.

Wolf, Eric. *Sons of the Shaking Earth: The People of Mexico and Guatemala—Their Land, History, and Culture*. Chicago: Phoenix Books, 1959.

SELECTED VIDEOS

Audiopedia. "Mestizo," YouTube video, 37:43, posted July 24, 2014, https://www.youtube.com/watch?v=Ry7yGbpET1I

Burton, Ryan. "The Color of America: Debating Racial Classification in the U.S. Census," YouTube video, 9:59, posted August 4, 2011, https://www.youtube.com/watch?v=jaw-xgpmNug

Caballero, María. "El machismo invisible y los micromachismos," YouTube video, 12:48, posted May 31, 2015, https://www.youtube.com/watch?v=-oLWb0021P8

meettheprimates's channel. "The history of racial classification," YouTube video, 4:43, posted September 25, 2011, https://www.youtube.com/watch?v=21saXbRo0XY

MrNapper1. "The Americas as 'New World'" (3), YouTube video, 1:49, posted November 18, 2015, https://www.youtube.com/watch?v=C3_WoRgNZrs

Red Rose. "Hombres que evitan educar a sus hijas, por machismo," YouTube video, 12:10, posted February 5, 2016 https://www.youtube.com/watch?v=vS6pY5y0kwI

The Skeptic Feminist. "George Carlin—On Patriarchy," YouTube video, 15:03, posted July 31, 2015, https://www.youtube.com/watch?v=dP5Pv4HthIk

Sweet, Frank W. "A Brief History of Census 'Race,'" YouTube video, 15:38, posted April 9, 2011 https://www.youtube.com/watch?v=KIEmR5cLVsk

TrueGeoPolitik. "Race and Intelligence: Science's Last Taboo," YouTube video, posted July 10, 2012. https://www.youtube.com/watch?v=5JLH9OKMnbU

Weese, Patricia. "Race and Gender Discrimination in the United States Work Place," YouTube video, 3:17, posted April 18, 2012. https://www.youtube.com/watch?v=WASXswcX9bA

The Wise Guy—Anthropology TV. "The Racial History of Latin America (Since 1492)," YouTube video, 8:06, posted August 20, 2014, https://www.youtube.com/watch?v=O6eK7y1yqRg

2

Race and Cultural Identity

BACKGROUND

Racism has consequences. When you live for generations in a caste you assume the personality and values of those who created the caste. This behavior comes out in ways that we are not aware of. Over 50 years ago when I was teaching in a high school, one of my students approached me, asking for the name of a classy restaurant; she wanted to take her prom date to dinner. I gave her the name of a good Mexican restaurant. The student answered, "No, I don't want cheap food." The answer bothered me, since her response probably reflected how she viewed Mexicans and their culture.

The San Fernando Valley (SFV) was white when I first moved there in the 1950s. By 2010, Latinas/os made up 42 percent of the population in the SFV—whites made up 41 percent. Diversity has brought about changes in numbers. In the 1960s Mexican food had not yet been assimilated and Mexican restaurants were mostly in Mexican enclaves. Mexicans were referred to as "chili eaters" and "beaners." At the Mexican restaurants catering to whites, salsa tasted like ketchup. By 2013, salsa was the nation's number one condiment; Latina/o foods and beverages (mostly Mexican) were an $8 billion market and growing.

Americans of all colors consumed 85 billion tortillas in 2000 (Hirsch, 2013; Galindo, 2011).

Next to Chinese cuisine, Mexican is the most diverse cuisine in the world. It has foods not originally available in other parts of the world such as the avocado. While Latinas/os have a common language, there is a great deal of diversity within their customs, ethnicity, intonations, and their food. The diversity in food, culture, and customs comes from the indigenous peoples of the Americas. What people do not take into account is that there were an estimated 100 million people in the Western Hemisphere. Mexico had an estimated population of 25 million, which made it larger than most European nations. What is today Mexico and Central America had considerable cultural and linguistic diversity. This awareness of cultural diversity is today more and more prevalent among younger Mexican Americans and some Latinas/os who are taking pride in this indigenous past. This pride is not only about language and culture but even about indigenous medicine such as herbs: "The Mexicans love to cook fresh food naturally but with an emphasis on diversity, color, spice and flavor. They're always keen to ensure that the food is presented nicely as we should always remember that we eat with our eyes as well as our stomachs. If you should wish you can wash your dinner down with some of the special local beverages. Tequila is of course famous but there are a number of homegrown breweries that specialize in beers that are very popular beyond the country's borders as well" (Ramírez, 2011).

How do numbers bring about a change in cultural and racial attitudes, or do they? How is food a good guide as to the diversity of a people?

Although Americans have historically boasted about being a "nation of immigrants," they have not always welcomed immigrants. Typically, Americans have assimilated their food but limited assimilating their culture or accepting them as full members of American society. Assimilation does not always mean acceptance; it means different things to different people. For some, assimilation is synonymous with Americanization, which the *Collins English Dictionary* defines as "becoming American in character, manners, methods, [and] ideals" (Collins). Many Americans have interpreted this to mean the total absorption of immigrant cultures into the main cultural body. In other words, immigrants were expected to reject their past and act American.

Do you believe that absorption enriches American culture? Does it matter if we label it assimilation or acculturation?

During the first decade of the 20th century, President Theodore Roosevelt wanted to Americanize immigrants so that they would not threaten American culture. Roosevelt believed that Americans had an exceptional culture and that the language and customs of foreigners corrupted it. Roosevelt had an "America: Love It or Leave It" attitude toward immigrants, and in his view, immigrants had to surrender their old-world culture and their historical memories, or they should go back to Europe. For Roosevelt the ethnic ghettos of his times were a threat to an American way of life, and he wanted to get rid of them.

The antipathy toward immigrants went beyond culture and race, and during the first two decades of the 20th century, most Americans, like Roosevelt, considered people of color and other cultures as threats to the American race, which at the time was considered to be composed only of people who spoke English, had British features, and were Protestant. Roosevelt said in 1906 that "race purity must be maintained" (Klarman, 2004, p. 66) and warned of the falling birth rate among native-born white women, saying that it amounted to "race suicide" and threatened the survival of the white race. Roosevelt did not consider Latin Americans white, and, therefore, they would not have met his definition of American (Roosevelt, 1902/2013).

Did Theodore Roosevelt and others believe Latinas/os would or could be assimilated? What did Teddy Roosevelt's "Big Stick" line really mean? Did it have any bearing on his views on assimilation?

Because large numbers of non-English-speaking and non-English-looking immigrants entered the country during the first two decades of the 20th century, Americans hotly debated the question of assimilation and what an American should be. For some, continued immigration of people who did not fit the White Anglo-Saxon Protestant (WASP) prototype was a danger to what their definition of American should be. The Daughters of the American Revolution, the Daughters of the Confederacy, and the League of the South were active in seeing that schools taught the official version of U.S. history (Pozzetta, 1991).[1] Groups such as the American Legion became active in advocating

Americanization after World War I. The Legion promoted American history, English language classes, and American cultural classes to immigrants. The end desire was to make them good Americans, to instill the Protestant ethic of hard work in them, and to have them accept the superiority of American values. For many the smell of garlic was unclean, un-American.

Why did the WASPs equate color and smell of food with cleanliness?

The 1921 and 1924 Immigration Acts were a response to this debate and represented an effort to preserve the American culture and race by controlling who would come in. They were a form of racial engineering. To this end, the National Origins (Discrimination) Act—1921 Act limited the number of immigrants entering the country to 350,000, and set a quota for each nationality in any fiscal year to 3 percent of the number of persons of such nationality who were residents in the United States according to the census of 1910. The 1924 Act lowered the ceiling to 165,000 immigrants and limited each nationality to 2 percent of the 1890 census and, as with the previous act, excluded Asians. Critics called the 1924 Immigrant Quota an effort toward social engineering (Nagi, 1999).

Is this form of social engineering racist, nativist, or both? What is the intended outcome? How are sexism and homophobia similar to racism?

Congress called these laws national origins because they placed countries on a quota system and gave preference to Northern Europeans, limiting the number of Central and Southern Europeans immigrating to the United States. Latin Americans, because of the opposition of the Western growers who were dependent on them to pick crops, were *not* put on the quota. The consequences of these acts were far-reaching, and over the next 40 years the United States, by limiting the immigration of Southern and Central Europeans, became culturally and racially homogeneous.

Meanwhile, the Southern and Central Europeans were pressured to adopt the majority culture and were assimilated or absorbed—the second and third generations rapidly outnumbered the immigrant population that remained ghettoized. Without immigrants reinforcing language and customs, most of the grandchildren of immigrants spoke only English by the third generation. In other words, most European ethnics had assimilated American customs and speech, and they thought of themselves as Americans. They differed from the Puerto Ricans who were American citizens and Mexicans who shared a 2,000-mile border with the United States.

Is nativism synonymous with racism? How do they differ?

How would it make any difference if Latinas/os were Scandinavian?

The assimilation of European immigrant groups did not end the debate over assimilation or Americanization. In the 1950s, there were still enclaves of Irish, Polish, Italian, Jewish, and other groups throughout the United States, and religion was still an issue in presidential elections. Moreover, their color allowed them to blend in. Latinos, Asian Americans, Native Americans, and African Americans also remained apart from the majority culture. Within each of these groups the rate of assimilation differed according to the size of the ethnic or racial enclave. Economic class also played a role in the assimilation of the different groups. For example, assimilated Europeans and Latinas/os with money were able to move out of the ghetto. Some assimilation in parochial schools also took place where children of different immigrant groups mingled.

Were the lighter more Americanized immigrants more quickly accepted? Is assimilation a matter of acceptance?

The 1960s renewed the question of identity as the children and the grandchildren of immigrants resurrected the notion of identity. Mexicans chose to call themselves Americans of Mexican descent, Spanish-speaking Americans, Mexican-Americans, Mexican Americans without a hyphen, and, toward the end of the decade, Chicanas/os. During the 1960s, many Americans grew conscious of the harsh treatment of immigrants, African Americans, and others in American history. Some Americans felt uncomfortable with the fact that the country had once excluded Asians, whom Congress was permitting to enter the country in limited numbers. In the context of the socially conscious

1960s, Congress passed the 1965 Immigration Act, which opened the door for Asians to enter the country on a quota.

For the first time, because of the insistence of nativists and American trade unions, Latin Americans were placed on a quota in 1965. Despite objections, the Act was considered a progressive step forward because it changed government immigration policy from national origins to family preferences and nullified anti-Asian provisions. Its purpose was to reunite families with the new immigrant families, and close relatives were given visas in preference to other applicants.[2] Throughout the 1970s and 1980s, large numbers of Asians and Latin Americans migrated to the United States to reunite with their families. The entry of large numbers of Asians, Middle Easterners, and Latin Americans renewed the arguments of nativists that separate national identities were creating division and making assimilation more difficult.

Meanwhile, African Americans, U.S. Latinos, women, and others challenged the prevailing paradigm and wanted programs to maintain their individual identities. This debate over identity shook not only nativists but moderate scholars who called for Americanization. One of the most prominent voices criticizing the demands of African Americans and other minorities to hold on to their identities was that of the American historian Arthur M. Schlesinger Jr., who wrote the following in his book *The Disuniting of America*:

> George Washington was a sternly practical man. Yet he believed no less ardently in the doctrine of the "new race." "The bosom of America," Washington said, "is open . . . to the oppressed and persecuted of all Nations and Religions." But he counseled newcomers against retaining the "Language, habits and principles (good or bad) which they bring with them." Let them come not in clannish groups but as individuals, prepared for "intermixture with our people." Then they would be "assimilated to our customs, measures and laws; in a word, soon become one people." (Schlesinger, 1992, p. 1)

Schlesinger argued that the United States had been relatively successful at avoiding the fragmentation that plagued Europe, and he cautioned that there was an alarming tendency among Americans to Balkanize their country. Schlesinger appealed to his brand of Americanism and posited that Americans should renounce old loyalties and melt away ethnic differences, saying that in this way Americans can forge a new culture and a new national identity (Schlesinger, 1992, p. 137).

Do you believe that Schlesinger purposely turned the national debate from race to culture? Why? Is this why such conflicts are called "culture wars" as opposed to race wars? Why was it a natural outcome that the debate was widened to include sexism and homophobia?

According to Schlesinger, having a set of common values was essential, which the nation could only accomplish through a common interpretation of a past and through a shared national identity and shared historical experiences. Schlesinger condemned the multiculturalists and minorities who harped at what was wrong with America, and he accused the multiculturalists and Afrocentric Black scholars of exaggerating past injustices. He argued that minorities should not teach history to promote group self-esteem, but instead they should teach history to promote an understanding of the world and the past. The role of the public school system was to Americanize students and teach them the American creed. It was the schools' job to unify Americans. An obsession with differences led to separatism, and "separatism nourishes prejudices, magnifies differences and stirs antagonism" (Eberly, 1998, p. 160).

In what ways are race and culture alike? How are racism and xenophobia the same?

Again, the question of assimilation and who should determine it is a debate that has been raging since the founding of the United States. This debate has fluctuated according to the times. When Schlesinger published his book in the 1990s, the country was in the midst of a culture war in which conservative scholars challenged the pluralistic model of many liberal scholars. They did not believe in racial or cultural fusion. Schlesinger and others favored the idea of American society as a melting pot whereas so-called multiculturalists looked at society as a salad bowl where people mixed but were not melted down. Immigrants and, by extension, their descendants were free to keep their individual identities while being part of the salad. The multiculturalists attacked the assimilationists, accusing them of wanting to impose conformity, while ultraconservatives accused both sides of being un-American and joining forces with Marxists to attack Western civilization.[3]

Is the United States a melting pot? In which ways are people segregating themselves or does government and economic policies separate them?

Calling Schlesinger a nativist would be incorrect, since his attack was not on immigrants but instead on the so-called identity politics of unassimilated minorities and others. He did not defend racial purity but American exceptionalism, a notion that is carried in the culture. Schlesinger's ideas in reality coincided with those of nativists who felt that immigration was threatening American culture and race. Historically, multiculturalists have called those against immigration nativists because they claim to be Native Americans and champions of American culture. Nativism had reemerged as a force in politics in the 1980s when nativists revitalized their attacks, fueled by private foundations and nativist organizations.

Nativists revived the question of assimilation and called for an immediate end to immigration. They argued that when immigrants moved to U.S. territory, they agreed to abide by an implied social contract, which American law, traditions, and heritage shaped. The immigrant agreed to assume a common identity—an American identity, agreeing to abandon the past in favor of a new reality. Nativists accused immigrants of straining the social contract by their refusal to surrender their languages and cultures.

On the other side, critics did not deny that a social contract existed, but they challenged the right of individuals or groups to define what the duties and obligations of the individual were under this social contract. According to them, the U.S. Constitution and laws formed the social contract and defined the parameters of behavior. Pro-immigrants and activists also challenged the broadness of the social contract's interpretation. Did the newcomers renounce their cultural past?

Did immigrants agree not to criticize anything American? Did the descendants of immigrants have the right to retain their ethnic and, for that matter, racial identity?

Americanization as a prerequisite to assimilation is as thorny as it is problematic. Many proponents of Americanization claim that unassimilated immigrants are ethnically Balkanizing America. As in the past, many of these nativists are concerned about having too many foreign-looking and foreign-sounding strangers in their midst and worry about the impact immigrants are having on what they consider unique American values. Nativists see this as a much greater threat than what took place during the first three decades of the 20th century when foreigners were clustered in eastern cities. Today the newcomers are more geographically dispersed, non- European, and darker than the early 20th-century immigrants.

This issue raises the question,"Will U.S. Latinas/os eventually go the route of the Irish, German, Polish, and Italian nationalities?" For many U.S. Latinas/os, identity is important, and consequently assimilation has been slower for them than for Europeans. Moreover, conditions are not the same for Latinas/os. While European immigrants had to cross an ocean at a time when travel was slow, Mexico shares a 2,000-mile border with the United States. Latin Americans can reach the United States in a matter of hours. Thus, U.S. Latinas/os have more contact with their homelands. Telephones also keep them in constant touch with relatives. Further, the masses of Latinos are darker than Europeans, and while Southern and Central Europeans could change their surnames and be assimilated, many U.S. Latinos remain unassimilated to the fourth and fifth generation from their original immigrant ancestors.

Will the universal use of the terms Hispanic or Latina/o accelerate the absorption process? Why is what we call ourselves important?

The experiences of the Irish, Poles, and Italians must be put into a historical context. Europeans came to the United States in response to the industrial revolutions of the 19th century and the uprooting caused by the transformations of their economies. Europeans arrived in the United States at a time when there was opportunity. Non-English-speaking Europeans suffered discrimination; however, the main obstacles to their assimilation were language, culture, religion, and economic class. European ethnics easily overcame the first two variables. Over time Americans became more tolerant of Catholicism, and the expansion of heavy industry allowed some upward mobility for European ethnics. Some of these immigrants changed their last names, and even their religions were accepted as American.

U.S. Latinos migrating to the United States had different experiences. Some Mexicans were in the United States before the Treaty of Guadalupe Hidalgo of 1848, which ended the Mexican War. Other Mexicans came to the United States throughout the 19th century, working on ranches and farms along the Rio Bravo. The railroad helped industrialize the Southwest and Mexico and both pushed and pulled Mexicans into the United States. Mexican migration was constant throughout the 20th century as labor contractors actively recruited Mexican workers for menial labor. Mexicans did not work in heavy industry in any significant numbers until World War II. Additionally, Mexicans assimilated into American society at varying stages. For example, lighter-skinned and middle-class Mexicans were accepted more readily than dark-skinned and working-class Mexicans.

Overall, U.S. Latinos have assimilated, just at different rates. The majority culture influences anyone who listens to TV or the radio or who goes to school. The question is what constitutes assimilation? Some of the factors that should be considered are as follows:

1. How well does the person speak English? What language is spoken at home?
2. Does the person have an accent?
3. What color skin does the person have?
4. What is the person's level of education and income level?
5. What generation is the person?
6. What type of food is eaten at home?
7. What type of music does the person prefer?
8. Where does the person live? Is it a segregated or integrated neighborhood?
9. What is the race or ethnicity of the person's friends?

Lastly, how much discrimination has the person suffered? Racism plays a determining role in assimilation. Within this quagmire, it is important to discuss the question of assimilation or acculturation.

Remember, not all immigrants are resisting assimilation or even absorption. What is often the case is that second-, third-, and fourth-generation Latinas/os are the ones resisting total surrender, as some put it. Some immigrants wish to forget the past entirely and others want to maintain their national identity. The reality is that once immigrants come into the United States they are part of the nation–state called the United States of America. Their nationality, however, does not change. For example, the Maya Indians in Mexico are part of the Mexican nation–state but they have a separate national identity and should. Ultimately the question is, do the immigrants who want to maintain their mother cultures have the right to preserve elements of the past, such as language and history, in the United States?

Should they be called race or culture wars, or both? Is assimilation good?

Other groups have undergone similar patterns, for instance, the Japanese Americans who went through generational cycles. The first generation was the Issei, the second Nisei, and the third Sansei. Each generation was less Japanese in culture and language maintenance. Although they are today into multiple generations, they have retained their group identity and culture if not the language. Most remember the internment of Japanese during World War II and actively oppose xenophobia toward groups, such as Muslims, maintaining a collective historical memory.

Has the Japanese Americans' physical appearance helped them to retain their identity? What role has a historical memory played in the retention of identity?

Meanwhile, while relations are played out with white Americans, there is a fusion among the disparate Latina/o groups with their various cultures, histories, customs, and identities as they assimilate. Professor Samuel K. Byrd has written about the music community in Charlotte, North Carolina—a relatively recent destination for undocumented immigrants—that is forming a sense of place (Byrd, 2015). Charlotte is unique because it is more than a melting pot of Latinos (Mexicans, Caribbeans, Central Americans, and South Americans) seeking economic mobility. They share the effects of restrictive immigration policies much as do marginalized societies throughout the globe. Byrd writes how their struggle is differentiated by generation, race, and class as well as ethnicity. They play a "Latin rock" that incorporates English, Spanish, and Portuguese. Byrd used musicians and their various venues as a guide to understanding the people and their struggles.

Lastly, Latinas/os appear to have more of a sense of color in their clothing and surroundings. When you visit a white neighborhood the ambience is different. The houses seem to be white or pastel colors. In contrast, Latinas/o houses vary in color, with some even painted purple, red, or black. The conformity of the homes of the dominant group is not apparent in Latinas/o neighborhoods. The only things that seem consistent are geraniums and a lemon tree or two. The same goes for the décor inside the homes where white homes are mostly painted in off whites. Latina/o homes stand out for their bold colors.

These differences carry over to dress and fabrics. As one source put it, colors create a sense of inner balance (Wax, 2016). Much of this phenomenon is seen in the patterns of indigenous clothes and is carried over to art. Again, the colors are reflections of conditions of the climates of many of the indigenous peoples who do not come from the austere climates of Northern Europe.

Cultural Fusion

When I was a kid, in many places the prevailing attitude was "white was right," and people would sometimes bathe their children in milk to lighten them. Children would be told to come out of the sun lest they get too dark. On sunny days many walked with umbrellas, not to shield themselves from the heat but to prevent themselves from getting too dark. Things have changed, and white people are now going to tanning studios or lying out in the sun or putting on tanning lotions. A growing number of whites realize that color should be or is an asset.

Culture, however, is another matter. For years, people tried to speak without an accent—that was before accents became sexy. But still the kind of accent is important. Western European accents are preferred—a British accent is the ultimate, a German accent shows intelligence, and a French accent is sexy. Mexican and Asian accents are still on the outs.

More and more sociologists are talking about "cultural fusion" in the new age of transnationalism, convergence, or cultural fusion. They call it "selective acculturation and contemporary multiculturalism as factors that decisively shape immigrants' life and health decisions" (Chiang-Hanisko, 2005). What they have found is that "older adult immigrants maintain a continuous link between their societies of origin and settlement thus creating a 'cultural fit' when it comes to making decisions about healthcare issues" (Chiang-Hanisko, 2005). Older immigrants acculturate at a slower rate. From the beginning immigrants made changes in American society. "[Jewish immigrants] defined a new way of freedom and American dress, and that took part in the late 19th and early 20th century, through mid-century, but even earlier," says Gabriel M. Goldstein, a historian who curated an exhibit for Yeshiva University Museum (Rivas, 2014). Blacks, Latinas/os, Asians, and Native Americans are making similar changes in fashion design.

Globally, national cultures are becoming more diverse. The impact of African American and African music is well documented and has been incorporated domestically and globally. Mexican and Latina/o music are producing new sounds and being beamed throughout the world. The sounds do not clash but are fused.

A good example of fusion or acculturation is the enrichment of what we eat. This form of acculturation is bringing people closer. I like going to the salsa bar and being nudged by Asians as they load up their plastic cups with red, green, and other mixed salsas, some of which are too hot even for me to consume. I can go to the neighboring sushi bar or eat Chinese, Thai, or Indian food. This diversity was uncommon 40 years ago when Mexican students were marked wrong when asked to unscramble the letters ACOT—the answer was COAT; TACO was the wrong answer as it was not yet a word.

Not all examples of fusion go well. For centuries, pizza was considered a peasant's meal in Italy. The Italians brought it to the United States and had a variety of recipes for it. These recipes were found mostly in Italian ghettos and were owned by Italians. Today pizza and its many variations have been totally fused into American culture, and instead of that exquisite garlic-based aroma and tomato sauce, there is ketchup. Pizza has been franchised; is it the taco's turn?

Is the taco going the way of the pizza? Does it matter? What will determine the rate of fusion? How will the franchising of the taco dilute Mexican culture?

ANOTHER POV (POINT OF VIEW)

Latino Is a Culture . . . . Not Yet

Jorge García, Emeritus Professor, Chicana/o Studies, California State University, Northridge

Latino is a word that has been around for many years but does not yet refer to a culture. We may be in the process of developing into a culture but have not reached the point where we can call these varied and disparate groups a culture. A culture is a shared way of thinking, believing, and acting that a group of people has developed over time through shared experiences. The various groups of people we call Latinos are peoples from 25 plus countries who allegedly share some cultural characteristics. However, in this case our differences divide us into different cultural groups. Political and marketing forces are pushing us toward a loose culturally superficial unity but thus far, the realities of our experiences are working to keep us separate.

I first became aware of this generic catchall term as a youth in the 1950s. All four of my grandparents migrated from the hill country of northern Jalisco, Mexico. All four of them always referred to themselves as Mexican and remained Resident Legal Aliens all their lives. My father was born in New Mexico and was brought to California before he was two years old. My mother was born in rural Central California. Both went to elementary school in a system that taught non-English speakers by keeping them in the first grade until they spoke English well enough to advance to the second grade. My father finished eighth grade at age 16 and left school to work. My mother started 10th grade but also dropped out to work at age 16. Both were literate in English and spoke Spanish.

Whenever an Anglo would make a negative comment about "you Mexicans . . . ," my parents would respond by saying, "We Latins . . . ." The word was also used as a modifier of Mexican music; for example, "Sunday night is Latin music night at the Rainbow Ballroom." Some community organizations also used the word in their titles. Oddly enough, the restaurants that served tamales and tortillas often called themselves "Spanish" such as Estrada's Spanish Kitchen. There were a few Spaniards in our midst who were always called Spaniards. There were also a few people from countries other than Mexico, primarily Central America, who were known by their place of origin: *puertorriqueño*, *guatemalteco*, etc. We all understood that Latin was a polite and defensive way of saying Mexican in English. As we grew up we learned the social cost of being Mexican in the United States. Our experiences do play a major role in shaping our cultural identity.

Today there are many more people in the United States who are from or are descendants of people from the 25 plus countries referred to as Latin America, and the word Latin is used to lump all 50+million of us together. Yet the majority of us are of Mexican origin. This combining of all of us is a political brokerage ploy to enhance political clout and influence. Imagine the case of a Cuban American politician in Southern California saying she represents 41,000 Cuban Americans in the region. Now imagine the same politician saying she represents 3.4 million Latinos in Southern California. This statement creates a different reaction. There are many more of us but the majority of Latinos are still Mexican, and that is easily glossed over as we try to put every one of us under the label Latino. However, these forces are at work for obvious reasons.

Commercial marketing ploys to sell us specific products and brands likewise become a factor in shaping our cultural identity. The marketers are facing a challenging situation. Consider the language used to sell products and brands to us. Is it Spanish, Spanglish, or English? When one markets to Latins, whose Spanish is used? Those who speak Spanish often do not seem to be speaking the same language. We

Mexicans call a particular type of sweetbread a *concha*. An Argentine will promptly tell you not to use that word in polite company because to her it is a euphemism for part of the female anatomy. What about the words that enter into the various national varieties of Spanish from the myriad of indigenous languages? Is a turkey a *guajolote, cocono, chompipe*, or a *pavo*? And what about those immigrants from Latin America who do not speak Spanish but speak their indigenous languages?

Goya is a major distributor of foods that supermarkets label as "Hispanic" or "Latino" in the United States. The majority of Latinos in this country are Mexican, and many of us are thankful for the pictures on the containers of *habichuelas, gandules*, and *judias verdes*. If you go to the Goya website you will see that the listings of food products are broken down into three major categories: Caribbean, Mexican, and Central and South American. Food is a major cultural marker, and the largest distributor of Latino food in the United States uses three distinct categories. Some would argue that there are regional differences within each category but the categories hold as to communalities within them. I acknowledge some of these differences even within the category Mexican. Mention tamales to a group of Mexicans and the discussion will invariably turn to corn husk versus banana leaf wrapping followed quickly by a discussion of fillings and ending with a debate about chopped versus shredded meats. These preferences will be debated endlessly, but we are all talking about tamales.

Language, music, and food are requisite basic cultural markers that the heterogeneous groups known as Latinos do not share. We Latinos are one people and one culture if you are willing to say the people of England, the United States, Canada, New Zealand, and Australia are one culture even though they do not share the same food, music, and, questionably, language.

And yet as the marketing and political forces continue to work on us, as 55 million of us are subjected to a society of consumerism and a political brokerage system in this country, we may be moving in fits and starts to the formation of a Latino culture. But we are not there yet.

Sin querer queriendo: *Latinx Should be a Race*

José Juan Gómez, Doctoral Student,
Arizona State University, Tempe

Race is a sociopolitical construct that determines power relations in our social experience as individuals and as communities. Such is the case that racism permeates our everyday social experiences, that in our interactions with others, we are predetermined to treat others based on their racial category. The preconceived ideas of others based on their race then leads to privilege. Privilege is eventually reflected in the demographics of institutions, economical status, and political representation. This pattern all comes back full circle to buttress (reinforce) the racist common sense that predetermines the privileges of those with lighter skin color while criminalizing darker hues. Such is the case within the United States, and such is the case with Latino/a (Latinx) racial common sense—a quick look at *novelas* will be sufficient evidence. With this premise (idea), Latino/a should be considered a race category for political purposes, but it will not be a solution to everyday racist practices.

The construction of race is problematic, and not until, as society, we deconstruct our notions of racial privilege will we be able to consider Latina/o a race without any contradictions. In the traditional sense, with the concept of Latino/a, many races are grouped together, and the same dynamic of privilege is repeated. Latinos/as most definitely are characterized by their colonial origins as a mixed-race population. Nonetheless, as the author suggests, many Latinos/as will not be hesitant to cover themselves from the sun with an umbrella, not out of fear of skin cancer but rather to protect the lighter skin from turning darker. One may ask why such occurrences take place, and the answer is not simple; it dates back to the colonial period when Europe invaded indigenous lands. The caste system, as in Willie Lynch's letter in 1712 where he explained the procedures of breaking down Africans and making them slaves, is a colonial structure that determined our racial common sense and the economical disposition of people of color based on a black and white spectrum.

Besides denoting political power, lighter skin also denotes economic status. Individuals with a decent established economic status have the privilege of seeking tanning salons in order to get darker, but just enough to highlight the color of their eyes and so that they do not cease to be white. However, some brown Latinos/as will look for ways to whiten their skin, be it a protective sun umbrella or creams, the purpose of which is to maintain the purity of their skin and resemble the hue of people in a better economical position. Is it a coincidence that the majority of political leaders in Latin America and the United States are light skinned? Since political power goes hand in hand with economic power and these are the results of colonial social structures based on the caste system, then lighter skin denotes power in our common sense. As a result, individuals are driven to aspire to whiteness as a marker of progress.

Thinking back to the author's reference to Arthur M. Schlesinger Jr.'s book on the "new race" of America, at first glance this new race appears promising, but readers must ask who is included and excluded in the concept of "our people." As long as political and economic institutions are not diversified in an attempt to reflect the demographics of the country, such a "new race" is impossible. Indeed, the United States is attractive to many people worldwide, and regardless of having an African American president, the country's image is centered in its European origins—whiteness and English are the faces of the United States of America. Similar to the sun umbrella and the creams, the cinema and other exported cultural productions obstruct the potentiality of that "new race" by erasing America's diversity.

By the 1960s, ethnic pride and the civil rights movement represented a significant attempt to counterbalance overt and institutional racism. For the Latino/a community, the 1960s also represented a significant sociopolitical shift from their predecessors who saw themselves as white in a failed attempt to claim equal treatment based on their whiteness. However, ethnic pride (i.e., Xicanx, Puerto Rican) gradually lost popularity to the more encompassing term *Latino/a*. The outstanding reason for the shift toward Latinidad was the potential inclusion of a much broader range of population, but the shift also involved the depoliticalization of the 1960s political movements. In this sense, Latinidad is a marker for the political reformist attitude of the United States' population of Spanish-speaking or indigenous descent. Nonetheless, as of today, Hispanic is a much more preferred label by governmental institutions, a term that is less commonly in use within the Latino/a population. The main criticism of both of these terms is that they contribute to the whitening of this population and to the erasure of an indigenous and African heritage and genetic makeup.

As of today, according to a Pew Hispanic Research report, 30 million of the 55 million people who selected Hispanic as their origin in the U.S. Census selected white as their race, while 19 million selected the option for "other" race. From these numbers, it is visible that many Latinos/as are not completely okay with being categorized as white; this despite the fact that "white" is commonly associated with progress (Taylor, López, Martínez, Velasco, 2012) Clearly, "white" is not a racial categorization representative of all Latinos/as, which is estimated at 17.3 percent of the U.S. population. Our current sociopolitical structure is determined by power relations that are reflected in the lack of racial diversity in our institutions. On one hand, racial categorization is important because it is used to discriminate institutionally and covertly through common sense. On the other hand, since the social structure and common sense are already racialized, a race can be useful to empower unprivileged communities and claim higher political and institutional representation. Ideally, race should not be a definite factor in any given society, but if in our society it is already a predetermining aspect of how we as individuals and communities engage with the world around us, then Latino/a should be a race representing *mestizaje*.

This topic is one of the most controversial in the Latino/a community; it is a pressing issue that can be approached from many conflicting perspectives. However, since race has political ends to itself and being political means to be engaged with everyday life around an individual, then the question should not be disregarded: should Latino/a be an additional racial category? If left unchanged, not only will the caste system based on white supremacy perpetuate its colonial sociopolitical structures, but Latinos/as will continue to select "white" as their racial category, and in the act, perpetuate a very limited representation of the diversity in the United States. If changed, Latinos/as as a race will not do much to modify the caste system permeating our society through notions of common sense, but they can attempt to equalize power relations by recognizing the potential political and economic influence that comes with a significant numerical presence of a group within a population. One way or another, the preponderance of race as a marker of class and privilege in our society is an extension of colonialism; Latino/a as a race can lead to a further erasure of darker hues, that is, indigeneity and blackness. In order to properly address racial privilege, microracism, racism, and institutional racism, we must first decolonize our way of thinking and of perceiving everyday reality. As a social body, we must all become conscious of the colonial symbolic system's hegemony over our contemporary conceptualization and understanding of the world through notions of common sense. Latino/a should be considered a race, but it is only a small and problematic step toward finding a solution for the injustices and inequalities of racism.

NOTES

1. The Daughters of the American Revolution were formed with the purpose of promoting understanding of the American Revolution. They have restricted their membership to people who can document that they are descended from someone in the American Revolution. This works to exclude non-Anglo-Saxon immigrants in the nineteenth and twentieth century. Critics accused the organization of bringing the idea of hereditary caste into America, being a blatant separatist group, and spawning Confederate organizations such as the United Daughters of the Confederacy and the Sons of Confederate Veterans. Arthur M. Schlesinger Jr., *The Disuniting of America* (New York: Norton, 1991, 1992).

2. "Immigrant Visas through Family," Immigralaw.com, http://www.immigralaw.com/english/familypref.shtml.

3. Schlesinger also headed a Committee of Scholars in Defense of History. The group criticized Afrocentricism and the growth of ethnic studies and women's studies programs and their attempted revision of U.S. history. According to the Committee of Scholars, minorities were in league with radical feminists and others determined to destroy Western civilization. Other scholars joined Schlesinger and accused multiculturalists and Afrocentric scholars of substituting "ethnic cheerleading" for scholarship. Many of the country's leading historians seconded the Committee of Scholars in Defense of History, which objected to the adoption by the state of New York of U.S. history books giving the so-called multiculturalist interpretation.

BIBLIOGRAPHY

Acuña, Rodolfo F. *Sometimes There Is No Other Side: Chicanos and the Myth of Equality*. Notre Dame, IN: Notre Dame University Press, 1998.

Acuña, Rodolfo F. *Anything But Mexican: Chicanos in Contemporary Los Angeles*. London: Verso, 1996.

America First Committee, United States History. http://www.u-s-history.com/pages/h1643.html

Byrd, Samuel K. *The Sounds of Latinidad: Immigrants Making Music and Creating Culture in a Southern City*. New York: NYU Press, 2015.

Chávez, Linda. "The New Politics of Hispanic Assimilation." In *Beyond the Color Line: New Perspectives on Race and Ethnicity in America*, edited by Abigail Thernstrom and Stephan Thernstrom, 383–390. Stanford, CA: Hoover Institution, 2002.

Chiang-Hanisko, Lenny. "Cultural Fusion: Rethinking Assimilation Theory in Older Adult Immigrants Healthcare Decisions." Midwest Nursing Research Society, Kent State University, 2005. http://hdl.handle.net/10755/160331

Collins English Dictionary. https://www.collinsdictionary.com/dictionary/american/americanize

Cruz, José E. *Identity and Power: Puerto Rican Politics and the Challenge of Ethnicity*. Philadelphia, PA: Temple University Press, 1998.

"The Diversity of Hispanic Cuisine, from Mexico to the Patagonia," MIC Food. http://www.micfood.com/blog/the-diversity-of-hispanic-cuisine-from-mexico-to-the-patagonia

Eberly, Don E. *America's Promise: Civil Society and the Renewal of American Culture*. Boulder, CO: Rowman & Littlefield, 1998.

Ennis, Sharon R., Merarys Ríos-Vargas, and Nora G. Albert. "The Hispanic Population: 2010." 2010 Census Briefs, May 2011. http://www.census.gov/prod/cen2010/briefs/c2010br-04.pdf

Farley, Reynolds and Richard Alba. "The New Second Generation in the United States." *International Migration Review* 36, no. 3 (Fall 2002): 669ff.

Galindo, René. "The Nativistic Legacy of the Americanization Era in the Education of Mexican Immigrant Students." *Educational Studies: A Journal of the American Educational Studies Association* 47, no. 4 (2011): 323–346.

Gordon, Milton. *Assimilation in American Life: The Role of Race, Religion and National Origins*. New York: Oxford University Press, 1964.

Hayes-Bautista, David E., and Gregory Rodriguez. "California: Cultural Assimilation Is Bad for Your Health." *Los Angeles Times*, December 17, 1995. http://articles.latimes.com/1995-12-17/opinion/op-16182_1_american-culture

Hirsch, J. M. "Tortillas And Salsa Are Outselling Burger Buns And Ketchup In The US." *Business Insider*, October 17, 2013, http://www.businessinsider.com/salsa-is-americas-favorite-condiment-2013-10

"Immigrant Visas through Family," Immigralaw.com. http://www.immigralaw.com/english/familypref.shtml

Klarman, Michael J. *From Jim Crow to Civil Rights: The Supreme Court and the Struggle for Racial Equality*. Oxford: Oxford University Press, 2004.

Kollenborn, K. P. "Who are the Issei, Nisei, Kibei, and Sansei?" http://kpkollenborn.blogspot.com/2010/11/who-are-issei-nisei-kibei-and-sansei.html

Lorenzo, Maria-Isabel. "Race, Gender, and Mexican Americanization: How Mainstream Anglo Assumptions Inspired Mexican Americanization in California, 1914–1939." Thesis, California State University, Fresno, 2012. 86 pp. http://gradworks.umi.com/15/31/1531238.html

Lynch, Willie. *The Willie Lynch Letter And the Making of A Slave*. La Vergne, TN: African Tree Press, 2011.

Nagi, Mae M. "The Architecture of Race in American Immigration Law: A Reexamination of the Immigration Act of 1924." *The Journal of American History* 86 (1) (1999): 67–92.

Nowrasteh, Alex. "The Failure of the Americanization Movement." Cato at Liberty, December 18, 2014. http://www.cato.org/blog/failure-americanization-movement

Ochoa, Alberto M. "Succeeding in America: Latino Immigrants are Finding a New World and More Challenges in Assimilating than Immigrants of a Century Ago." *San Diego Union-Tribune*, July 20, 2003.

Orfield, Gary. "The Resegregation of Our Nation's Schools: A Troubling Trend." *Civil Rights Journals*, no. 1 (Fall 1999): 8ff.

Orfield, Gary, and Susan E. Eaton. "Back to Segregation." *The Nation* 276, no. 8 (March 3, 2003): 5ff.

Pozzetta, George E. *Americanization, Social Control, & Philanthropy (Immigration and Ethnicity Series)*. New York: Routledge, 1991.

Ramírez, George. "Regional Diversity Influences Mexican Cuisine." submityourarticle.com, posted August 9, 2011. http://articles.submityourarticle.com/regional-diversity-influences-mexican-cuisine-203169

Rivas, Jorge. "How Immigrants Are Fueling America's Cultural History Through Fashion." *Fusion*, June 24, 2014. http://fusion.net/story/6009/how-immigrants-are-fueling-americas-cultural-history-through-fashion

Rodríguez, Gregory. "150 Years Later, Latinos Finally Hit the Mainstream." *New York Times*, April 15, 2001.

Roosevelt, Theodore. "Theodore Roosevelt's 1902 letter on 'race suicide' to Marie Van Horst," White House, Washington, October 18, 1902, progressingamerica, June 14, 2013. http://progressingamerica.blogspot.com/2013/06/theodore-roosevelts-1902-letter-on-race.html

Rosales, Rodolfo. *The Illusion of Inclusion: The Untold Political Story of San Antonio*. Austin: University of Texas Press, 2000.

Taylor, Paul, Mark Hugo Lopez, Jessica Martínez and Gabriel Velasco, "II. Identity, Pan-Ethnicity and Race," Pew Research Center, April 4, 2012. http://www.pewhispanic.org/2012/04/04/ii-identity-pan-ethnicity-and-race/

Schlesinger Jr., Arthur M. *The Disuniting of America: Reflections on a Multicultural Society*. New York: W. W. Norton, 1992.

Sloan, Jane, and Carlos E. Cortés. *Multicultural America: A Multimedia Encyclopedia*. Thousand Oaks, CA: Sage, 2013.
"The Social Contract and Constitutional Republics." Constitution Society, 1994, 2007. http://www.constitution.org/soclcont.htm
Upchurch, Michael. ArtXchange show gives a sense of depth, breadth of Latino art in the NW, *The Seattle Times*, March 11, 2010.

SELECTED VIDEOS

Listen to the Videos. How are they Examples of Fusion? Can You Provide More Examples?

Blanco, Robbin. "Mexican Fusion—Quemazón by Robbin Blanco Power Trio," YouTube video, 5:37, posted February 5, 2015. https://www.youtube.com/watch?v=8B2IU-zHIbI
"East LA Taiko Featuring Lysa Flores—Love Will Tear Us Apart," YouTube video, 3:57, posted February 21, 2012. https://www.youtube.com/watch?v=I5s7HmKpGfk
Ellekuruda's channel. "The ASEAN Community by 2015," YouTube video, 6:22, January 10, 2010. https://www.youtube.com/watch?v=YrnK5UQDdO0
Gorodezky, Alexander. "Ethnic jazz fusion. Romany (Gypsy) tune," Via Romen band, YouTube video, 3:46, posted March 15, 2013. https://www.youtube.com/watch?v=pe6P_cu11nc
Poulsen, Ryan. "Little Rock—School Integration," YouTube video, 5:45, posted April 18, 2013. https://www.youtube.com/watch?v=Qk1tTCk2Kks
Salsadura. UK. "History of Salsa From Africa to Newyork 1 of 3," YouTube video, 8:16, posted March 13, 2011. https://www.youtube.com/watch?v=HtJKDvhA7YM
Seder, Sam. "Latino Immigrants Assimilate No Slower Than Other Immigrants," YouTube video, 2:44, posted January 31, 2013. https://www.youtube.com/watch?v=vWGE5Zg5j_Y
Suárez, Ray. "Integration and assimilation of Latinos," YouTube video, 5:56, posted February 18, 2011. https://www.youtube.com/watch?v=3R6FXZ_lpQo
Stay See. "Hip Hop 'Funk' Jazz—Ours Samplus," YouTube video, 54:28, posted October 16, 2014. https://www.youtube.com/watch?v=9ka5bgHnHyg
TeleSUR English. "Cultura Latina—Latin Swing and Jazz Fusion," YouTube video, 12:42, posted May 29, 2015. https://www.youtube.com/watch?v=ApE3-PhiXho
UNAS United. "Social Integration," YouTube video, 3:56, posted March 15, 2015. https://www.youtube.com/watch?v=h_Km9IG8t3o

3

Cultural and Linguistic Diversity in Education

BACKGROUND

In December of 2014, *Atlantic Magazine* reported that despite the benefits of bilingualism, "U.S. Schools Are Saying Goodbye to Foreign Languages." The Success Academy Charter Schools that enroll about 9,000 students in 32 charter schools around New York City dropped their foreign language requirement at a time when a high demand existed for foreign language speakers. In an interview the school's CEO apologized, explaining, "So something's got to go. We picked—and you know this may be shocking to this audience—we picked foreign languages [to eliminate]. People say 'Don't you believe in foreign languages?' I love multilingualism. I speak French, but something had to go . . . . We can't do everything. And by the way, Americans don't tend to do foreign languages very well. I think if I were doing schools in Europe I might feel differently. But my son took three years of French and he could barely say, 'How are you?' . . . I really believe whatever we do we should do it exceptionally well and I wasn't sure that I could find foreign language instructors that were really good and could do it at a very high level" (Kohli, 2014).

Why has the instruction of Spanish declined in the public schools given the increase of the Latina/o student population? How is the elimination of Spanish language learning a slight to Latin America? Why are people who know a foreign language less apt to be xenophobic?

This development was baffling to many because "the majority of colleges expect a student to have a minimum of two years of foreign language when applying to college" (Barber, 2015). The fact is that fewer colleges are requiring a foreign language. Explanations range from xenophobia to declining grade point averages. Politicians have worsened the situation by passing legislation allowing students to substitute coding classes such as computer science for the foreign language requirement—the reasoning is that everyone speaks English. "The rationale . . . is rooted in the rapidly changing world of information technology. Jobs in programming and various information technology fields continue to be in high demand. Nonprofit K–12 advocates at Code.org say that the number of computer science graduates in 2015 cannot fill the demand in the industry. "There are 38,175 new graduates to fill 618,000 open jobs" (Avelino, 2016). It doesn't help foreign languages that "President Barack Obama called for a $4 billion increase in funding for computer science programs for high schools, citing the need to meet the drastically under filled demand" (Avelino, 2016). Universities show very little leadership and follow the money.

What is the relationship between the decline in Spanish instruction and economics? Why would coding classes trump foreign languages?

In the past, foreign languages were one of the few examples of bilingualism and multiculturalism in high school and college classes. A correlation between the teaching of foreign languages and lip service to ethnic diversity exists at the university level. Publicly universities praise diversity, although critics doubt whether they know what it is. Columbia University President Lee C. Bollinger claims: ". . . the diversity of our University community makes it possible for students, faculty, alumni, and neighbors to interact with—and thus be transformed by—the multiplicity of human perspectives" (Multicultural Affairs). In reality the number of students and faculty of color remains low. In Bollinger's view diversity comes about by recruiting highly gifted minority and international students. They are given space within the university—almost always in the Student Union. Diversity to most university administrators means more brown and black faces and taco night once a week.

What is your opinion of Columbia University's multicultural paradigm? Will it achieve multiculturalism? Can diversity be achieved without a balance of diversity in students and faculty?

Although California has a sizable Latino population, the approach is no different at the California state universities (CSU). The CSU paradigm resembles that of the Ivy League schools; the only difference is that, for the most part, the CSUs do not attract students from the ranks of the elite. However, what the CSU calls cultural identity boils down to token brown and black faces. They sponsor taco nights and Black History months, and occasionally fraternities mock minority cultures. In the end, diversity is measured by the color of faces. Not many changes, however, have taken place, and cultural diversity amounts to smoke and mirrors.

How do public state universities differ from Ivy League universities? Do classes and special events socialize students to accept different people and cultures? Evaluate diversity at your school.

CSUN services an area with a large Mexican/Latino population and its mission is to educate an economically diverse population. Part of its mission is to educate competent teachers for this diverse population. Most studies prove that this mission is best achieved by employing minority teachers who know those communities and can train teachers, teach and motivate Mexican and Latino students.

Why would white faculty members resist hiring professors of color? How is faculty diversity a key to institutional diversity?

LINGUISTIC DOMINATION

Like race, culture has essentially been used as a weapon of domination. It has been said that man invented culture but that culture controls us. Culture represents power and influences us in imperceptible ways, shaping our lives and relationships. Culture is much more than just language, dress, or food. It is constantly changing, manipulated by the media and the elite who have reduced it to a commodity. Culture gives meaning to our identities. Language sends cultural messages. In the 1960s we were well aware of the role of culture that went beyond language. Our collective awareness has been erased by time and the manipulation of language.

How does culture reinforce and maintain xenophobia, sexism, and homophobia? How does a collective memory aid a positive reform of culture?

During the 1960s, I was intellectually tickled by the lectures of Leonard Olguín, a high school teacher who later taught at Los Beach State College. The title of his book was *Shuck Loves Chirley* (Olguin, 1968), which summed up an essential linguistic conflict. I recalled my own childhood when the teacher would grab my chin and yell at me, "Look at me straight in the eyes; don't be shifty eyed, and don't be defiant." With a sore neck I would go home and when my father scolded me, not wanting to be defiant, I would look straight into his eyes, and he would yell at me, "Look down. Don't be defiant." The lessons stayed with me, and one of the first courses I designed for Chicano Studies was called "Cultures in Conflict" (Acuña, 1970).

Language is frequently used in culturally and ideologically biased contexts. Accents are often graded according to the prestige of the speakers' country of origin. "In the context of globalization, immigration, and perceptions about its prestige and power, there is an immense" value in English; after all, it is the language of the colonizer (Waseem, 2013). Language corresponds to power domains, and it is a doorway to economic and educational opportunities. English is the language of the International Monetary Fund and the World Bank. In fact, Northern European languages fall into this same orbit. On a daily basis, the teacher dominates the student through the use of language. In most cases, colonial languages suppress the connection to and the development of other languages. They contribute to making the colonized languages extinct. It is common in colonial situations to forbid the use of native languages, prioritizing instead the use of the language of the colonizers. A policy is imposed limiting communication in the national or colonial language. For example, during the dictatorship of Spanish dictator Francisco Franco, the Catalåns or Basques were forbidden to use their languages. Accordingly, they reasoned Mexicans lacked intelligence. IQ testing played a major role in justifying remedial programs that trained Mexicans for subordinate roles in American society. During the 1920s about half of Mexican students attended segregated Mexican schools. Not all Protestants supported the jingoist strategy of cultural annihilation. Many reformers pushed for programs stressing the cultural needs of Mexican children. Some reformers advocated compassionate Americanization programs based on stressing the positive assets of Mexican culture, and they sponsored cultural and teacher exchanges with Mexico.

Protestant ministers such as the Reverend Robert N. McLean, an associate director of the Presbyterian Board of Missions in the United States, were active in the Mexican and Puerto Rican communities, writing studies and establishing schools. They played important advocacy roles. Mexicans also opposed the English Only teaching requirements enforced in Texas and other states during World War I, which increased segregation.

During the 1920s, Mexican organizations established *escuelitas* (little schools) dedicated to teaching reading and writing instruction in Spanish to preschoolers. A bridge between these early scholars and bilingual education and Chicana/o studies was University of Texas Professor George I. Sánchez. Born in New Mexico, educated in Jerome, Arizona, Sánchez taught in public schools and earned an EdD from the University of California at Berkeley. Sánchez later taught at the Universities of New Mexico and Texas and was a crusader for equal education for Mexican Americans. He was a gradualist—in line with labor-oriented progressives of his time. In the fall of 1957, American education entered an era of intense educational reform.

SPUTNIK

The Soviet Union sparked a revolution when it launched Sputnik in October, 1957, which led to cries for educational reform—the Russians had beaten the United States in the race to outer space. The reaction was that the United States spent billions of dollars into reforming the teaching of math and science, and a substantial amount went into funding of the humanities and the social sciences. For a time, higher education spurred by government grants was interested in reforming language teaching methods.

By the mid-1960s, the National Education Association published *The Invisible Minority* to address the 60 percent dropout problem among Mexican Americans. The NEA based many of its findings on a survey of Tucson schools. Aside from the teaching of bilingual education, the report recommended the building of pride in Mexican American students. The report quoted an essay by a 13-year-old eighth grade Mexican American:

> ME
>
> To begin with, I am a Mexican. That sentence has a scent of bitterness as it is written. I feel that if it weren't for my nationality I would accomplish more. My being a Mexican has brought about my lack of initiative. No matter what I attempt to do, my dark skin always makes me feel that I will fail. Another thing that "gripes" me is that I am such a coward. I absolutely will not fight for something even if I know I'm right. I do not have the vocabulary that it would take to express myself strongly enough. Many people, including most of my teachers, have tried to tell me I'm a leader. Well, I know better! Just because I may get better grades than most of my fellow Mexicans doesn't mean a thing. I could no more get an original idea in my head than be President of the United States. I don't know how to think for myself. I want to go to college, sure, but what do I want to be? Even worse, where do I want to go? These questions are only a few that trouble me. I'd like to prove to my parents that I can do something. Just because I don't have the gumption to go out and get a job doesn't mean that I can't become something they'll be proud of. But if I find that I can't bring myself to go to college, I'll get married and they'll still get rid of me. After reading this, you'll probably be surprised. This is the way I feel about myself, and nobody can change me. Believe me, many have tried and have failed. If God wants me to reach all my goals, I will. No parents, teachers, or priest will change the course that my life is to follow. Don't try. (National Association of Education, 1966)

The purpose of the report was to encourage schools to implement pedagogies addressing the high dropout rate of Mexican American students. According to the NEA, the way was not to Americanize and take away the student's identity. It asked: "Is there something inherent in our system of public schooling that impedes the education of the Mexican-American child—that indeed drives him to drop out?" The

NEA report found the schools complicit; Mexican Americans were schooled to fit a stereotype in the process, as witnessed by the haunting words, "I feel if it weren't for my nationality I would accomplish more" (National Association of Education, 1966).

In 1967 California Governor Ronald Reagan signed Senate Bill 53 that ended a 95-year-old state education mandate requiring schools to carry out instruction in English. The next year President Lyndon Johnson signed Title VII of the Elementary and Secondary Education Act that provided funds for students with limited English skills. There was no English Only requirement. Even bilingual education critics conceded that bilingual education was "a special effort to help immigrant children learn English so that they can do regular schoolwork with their English-speaking classmates and receive an equal educational opportunity" (Porter, 1998).

Congress passed the Bilingual Education Act of 1968 in an era of growing immigration and a militant civil rights movement. It allocated federal funding to encourage local school districts to try approaches incorporating native-language instruction. Most states followed the lead of the federal government, enacting bilingual education laws of their own or at least decriminalizing the use of other languages in the classroom. The notion came from President Lyndon Johnson, who, according to former U.S. Rep. Edward R. Roybal, raised the idea of bilingual education on an Air Force One flight. Johnson based his opinions on his teaching experience in a Mexican school where he observed that Mexican children were smart but that they did not know how to speak English. This problem would keep them in the same grade year after year and falling behind in crucial subjects like math and science, which Mexican students could understand in Spanish. Mexican American educators also pointed out that teachers often punished Mexican students for speaking Spanish in school. Studies showed that school districts would often label non-English-speaking Mexican American students as mentally retarded.

Lau v. Nichols based its decision on Title VI of the Civil Rights Act (*Lau v. Nichols*, 1974). The ruling stated the following: "There is no equality of treatment and provided funds for facilities, textbooks, teachers and curriculum for students who did not understand English" ("Evolution of Important Events in California Bilingual Education Policy"). After this point, nativist organizations and the Republican Party made the defeat of bilingual education a priority, and in 1998 voters passed Proposition 227, the so-called English for the Children initiative, which eliminated bilingual education.

Is K-12 education a right or a privilege? Does bilingual education go to the right of all students to learn? Is it good education for a student to sit in class not understanding what the teacher is saying?

THE WAR ON BILINGUAL–BICULTURAL EDUCATION

According to the then University of Colorado law professor Richard Delgado, a string of ultra-right-wing foundations financed the English Only movement, of which Proposition 227 was part (Stefanic and Delgado, 1996). Opponents argued that Proposition 227 was confusing voters and that bilingual education was pedagogically sound (Stefanic and Delgado, 1996). Bilingual education had two goals: the development of academic English and school success and the development and maintenance of the student's first language.

Educator Stephen Krashen argued that it made no sense to let students sit in a class and have a limited grasp of the subject matter while they learn English. According to Krashen, a "child who understands history [in his native language] . . . will have a better chance understanding history taught in English than a child without this background knowledge" (Krashen, 1999). Krashen posited that "there is strong evidence that literacy transfers across languages, that building literacy in the primary language is a short-cut to English literacy" (Krashen, 1999).

White voters overwhelmingly approved Proposition 227. Latinos voted by a margin of 2–1 against the initiative, with many describing it as discriminatory; 37 percent voted yes, and 63 percent voted no. The tally was reversed with white voters. Bilingual education, like immigration, was a red button issue.

Is the opposition to bilingual education pedagogical or political and racial bias?

What then makes bilingual education so controversial? Is bilingual education the invention of the 1960s or of U.S. Latinas/os? In reality, bilingual education has been part of the European immigrant tradition. Newcomers often enrolled their children in bilingual or non-English-language public and private schools. They wanted to keep their native languages alive. In 1839, Ohio adopted a bilingual education law authorizing German–English instruction at parents' requests. In 1847

Louisiana authorized the teaching of French and English, and the New Mexico Territory did so for Spanish and English in 1850. By the end of the 19th century, around a dozen states passed bilingual education laws. These states were not unique, and many smaller localities offered bilingual instruction in languages as diverse as Norwegian, Italian, Polish, Czech, and Cherokee.

Why does the attitude of American corporations doing business in Latin America and the majority of the American public toward learning Spanish differ? If you had a market in a Spanish-speaking neighborhood, why would it be good business to hire Spanish-speaking employees?

Before World War I, at least 600,000 public and parochial school students received some or all of their schooling in German—some 4 percent of all American children in the elementary grades—which was larger than the percentage of students enrolled in Spanish–English programs today. World War I changed this, and an anti-German sentiment led most states to enact English- only laws designed to Americanize foreigners. People of German extraction even changed their last names to Americanized versions, and local school boards banned the study of foreign languages in the early grades, which the courts declared unconstitutional in 1923. By the mid-1920s, school districts had largely dismantled bilingual schooling. School authorities expected immigrant children to learn in English only, and they prohibited them from speaking Spanish or any other foreign language in school. Teachers often punished Latina/o students when they broke the no-Spanish-spoken rule. Schools called this method of teaching English "sink or swim," or the immersion method.

From the beginning, the process was fraught with politics, with some educators and politicians opposing the Bilingual Education Act of 1968 unless it taught English as a second language. Eventually, the bill passed, ironically with little support from the White House (Stewner-Manzanares, 1988). This lack of support was because of President Johnson's problems with the Vietnam War and the politics of the War on Poverty. Much of the funding for the first bilingual program came from the media giant, the Hearst Corporation (Pycior, 1997).

After Congress passed the Bilingual Education Act of 1968, the U.S. Supreme Court held in *Lau v. Nichols* that leaving limited-English students in English Only classrooms to sink or swim made "a mockery of public education." The court held that education should be equally available to all students. *Lau v. Nichols* (1974) required schools to take "affirmative steps" to overcome language barriers hampering children's access to the curriculum. Congress immediately reinforced this in the Equal Educational Opportunity Act of 1974 (*Lau v. Nichols,* 1974). Neither the Bilingual Education Act nor the Lau decision required any specified methodology for teaching limited English students. However, bilingual education was clearly considered a civil right that required educational programs to offer equal opportunities for limited English children. The universities and schools in turn supported bilingual education for as long as federal monies fueled them.

Postscript: The 1968 law was passed as a result of World War II and Sputnik (1957), which showed that the United States was woefully unprepared to lead the world because of its lack of bilingual experts. It passed also because of the Civil Rights Movement of the 1960s and numerous education studies showing that it contributed to the success of Mexican American children.

SPEAK AMERICAN

Influencing the discourse on bilingual education was the notion that most Americans have never been fond of foreign languages although its leaders have given lip service to it. In 2004, "President George W. Bush . . . said that diversity is one of America's greatest strengths and . . . encouraged the development of race-neutral alternatives to achieve diversity in educational institutions. Diversity, broadly understood, gives students an enriching insight into the lives and worldviews of a wide variety of people. Exposure to students from different backgrounds gives students a larger context within which they may analyze competing views. There is no substitute for allowing young people the opportunity to exchange ideas with others who have talents, backgrounds, viewpoints, experiences and interests different from their own" (U.S. Department of Education Office for Civil Rights).

While business became more global, most institutions of higher learning became more insular and dropped or lowered foreign language requirements. Between 1966 and 1979, U.S. colleges and universities scaled back requirements for foreign language as a qualification for admission, and the number of institutions of higher education requiring a foreign language for admission dropped from 34 percent to 8 percent. Meanwhile, many children of European ethnics who were becoming teachers resented that many school districts were requiring some knowledge of Spanish and said if people lived in the United States, they should speak English. They believed it was up to the students to adjust to the system. To make their point, they raised the illusion of how their grandparents had come to the United States and how they had to learn English.

Many U.S. Latina/o leaders countered that Americans had a low opinion of the Spanish language and culture and that the best way to counteract this ethnocentrism was to give Spanish language and culture greater importance in the educational scheme. By this time, Mexican Americans and Asians were not the only U.S. proponents of bilingual education. Cuban immigrants, many of them highly educated, called for quality schooling for their children, an education that would preserve the Cubans' Spanish culture. Puerto Ricans were equally outspoken in their demands. In New York City, ASPIRA (ASPIRE), a Puerto Rican cultural organization, sued the school board for effective bilingual programs.

Meanwhile, the dreams of many Latinos that everyone would speak two languages were scaled back, and by 1983 the National Association for Bilingual Education advocated transitional bilingual programs and abandoned its demand for language maintenance. It accepted the primacy of English and said the native tongue should be considered a second language. The American Federation of Teachers (AFT) opposed bilingual education because its leader believed it was keeping Latinos from assimilating. Although U.S. Latinas/os had increased in population, they lacked the voting and economic power to fight back the pressure of English Only groups.

The fluctuation in the economy in the 1980s and 1990s increased strains and heightened nativist sentiments throughout the United States. Deindustrialization, that is, the sending of factories overseas, severely curtailed the stepping stone many working-class Americans had into the middle class by eliminating higher-paying union-scale jobs. Rising property values also made it more difficult to qualify for purchasing a house. With this downturn, nativism increased, and bilingual education came under heavy fire as funding for education decreased, from kindergarten through to institutions of higher learning.

Conservative think tanks played an important role in cultivating this discontent and associating the disaffectedness and the decline in education with many reforms of the 1960s. The rising conservatism expressed itself through a growing resistance to taxes, blaming unemployment on immigrants, and growing resentment toward immigrants and bilingual education. A feeling that foreigners were trying to take something away from Americans seemed to justify the curtailing of special programs such as bilingual education and ethnic studies.

Within this context, a polarization occurred in American society. A conservative surge negated the civil rights reforms of the 1960s, and in the late 1970s, ultraconservatives became much more active in forming think tanks and organizations. According to University of Colorado law professor Richard Delgado, "The Reagan era was a time of consolidation and experiment. Supply-side economics came and went. Religion, family values, and patriotism came to stay" (Stefanic and Delgado, 1996, p. 3).

These struggles thrust Latinas/os into the mainstream political movement in the early 1990s, fanned by a severe recession that encouraged many politicians to scapegoat immigrants for the economic recession. Former California Governor Pete Wilson resurrected his political career by blaming immigrants for California's problems. Wilson contributed greatly to Proposition 187, the anti-immigrant initiative, in 1994; Proposition 209, the anti-affirmative action initiative, in 1996; and Proposition 227, the anti-bilingual education initiative in 1998. Meanwhile, most U.S. Latinos became more defensive, interpreting the anti-bilingual education mood as directed against them.

Prior to the 1980s, why did most references, academic and popular, refer to Mexican Americans and not Latinas/os? Why would these groups become defensive?

"The diversity question in America now is not 'Whether?' but 'How?'" (U.S. Department of Civil Rights, 2004). The fight for bilingual education continues as does the fight to achieve student and faculty diversity through affirmative action. Many U.S. Latinas/os believe that knowledge of the Spanish language is a strong part of their identity and essential in this era of globalization. The issue of bilingual education binds most U.S. Latina/o organizations with a common cause. ASPIRA (New York), the Puerto Rican Legal Defense Fund, and the Mexican American Legal Defense and Education Fund all filed amicus briefs in *Lau v. Nichols* (Rodríguez, 1991, p. 140).

Puerto Ricans had a strong sense of identity even before being incorporated into the United States in 1898 (Rodríguez,1991, p. 29). In New York City in 1980, 91 percent of Puerto Ricans spoke Spanish at home compared with 90 percent of Cubans and 64 percent of Mexicans. Why?

In the past, Puerto Rico's isolation from the mainland allowed for the formation of close family and cultural ties. However, probably more important was the role of U.S. colonialism and American racism both on the island and on the mainland.

Mexicans have a different experience with racism than other Latinas/os, engendering a strong sense of identity among Mexicans. The Mexican Revolution of 1910 contributed to the forging of this identity. The constant waves of Mexicans coming from Mexico have revitalized their sense of Mexicanness; intermarriage between immigrants and citizens has been common throughout the generations. Identity is also important to Cubans and has been reinforced by their exile status.

In addition, most South Americans and Central Americans are recent arrivals and also have a strong sense of identity, having gone through almost 200 years of nation–state building. Salvadorans, for example, come from a densely populated area, and a war and their collective migrations to the United States have reinforced Salvadoran identity.

Because of this, the victory of the English Only forces in California did not end the debate over bilingual education. Thus, as Latinos got more political clout and more of them were elected to office, Latina/o politicians and organizations began to challenge the act. The way they saw it was that an estimated 1.5 million public school students in California spoke little, if any, English, and that this problem had to be addressed. The powerful state senator, Richard Polanco, D-Los Angeles, chair of the Latino Legislative Caucus in 2001, pushed legislation that would require "appropriate instruction, curriculum, and materials" for limited English students (Guthrie, 2002).

Just 12 percent of California's 1.5 million language minority students remained in bilingual programs, and this number declined without substantial federal support. One reason for this decline was the negative publicity given to bilingual education. Another was the inability of the state to hire adequately trained Spanish-speaking teachers. Yet another reason was that many school districts failed to inform parents of the option to keep their children in bilingual programs (Helfand, 2002; Geyer, 2001).

Out of the discourse on bilingual education a third camp has emerged, which recognizes that both immersion and bilingual programs have been deficient. This camp states that test scores can go either way and that many teachers are not teaching the subject matter by training students to take particularized exams. They point to the inequality of schools and cite the lack of certified teachers in Latino and African American schools. Because of this, the American Civil Liberties Union (ACLU) sued 18 California school districts, alleging that "the state is providing its poorest students with an inferior education." The ACLU expected to expand its suit to cover all the state's 1,100 districts and their 5.8 million students ("Eighteen Calif. School Districts Sued," 2000).

The future of bilingual education is uncertain because of the backlash it produced. A major weakness was that from the beginning it was inadequately funded, and higher education was not prepared to train bilingual teachers. It was seen as a Mexican program and thus not given importance. It came about as a result of inequities and failures of the American educational system. Educators such as Dr. George I. Sánchez envisioned a better world where students would be bilingual–bicultural (Chaudhry, 2010). It was part of the quest for equality. Finally, cultural diversity cannot be achieved without affirmative action. Most Latinas/os view arguments that race-based criteria are not legitimate as racist arguments. These court decisions have delayed diversity.

SUMMING UP

The argument of those for bilingual education and diversity is the following: Most Americans do not know what bilingual education or what cultural diversity are. They are instinctively against both because they sound foreign and they interpret them as forced integration. They also oppose affirmative action and faculty diversity because they fear a loss of control of THEIR institutions. Accordingly, Americans feel threatened by other languages and by integrating their faculties because having an irrational fear of foreigners drives them to oppose bilingual education and affirmative action. However, this is at a time when business and government want more people proficient in foreign languages.

Saying that the reason for opposing bilingual education is based on the needs of the child is disingenuous. The common argument that people have succeeded without bilingual education is open to question. For example, many German Americans received bilingual education, and they were among the most successful of the European immigrants. Jewish Americans have had Hebrew schools that supplemented their public education, as did Japanese Americans, and that education did not detract from their learning or assimilation into society. Many other ethnic groups, such as the Italians and Poles, did not have as extensive bilingual education networks, but that is no reason for Latinos or any other newcomers to suffer through their language barriers.

What it comes down to is that Latina/o children have certain needs. Many studies show that students coming from places such as Mexico do better in school than U.S.-born Mexicans, and that those coming to the United States having completed the first six grades do better than those having completed only one grade. An ability to read in any language transfers across languages even when the writing systems are different. Instead of blaming bilingual education for the system's failure, educators should study what it is in American education that takes away a child's motivation to learn. An exposure to other cultures produces an appreciation for them.

Limited-English-speaking children would benefit from bilingual education just as most Americans would benefit from knowing two languages. Latinas/os know that Latina/o children have problems and that their schools are in bad shape, which is why Latinas/os want to improve bilingual education. That is why they want to improve teacher education. Frankly, if the schools were doing an excellent job of educating non-Latina/o students, it would be easy to say, "Give it a try." If those people who oppose bilingual education really had Latina/o children's interests in mind, it would be easy to say, "Give it a try." However, people who are anti-bilingual usually oppose immigration, affirmative action, and civil rights.

Society is beyond the times when people would throw their kids into a river and tell them to sink or swim. If society wants to help Latinas/os children, then it needs to provide their parents with better job opportunities, improve housing, bring schools up to the level of the best schools in the state, and provide certified teachers. Between 1952 and 1972, government spending for education in schools and colleges increased more than 700 percent, from $8.4 billion to $67.5 billion. During that period, the school median of white students increased substantially. It was not until the 1970s, when Latinos and other minorities started to approach a majority in many local school districts dominated by white school board officials, that support for education was abandoned.

Does family income play a role in the success or failure of Latina/o students in school? Who has more of a responsibility: the schools or the parents?

The irony is that despite wasted money and wasted years, diversity will come about but only after struggle. The Latina/o population will continue to grow. They already number 55 million. They will eventually question the competency of the system to produce competent teachers. Diversity is part of the solution, not having whites eating jalapeños.

ANOTHER POV (POINT OF VIEW)

Cultural and Linguistic Diversity in Education

Lydia Soto, National Board Certified Teacher, Social Studies, AMAE State President, 2012 (Association of Mexican American Educators), Political Activist

There are over 90 primary languages spoken by students in the Los Angeles Unified School District (LAUSD)! This school district, second largest in the nation, is a reflection of the county of Los Angeles, second largest city in the nation. Statistics show that Spanish-speaking students make up 94%, followed by Korean-speaking students, 1.1%, and Armenian-speaking students, 1.1%. These numbers illustrate the diversity of languages and cultures prevalent in the Southwest. The City of Los Angeles itself is a prime example of people from various cultures interacting with one another. There are pockets of cultures where outsiders visit and engage with the locals of that area: Chinatown, Little Tokyo, and Olvera Street, to name a few (Krovoza, 2013).

An integral part of culture is language. Values and behavioral styles are expressed through language, and language provides for the transmission of knowledge. However, the challenge is educating students of diverse cultures and languages. The issue of educating culturally and linguistically diverse students is a controversial one.

One of the primary issues essential for the successful implementation of culturally and linguistically diverse programs is to accept the necessity of such programs. As globalization continues to take place, it is common to find classes where there is more than one language and culture represented, and the educational system has an obligation to teach all students. Interaction and communication with all students regardless of their culture is an integral part of teaching and as society and cultures evolve, so must the educational system.

A secondary issue is the current population trend in the Southwest. The Latino population has doubled in the past 20 years and continues to grow. The African American population is also increasing, while the birth rate of whites has declined to an estimated one-fourth of the population. Yet, these trends are not reflected in graduation rates, test scores, or non-whites pursuing a higher education. In fact, it is quite the contrary! And that, of course, is another issue.

Statistics show that non-white students perform worse than their white counterparts. The main reason for this discrepancy is low teacher expectation. Studies demonstrate that culturally and linguistically diverse students receive less interaction from teachers because such teachers expect less from those students. Such teachers equate poverty with ignorance and expect a lack of educational support from the home. They do not motivate culturally and linguistically diverse students with challenging work, resulting in such students being ignored and demoralized by the education system.

The issue of low teacher expectation can be addressed by implementing various policies. The institutions of higher education can make diversity a content standard in education courses. Inclusion of culturally and diverse students can become district policy and a part of the evaluation requirements for teachers. Outside of the educational systems teachers can embrace diversity by interacting with the community, such as attending local events.

Administrative classroom observations of teachers must periodically focus on the successful implementation of addressing learning styles and effective teaching. Not all students learn in the same style. Though many are auditory or active learners, the majority are visual learners. Effective teaching addresses these styles by verbally explaining concepts, then reinforcing them with visuals such as illustrations, worksheets, and charts. For the active learner teachers can create assignments allowing for student interaction. All these styles and more can easily be implemented. At the high school level, group projects can be assigned where students must utilize a minimum of three forms of media for presentations, or for an economics class groups can create a new product that includes a business plan and marketing pitch. These challenging types of activities allow for inclusion, interaction, and most importantly, learning by everyone.

The National Council of Teachers of English (NCTE) embraces cultural and linguistic diversity and offers a myriad of activities, assignments, and references for grades K–12. These are strategies for good teaching that can easily become part of a teacher's lesson plans. Their views and activities can be easily incorporated into all subjects, not just English. There are also endless lessons on the Internet that can be accessed.

Low performance by culturally and linguistically diverse students is another key issue. A major reason is the hidden biases on standardized tests, administered three times during K–12 education. Unfortunately, these biases have become quite a problem and many communities question the validity of these tests. Test bias is evident in what may appear to be a simple question in everyday living, such as associating a cup with either a saucer or a table (some families do not use saucers for their cups). Tests relegate the poorly performing student as one with learning disabilities and place him or her in Special Education classes. These tests channel such students into a lower quality of education, affecting them for life. Students are treated as though they are not intelligent and end up expecting little from themselves. They have little if any aspirations to attend a college or university, thereby affecting their career, annual income, and ultimately, their quality of life.

The issue of culturally biased tests can be easily remedied. The creation of local groups of community members could be formed, and they in turn would be charge of reviewing standardized tests, ensuring that there are no cultural biases.

Another reason that culturally and linguistically diverse students perform poorly is that less experienced and less qualified teachers are placed in low socioeconomic schools. These are teachers that have yet to develop their teaching strategies, and if administration members rarely go into their classrooms to observe them, then they are pretty much able to do what they want. An example of poor teaching would be where a teacher regularly gives handouts or the students are told to read individually and answer the questions at the end of the chapter. These passive approaches result in a lack of interaction between the teacher and the student and a lack of collaboration among the students themselves. Again, we see that the teacher does not motivate the students to learn.

The school districts should play an integral part in addressing the issue of providing equal opportunity in education. By providing a more equal distribution of experienced teachers throughout the district, the inexperienced teachers can use them as mentors. This approach would enhance the inexperienced teachers' teaching strategies thereby resulting in a better quality of teachers.

The concept of inclusion of culturally and linguistically diverse students as a goal was globally realized after September 11, 2001 when the United States was attacked. UNESCO, the United Nations Educational, Scientific and Cultural Organization, an agency of the UN, created the Universal Declaration of Cultural Diversity. The UN has taken this approach for intercultural dialogue as opposed to the possibility of inevitable conflict between cultures. This document's "purpose is to contribute to peace and security by promoting international collaboration through educational, scientific, and cultural reforms in order to increase universal respect for justice, the rule of law, and human rights along with fundamental freedom." UNESCO has recognized that cultural and linguistic diversity should be preserved and embraced as globalization continues to take place. These are a few of the Articles in the document:

Article 1—Cultural diversity: the common heritage of humanity
Article 2—From cultural diversity to cultural pluralism

Article 3—Cultural diversity as a factor in development
Article 4—Human rights as guarantees of cultural diversity
Article 5—Cultural rights as an enabling environment for cultural diversity
Article 6—Toward access for all to cultural diversity
Article 7—Cultural heritage as the wellspring of creativity

Thus, we see that embracing cultural and linguistic diversity allows for understanding and peace as opposed to rejecting diversity, which opens the door to ignorance and conflict.

Latinas/os Should Not Assimilate or Acculturate

Elías Serna, Doctoral Student, University of California, Riverside and Founding Member, The Chicano Secret Service

The Nican Tlaca people of Turtle Island, including a band of Xican@s, recently declared that they will continue to live as caretakers of the land, produce their culture, and pass it on to their descendants for seven generations to come. Without relying on permits or permissions from any state or administration, this declaration of sovereignty (discussed later) was a manifestation of a powerful decolonial revolutionary concept: self-determination.

Self-determination declares that a people will determine their own destiny. United States Latinas/os, in other words, having indigenous origins throughout the Americas, have very meaningful histories that must be remembered and unique cultures that should be preserved. We should not assimilate because assimilation in this country has historically meant cultural destruction and systemic violence that whites have inflicted on non-white peoples. Acculturation is inevitable because groups coexist and interact. That I'm writing this essay in English is acculturation; if I wrote in English because I was ashamed of speaking Spanish that would be assimilation.

In the United States, assimilation, as the introduction explains, implies the surrender and destruction of Latino languages and cultures. The author details xenophobic attacks on the Spanish language and Latino struggles to maintain culture and improve educational experience. In addition to language, indigenous identity and decolonization should be considerations when discussing assimilation.

To be clear, Nican Tlaca is a Mesoamerican expression meaning "we people here" and refers to all peoples with indigenous roots throughout the Americas. "Turtle Island" is an Iroquois term referring to the American Continent. "Xican@" is a term developed in the 1990s that combined the political consciousness of "Chicano" with a growing indigenous and decolonizing identity/worldview. These terms grew in popularity during and after the first Peace and Dignity Run.

In 1992 the United States joined European and Latin American nations to celebrate 500 years of "progress" since Christopher Columbus' 1492 voyage of "discovery" of the New World. At the grassroots level, artists, scholars, and indigenous groups were convening more reflective and critical gatherings on the topic. When the first replica boats arrived in Puerto Rico, they were attacked by protesters, ruining the commemoration. The Los Angeles Riots that April, which spread globally, were also spurred by a critical quincentenary consciousness. The UCLA Hunger Strike for Chicano Studies sparked student activism in 1993. In 1994 the Zapatistas rebelled in Southern Mexico. Alongside this evolvement and politics, the 1990s also witnessed the "criminalization" of black and brown youth and repressive laws against bilingual education, affirmative action, citizenship, and human rights. Suffice to say, the 1990s politicized a generation and influenced a Xican@ awakening.

Indigenous groups also came together in 1992 for a continental ceremony to reflect on the history, present and future, of the native peoples of the Americas. Numerous groups, including Chicanos in the Southwest, declared their indigenous identity and participated in a hemispheric run that departed from both tips of the Americas (Alaska and Chile) and convened at the ancient center of Mesoamerica, Teotihuacan. Repeated every four years since the initial run, the Peace and Dignity Run has continued to join indigenous groups and remind U.S. Latinos that they possess a more deep-rooted, productive, and meaningful allegiance than the pledge of allegiance to the United States.

Assimilation happens through "state apparatuses": schools, books, mass media, and social conditioning. When we see that most main actors and superheroes are blonde and white, when the main characters in our schoolbooks are Anglo-Saxons, we grow up with inferiority complexes. These images also reflect the patterns and goals of a Eurocentric society. In this way, assimilation fails Latinos and is also the reason many educators and high school students are calling for "ethnic studies now." They want to see a curriculum that they control, that includes their faces, and one that is more truthful and critical of the past. Chicana/o Studies and Ethnic Studies curricula have been proven to increase student self-esteem, academic engagement, test scores, critical thinking, civic engagement, and a college-bound identity. Assimilation is not the "final frontier" for Latinos and it contains no guarantee. Preserving our culture preserves our ties to ancestors and builds community. These values serve the social and biological health of everyone for generations to come. As Bonfil Batalla argued in *Mexico Profundo*, we have a powerful life-sustaining culture—featuring healthy foods, reflective ceremonies, and sustainable economies—that puts people in front of profit and is as old as the rocks. Colonization failed to destroy it. We shouldn't throw it away.

BIBLIOGRAPHY

Acuña, Rodolfo, F. *The Making of Chicano Studies: In the Trenches of Academe*. New Brunswick, NJ: Rutgers University Press, 2011.

Acuña, Rodolfo, F. *Corridors of Migration: The Odyssey of Mexican Laborers, 1600–1933*. Tucson: University of Arizona Press, 2007.

Acuña, Rodolfo, F. *Occupied America: A History of Chicanos*. 8th ed. New York: Pearson, 2000.

Acuña, Rodolfo, F. *Cultures in Conflict: Problems of the Mexican Americans*. Los Angeles: Charter Schools Books, 1970.

Acuña, Rodolfo F. and Gregory Rodriguez. "Who Killed Bilingual Education? (Pro and Con Arguments Concerning What Led to the End of Bilingual Education in California)." *The Nation* 266, no. 23 (June 29, 1998): 2.

Avelino, Gerald. "Coding is not a suitable substitute for learning a foreign language." *Daily Titan*, February 16, 2016. http://www.dailytitan.com/2016/02/coding-is-not-a-suitable-substitute-for-learning-a-foreign-language

Banks, James A., and Cherry A. McGee Banks. *Multicultural Education: Issues and Perspectives*. 8th ed. Hoboken, NJ: John Wiley, 2012.

Barber, Ramona. "Tackling foreign language requirements for college." *The Des Moines Register*, February 22, 2015. http://www.desmoinesregister.com/story/news/education/2015/02/22/college-foreign-language-requirements/23689343

Boada, Irene. "How Catalan Survived. Banning a language may be an effective way of preserving it." *The Atlantic*, September 26, 2015. http://www.theatlantic.com/international/archive/2015/09/catalan-spain-independence-vote/407446

Brilliant, Mark. *The Color of America Has Changed: How Racial Diversity Shaped Civil Rights Reform in California, 1941–1978*. Oxford: Oxford University Press, 2012.

Chaudhry, Kelly. "Bilingual Education: Past, Present, Future." *NCPEA National Council of Professors of Educational Administration, International Journal of Educational Leadership Preparation* 5, no. 1 (January–March 2010).

Darder, Antonia, Rodolfo D. Torres, and Henry Gutierrez (eds.). *Latinos and Education: A Critical Reader*. New York: Routledge, 1997, pp. 163–165.

"Eighteen Calif. School Districts Sued; Shoddy Classrooms, Textbook Shortages, Teacher Quality Cited." *The Washington Post*, December 13, 2000.

Espinoza Dionne, Lionel Maldonado, Ester Hernandez, and Richard Rodriguez. *Chicanos, Latinos, and Cultural Diversity: An Anthology*. Dubuque, IA: Kendall Hunt Publishing, 2004.

"Evolution of Important Events in California Bilingual Education Policy." http://web.stanford.edu/~hakuta/www/policy/ELL/timeline.html

Galindo, René. "The Nativistic Legacy of the Americanization Era in the Education of Mexican Immigrant Students." *Educational Studies* 47, no. 4 (2011): 323–346.

Geyer, George Anne. "Even Liberals See Failures of Bilingual Education." *The Denver Post*, January 14, 2001.

Gray, Lisa. "Principal who told kids not to speak Spanish will lose job: Hempstead issue sharpens focus on rising state Latino Enrollment." *Chron*, March 19, 2014. http://www.chron.com/news/education/article/Principal-who-told-kids-not-to-speak-Spanish-will-5327528.php

Guthrie, Julian. "Bilingual-Education Showdown: California Board Is Considering Modifications of Prop. 227 Law." *The San Francisco Chronicle*, March 2, 2002.

Helfand, Duke. "The Bilingual Schooling Battle Flares Anew; Education: Author of Prop. 227 Accuses State Board of Weighing New Rules that Would Nullify the Law." *Los Angeles Times*, February 20, 2002.

Kohli, Sonali. "U.S. Schools Are Saying Goodbye to Foreign Languages." *The Atlantic*, December 13, 2014. http://www.theatlantic.com/education/archive/2014/12/us-schools-saying-goodbye-to-foreign-languages/383691

Krashen, Stephen. "Bilingual Education: Arguments for and (Bogus) Arguments Against." *Georgetown University Roundtable on Languages and Linguistics*, May 6, 1999. http://www.languagepolicy.net/archives/Krashen3.htm

Krovoza, Charlotte Rose. "In the Trenches: Reflections on the Pedagogy and Policy of Teaching Los Angeles' English Language Learners." Urban and Environmental Policy. Senior Comprehensive, UCLA. Spring 2013. https://www.oxy.edu/sites/default/files/assets/UEP/Comps/2012/2013/Krovoza%20Senior%20Comprehensive_Part1.pdf

Lau v. Nichols, no. 72-6520 S.Ct. 414 U.S. 563; 94 S. Ct. 786; 39 L. Ed. 2d 1; 1974 U.S. LEXIS 151, December 10, 1973, Argued, January 21, 1974, Decided.

Lorenzo, María-Isabel. *Race, Gender, and Mexican Americanization: How Mainstream Anglo Assumptions Inspired Mexican Americanization in California, 1914–1939*. Fresno, CA: California State University Fresno, 2012.

Macedo, Donaldo, and Lilia I Bartolomé. "Multiculturalism Permitted in English Only." *International Multilingual Research Journal* 8, no. 1 (2014): 24–37.

"Mexican Americans and Religion." *The Handbook of Texas*. https://tshaonline.org/handbook/online/articles/pqmcf

Mignolo, Walter. "English Only." *Radical Society* 29, no. 4 (2002): 10.

"Multicultural Affairs (OMA)." Columbia College. https://www.cc-seas.columbia.edu/OMA

National Association of Education (NEA). "The Invisible Minority." Report of the NEA–Tucson Survey on the Teaching of Spanish to the Spanish-Speaking. National Education Association, Washington, DC, 1966. http://eric.ed.gov/?id=ED017222

Olguín, Leonard. *Shuck Loves Chirley: A Non-technical Teaching Aid for Teachers of Bilingual Children*. rev. ed. Golden West Publishing House (defunct), 1968.

Phillison, Robert, and Tove Skutnabb-Kangas, Bhatia. "Linguistic Imperialism and Endangered Languages." In Tej K. Bhatia, and William C. Ritchie, eds., *Blackwell Handbooks in Linguistics: The Handbook of Bilingualism and Multilingualism*, 2nd ed., 2012.

Porter, Rosalie Pedalino. "The Case Against Bilingual Education: Why Even Latino Parents Are Rejecting a Program Designed for Their Children's Benefit." *The Atlantic Monthly* 281, no. 5 (May 1998): 28–39. http://www.theatlantic.com/magazine/archive/1998/05/the-case-against-bilingual-education/305426

Pycior, Julie Leininger. *LBJ and Mexican Americans: The Paradox of Power*. Austin, TX: University of Texas Press, 1997.

Rodríguez, Clara E. *Puerto Ricans: Born in the U.S.A.* Boulder: Westview Press, 1991.

Rodríguez, Gregory. "English Lesson in California: In the Face of a Ballot Challenge, Support for Bilingual Education Is Wavering." *The Nation* 266, no. 14 (April 1998): 15(4).

Rodríguez, Richard. *Hunger of Memory: The Education of Richard Rodriguez*. Reissued ed. New York: Bantam Books, 1983.

Salas, Miguel Tinker. *In the Shadow of the Eagles: Sonora and the Transformation of the Border During the Porfiriato*. Berkeley: University of California Press, 1997.

Sleeter, Christine E. *Multicultural Education, Critical Pedagogy, and the Politics of Difference*. New York: State University of New York Press, 1995.

Stefanic, Jean, and Richard Delgado. *No Mercy. How Conservative Think Tanks and Foundations Changed America's Agenda*. Philadelphia: Temple University Press, 1996.

Stewner-Manzanares, Gloria, "The Bilingual Education Act: Twenty Years Later." The National Clearing House for Bilingual Education, no. 6, 1988. https://ncela.ed.gov/files/rcd/BE021037/Fall88_6.pdf

UNESCO. Universal Declaration on Cultural Diversity, Cultural Diversity Series No. 1: A Vision, A Conceptual Platform, A Pool of Ideas for Implementation, A New Paradigm." 2002. http://unesdoc.unesco.org/images/0012/001271/127162e.pdf

U.S. Department of Education, Office for Civil Rights. "Achieving Diversity: Race-Neutral Alternatives in American Education." U.S. Department of Education, 2004. https://www2.ed.gov/about/offices/list/ocr/edlite-raceneutralreport2.html

Waseem, Filza, and Saeeda Asadullah. "Linguistic domination and critical language awareness." *Procedia—Social and Behavioral Sciences* 70 (January 25, 2013): 800.

SELECTED VIDEOS

Al Jazeera English. "Riz Khan—Linguistic imperialism?" YouTube video, 22:30, posted October 21, 2010. https://www.youtube.com/watch?v=c3TJe4jnqFo

AntiDagger. "6 Reasons You Should Learn Spanish," YouTube video, 2:15, posted March 10, 2010. https://www.youtube.com/watch?v=ZV2h5XbAqXI

Big Think. "How are language and identity connected?" YouTube video, 6:18, posted April 23, 2012. https://www.youtube.com/watch?v=D5pu47-iQ8E

Corbettreport. "Language, Imperialism and Culture—Dr. Thorsten Pattberg on GRTV," YouTube video, 12:15, posted February 27, 2012. https://www.youtube.com/watch?v=gvbf7wqwlbs

Destination Casa Blanca. "A historic background of bilingual education," YouTube video, 6:00, posted May 22, 2009. https://www.youtube.com/watch?v=0tIppleeIjk

Galne Gunnar TV. "The Fraud of Multiculturalism," YouTube video, 7:49, posted June 7, 2010. https://www.youtube.com/watch?v=H-eNXWtXRQI

HelpSaveWhiteRace. "History of Multiculturalism," YouTube video, 5:24, posted June 21, 2012. https://www.youtube.com/watch?v=niicDbbSky0

JASLLife. "English In The Deaf Community Ch. 3." YouTube video, 5:58, posted December 17, 2009. https://www.youtube.com/watch?v=Y0HeAPXVH8c

LibertyPen. "Thomas Sowell—The Reality Of Multiculturalism," YouTube video, 15:00, posted July 12, 2013. https://www.youtube.com/watch?v=9ESlS2jrhXY

List25. "25 Unbelievable Things You Didn't Know About Language And Linguistics," YouTube video, 4:18, posted March 24, 2015. https://www.youtube.com/watch?v=ceEzrjC6i0Y

The MacMillan Center, Yale University. "Linguistics in a Colonial World: A Story of Language, Meaning, and Power," YouTube video, 13:53, posted February 9, 2012. https://www.youtube.com/watch?v=xwsj9AZnaaE

MEMETROPOLIS. "Some Linguistic Differences 2," YouTube video, 00:46, posted July 19, 2013. https://www.youtube.com/watch?v=vn8cwrjrZsM

Polka23dot. "Jared Taylor—racial diversity leads to violence," YouTube video, 11:32, posted March 2, 2012. https://www.youtube.com/watch?v=QXz3gsYW9hM

SAARA. "What Languages Sound Like To Foreigners," YouTube video, 1:44, posted March 3, 2014. https://www.youtube.com/watch?v=ybcvlxivscw

Stanford. "Student Voices: Why Faculty Diversity (Humanities)," YouTube video, 14:28, posted November 11, 2014. https://www.youtube.com/watch?v=-PsY6UKIh6k

TEDx Talks. "Why cultural diversity matters | Michael Gavin | TEDxCSU," YouTube video, 17:52, posted November 7, 2014. https://www.youtube.com/watch?v=48RoRi0ddRU

TEDx Talks. "Inclusion, Exclusion, Illusion and Collusion: Helen Turnbull at TEDxDelrayBeach," YouTube video, 13:15, posted September 18, 2013. https://www.youtube.com/watch?v=zdV8OpXhl2g

TEDx Talks. "Inclusion, belonging and the disability revolution: Jennie Fenton at TEDxBellingen," YouTube video, 23:01, posted September 18, 2013. https://www.youtube.com/watch?v=VAM9nh8WC-8

4

Chicana/o and Latina/o Studies

In 1968, approximately 50 Mexican Americans had doctorates in the United States. The doctorate is important because it qualifies a person to become a tenure track professor at a university. That year,

1. The average Mexican American child in the Southwest dropped out of school by the seventh grade. In Texas, 89 percent of the children with Spanish surnames dropped out before completing high school.
2. [I]n California . . . some schools more than 50 percent of Mexican American high school students dropped out between grades 10 and 11; one Texas school reported a 40 percent dropout rate for the same grades.
3. Mexican Americans accounted for more than 40 percent of the so-called "mentally handicapped" in California.
4. Although Spanish-surnamed students made up more than 14 percent of the public school population of California in 1968, less than one-half of 1 percent of the college students enrolled in the seven campuses of the University of California were of this group. (ERIC, The Mexican American, 1968).

By the late 1960s, only a handful of Chicana/o students attended universities; access was tied to a high school diploma, and many barrio high schools did not offer the requisite classes to be admitted to college. Counselors discouraged Chicana/o students from applying for college, saying "You are not college material" (Cranmore, 2010; Thys, 2002; Acuña, 2010b).

How would this reality lead to a negative self-image? How did this portrait lead to student failure? Is everyone equal in America?

Departments of Chicana/o studies were formed to address the failure of school systems to educate Mexican Americans and the pushing of Mexican Americans out of schools. Chicana/o studies is as much an adherence to a pedagogical method as it is the study of Chicanas/os. It deals with identity and with motivating students to acquire the skills to think critically and motivate then to learn other skills to succeed in college.

Chicana/o studies came about when students demanded access to higher education. A series of school walkouts began in East Los Angeles in 1968 and spread throughout the Southwest, Midwest, and Northwest (Acuña, 2011). Over 50 walkouts occurred in Texas. Simultaneously, students already admitted to colleges began to agitate for the admission of more Mexican Americans and other Latinas/os. Outreach programs brought in more students but only after more confrontations (Acuña, 2011). Chicana/o studies and Latina/o departments and programs were commonly established in areas with large Mexican American populations. They were called "Chicana/o Studies," whereas departments established in areas that were shared with other Latinos/as were called "Latino Studies" (Torres, 2015; Oboler, 2012; Caban, 2007).

Do students have the right to protest inequities? Does protesting demonstrate that they care about their education?

These events contributed to the growth of a Latina/o middle class during the 1970s (Acuña, *counterpunch*, 2012). Indeed, the growth of the Latino middle class is a legacy of the Chicana/o Generation. This growth of a critical mass of Mexican American students put pressure on the universities and, for that matter, the public schools. The times produced a "collective memory" that created a communitarian bond among the students and the Chicana/o/Latino community. Indeed, the name *Chicano* at the time symbolized the unity of students and their commitment to improving the lives of those who did not have an education.

How does this "collective memory" help the entire community regardless of race? How is the "collective memory" of Mexican Americans and Latinas/os similar to the nation's "collective memory" of the Boston Tea Party?

The horrendous dropout rate in the public schools deepened student disenchantment with education. There were few Chicana/o students who went to college before 1960 who don't remember not being punished for speaking Spanish on the school grounds or who were told that they were not college material. When they became aware of the dropout problem and the inequities in education, they expressed moral outrage that resulted in a collective movement against what was unfair and unequal. The civil rights and anti-war movement also deepened the realization that Mexican Americans and Puerto Ricans were dying for the United States while they were being shut out of America's so-called dream.

From the beginning, Chicana/o and ethnic studies were controversial. The lack of institutional support and the negative attitude of the universities resulted in a negative reaction to the studies programs. As in the case of bilingual education, college faculty members, the general public, and parents questioned the value of taking classes on Mexican Americans and rejected the studies programs. However, Chicana/o educators felt that it was important to make students feel proud of themselves so that they could master skills such as reading, writing, and critical thinking.

If you do not understand English, does this affect learning to read? Why is a positive self-image essential for success?

Because of institutional resistance and xenophobia, the new programs were not properly supported. The academy ignored fundamental epistemological questions such as what their corpus of knowledge was and whether the new classes were a discipline or an area of study. This negligence and institutional racism made the development of Chicano studies uneven. To this day, for example, geography is neglected and has not been incorporated into Chicana/o studies courses, although place is fundamental to the study of Mexican Americans and Latinas/os. Consequently, the geography of places like Texas and California were and are ignored along with the study of how unique cultural formations took place in disparate parts of the country.

What is a sense of place? Is it the same as a sense of community? Look up gentrification. What is it? How does it erase the sense of place?

Chicana/o studies, instead of studying regions or individual countries through single disciplines, study disciplines through a multidisciplinary lens. Many Chicana/o educators believed that the single-discipline Eurocentric model did not meet the needs of students in the 1960s. Simply put, a holistic and more efficient approach was needed to teach the corpus of knowledge of not only foreign countries, but of increasingly multicultural America. Chicana/o educators, such as George I. Sánchez, added a bicultural component to bilingual education. Learning the language was not enough for teachers; they had to know the history and culture of Mexican American children.

Institutional racism prevented ethnic studies scholars from developing balanced programs. A major problem was that administrators had difficulty understanding or conceptualizing its pedagogical nuances. Many still erroneously believed that studying history or other disciplines from a Mexican American or Latina/o perspective does not have value. A lack of research on Chicana/o studies programs kept many programs in an inchoate state of development. As a consequence, many programs are today defined by individual courses in traditional disciplines rather than within a comprehensive program of study. For instance, contrary to popular belief, Chicana/o history is not Chicana/o studies, Chicana/o history is a field within the discipline of history that uses common historical methods for research as well as teaching that corpus of knowledge. In the same vein, Chicana/o literature does not study, research, or teach Chicana/o studies; Chicana/o literature is a field within the discipline of literature. History and literature are necessary parts of Chicana/o studies.

What is institutional racism or resistance? Why do colleges and universities spend millions of dollars supporting centers that serve few students and refuse to support programs for underserved students?

Putting Chicana/o studies into context: after World War II, the United States was totally unprepared to assume a world leadership role. Its ignorance of other nations and its competition with the Soviet Union exposed glaring weaknesses in its education system. Few educated Americans knew a foreign language or had even a tourist's knowledge of countries outside the northern European orbit. As a result, Area Studies was established. The weaknesses of the American education system were well known to many leaders in the American political and business communities and they called for reforms. Unfortunately, most educators turned the other way. The attitude of most Americans was that the system was good enough just as long as they didn't have to pay higher taxes. This wrongheaded thinking was bolstered by the ignorance or pseudo common sense of the average American who did not recognize that reforms were in their interest.

Even before the United States entered World War II, the U.S. Army recognized flaws in the American educational system and established the Defense Language Institute Foreign Language Center (DLIFLC) in Monterey, California in November of 1941. It was a secret school near the Presidio of San Francisco and was initiated to teach Japanese. The number of languages offered soon grew to include other languages; the school was unique and a person could become conversant in a foreign language in six months. Because of the success of the Monterey School, a cluster of private language schools was established around this school, emulating its language instruction methods. Consequently, the Monterey Institute for Foreign Studies was established in 1955 and was later renamed the Monterey Institute of International Studies. Spin-offs, such as the Thunderbird School of Global Management in Glendale, Arizona, were established.

Why is knowing someone's culture and language important in business and in government?

The purpose of the schools was initially to train military personnel; why was it equally important in training teachers?

It was evident that Americans were also woefully deficient in their knowledge of the history and culture of other nations. A few American educational reformers moved to modify the curriculum in higher education. The single discipline–Eurocentric model did not meet the needs of the truly educated American. However, language was just one component in learning about other people and geographic places. Reformers felt that the approach had to be holistic and include history and culture. These proposals met resistance. Most Americans felt that the world revolved around the United States and Western Europe. When reformers, for instance, wanted to substitute a course in World History for one in Western Civilization, an intense culture war broke out. Americans believed knowing only one language enhanced their Americanism. At the same time, students did not want to put forth the effort of learning a foreign language, often because they feared failure and that such courses would lower their GPA.

Given the shrinking size of the world and diversity of the United States, is it practical to view society through Eurocentric lenses?

Many Chicana/o studies programs followed this pedagogy. Ethnic studies programs are not just about feeling good about oneself but about getting to know disparate ethnic groups in order to develop more effective teachers and more effective methods. Chicana/o studies, for example, are used to motivate students to acquire skills. It is reasonable to assume that if the military and the State Department use this method to train their professional employees, then it is an effective way to teach minority students. Teacher competency is at the root of student failures.

Chicana/o studies is not defined by its content or discipline. It is a course of study that motivates and facilitates students in acquiring critical thinking and other essential skills. It is bound together by a pedagogy that defines that purpose. Chicana/o studies is the platform used to motivate and to teach Latina/o students. Again, the content is part of a motivational tool to inspire students to learn, to correct negative self-images that came about through colonialism, and, yes, to accumulate more knowledge and search for the truth. This platform is not unique to Mexican Americans or Latinas/os. Hence, content fields studying Chicana/o study programs should develop pedagogy within their contexts of study, not disciplines.

Is the Area Studies model reasonable? How does it improve learning about a people?

Learning Spanish alone does not prepare teachers to teach Mexican American children. It would be dumb to send a foreign diplomat to a country when she did not know the language, history, or culture of that country. It is also dumb to send teachers to teach Latina/o students while not knowing them. It is a matter of competency. It raises the question, if it is an efficient method to educate diplomats and military personnel, why shouldn't this pedagogy be used to train teachers to teach Chicana/o students? The reality is that many teachers view Latina/o students as a foreign population. It logically follows that this pedagogy is also an effective method to deal with the negative self-images of many Mexican American and Latina/o students. Indeed, in order to acquire skills, a student has to have a positive self-image.

Should the education of teachers of Latina/o students be held to the same standard as the education of diplomats?

In the 1960s and 1970s, white racists accused Chicana/o education reformers of imitating Afrocentrism, which they labeled racist (Asante, 2009). Heated debates broke out and many Chicana/o educators asked, if Afrocentrism is racist, why isn't Eurocentrism racist? The programs were not only multidisciplinary, they also offered an analysis that explored American history from the point of view of Mexican insight. Chicana/o studies went beyond the norm. Moreover, Mexican American studies led to an appreciation of other cultures and people and connected them through a sense of communitarian appreciation of each other (Freire, 2000).

The only example of Mexican American studies for the K–12 level was the Tucson Unified School District's Mexican American Studies program (MAS). The beginning of the end came when the State of Arizona passed HB 2281 in 2010, which claimed that the La Raza program was un-American. Republicans attacked the program despite the fact that it was highly successful in graduating and preparing students for college. Elected officials used Mexicans as a bogeyman to spread fear through unfounded accusations that Mexicans were preparing to take back the southwest. Conservatives and neo-Nazis attacked Mexicans, blurring the reality of the program's successes. They claimed that students were being taught critical thinking using the methods of Paulo Freire (Freire 2000), John Dewey, and Edwin Fenton.

Was the opposition to the Tucson MAS program political or pedagogical? Is critical thinking un-American? Why would some people think it is?

Further, the Tucson program came under attack because it taught about the Mesoamerican past. Students were exposed to the contributions of these civilizations, thus building students' self-identity. They were taught to think critically about that past as well as the present. As mentioned, at the core was the pedagogy of Paulo Freire, who wrote that the educational process was never neutral and that students should never be used as passive recipients of knowledge. Teachers should engage them through "problem-posing." Accordingly, knowledge was linked to action that solved problems and changed their communities (Freire, 1986). As mentioned, many Arizona politicians found critical thinking threatening. They believed that if students did not discuss racism, racism would not exist.

Why is critical thinking necessary? Why do the most prestigious law schools use the Socratic method? Why would they find critical thinking threatening?

An underlying motive for the assault on Tucson MAS was its success. The white establishment felt threatened by the growing Mexican voting population and therefore opposed any program that would allow students to be critical and eventually vote them out of office. It did not matter to them that, nationwide, Latino and African American males had the lowest third- grade scores on reading tests. No matter to them that the Latina/o high school dropout rates nationwide hovered around 56 percent and higher if the dropouts from middle school to high school were counted. Only about 24 percent of graduating Latinas/os went to college, and mostly to community colleges. Tucson's Unified School District's Ethnic Studies and Mexican American Studies program reversed these trends: the dropout rate in the MAS program was 2.5 percent. Students in the program significantly outperformed their peers on the state's standardized AIMS tests, and 66 percent of these students went to college. The key to its success was that "The classes [were] designed to be culturally relevant—to help the students see themselves in the curriculum and make them see why education is important for them. If they see themselves in the educational literature, they find more reasons to read and write, to research and draw conclusions" (Cabrera, Meza, and Rodríguez, 2012).

Why is the demolition of successful teaching programs an insult to taxpayers? Does teaching to tests change anything?

In fact, the Socratic method, although a powerful teaching tool, was controversial. As mentioned, the better law schools prepare American law students by using Socratic questioning. Although effective, critical thinking methods threatened many white Americans who believed that education was to teach students to be good Americans, which meant to them to practice blind patriotism. Critical thinking was controversial before HB2281 began the controversy. In the late 1960s, California Superintendent of Schools Max Rafferty called a reform movement that advocated a similar inquiry method of teaching social science "subversive" because, according to Rafferty, it taught students to question (Fort, 2010, p. 103).

Why was critical thinking considered dangerous? What is your opinion? How is the opposition linked to the growing Mexican/Latino voting population?

In 2010, the 12th Annual Institute for Transformative Education was sponsored by La Raza Studies, in partnership with the University of Arizona School of Education. The Institute featured educators from across the United States. The presenters and the participants were multiracial and featured scholars such as Pedro A. Noguera, Executive Director, Metropolitan Center for Urban Education, New York University and Angela Valenzuela, University of Texas, Austin. Their mission was to improve teaching effectiveness. In contrast, enemies of ethnic studies knew nothing about the students or how to deal with their learning problems. Thus, by abusing the legal process, they killed ethnic studies courses in Tucson schools (Buelna, 2012).

How is the ban on the teaching of MAS a violation of the Fourteenth Amendment's equal protection clause? Do the Tucson schools want Mexican American students to succeed?

Every reform measure designed to better teach U.S. Latinas/os has been shot down by the American electorate—bilingual education, affirmative action, racial integration, smaller class sizes, etc. The tragedy of La Raza Studies was that it was a proven program. The decision to end it was political, not educational. Educators of all colors know that if given the right resources, ethnic studies will improve the performance of students of color and enhance and enrich the education of all students.

The importance of the California State University, Northridge, Department of Chicana/o Studies Department is that it proves that MAS and Latina/o programs are viable when properly constructed and institutionally supported. The CSUN program has 26 tenure track professors and over 40 part timers offering 166 courses per semester (Chicana/o Studies Web Page, 2016). Most students taking the classes are Mexican American; however, classrooms resemble the United Nations and mirror the population in the Los Angeles area. What is unique about the department is that it is still experimenting, teaching Nahuatl and occasionally Mayan along with the arts and music. The classrooms are covered with student-painted murals, and the program has a *jarocho conjunto*, a *mariachi*, and a *ballet folklorico*. Students in the past also formed jazz ensembles and Andean music groups. These activities integrate with the social sciences and humanities. An experimental class also teaches Latin to Spanish speakers to enrich vocabulary, since most English words are derived from Latin. Cultural events such as *El Día de Los Muertos* draw over a thousand guests.

How does Chicano studies bring about racial and cultural diversity?

Every civilization has had a method of verification that resolves negations. The Greek philosophers used a method of inquiry 5,000 years before the birth of Christ. Scholasticism as a method was used in medieval universities from roughly 1100 to 1500 (Makdisi, 1974). It was a tool and method for learning and testing knowledge, which emphasized dialectical reasoning. And in the 1950s, when the Russians launched Sputnik into orbit, critical thinking and the Inquiry method were once more popularized by the writings of Edwin Fenton (Fenton, 1966). This reform was quashed by an America First movement.[1]

Meanwhile, most states, when they thought about it, struggled with student and faculty diversity. School enrollment, based on the service areas of the schools, was and is segregated—de facto, but nevertheless segregated. Segregation is the result of institutionally racist housing and economic separation. In 2012, the Civil Rights Project at UCLA reported, "More than half of Latino students in California attend 'intensely segregated' K–12 schools, or those that have a white population of 10 percent or less" (Gazzar, 2014). According to Gary Orfield, co-director of the Civil Rights Project at UCLA, "What we've seen for Latinos is an incredible increase in isolation from white and Asian students and an extremely high exposure to poverty . . . . We also see a significant exposure to linguistic segregation, which we call triple segregation (after race and income levels). It's gotten much worse" (Orfield, 2014). Latinas/os had fewer white classmates than Latinas/os in any other state. Black and Latina/o students on average attend schools where two-thirds were poor students. This situation has resulted in racial and class isolation and is true of parochial schools as well, many of which have become havens for white flight, catering to middle- and upper middle-class students.

Should the decline in Black students on campuses be everyone's concern? What does the decline tell us about higher education? What does it tell us about the future?

United States prestigious public and private universities resemble Republican conventions. Public universities, although public, are also separated by economic class. In California, the University of California system shows shades of white and yellow, the California State universities a light tan, and the community colleges darker shades of black and brown. Students in K–12 do not mingle much outside the classroom. This pattern is maintained at state college institutions where integration varies according to student majors. Walk out onto the yard or eating areas of universities such as California State University, Northridge and you will see that students group mostly white on white and brown on brown, which is so even though Latinas/os comprise over 40 percent of the students (up from about 1 percent in the spring of 1969).

Classrooms are similarly segregated. Almost 50 years ago when I began teaching at San Fernando Valley State (now California State University, Northridge), Latina/o faculty, according to the administration, was over 10 percent of the faculty. After a year of protests, we were finally given the list of Mexican American faculty—like they say on Facebook, "lol" (laugh out loud). The list was laughable since the names of every Italian on campus were included—one name stood out, Warren Furomoto—a friend. His name had been included because his name ended in a vowel. Warren is Japanese American. After years of wrangling, the administration still refuses to hand over the hard data or identify Mexican American faculty, which we estimate at about 3 percent. Over 75 percent of the academic departments do not have a single professor of Mexican origin, and 90 percent do not have a course drawing from that corpus of knowledge. Curricular changes have been superficial and rare since 1969.

Why are precise statistical data of Mexican Americans and Latinas/os important? What does the lack of progress in hiring Mexican American and Latino faculty at CSUN tell you about the institution's commitment to diversity?

The lack of faculty of color does not faze white faculty members. In 2014, the sole Latina/o member of the Department of Psychology (out of 50 tenure track professors) brought up that one of the goals for hiring new faculty should be to balance the professor–student ratio. Psychology majors are 50 percent Latina/o students. This suggestion began a stir, with faculty accusing the professor of creating dissention and claiming that they did not look at color. They wanted to hire the most qualified applicants. However, there is only one Latina/o administrator. Diversity, from my experience, is an ideal of equal justice as defined by the Fourteenth Amendment to the Constitution, which has been perverted by the Supreme Court and society. Rudy Rosales, a San Antonio colleague, aptly called diversity the "illusion of inclusion" (Rosales, 2000).

What is the illusion of inclusion?

One of the biggest tragedies in California in recent years is the decline of the African American student population. In 2014 the enrollment of blacks fell to 5.8 percent at CSUN and to 3 percent at the University of California, Los Angeles. In 2006, "Nearly 10,000 African American students graduated from high school last month in Los Angeles County. This fall, only 96 of them will attend one of the state's most prestigious universities, the University of California, Los Angeles . . . . The number of black students at UCLA has also been falling for years, partly due to a ballot measure that ended racial preferences in admissions" (Korry, 2006).

Chicana/o studies is part of the solution in respect to diversity. If Chicano studies were not in the mix, there would be almost no classes on Mexico, Latin America, or U.S. Latinas/os. There would be no Central American Studies and the number of Mexican American faculty would be slightly above 1 percent. There would be no murals and no cultural activity. But more importantly than that is that there would be less interaction among the students. The classroom, no matter at what level of education, has always been a melting pot. This *was* one of the values of parochial schools, where Mexicans came into contact with Irish and white Catholics.

If Chicana/o studies did not exist, the likelihood of a student attending a class with a Mexican American or Latina/o professor would be negligible. Coming into contact with minority role models—female and male—is important. For Latinas/os, being in contact with a positive role model heightens students' professional aspirations. If it weren't for Chicana/o studies, fewer students would come into contact with a Latina/o professor or students of color. Frequently young people compare themselves with others. The availability of role models is critical. It is important to see people of color in positions of power.

Are minority professors role models important? I first came to realize that I could go to college when I attended an integrated high school. Why?

Students interact in a class and are given the opportunity to know each other. My classes are about 50 percent Latina/o and a combination of Armenians, Middle Easterners, and whites. Aside from the academic work, reading, and research, students are given the opportunity to learn about Mexican Americans through attendance at lectures, events on campus and in the community, and cultural events. They are even given the opportunity to go to political events. Two years ago 60 Asian and Latina/o students took three trips to Arizona, giving students the opportunity of visiting the Wall at Nogales.

If Paulo Freire would have had an Anglo name and his book a different title, would the reaction have been different? In the view of Arizona politicians, exposing students to inequities such as the American Wall separating the United States from Mexico is un-American. Discuss.

The arguments against ethnic studies programs are in great part emotional and unsubstantiated. The former Superintendent of Public

Instruction and then Attorney General, Tom Horne, said the [Mexican American] "courses, focused on controversial issues like racism and socioeconomic inequality and widely used books written by Latino authors, bred resentment against whites" (Planas, 2014). He alleged that the MAS program caused divisions among students because it was directed at a specific group, even though Horne never visited the program. Horne made these accusations although "An independent audit and education researchers credited the program with developing critical thinking schools and boosting student achievement." Horne's objection was based on the notion that the courses focused on controversial issues like racism and socioeconomic inequality and used books widely written by Latino authors" (Planas, 2014). The result was that state authorities banned books used in MAS classes.

HB 2281 summed up Tea Party arguments against MAS:

1. Promote the overthrow of the United States government;
2. Promote resentment toward a race or class of people;
3. Are designed primarily for pupils of a particular ethnic group; or
4. Advocate ethnic solidarity instead of the treatment of pupils as individuals.

Huppenthal visited the Tucson program and then claimed it was a cult because students used the farmworker hand clap.

In an online interview in July of 2015, Curtis Acosta, a high school ethnic studies teacher in Tucson and part of the group SaveEthnic Studies.org, said, "The purposes of our classes are varied, but our main objective is to dehumanize the academic experience for our students through culturally and socially relevant curriculum. It is no news flash that Latin@, African American and Native American students have been historically marginalized and ignored in mainstream public school curriculum, and that the drop-out/push-out rates for our communities are far out of proportion compared to European–American students. The numbers are disturbing, unsettling, and as educators we have an obligation and responsibility to offer progressive pedagogical and curriculum changes to promote academic equality and achievement for all our students" (Sleeter, 2011).

MAS Teacher Rene Martínez went on, "In our school district, we are 63 percent Latino students. So they really have grabbed on. And it's been effective academically. In this era of standardized testing, students who have participated in our ethnic studies classes, regardless of ethnic background, they outperform their peers on the state standardized tests. But yet we continue to be scrutinized and attacked by our state legislators." Martínez said that one of the things the program instills is captured by the African proverb: "Until the lions have their historians, tales of the hunted will always glorify the hunter." Martínez said, "We talk about how we come from the lion's perspective, from the story that's never told. We emphasize the whole history, which historically and even now, continues to be left out" (Avakian, 2011). It should be noted that learning about history—including the brutal oppression of black, Latino, native, and other people in the United States—is good for all students, including white students.

What did Rene Martínez mean by "Until the lions have their historians, tales of the hunted will always glorify the hunter"?

Critics claim that ethnic studies leads to the Balkanization of American society and to internecine ethnic wars like those of Yugoslavia and the Middle East. Ward Connerly, an African American leader in the fight against affirmative action, took aim at ethnic studies. Suspicious of women's studies and gay and lesbian studies, Connerly went after Black Welcome Week, Latino orientation day, separate graduation ceremonies, and ethnic "theme houses," which, according to Connerly, are "Balkanizing" the campuses of California's state universities. Connery and his ilk claim that ethnic studies lead to intellectual confusion. They especially chafe at what they call "political correctness or PC. They blame the U.S. media" (Losey and Kurthen, 1995).

REPEATING: Chicana/o studies is not a discipline; it is an area studies program with disciplines within the program. Area studies did not become popular in American academies until after World War II. Prior to that, the curriculum revolved almost exclusively around Euro-American studies. Indeed, the required general education course was Western Civilization, not World History. That is a product of the post-1960s.

ANOTHER POV (POINT OF VIEW)

Chicana/o Studies Should Not Be Mandatory

Celina Fernández-Ayala, Chicanx-Boricua, Undergraduate Student, California State University, Northridge

Mandatory classes are a given in the U.S. educational system, demonstrated by requirements for math, science, history, and English. The country's changing demographics, increased awareness of civil rights abuses, and the outlawing of ethnic studies in some areas (e.g., Arizona House Bill 2281, which banned Mexican American Studies in the Tucson Unified School District) have stimulated dialogue around making Chicana/o studies mandatory. Albeit well intentioned, Chicano/a studies should not be mandatory because that would remove an opportunity for students to build their own academic values. Furthermore, Chicano/a studies cannot become a requirement unless all ethnic studies are required. Should an area of study be mandated, preconditions must exist in order to best benefit the students and the discipline.

Chicana/o studies should not become mandatory just as no field of study should be mandatory. "Mandatory" means an authority has determined the subject to be important or "essential" for students. With educational institutions as sites for potential intellectual growth, course requirements automatically inform students as to what has or does not have academic value. By that fact, requirements also dictate what is or is not worthy of intellectual pursuit. Educational institutions additionally function as social institutions, using academia as a means to enforce specific values and beliefs. Therefore, mandatory courses do not just assert the importance of a subject, but enforce the values and/or beliefs present in that subject's content. Although students take required courses for the short-term, generally speaking, the association between "mandatory" and "important" shapes students' values both academically and personally. Mandating a course or an area of study determines how and what students consider significant in their lives and to education.

Chicana/o studies, as is the case with any other subject, should not be mandatory because students should determine for themselves what is academically valuable and relevant. Students need an education that orients them within their specific experiences and their world. Mandating courses creates a hierarchy not just in terms of assigning greater value to some courses over others, but in the educational process itself. School boards merely inform students as to which subjects they must take, forcing the students to passively accept the requirements in order to graduate and continue in the educational system if they so desire. This structuring creates disengagement, as students take classes simply because they "have to," while also internalizing the idea that certain knowledge is more crucial than other knowledge. Allowing students to make their own decisions about their education invites them to become active participants in their pursuit of knowledge instead of passive recipients of information. Without requirements, students are invited to think more critically about their education, themselves, and their world. Even if students do not do so, they at least have the opportunity to reflect on why some courses are more important than others, what motivates them to take certain classes, and why they think they should or need to take the classes they choose.

Specifically enforcing Chicana/o studies creates a problem because the decision to include involves the decision to exclude. Chicano/a studies cannot become mandatory unless all ethnic studies courses become mandatory. Requiring students to take Chicana/o studies but not black studies, Asian American studies, Native American studies, and so forth, prioritizes certain experiences over others. This decision would effectively recreate the same oppression that many ethnic minority students experience because of the standardization of Euro-American perspectives and experiences in mainstream curriculum. Chicana/o studies came about because students demanded the inclusion of alternative perspectives in education. Therefore, requiring Chicano/a studies without requiring all ethnic studies courses does a disservice to the history of Chicana/o studies and ethnic studies as a whole.

Many of those who argue in favor of mandating Chicano/a studies, and ethnic studies in general, emphasize the skills that students gain from such areas of study, especially critical thinking skills. Although Chicano/a studies and other ethnic studies' presentations and analyses of different perspectives do foster critical thinking, they should not be the exclusive domain of ethnic studies. In other words, students should not have to depend on any specific subject to learn how to think critically. As sites for intellectual growth, the acquisition of critical thinking skills should be an integral part of the curriculum for all courses at all schools. Failure to teach students how to think critically fails the purpose of education.

Before any course or area of study becomes mandatory, preconditions must exist in order to ensure that students receive the best education possible and to maintain the academic rigor of the discipline. Preconditions function as a form of quality control, giving the newly required classes a sense of legitimacy with the demand for certain standards to be met. In addition, preconditions set a standard and expectations for how the course should run, and which skills the students should gain by the end of the course.

Mandatory courses require competent teachers who demonstrate mastery in their understanding of the subject and present diverse viewpoints pertaining to the material. For example, a literature course may focus on a specific novel but should include readings by those who analyze the strengths of the novel and those who critique the novel.

Students cannot build critical thinking skills unless the instructors exhibit their own ability to do so. Teachers must also be able to professionally and intelligently respond to students who challenge the instructor and the necessity of the course. The teachers' abilities to handle questioning can either isolate students or invite them to engage with the courses' content more deeply as students and instructors explore the answers to the challenges posed. Interpersonal skills are just as important as the padding on the résumé because education does not occur in a vacuum. Even the most intelligent and knowledgeable professor would be ineffective without the ability to engage with their students.

Chicano/a studies, just as any other area of study, should not become mandatory because a less regimented or restrictive educational system would allow students to decide for themselves what is academically significant—which is a means available to them to exercise their intellectual curiosity. Making Chicano/a studies a requirement without requiring all ethnic studies courses would cause an injustice to the very history of ethnic studies, and all courses should be obligated to help students build their critical thinking skills. In the event that an area of study becomes mandated, the existence of preconditions is essential to best serving the students and maintaining the area's legitimacy. The most important precondition falls upon the quality of the instructors who bear the responsibility of shaping students' minds.

Chicana/o–Latina/o Studies Should Be Mandatory in Schools

Sean Arce, High School Teacher, Chicana/o-Latina/o Studies, Azusa Unified School District, Educational Consultant Xican@ Institute for Teaching and Organizing, Former Director of La Raza Studies, Tucson Unified School District

Chicana/o–Latina/o studies should be mandatory in schools because this program addresses the demographic imperative for Chicana/o–Latina/o youth; it operates to rectify the historical and contemporary oppressive educational policies, processes, and practices which have and continue to plague Chicana/o–Latina/o youth; and it improves the academic and social outcomes of Chicana/o–Latina/o and other youth. In order to discuss why Chicana/o–Latina/o studies should be mandatory in schools, it is first necessary to define Chicana/o–Latina/o studies and state its objectives.

Chicana/o–Latina/o studies presents an in-depth interdisciplinary study of the major developments in the distinct history, culture, and experiences of Chicanas/os–Latinas/os in the United States within the greater context of the Americas. In Chicana/o–Latina/o studies students critically examine how notions of power, culture, and identity intersect with constructs of race, class, gender, and sexuality as influencing the Chicana/o–Latina/o communities in their struggles for social justice. The objectives of an effective Chicana/o–Latina/o studies program are:

- To develop critical analyses of the Chicana/o–Latina/o historical, cultural, social, political, and economic experience in the United States.
- To develop critical thinking, reading, writing, and speaking skills through the study of the Chicana/o–Latina/o experience.
- To develop in Chicana/o–Latina/o youth a positive image of self and community.
- To develop critical literacies and skills which afford Chicana/o–Latina/o youth to articulate, address, and act upon issues facing Chicanas/os–Latinas/os so as to improve the conditions of their communities.

Current demographics indicate that Chicanas/o–Latinas/os are the largest ethnic minority in the United States, with those of Mexican origin comprising the largest subgroup within this minority. Urban public schools are experiencing a demographic shift wherein the Chicana/o–Latina/o student population is rapidly increasing—with a significant number of urban school districts now comprised of a Chicana/o–Latina/o majorities—while the white student population is rapidly decreasing. Also important to note is the divestment in public schools and an investment in both public and private sectors of the prison industry. Equally alarming, Chicanas/os–Latinas/os continue to have the lowest educational attainment of any racial or ethnic group in the United States, with the exception of Native American youth. These harmful demographic shifts and trends are often driven by the criminalization and marginalization of Chicanas/os–Latinas/os, leaving them vulnerable to economic exploitation with few viable opportunities to earn a sustainable wage to support themselves and their families.

The combination of these demographic shifts, divestment in public education, and low educational attainment of the largest ethnic minority in the United States presents public schools—specifically the Chicana/o–Latina/o youth who attend them—with a major crisis and a demographic imperative that requires prompt and adequate measures to address these damaging trends. Mandatory Chicana/o–Latina/o studies in schools is an effective way to address this demographic imperative, for they serve as an empowering and culturally and socially responsive approach to meet the academic and social needs of a rapidly increasing Chicana/o–Latina/o student population who have been traditionally forced into a disempowering educational system where they are pushed out of the system.

For over a century and a half the policies, processes, and practices of schooling have adversely impacted Chicana/o–Latina/o youth. Given this reality of schooling, Chicana/o–Latina/o studies in schools should be mandatory because they operate to rectify past schooling practices and effectively counter current schooling conditions that are detrimental to the learning, academic achievement, and well-being of Chicanas/os–Latinas/os.

Schools have traditionally and continually operated as primary sites of deculturalization, assimilation, and colonization, perpetuating a school experience where Chicanas/os–Latinas/os do not see themselves in the curriculum. Schools leave them with distorted cultural identities, underdeveloped academic identities, and underdeveloped critical reading, writing, and speaking skills and literacies. These schooling conditions have led to Chicana/o–Latina/o school failure that is defined as "their persistently, pervasively, and disproportionately low academic achievement" (Valencia 2011). Essentially, schools have and continue to serve as institutions that reproduce inequality for Chicana/o–Latina/o youth. Chicana/o–Latina/o school failure is attributable to systemic racism in schools that is propagated through oppressive schooling conditions, including the following: (1) prevalent attitudes such as deficit thinking, which is placed upon Chicanas/os–Latinas/os; (2) institutional processes that privilege white students and disadvantage Chicanas/os–Latinas/os; and (3) outcomes wherein educational attainment for white students is significantly higher than for Chicanas/os–Latinas/os. As an antiracist educational project, Chicana/o–Latina/o studies addresses institutional racism in schools and society, fostering the development of historical and critical consciousness in students wherein they can act upon inequality to transform current schooling conditions to meet their academic and social needs.

As public school records attest, Chicanas/os–Latinas/os cannot afford to wait any longer for schools to work in their best interests. Consequently, Chicana/o–Latina/o studies should be mandatory, for it is one of few proven educational methods to effectively counter and transform the pernicious schooling conditions for Chicana/o–Latina/o youth.

Chicana/o–Latina/o studies should be mandatory in schools because it has been demonstrated to improve academic and social outcomes for Chicana/o–Latina/o and other youth. Whereas mainstream curricula remain Eurocentric, contributing to the academic disengagement of Chicana/o–Latina/o youth, Chicana/o–Latina/o studies has reversed that disengagement through a historically, culturally, and socially responsive curriculum and pedagogy that is academically rigorous. Whereas mainstream curricula and pedagogy have perpetuated inequality between white and Chicana/o–Latina/o youth, Chicana/o–Latina/o studies effectively works to counter inequality by facilitating the closing of the persistent and pervasive achievement gap between Chicana/o–Latina/o youth and white youth. Lastly, whereas mainstream Eurocentric curricula and pedagogy have served to marginalize and in many instances erase the identities of Chicana/o–Latina/o youth while simultaneously perpetuating prejudice, bias, and racist ideologies in white youth, Chicana/o–Latina/o studies develop strong academic and cultural identities in Chicana/o–Latina/o youth while also reducing prejudice, bias, and racist ideologies in white youth.

The demographic imperative of Chicana/o–Latina/o youth, the oppressive schooling conditions of Chicanas/os–Latinas/os, and the academic and social well-being of Chicana/o–Latina/o youth provide evidence and the rationale that Chicana/o–Latina/o studies should be mandatory in schools. Few, if any, educational approaches or methodologies have proven to be as successful as Chicana/o–Latina/o studies in effectively addressing these significant areas of Chicana/o–Latina/o education.

NOTE

1. It is fair to interject that education reform and experimentation were popular for a brief time, sustained by government and private funding. However, they were cut short by corporate-led cutbacks in funding for higher education. The cutbacks had very little to do with the success of the programs, but rather with the profit-making culture of higher education which, in the end, undermined teacher training competency.

BIBLIOGRAPHY

Acuña, Rodolfo F. "Forgotten Memories Wasted Years." *WordPress*, November 5, 2015. (a) http://rudyacuna.net/forgotten-memories-wasted-years-2

Acuña, Rodolfo F. "Redundancy and Chicana/o Studies." *WordPress*, December 22, 2015. (b) http://rudyacuna.net/redundancy-and-chicanao-studies-12-22-15

Acuña, Rodolfo F. "The Identity Crisis of Mexican Americans." *counterpunch*, October 25, 2013. http://www.counterpunch.org/2013/10/25/the-identity-crisis-of-mexican-americans

Acuña, Rodolfo F. "What Happened to Chicano Studies?" *LA Progressive*, March 10, 2013. https://www.laprogressive.com/chicano-studies

Acuña, Rodolfo F. "The Illusion of Inclusion." *counterpunch*, June 1, 2012. http://www.counterpunch.org/2012/06/01/the-illusion-of-inclusion/

Acuña, Rodolfo F. "The Role of the Middle Class, Revisited." *counterpunch*, April 20, 2012. http://www.counterpunch.org/2012/04/20/the-role-of-the-middle-class-revisited

Acuña, Rodolfo F. "Critical Thinking: The Basis of Scientific Thought." *LatinoLA*, June 11, 2011. http://www.latinola.com/story.php?story=9586

Acuña, Rodolfo F. *The Making of Chicana/o Studies: In the Trenches of Academe*. New Brunswick: Rutgers University Press, 2011.

Acuña, Rodolfo F. "Forty Years of Chicana/o Studies: When the Myth becomes a Legend." October 2010a. http://forchicanachicanostudies.wikispaces.com/Chicana+Chicano+Studies

Acuña, Rodolfo F. "Mexicans Are Not Dumb, the Schools Fail." *Reader Supported News*, June 24, 2010b. http://readersupportednews.org/opinion/124-124/2280-mexicans-are-not-dumb-the-schools-fail

Acuña, Rodolfo F. "The Search for Reason in Arizona." *Reader Supported News*, June 20, 2010c. http://readersupportednews.org/opinion/42-42/2246-the-search-for-reason-in-arizona

Asante, Molefi Kete. "The Role of an Afrocentric Ideology." Web Page, July 29, 2009. http://www.asante.net/articles/42/the-role-of-an-afrocentric-ideology

Avakian, Bob. "The Fight Over Ethnic Studies in Tucson, Arizona." *Revolution #223*, January 23, 2011. http://revcom.us/a/223/ethnic_studies-en.html

Biggers, Jeff. "Why Arizona's Ethnic Studies Crisis Should Matter to All Educators: Interview With Dr. Rudy Acuna." *Huffington Post*, August 10, 2011. http://www.thenation.com/article/why-arizonas-ethnic-studies-crisis-should-matter-all-educators-interview-dr-rudy-acuna

Britton, Dee. "What is Collective Memory?" *WordPress*, June 2012. http://memorialworlds.com/what-is-collective-memory

Buelna, Gabriel. "Outlawing Shakespeare: The Battle for the Tucson Mind." *The Non-profit Network*, October 30, 2012. https://www.youtube.com/watch?v=anChx_9TF-Q

Cabán, Pedro. "Black and Latino Studies and Social Capital Theory." *Sage Race Relations Abstracts* 32, no. 3 (2007): 5-29.

Cabrera, Nolan L., Elisa L. Meza, and Roberto Dr. Cintli Rodríguez. "The Fight for Mexican American Studies in Tucson." *NACLA*, January 9, 2012, https://nacla.org/article/fight-mexican-american-studies-tucson

Connerly, Ward. "The Sacramento Crusader against Affirmative Action, Has Turned His Sights on a New Target: Ethnic Studies." *Chicago Tribune*, June 21, 1998. http://articles.chicagotribune.com/1998-06-21/news/9806210105_1_ethnic-studies-balkanizing-ward-connerly

Cranmore, Jeff. "School Counseling: Turning Potential Dropouts Toward a College Going Culture." http://media.collegeboard.com/digitalServices/public/School-Counseling-Turning-Potential-Dropouts.pdf

Defense Language Institute Foreign Language Center–Official Site. http://www.dliflc.edu

Department of Chicana and Chicano Studies Web Page. California State University, Northridge. http://www.csun.edu/humanities/chicana-chicano-studies

Fenton, Edwin. *Teaching the New Social Studies in Secondary Schools: An Inductive Approach*. Milwaukee: International Thomson Publishing, 1966.

Freire, Paulo. *Pedagogy of the Oppressed,* 30th Anniversary Edition. New York: Bloomsbury Academic, 2000.

Gazzar, Brenda. "California's Latino Students Among the Most Segregated in the Country, Says UCLA Report." *Los Angeles Daily News,* May 22, 2014. http://www.dailynews.com/social-affairs/20140522/californias-latino-students-among-the-most-segregated-in-the-country-says-ucla-report

Korry, Elaine. "Black Student Enrollment at UCLA Plunges." *Morning Edition,* NPR, July 24, 2006. http://www.npr.org/templates/story/story.php?storyId=5563891

Losey, Kay M., and Hermann Kurthen, "The Rhetoric of 'Political Correctness' in the U.S. Media." *Amerikastudien/American Studies* 40, no. 2 (1995): 227–245. http://www.gvsu.edu/cms4/asset/2EF13597-D42F-119E-4BC17F1486F70448/losey__kurthen_-_the_rhetoric_of_political_correctness_in_the_u.s._media_1995.pdf

Makdisi, George. "The Scholastic Method in Medieval Education: An Inquiry into Its Origins in Law and Theology." *Speculum* 49, no.4 (Cambridge University Press, 1974): 640–661.

The Mexican American: Quest for Equality, Report from National Advisory Committee on Mexican American Education, Washington, DC, 1968. http://eric.ed.gov/?id=ED049841

National Education Association, Research Department, 2011. http://www.nea.org/assets/docs/NBI-2010-3-value-of-ethnic-studies.pdf

Oboler, Suzanne. "Revisiting the State of the Field: Some Reflections on the 10th Anniversary of Latino Studies." *Latino Studies* 10, no. 3 (2012): 281.

Orfield, Gary. *The Civil Rights Project.* Los Angeles: UCLA, 2014. http://civilrightsproject.ucla.edu/about-us/staff/gary-orfield-ph.d

Paul, R., and L. Elder. "Socratic Teaching." The Critical Thinking Community, April 1997. http://www.criticalthinking.org/pages/socratic-teaching/606

"Paulo Freire." Freire Institute. http://www.freire.org/paulo-freire Christine E. "The Academic and Social Value of Ethnic Studies: A Research Review."

Soldatenko, Michael. *Chicano Studies: The Genesis of a Discipline.* Tucson: University of Arizona Press, 2011.

Thys, Fred. "Why The Best Low-Income Students Often Don't Apply To The Most Competitive Colleges." *WBUR Boston,* February 27, 2002. http://www.wbur.org/2014/02/27/low-income-students-college-applications.

Torres, Lourdes. "New Directions in Latino Studies." *Latino Studies* 13, no. 3 (2015): 313.

Valencia, Richard R. (ed). *Chicano School Failure and Success: Past, Present, and Future* 3rd ed. New York: Routledge, 2011.

Zalaquett, Carlo P., and Miguel E. Gallardo. "The National Successful Latina/o Students Project: Providing Role Models to Latina/o Students." National Successful Latina/o Students, 2004. http://www.coedu.usf.edu/zalaquett/s/p.html

SELECTED VIDEOS

Buelna, Gabriel. "Outlawing Shakespeare: The Battle for the Tucson Mind," The Nonprofit Network. YouTube video, 41:52, posted October 30, 2012. https://www.youtube.com/watch?v=anChx_9TF-Q

Cancerleo79. "Chicano! PBS Documentary—Taking Back the Schools," YouTube video, 14:37, posted August 30, 2011. https://www.youtube.com/watch?v=NL4rQHKza9Y

"Crystal City Walkout state competition," YouTube video, 9:56, posted by 1025hamblin, April 29, 2014. https://www.youtube.com/watch?v=eDfEbr8NKHU

"Daily Show's satirical take on the Mexican-American studies controversy," YouTube video, 3:48, posted by KGUN9, April 3, 2012. https://www.youtube.com/watch?v=y1miLXqpcGs

"Defense Language Institute Foreign Language Center," YouTube video, 6:30, posted by DLIFLC Monterey, March 22, 2010. https://www.youtube.com/watch?v=rskKXpSV9Ww

"MAS students speak out about their classes and books being banned in Tucson," YouTube video, 32:43, posted by ThreeSonorans's channel, January 15, 2012. https://www.youtube.com/watch?v=-OUSbELFpX8

"San Francisco State Strike 1968, Black Students & Third World Liberation Front," YouTube video, 19:50, posted by Saul Rouda, July 6, 2014. https://www.youtube.com/watch?v=YMDPk29XUvw

"The Storm At Valley State," YouTube video, 35:16, posted by CSUN EOP, July 8,2014. https://www.youtube.com/watch?v=RWXlSdLFuKw

TEDx. "Why ethnic studies matters | Ron Espiritu | TEDxAmherstCollege," YouTube video, 17:51, posted December 18, 2014. https://www.youtube.com/watch?v=XvvMgujD4i8

UAW. "Rodolfo Acuña on his banned book, 'Occupied America: A History of Chicanos,'" YouTube video, 4:15, posted October 7, 2011. https://www.youtube.com/watch?v=tJKOzA3TAvs

Univision. "Eduardo Padrón: Only 8% of teachers in the US are Hispanic," YouTube video, 3:54, posted October 21, 2011. https://www.youtube.com/watch?v=UHIzUREHAwo

Unrest Documentary: Full Movie, YouTube video, 1:00:36, posted by Tlanvision, May 12, 2012. https://www.youtube.com/watch?v=erf3j3UOmWE

Zalaquett, Carlos P., and Miguel E. Gallardo. "The National Successful Latina/o Students Project: Providing Role Models to Latina/o Students," 2004. http://www.coedu.usf.edu/zalaquett/s/p.html

5

Open Borders: Where the Third World Begins

BACKGROUND

Mexico shares just shy of 2,000 miles of border with the United States; it is where the Third World begins and the First World ends. Immigration affects all U.S. Latinas/os, even Puerto Ricans who are U.S. citizens, because in truth, Puerto Ricans are targets of American racist nativism directed at Latina/o immigrants. Since the early 1970s, anti-immigrant organizations and politicians have fanned nativist fears in reaction to the heavy migration of people from Mexico, Central America, and Asia. The rise of immigration swelled the ranks of nativist organizations devoted to immigration control. The Internet helped this growth, and entire Web pages warn about the impending silent invasion onto American soil of criminal aliens.

> **Why do Latinas/os resent being called criminal aliens? Do they look like ET? Criminals? Why would some Americans want to forget how the present border came about?**

Much of the literature on immigration is inflammatory and plays on American angst. For example, Matthew Campbell writes, "The year is 2100. America is in ferment. The second civil war has ended in defeat for English-speaking whites, encircled in their heartland in the Midwest. The southwestern states of California, Arizona, New Mexico, and Texas have broken away from the union to form provinces in the new, Hispanic country of Aztlan. Unlikely as this vision of the future may seem, the break-up of the United States within the next 100 years is regarded by some people as an entirely plausible consequence of a new wave of immigration" (Campbell, 2000).

What is inflammatory about the Matthew Campbell statement?

Pat Buchanan, during the 2000 presidential campaign, screamed, "Stop this massive illegal immigration cold. . . . I'll build that security fence and we'll close it, we'll say 'Listen Jose, you're not coming in'" (Bennet, 1996). Buchanan used the undocumented as scapegoats, saying: "All I'm saying is that our levels of immigration now in the last 30 years have been enormous. It's almost over a million legal immigrants a year, and half a million illegals that come here and stay. And you're rapidly changing the nature of the entire country; we speak 300 languages. Unless we do something and make sure the things that unite us are elevated—like language and history and all the rest of it—we're gonna lose our country, my friend" (Janofsky, 2000). Buchanan's rhetoric set the tone for other Republican candidates who wanted to score easy points with nativists—immigrants were easy targets—they could not vote or mostly voted Democrat.

The rhetoric has deteriorated in the past 16 years. Republican presidential candidate Donald Trump said:

> The U.S. has become a dumping ground for everybody else's problems. [Applause] Thank you. It's true, and these are the best and the finest. When Mexico sends its people, they're not sending their best. They're not sending you. They're not sending you. They're sending people that have lots of problems, and they're bringing those problems with us. They're bringing drugs. They're bringing crime. They're rapists. And some, I assume, are good people. (Capehart, 2015)

Trump did not invent these racist cheap shots. The anti-immigrant laws and campaign speeches gave wings to this virulent nativism. Candidates learned that they could call Mexicans drug dealers, rapists, and whores and not pay a political price.

Why would Latina/o immigrants consider Buchanan and Trump's statement inflammatory? Do they indicate how they view Latinos in general?

Many Latina/os resented these cheap shots and felt under siege. At the gut level Mexican Americans responded, "WE DIDN'T cross the border, the border crossed us" (D'Amato, 2006). Recalling the fact that the Southwest once belonged to Mexico, immigration activists resented the term *illegal alien* as offensive because it conjured up the image of criminals and aliens from outer space invading the United States. The word *illegal* criminalizes poor people who want the same things all Americans do, which is adequate food, shelter, and clothing. They counter that the word *alien* dehumanizes them and encourages violence toward them. Latinas/os prefer the term *undocumented worker* or at the very least *unauthorized immigrants*. The Latinas/os' reactions to nativist attacks vary from ignoring them to militantly confronting their statements.

Discuss the statement "WE DIDN'T cross the border, the border crossed us."

Among the various Latina/o groups, Mexican Americans are the most vocal, largely because Mexicans are the largest Latina/o group and numerically most affected. They have been here the longest and thus have a larger organizational network. They also share a 2,000-mile border with the United States. Mexican Americans also have the largest network of elected officials. Within the Mexican American community, there are divisions on how to deal with nativists. For example, the more militant sector responds that they are indigenous to the land and that the nativists are the illegal aliens. Mexica Nation, a nationalist group, believes that as indigenous people, Chicanas/os form a nation, and they declare in the Mexica Manifesto: "[w]e do hereby declare the following manifesto in order to free our people from the descendants of Europeans (Anglo-American, Latinos-Hispanics, Euro-Mexicans and other 'whites') who have illegally and stubbornly remained on our land through their deceit, the enslavement of our people, racial rape, and the cultural castration of our people. They have fortified their position as trespassers and thieves by destroying our identity, history, heritage and independent Anahuac [the Aztecas were part of this linguistic group] Indigenous thought."[1]

More and more the question arises, would Americans be illegal aliens if climate change made large parts of the United States uninhabitable; if terrorists bombed the border states and they moved to Mexico?

While the approaches differ, over 70 percent support the undocumented and oppose massive roundups and deportations that separate families. The sentiment of many Mexican Americans is that the United States illegally seized more than half of Mexico's land and three-quarters of its water. They are only demanding just treatment for immigrants and the recognition that Mexicans have just as much, if not more, right to be in the United States as Europeans do. Immigrant groups are lobbying for laws, making arguments to counter the nativist propaganda generated by anti-immigrant groups, and establishing organizations to protect the rights of the foreign-born.

Sum up the Latina/o positions on immigration. What did Mexican President Porfirio Díaz's statement, "Pobre Mexico tan lejos de Díos y tan cerca a los Estados Unidos" [So far away from God and so close to the United States], mean?

The Catholic Church has played a leading role in the protection of the immigrant. Indeed, former Cardinal Roger Mahony of Los Angeles said, "The divisive rhetoric of the immigration debate is harmful in itself. It plays upon fears and emotions; it affirms the racism and prejudices deeply ingrained in the hearts and minds of people. But when individuals seek to further embody this rhetoric in social policy, then the evil of this rhetoric becomes institutionalized. It is given life. It is what we call social sin" (Klein, 1993). The Church's interest in Latinos had much to do with the fact that "Latinos now make up 34% of American Catholics—and their number is only expected to grow as the church's declining white majority ages. Already, nearly half of all American Catholics younger than 30 are Latino." A total of 70 percent of the nearly 5 million parishioners in the Los Angeles Archdiocese is Latinos (Duara and Parvini, 2015).

Trump's rhetoric of building a higher wall and vowing to have Mexico pay for it drew a reaction from Pope Francis. When a reporter asked him about Mr. Trump on the papal airliner as he returned to Rome after his six-day visit to Mexico, the Pope said, "A person who thinks only about building walls, wherever they may be, and not building bridges, is not Christian." The Pope added: "I say only that this man is not Christian if he has said things like that . . . . We must see if he said things in that way and in this I give the benefit of the doubt" (Yardley, 2016).

Was the Pope's answer political or based on morality?

Racist xenophobia is called "nativism." In the 1850s this movement was called "Know Nothings." The negative reaction of Americans to immigrants is a product of American history dating back to the Alien and Sedition Acts of 1798 (Smith, 1954). Historically it is the response of mainstream Americans to the successive waves of immigrants coming into the country from Europe, Asia, and Latin America. During the colonial period, the British formed colonies along the tidewater of the Atlantic Ocean, thinking of themselves as native while ignoring that the Indians were the natives and that the African was part of the migration process. Later, Scotch–Irish immigrants arrived and were forced into the backwoods, the Western frontier region. At the same time, Germans immigrated to the United States as well as more African slaves. Americans felt that they were threatened, conducted anti-Catholic crusades, and preached that the Pope wanted to control the United States.

How does nativism go beyond race in targeting culture and religion? Is the present revolt of many white Americans based on race, culture, or both?

About 450,000 enslaved African Americans lived in the 13 colonies. African Americans lived throughout the colonies by 1775. The transformation of the economy during the first part of the 19th century brought a second wave of immigration in the 1820s; immigrants were pulled by the lure of jobs and pushed by conditions in their own countries. From 1820 to 1860, Europeans arrived from Great Britain, Ireland, and western Germany, with a few immigrants from Norway, Sweden, and the Netherlands. Many were Catholic, and the White Anglo-Saxon Protestants (WASPs) rejected them.

Anti-immigrant riots broke out in cities such as Philadelphia and New York and spread throughout the Northeast. In this context, the Texas filibuster (1836) and the Mexican American War (1848) added to growing nationalism among Americans and reinforced anti-foreign and anti-Catholic sentiments. Events such as the battle at the Alamo (1836) and the Mexican American War (1845–1848) typed the Mexican as the enemy. In the 1850s, anti-immigrant voters formed the Native American Party, popularly known as the Know Nothing Party, which called for the exclusion of immigrants and advocated anti-immigrant policies. After the Civil War, spurred by the building of railroads and technological innovations such as electricity, more Irish, Germans, Poles, Italians, Jews, and other central and southern Europeans were pulled into the country. The uprooted immigrants struggled against poverty and discrimination in cities.

Does nativism cast a bright light on the description that the Unites States is a nation of immigrants?

The first immigrants officially excluded were the Chinese. The Chinese Exclusion Acts of 1882, 1892, and 1902 eliminated the Chinese, and then the Gentlemen's Agreements with Japan of 1900 and 1907 reduced and then eliminated the Japanese as immigrants. Until 1895, most immigrants came from northern or western Europe. After this point, most immigrants came from southern or eastern Europe, primarily from Austria, Hungary, Italy, and Russia. The most offensive was Italian immigration: "In the 1880s, they numbered 300,000; in the 1890s, 600,000; in the decade after that, more than two million. By 1920, when immigration began to taper off, more than 4 million Italians had come to the United States, and represented more than 10 percent of the nation's foreign-born population" ("Immigration Italian"). These changes made many Americans nervous, since the new immigrants were darker, spoke foreign languages, had different customs, and were Catholic and Jewish.

Can Trump's wall be described as a color line? How is it similar to the Berlin Wall?

Convinced that immigrants were responsible for crime, violence, and industrial strife, and that they could not easily assimilate into American society, Congress passed the Literacy Act of 1917, largely to keep European immigrants out of the country. Congress aimed the

1921 Immigration Act at immigrants from southern and central Europe and established an annual quota of 3 percent of each nationality, based on the 1910 census. Only 375,000 immigrants could be admitted annually. Great Britain, Ireland, and Germany received more than 70 percent of this quota, which was rarely filled. The purpose was to preserve the American racial mix of predominately northern Europeans. In 1924, Congress passed another act, setting the limit at 2 percent for each nationality, based on the 1890 census, when the percentage of southern and eastern Europeans was much lower. The law limited the number of immigrants to the United States to 165,000 annually. The act discriminated against immigrants from southern and eastern Europe and barred Asians completely (Ngai, 1999).

How did the immigration acts maintain the color line? Was it American?

The Immigration Act of 1924 did not limit Mexicans or other Latin Americans. Agricultural interests needed Mexican labor and many U.S. corporations were interested in promoting Pan-American trade. United States Representative Martin Madden of Chicago, chair of the House Appropriations Committee, complained by stating, "The bill opens the doors for perhaps the worst element that comes into the United States—the Mexican peon. . . . [It] opens the door wide and unrestricted to the most undesirable people who come under the flag." Senator Matthew M. Neely of West Virginia charged, "On the basis of merit, Mexico is the last country we should grant a special favor or extend a peculiar privilege. The immigrants from many of the countries of Europe have more in common with us than the Mexicanos have" (Neal, 1941, p. 113).

The incessant demand for labor and the shortage of workers created by the restriction of European immigration also led to the migration of African Americans from the South to the factories of the Northeast and Midwest. The dependence on Mexican labor did not shield Mexican workers from discrimination, however. In early 1921, the bottom fell out of the economy, and Mexicans became the scapegoats for the failure of the U.S. economy. American authorities shipped thousands back to Mexico. This act set the stage for the Great Depression of the 1930s, when deportation and repatriation programs sent an estimated one million Mexicans back to Mexico (Balderama and Rodriguez, 1995).

Many Mexicans had been in the American Southwest since before the American takeover. Others entered the United States throughout the 19th century for political and economic reasons. As the Southwest industrialized at the turn of the century, thousands of Mexicans were pulled north. Conditions in Mexico also pushed Mexicans northward. United States and European capitalists invested in railroads, mines, agriculture, and other industries that transformed the Mexican economy and society and led to a mass exodus from farm work. Labor contractors went into Mexico and recruited uprooted Mexican workers to come to what had become the American Southwest. The demand for Mexican labor increased as U.S. policy restricted Asians and Europeans from entering the country and as agriculture, the railroads, mining, and manufacturing became more dependent on Mexican labor. In addition, the building of a railroad that connected Mexico with the United States transformed Mexico's economy, uprooting many Mexicans from farms and pushing them north in search of work (see Acuña, 2015; Balderama and Rodríguez, 1995).

While the events with Mexican immigrants were taking place, between 1915 and 1930 some 50,000 Puerto Ricans came to the United States. Another wave followed between 1940 and 1969, and an additional 800,000 Puerto Ricans migrated, principally to the New York City area. The demand for labor strengthened the pull of Puerto Ricans to the United States. This new wave went to New York but also migrated to rural areas where they were employed as farm workers.

The Jones Act (1917) made Puerto Ricans citizens of the United States. Puerto Rican migration to the mainland coincided with the decline of European immigration. Americanization programs attempted to remake Puerto Ricans, who became even more determined to preserve their identity and strengthen bonds with their homeland. Some suggest that part of that glue which held the community together was Puerto Rican salsa (dance) and dance clubs (Padilla, 1990; Bloom, 2007).

What was the Jones Act? Discuss its good and bad aspects.

World War II accelerated Mexican and Puerto Rican migration because of the abundance of jobs in the United States. The Mexican bracero program brought several million contract laborers to the United States from Mexico from 1942 to 1964. Other Mexicans came both with and without documents. Puerto Ricans also were encouraged to migrate, not only to New York City but to Chicago and even to the tanneries of Milwaukee. Americans did not meet these waves of Latinos with open arms, and the U.S. government, in response to a wave of nativism, shipped more than one million Mexicans back to Mexico annually from 1953 to 1955 in what was called "Operation Wetback." Nativism followed a pattern, worsening in times of economic stress when nativist sentiment made the immigrant the scapegoat for the nation's economic problems (Hernández, 2006).

Congress passed the Immigration Act of 1965 during the civil rights era of the 1960s and, more significantly, in times of relative prosperity. For the first time, Congress put Latin Americans under a quota, and it allowed Asians to immigrate to the United States. Policy changed from basing immigration on national origins to admitting immigrants based on family preferences. Most liberal Americans saw the former immigration policy of national origins as racist and based on an attempt to engineer race in the United States. Most Americans believed that large numbers of western Europeans would continue to immigrate to the United States. However, the improvement of the European economy contributed to a slowing of European immigration (Ngai, 2015).

Despite the fact that the 1965 Immigration Act had inequities, why was it an improvement on national origins?

From 1930 to 1960, about 80 percent of U.S. immigrants came from European countries or Canada, but by 1977 to 1979, only 16 percent came from Europe and Canada, with Asia and Latin America accounting for about 40 percent each. The new Act was allegedly indifferent to ethnic origin and gave attention to family ties and the reunification of families.

As Americans saw more darker-skinned immigrants in the streets, panic spread among white Americans that the country was becoming darker. Congress responded by putting caps on legal Mexican and migration from other countries. These limitations encouraged the rise of nativist groups who promoted the notion that illegal aliens were invading the country. The intensity of the attacks led to the formation of pro-immigrant defense groups, which responded by saying that immigrants were neither criminals, that is, illegal, nor were they Martians (aliens). Latino immigrants were human and consequently were simply undocumented workers.

Why did the 1965 Act raise panic among white Americans?

Also, Cuban immigration picked up sharply during the 1950s because of political conditions in Cuba. For decades, Cubans had fled tyranny from right-wing dictators. After 1959 many fled Castro's revolution. Many in this wave were from wealthier families and were well educated. The United States granted them asylum and assisted qualified applicants in finding homes, finding jobs, and paying them health benefits and stipends. Most of the later waves of Cuban immigrants were relatives of the first group or were poor people looking for work. Most were white. About 125,000 *marielitos* came in the 1980s. Cuban Americans called themselves *marielitos* because the Cuban government put them aboard boats at the Cuban port of Mariel and sent them to Miami. The *marielitos* included many unskilled workers, criminals, and mentally ill people. They also included many Cubans of African ancestry who were hardworking people (Aguirre and James, 1997).

Why did Americans not comment on the fact that the great majority of the early Cuban immigrants were white? Would there have been a different response if they were Black? Why was there a negative reaction to the arrival of the marielitos?

Simultaneously, beginning in the early 1970s, internal crises pushed Central Americans and South Americans to the United States. The CIA-sponsored military overthrow of constitutionally elected Chilean President Salvador Allende in 1973 brought Chilean refugees to the United States. Over the past 10 years, civil war forced many Colombians to flee their homes.

In 1979, Nicaraguans overthrew dictator Anastacio Somoza, which set off a series of revolutions in Central America. The wars pushed political refugees from El Salvador and Guatemala as well as other Central American countries into the United States. In the 1980s the world saw increased military repression and rural counterinsurgency warfare programs supported by the United States. The result was numerous massacres, forced displacement, assassinations of political, religious, labor, student, and peasant leaders, and the disappearance of thousands. By the mid-1980s, about 300,000 Salvadorans and 50,000 Guatemalans lived in Los Angeles alone.

How did the U.S.-sponsored wars drive Central American migration to the United States?

The United States refused to recognize Salvadoran and Guatemalan immigrants as political refugees. However, the United States recognized

Nicaraguan refugees fleeing the revolution that overthrew Somoza, maintaining that the Salvadoran and Guatemalan insurgencies were communist inspired. Thousands of Salvadorans and Guatemalans who entered the United States without documents filed for political asylum and were routinely denied. United States churches, immigration lawyers, and activists won a class-action suit against the Immigration and Naturalization Service (INS) for discrimination. The government settled the suit in 1990, when the INS granted temporary protective status for these refugees, allowing them to work in the United States but leaving them with an uncertain legal future. In 1997, Congress attempted to resolve the issue and passed the 1997 Nicaraguan Adjustment and Central American Relief Act (NACARA). NACARA gave preference to Nicaraguan and Cuban refugees, who received a blanket amnesty and the right to apply for permanent residency because they were supposedly anti-Marxist.

In the late 1990s, Salvadorans and Guatemalans won the right to go before an immigration judge to prove, on a case-by-case basis, that returning to their countries would cause them to suffer extreme hardship. Previously, these refugees faced costly legal battles with no guarantee that the United States would accept their petition. Under new rules, the U.S. government presumed that returning these refugees would pose an extreme hardship for them. An INS official, rather than a judge, heard the cases. The Salvadoran and Guatemalan communities in the United States had formed political and refugee organizations and integrated into the Protestant and Catholic refugee relief network. North American groups, such as the Committee in Solidarity with the People of El Salvador (CISPES),[2] formed along with human rights organizations, such as CARECEN (the Central American Refugee Center) and El Rescate, but simultaneously reached out to solidarity committees, politicians, and community and neighborhood associations.

Were all Central Americans treated equally? Why were Guatemalans and Salvadorans treated differently from Nicaraguans and Cubans?

The first years of the new millennium found the question of immigration unanswered. Because of relative prosperity, most Americans did not have strong feelings about the issue. The two militant sectors, those vehemently for and against immigration, remained adamant in their positions. The issue is one that lies beneath the surface and will become an issue when there is a downturn in the economy. The legacy of Latina/o activists especially was that they had not abandoned the foreign-born and pressured labor and civil rights groups to make immigration and the foreign-born a priority. Noteworthy was the work of Bert Corona and Hermandad (Ramos, 2001).

The anti-immigrant hysteria was fanned by powerful so-called nonprofit foundations funded by some of the most prominent American billionaires who, in turn, funded anti-immigrant, antibilingual education, and human rights campaigns. They in turn received millions of dollars to fight for border control (Stefanic and Delgado, 1996). Many of these foundations funded Proposition 187 in California in 1994, which was passed by two-thirds of Californians. They voted for draconian measures that targeted immigrants, taking away many social services and access to human rights, such as education. Proposition 187 polarized Californians, with those opposing it noting that "187" was also the police code for murder in progress. The effects were devastating, but they did unify Latinas/os who saw the Republican Party as the enemy and this view has prevented a Republican candidate for a high state office to be elected (Stefanic and Delgado, 1996).

How did Proposition 187 politicize Mexican Americans and why other Latinos?

Proposition 187 also politicized another generation of activists. Feeling the racism and injustice, many middle school and high school students walked out of schools and took to the streets in 2006 when a federal draconian law was proposed. On April 10, 2006, millions of people, mostly immigrants, took to the streets of 140 cities across the nation. It was one of a series of marches. They were tired of being afraid and intimidated by U.S. Immigration and Customs Enforcement (ICE) and potbellied bullies who called themselves "minutemen." The protests began in response to a proposed legislation known as H.R. 4437, an extreme measure that would criminalize not only unauthorized immigrants but anyone who helped them. The undocumented would be classified as felons, among other punitive measures. Over one million showed up in Los Angeles, several hundreds of thousands in Dallas, and upwards of 300,000 in Chicago. Despite provocation by some racist nativists, the march was peaceful. Marches held on March 26 had paved the way for these marches, which not only protested H.R. 4437 but also called for immigration reform.

After this period, undocumented immigrants came out and openly, as a group, demanded justice. The Latino population in 2011 numbered an estimated 52 million—a growth of over one million a year. In California alone, Latinos numbered 14 million. Texas followed with 9.7 million, Florida with 4.2 million, New York with 3.4 million, and Illinois with 1.2 million. Latinos grew by 43 percent from 2000 to 2010, four times the national growth rate; they comprised 26.3 percent of the population younger than age 1. An estimated two-thirds to 70 percent of these totals were of Mexican origin. The numbers were significant in the presidential elections of 2008 and 2012. Add to this that in 2012, Latinos were concentrated in three states with large Electoral College votes: California (55), Texas (38), and Florida (29). In the first two states, the Mexican-origin population reached a plurality of their total population ("Pro-Immigrant Marches Surging Nationwide," 2006).

Some observers say that by 2006 Latinas/os had lost their fear? Why is this important?

Critics of U.S. border policy say that the United States created border tensions. Many informed persons on both sides of the border criticize the War on Drugs, charging that it is being used by the United States, in a similar manner as the so-called War on Terror, to frighten people into supporting assaults on basic freedoms. This war has corrupted Central American and Mexican officials and given rise to drug cartels. Before the War on Drugs, illegal merchandise was shipped by sea and air. These countries were unprepared to control this contraband. Moreover, Mexico had been disoriented by the North American Free Trade Agreement that went into effect in 1994.

At the same time, hundreds of millions of dollars were spent to shut down ocean drug corridors, diverting the drugs through Central America and Mexico and thus corrupting their governments and civil societies. Closing off the corridors migrants took through Texas and California channeled these migrants through the deserts of Sonora and Arizona, leaving men, women, and children to die of hunger and thirst. The drug trade created a huge demand in the U.S. drug market. The situation was worsened by the deportation of thousands of gang members to their homelands in Central America and Mexico. Most of the deportees were raised in the United States and inducted into crime in the U.S. prison system. The enormous profits in drugs spawned cartels and caused internal wars among the cartels and with local, state, and federal authorities:

> The Mexican government released new data showing that between 2007 and 2014—a period that accounts for some of the bloodiest years of the nation's war against the drug cartels—more than 164,000 people were victims of homicide. Nearly 20,000 died last year alone, a substantial number, but still a decrease from the 27,000 killed at the peak of fighting in 2011. (Breslow, 2015)

The United States blames Mexico for this war!

What was the role of the War on Drugs in creating the border crisis? If there was no American demand for drugs would there be a need for a War on Drugs?

Everything revolves around profit. Trump's border wall is projected to cost almost $50 billion, which will go into the pockets of building contractors. The War on Drugs has created an industry where gun dealers sell guns to the cartels. Banks launder the gun and drug profits and thousands of Mexicans and other Latin Americans die trying to make it into the United States. Human rights activists point out the contradiction that the Berlin Wall that separated East and West Germany came down in 1989, but the United States has built its own wall separating it from the Third World. Border patrols are increasing their abuse of people attempting to escape hunger. The official line—that the Border Patrol was fighting the War on Drugs—gave the agency tremendous latitude in violating human rights.

In 1990, one year after the Berlin Wall came tumbling down, the Defense Department built an 11-mile fence in the San Diego area as part of the War on Drugs. Two years later, the Army Corps of Engineers announced plans to place scores of floodlights along a 13-mile strip of border near San Diego to "deter drug smugglers and illegal aliens." A 1992 *Atlantic Monthly* piece posited, "It would not require much killing: the Soviets sealed their borders for decades without an excessive expenditure of ammunition," adding that a systematic policy of shooting illegal immigrants would deter most Mexicans, but "adopting such a policy is not a choice most Americans would make. Of course, there would be no question of free trade" (Langwiesche, 1992, p. 69).

Estimates of the number of people killed at the Berlin Wall vary. Berlin's privately run Checkpoint Charlie museum estimates 238 were killed; other estimates put the number at more than 1,000 people between 1961 and 1989. Much has been made of President Ronald Reagan yelling, "Mr. Gorbachev, tear down this wall!" in the mid-1980s. People seem to raise no contradictions that over 2,000 have died on the Arizona section of the U.S. border wall alone since 1990. The Binational Migration Institute reported the following: "Between FY 1990 and 2012, the PCOME [Pima County Office of the Medical Examiner] examined the remains of 2,238 migrants. Over a third of these decedents, or 761 cases, remained unidentified at the publication of this report, and thus their status as unauthorized migrants is predicted rather than certain" (Binational Migration Institute).

When a group of California State University Northridge Chicana/o students visited the wall at Nogales in 2012, a student commented at the wall between the two Nogales: "It was an odd feeling being so close to something that has sparked so many debates," said Daniel Mulato, 22, a senior double majoring in psychology and Chicana/o studies, about the Nogales border. "It really hit me when I saw a baby shoe left right at the border. This could be someone's little sister's shoe" (Acuña, 2012).

In the context of the Berlin and American Walls, why do many critics say that the United States is being hypocritical? What drives the drug market?

Currently, the toxic anti-immigrant rhetoric has polarized the overwhelming majority of U.S. Latinas/os and most compassionate Americans, reminding them of Dwight Eisenhower's Operation Wetback (1953–1955), which set a template for dealing with *those* dangerous people. His Attorney General, Herbert Brownell, deployed hate propaganda as a strategy. His message was that America's frontier with Mexico was out of control. We were being overrun by dangerous people. Brownell allegedly hinted to newspaper publishers that the best way to seal the border was to shoot down a couple of "wetbacks," supposedly to scare the others away. Through a campaign of fear and gross violation of human rights in the guise of "Operation Wetback," the U.S. Border Patrol supposedly halted "illegal immigration" across the entire 2,000-mile U.S.–Mexico frontier. In the 2016 Republican primaries, the candidates appeared to want to "trump" Brownell. Donald Trump has called immigrants "criminals" and "rapists." He has called them "killers," blaming them for violent crimes (Moreno, 2016).

How has the Republican hysteria made a solution more difficult?

Those advocating "The Wall" don't know history. Herbert Eugene Bolton (1870–1953) was one of the first American historians to stress the importance of a hemispheric rather than a national concept of the Americas. Bolton was the acknowledged leader of borderlands studies. In 1932, as president of the American Historical Association, Bolton said:

> There is need of a broader treatment of American history, to supplement the purely nationalistic presentation to which we are accustomed. European history cannot be learned from books dealing alone with England, or France, or Germany, or Italy, or Russia; nor can American history be adequately presented if confined to Brazil, or Chile, or Mexico, or Canada, or the United States. In my own country the study of thirteen English colonies and the United States in isolation has obscured many of the larger factors in their development, and helped to raise up a nation of chauvinists. Similar distortion has resulted from the teaching and writing of national history in other American countries. (Bolton, 1933)

Open the borders! Keeping people out of the United States at a time when the so-called free market is going global is ridiculous. Further, Americans cannot condone the violence that is taking place at the U.S.–Mexica border, much of it caused by the U.S. Border Patrol. Anti-immigrant sentiment has created a large-scale industry of unscrupulous coyotes, smugglers of undocumented immigrants into the United States who transport human cargo over often as many as five borders. Some Arizona ranchers are playing vigilante on the border while the government stands by and does nothing.

Even *Business Week*, a conservative magazine, points out that the graying of many European nations will reach the critical stage by the year 2050 when, for example, the median age in Spain will reach 55. *Business Week* posits that European nations will at that point be forced to import workers because of the old age of their populations. The current economic recession in Japan is partly attributed to the aging of the nation and the lack of expansion in its production. In contrast, the United States has grown because it takes in a million immigrants annually. The article says immigration "is one key reason economic growth has averaged 3.7 percent a year for the past decade" (Baker, 2002, pp. 138–140).

Consequently, many nations are reconsidering their immigration policies. The Pew Global Center reported the following:

> Although the population in the U.S. is getting older and growing more slowly than in the past, the demographic future for the U.S. is robust in comparison with other countries. In particular, the U.S. population is

> projected to grow faster and age slower than the populations of its major economic partners in Europe and Asia. These demographic trends may enhance future opportunities for the U.S. in the global economy. (Pew Research Center, 2015)

The reason why the U.S. economy will remain robust is in large part because of immigration. "Immigrants have added to the U.S. population generally and to the population of women in their childbearing ages. They also have brought relatively higher fertility rates with them" (Pew, 2014). Latina/o immigrants and Mexicans in particular are young. European nations are graying.

The fact is that immigration creates new jobs and makes expansion possible. Almost the entire country suffered a severe recession in the 1980s due to deindustrialization. Los Angeles was the exception. Undocumented workers subsidized the garment and electronics industries, creating jobs for better-paid workers. Immigrants buy goods as well as sell goods, so the number of jobs expands as the number of workers expands. When immigrants send their children to school, immigrants create jobs and keep schools open in areas where there are not enough white children to fill them.

Immigrants contribute to the system by paying local, state, and federal income taxes and indirect taxes such as sales taxes. Most data also show that most immigrants work; they are not on welfare. When immigrants and their families use emergency medical facilities, it is not because they are not working, but because they don't have medical insurance because their employers refuse to pay for the cost of social production, as in other industrialized countries, where employers do pay for medical insurance. Indeed, undocumented workers pay taxes and often get nothing in return. An example is Social Security to which they make contributions and rarely collect entitlements.

As mentioned, the undocumented worker is also younger than the general population and is paying for the retirement of the aging baby boomers. By the year 2030, people 65 and over will increase from 34 million to 69 million. Latinos will make up a disproportionate share of active workers. These baby boomers will live longer than any other generation and thus will collect more, paid for largely by minorities. Today the elderly population, not the undocumented, is straining Medicare. The fact is that the United States and Europe lack population, and they have to attract immigration to remain economically strong and prosperous. Americans are not having babies in great enough numbers for population growth, so it makes sense to integrate these immigrants and educate them for the future of the country.

Hate always draws a crowd. People believe the worst, and politicians exaggerate the truth to get votes. More importantly, hate makes money, and there are racist organizations, too. The Federation for American Immigration Reform (FAIR) received $1.1 million from the Pioneer Fund between 1982 and 1992. The latter foundation funds literature that attempts to prove the genetic inferiority of nonwhite people. FAIR has an annual budget of around $5 million and has some 40 other foundations contributing money to the anti-immigrant cause. It also receives money from individual donors who want to preserve their vision of America.

Only the most disingenuous person would deny that people want to close the border because they want to keep dark-skinned people out. Until September 11, 2001, the border patrol all but ignored the Canadian border. The nativist did not worry about white Canadians coming over the border.

It is hypocritical to discuss border control when it is the United States that has historically magnetized the border. The incessant pull for agricultural, mining, and railroad jobs created a demand. In recent times, the border was magnetized by the U.S. Border Patrol, which ignored the flow of labor during peak times. The bracero program magnetized the border and the United States insisted on doing the recruitment of braceros to the border thus magnetizing it. Moreover, the maquiladoras magnetized the border. Regarding the U.S. War on Drugs, the United States, unwilling to control the flow of drugs and interfere with gun dealers and banks, channeled the traffic of drugs through Middle America. The War on Drugs has destroyed the economies of Central American nations and created the cartels. Latin Americans are not the major consumers of drugs, Americans are.

Finally, the North American Free Trade Agreement has uprooted millions of rural workers who have no choice but to go north. The day that NAFTA went into effect on January 1, 1994, the Zapatistas rose up in rebellion in Chiapas. David Bacon tells how "U.S. policies fueled Mexico's great migration." Bacon tells the story of Roberto Ortega, a displaced Veracruzana butcher. NAFTA opened up Mexican markets to massive pork imports from U.S. companies like Smithfield Foods. Ortega, a small-scale butcher, was wiped out as prices dropped. In 1999 he was forced to migrate to Tar Heel, North Carolina, where, ironically, he worked for Smithfield in the world's largest pork slaughterhouse. "Tens of thousands left Mexico, many eventually helping Smithfield's bottom line once again by working for low wages on its U.S. meatpacking lines" (Bacon, 2012). Under NAFTA, Smithfield had access to subsidized U.S. corn, an advantage that drove many Mexicans out of business, as U.S. corn "was priced 19 percent below the cost of production." NAFTA allowed Smithfield to import pork into Mexico. By 2010 pork imports grew more than 25 times, to 811,000 tons. Mexico lost 4,000 pig farms and 120,000 jobs. Rural poverty rose from 35 percent in 1992–1994 to 55 percent in 1996–1998. By 2010, 53 million Mexicans were living in poverty—half the country's population, almost all in rural areas. Some workers went to the United States on a contract—those who did not have contracts were forced to migrate to the border or starve.

ANOTHER POV (POINT OF VIEW)

Are We Ready for Open Borders?

Ernesto Vigil, Independent Scholar, Historian, and Author

I firmly believe the United States, like all nations, has the right to control its borders, but candidates in many recent election campaigns speak as though advocates for humane immigration policies believe otherwise. The public hears speeches about the need for the United States "to take control of its borders" because "liberal" immigration policies have created "sanctuary cities" where "illegal immigrants" have "anchor babies" to reap undeserved benefits from America's "open borders" policy. People need to understand, and challenge, the terms and context of these debates, and to the extent an "immigration problem" exists, it must be discussed honestly and intelligently in appropriate terms.

The public has been told, with increasing frequency and volume since the 1960s, that the solution to "illegal immigration" would be the passage of new and stricter laws to punish undocumented migrants and their employers by making their employment illegal and requiring employers to check their workers' immigration status. The first law to do so, the 1986 Immigration Reform and Control Act (IRCA), was supposed to "solve" the immigration "problem" with new rules and punishments. And like nearly every immigration law since then, IRCA militarized the border, increased the funding and personnel for immigration authorities, and fueled the incarceration of undocumented people.

Young single males were the typical undocumented workers of that era and typically worked a few short years before returning to Mexico or other homelands. Since the passage of IRCA, it was now more expensive and dangerous to enter the United States illegally, so married workers now brought their families and stayed for longer durations. Instead of stopping undocumented immigration, these new laws increased the numbers of people who had never before migrated in large numbers: women and children. Worse, militarizing the border where most immigrants entered the country, Juárez/El Paso and Tijuana/San Diego, immigrants were forced to enter through isolated rural areas of Texas and Arizona's blazing desert where untold thousands have since died. Ignoring the futility and inhumanity of their policies, anti-immigrant forces currently merely demand more of the same. What few will openly admit is that racism is a major motivation driving immigration policy; racist Americans fear the browning of America.

It has been known since the 1960s, for example, that the Spanish-surnamed population in the southwestern states of America would become a regional majority and, in fact, was already a majority in some regions of Colorado, New Mexico, and Texas since the 1950s or earlier. However, the region was comprised of people of Mexican descent who were neither "foreigners" nor "immigrants," but descendants of Mexicans who lived here before the United States crossed the Mississippi River. History provides a context in which immigration can be understood, including the recent history of both countries, and the details are sometimes little known and ominous.

For example, when ex-CIA Director William Colby was interviewed in July 1978, he was asked about the "greatest threat to America today," with the interviewer thinking Colby would point to China, the USSR, or a similar rival. Instead, Colby said "the most obvious threat is . . . that there are 60 million Mexicans today [and there will be] 120 million [at] the end of the century [and] there are 7 to 8 million . . . in the United States today." Interestingly, he made no distinction between Mexicans who were born here and those who weren't, and then he said Mexico's growing population would result in an additional "20 million of them . . . living in this country." He added, "We can reinforce the Border Patrol and they don't have enough bullets to stop them." Although entering the United States without papers has never openly been a crime punishable by death, nor should it be, his suggestion that it might be an option was balanced with kinder words. He added that "we can . . . help [Mexicans] develop their own country" so they could find employment at home (Gonzales, 1978). American history, however, doesn't show it helps nations develop their economies. To do so would help these nations compete with American enterprise, so U.S. policy and practice keeps such nations at a perpetual disadvantage. In fact, the North American Free Trade Act (NAFTA) is a prime example directly related to the so-called immigration problem and promised to solve it.

NAFTA, the brainchild of U.S. economic elites and their political representatives, promised its 1994 enactment would bring greater economic growth and prosperity to the United States, Canada, and Mexico, with Mexico joining the ranks of First World countries like America. The promises sounded as if NAFTA truly intended to raise Mexico to a position of economic equality. Soon after NAFTA's passage, however, the growth of Mexico's economy slowed, wages declined, and the sale of cheap corn produced by U.S. corporate agriculture undermined Mexico's historic agricultural economy. Millions of small farmers, especially Mexican Indians from southern Mexico, went broke, lost their lands, and began migrating to the United States without papers. Instead of creating Mexican prosperity, which its critics said would never happen, NAFTA clearly further impoverished Mexico and created more "illegal immigration," the "problem" it promised to cure.

What should now be obvious is that immigration can be discussed and described without using emotional and bigoted terminology about "anchor babies," "open borders," and nonexistent "sanctuary cities." The longer that inappropriate, ignorant, and silly terminology is used in hysterical debates about immigration, the longer it will take to solve the actual problems involved. In fact, some of the immigration debates sound like schoolyard squabbles between 10-year-old boys arguing whether Superman could beat the Incredible Hulk in a fistfight. Since neither character exists, the arguments are inane, irrelevant, and pointless. However, arguments over Superman and the Incredible Hulk, while not intellectually superior to immigration debates, are far more benign and moral. No one is dying in the Arizona desert over Superman or the Incredible Hulk.

The same cannot be said for American immigration policy and practice.

¡LA CLASE OBRERA NO TIENE FRONTERA!

Eliot Lee Grossman, Attorney-at-Law. Academic Member, Permanent Seminar on Chicano and Border Studies, Department of Ethnology and Social Anthropology, National Institute of Anthropology and History (DEAS-INAH), Mexico City

Any debate or discussion of whether the border between the United States and Mexico should be open must begin with an understanding of its history. The border was put into place in 1848 as the result of a war of imperialist aggression against Mexico by the United States, which stole half of its territory to form the states of California, New Mexico, Arizona, Nevada, Utah, and parts of Oklahoma, Wyoming, and Colorado. Abraham Lincoln voted against the war as a first-term congressman and denounced it for being immoral, pro-slavery, and a threat to the nation's republican values. The border was artificially demarcated in the Treaty of Guadalupe-Hidalgo by combining the course of the Rio Grande River in the West with straight lines arbitrarily drawn in the East between El Paso, the Gila River, the junction of the Colorado and Gila Rivers, and San Diego Bay.

Viewed from an historical perspective on the illegal manner in which the border was imposed, it could be argued that it is the Anglos—and not the Mexicanos—who deserve the label of "illegal aliens," and it is hypocritical of them to insist that what is an illegal border in the first place be closed to the people whose land was unlawfully taken to create it.

Although the border was put into place by a war of aggression, it was not enforced or patrolled for over 50 years. The U.S. Border Patrol was not created until 1924, after the Mexican Revolution and World War I caused concern about controlling the passage of persons and goods between the two countries.

The virulent anti-immigrant discourse motivating shouts of "Build the Wall!" by Donald Trump's minions blames undocumented Mexicans for social and economic problems that are the result of processes of globalization and international economic restructuring, which themselves are causative of the undocumented immigration being decried. There is a world labor market created by globalization which requires a transnational working class to serve its needs. Immigration from "less developed" to "more developed" countries (and xenophobic reactions to it by reactionary sectors of the local populace) does not occur only from Mexico to the United States, but also to Europe from its former colonies in Africa, the Middle East, and Southeast Asia.

It should be understood, however, that the real purpose of the anti-immigrant repressive measures presently in place (and the more severe ones being urged) is not really to halt so-called illegal immigration, but rather to create and reproduce a permanent underclass of "outlaws" (in the sense of those who are "outside" the protections of the law) who are particularly vulnerable to superexploitation. Imposing the label of "illegal aliens" on these workers serves the interest of those who profit from their inferior status. This is contrary to the interests of the working class as a whole, which should unite to defend the rights of the undocumented. *"¡La clase obrera no tiene frontera!"*

NOTES

1. Excerpt of Mexica Manifesto, http://www.mexica-movement.org
2. The FBI admitted misconduct during its probe of CISPES. CISPES sued in 1988.

BIBLIOGRAPHY

Acuña, Rodolfo F. *Occupied America: A History of Chicanos*, 8th ed. New York: Pearson, 2015.

Acuña, Rodolfo F. "The Tucson-Nogales Trip: Learning experience of CSUN MEChA and students from the Asian American Studies Department spans three trips to ground zero." *LatinoLA*, March 6, 2012. http://latinola.com/story.php?story=10455

Acuña, Rodolfo F. "The Illusive Race Question & Class: A Bacteria That Constantly Mutates." Occasional Paper No.59, Julian Samora Research Institute, November 2005. http://www.jsri.msu.edu/upload/occasional-papers/oc59.pdf

Acuña, Rodolfo F. "Murder in Arizona It's Only The Third World." ForChicanaChicano Studies, June 18, 2000. https://forchicanachicanostudies.wikispaces.com/Acu%C3%B1a,+%E2%80%9CMurder+in+Arizona

Acuña, Rodolfo F. *Anything but Mexican: Chicanos in Contemporary Los Angeles*. London: Verso, 1996.

"African Americans In the Revolutionary Period." American Revolution, National Park Service, U.S. Department of the Interior. http://www.nps.gov/revwar/about_the_revolution/african_americans.html

Aguirre, B., Rogelio Sáenz, and Brian Sinclair James. "Marielitos Ten Years Later: The Scarface Legacy." *Social Science Quarterly* 78, no. 2 (1997): 487-507.

"Attitudes about Aging: A Global Perspective: Chapter 2. Aging in the U.S. and Other Countries, 2010 to 2050." Pew Research Center, January 30, 2014. http://www.pewglobal.org/2014/01/30/chapter-2-aging-in-the-u-s-and-other-countries-2010-to-2050

Bacon, David. "How US Policies Fueled Mexico's Great Migration." *The Nation*, January 23, 2012. http://www.thenation.com/article/how-us-policies-fueled-mexicos-great-migration

Baker, Stephen. "The Coming Battle for Immigrants." *Business Week*, August 26, 2002, 138–140.

Balderama, Francisco E., and Raymond Rodríguez. *Decade of Betrayal: Mexican Repatriation in the 1930s*. Albuquerque, NM: University of New Mexico Press, 1995.

Bennet, James. "Politics: Patrick J. Buchanan: Candidate's Speech Is Called Code for Controversy." *New York Times*, February 25, 1996. http://www.nytimes.com/1996/02/25/us/politics-patrick-j-buchanan-candidate-s-speech-is-called-code-for-controversy.html?pagewanted=all

The Binational Migration Institute. "A Continued Humanitarian Crisis at the Border: Undocumented Border Crosser Deaths Recorded by the Pima County Office of the Medical Examiner, 1990–2012." The University of Arizona, June 2013. http://bmi.arizona.edu/sites/default/files/border_deaths_final_web.pdf

Bloom, Julie."Salsa Spins Beyond Its Roots." *New York Times*, July 29, 2007. http://www.nytimes.com/2007/07/29/arts/dance/29bloo.html?_r=0

Bolton, Herbert E. "The Epic of Greater America." *American Historical Review* 38, no. 3 (April, 1933): 448–474. https://historians.org/about-aha-and-membership/aha-history-and-archives/presidential-addresses/herbert-e-bolton

Breslow, Jason M. "The Staggering Death Toll of Mexico's Drug War." PBS's *Frontline*, July 27, 2015. http://www.pbs.org/wgbh/frontline/article/the-staggering-death-toll-of-mexicos-drug-war/

Brown, Anna, and Eileen Patten. "Hispanics of Colombian Origin in the United States, 2011." Pew Research Center, June 19, 2013. http://www.pewhispanic.org/2013/06/19/hispanics-of-colombian-origin-in-the-united-states-2011

Butler, Paul, "A Mix of Colors: Country's Swirling Demographics Put New Twist on Meaning of 'Minority.'" *Dallas Daily News*, June 3, 2001.

Campbell, Matthew. "Hispanic Influx Threatens to Change Face of America." *The Times*, July 9, 2000. http://americanpatrol.com/RECONQUISTA/LondonTimesRecon000709.html

Campoy, Ana. "Power in Numbers: Mexico Has Started Counting Its Afro-Mexican Population." *Quartz*, December 10, 2015. http://qz.com/569964/mexico-has-started-counting-its-afro-mexican-population\

Central Intelligence Agency. *The World Factbook*. 2010. https://www.cia.gov/library/publications/the-world-factbook/geos/mx.html#People

Capehart, Jonathan. "Donald Trump's 'Mexican rapists' rhetoric will keep the Republican Party out of the White House." *Washington Post*, June 17, 2015. https://www.washingtonpost.com/blogs/post-partisan/wp/2015/06/17/trumps-mexican-rapists-will-keep-the-republican-party-out-of-the-white-house/

Chávez, Leo R. *Shadowed Lives: Undocumented Immigration in American Society*. San Diego: Harcourt Brace Jovanovich, 1992.

Collier, Melvin J. "African Americans and Mexicans Are Cousins." *Roots Revealed* (blog). June 9, 2013. http://rootsrevealed.blogspot.com/2013/06/african-americans-and-mexicans-are_9.html

Cuban Information Archives. "Background Paper on Cuban Immigration into Dade County." Metro-Dade County Planning Department, Research Division, January 6, 1985. http://cuban-exile.com/doc_051-075/doc0072.html

D'Amato, Paul. "The border crossed us." *Socialistworker.org*, April 28, 2006. http://socialistworker.org/2006-1/586/586_13_Border.shtml

Duara, Nigel, and Sarah Parvini. "Latino influence on Catholic Church is a backdrop to Pope Francis' visit." *Los Angeles Times*, September 22, 2015. http://www.latimes.com/nation/la-na-pope-visit-latinos-20150922-story.html

Etzioni, Amitai. "Inventing Hispanics: A Diverse Minority Resists Being Labeled." *Brookings Institution* 10, no. 1 (Winter 2002).

Glickman, Paul. "New US policy on Nicaraguan refugees assailed as 'subterfuge.'" *Christian Science Monitor*, July 10, 1987. http://www.csmonitor.com/1987/0710/aref.html

Gonzales, Laurence. "Interview: William Colby." *Playboy Magazine*, July 1978.

Grieco, Elizabeth M., and Rachel C. Cassidy. "Overview of Race and Hispanic Origin: Census 2000 Brief." March 2001. https://www.census.gov/prod/2001pubs/c2kbr01-1.pdf

Haney-López, Ian F. *Racism on Trial: The Chicano Fight for Justice*. Cambridge, MA: Belknap Press, 2003.

Haney-López, Ian F. "Race, Ethnicity, Erasure: The Salience of Race to LatCrit Theory." *California Law Review* 85, no. 5 (1997): 1143–1211.

Haney-López, Ian F. *White By Law: The Legal Construction of Race*. New York: NYU Press, 1996.

Hernández, Kelly Lytle. 2006. "The Crimes and Consequences of Illegal Immigration: A Cross-Border Examination of Operation Wetback, 1943 to 1954." *Western Historical Quarterly* 37, no. 4 (2006): 421–444.

Howard, Adam. "Pro-Immigrant Marches Surging Nationwide." *The Nation*, April 10, 2006. http://www.thenation.com/blog/pro-immigrant-marches-surging-nationwide

Humes, Karen R., Nicholas A. Jones, and Roberto R. Ramirez. "Overview of Race and Hispanic Origin: 2010 Census Briefs." March 2011, p. 2. http://www.census.gov/prod/cen2010/briefs/c2010br-02.pdf

Janofsky, Michael."Unlikely Ally Ends Her Ties To Buchanan." *New York Times*, June 20, 2000. http://www.nytimes.com/2000/06/20/us/unlikely-ally-ends-her-ties-to-buchanan.html

Klein, Dianne. "Curbs on Illegal Immigration Are 'Social Sin,' Mahony Says." *Los Angeles Times*, December 11, 1993.

Langwiesche, William. "The Border." *Atlantic Monthly*, May 1992, 69.

López, Luisa, and Blanca Vázquez. "'I Was More of a Citizen': A Puerto Rican Garment Worker Describes Discrimination in the 1920s." History Matters: The U.S. Survey Course on the Web. Source: "Nostras Trabajamos en La Costura." Center for Puerto Rican Studies, Hunter College, CUNY. http://historymatters.gmu.edu/d/121

Ludden, Jennifer. "Hundreds of Thousands March for Immigrant Rights." *Morning Edition*, NPR, April 10, 2006. http://www.npr.org/templates/story/story.php?storyId=5333768

McCaa, Robert. "The Peopling of Mexico from Origins to Revolution." In *The Population History of North America*, edited by Richard Steckel and Michael Haines. Cambridge: Cambridge University Press, 1997.

Mexica Manifesto, accessed 2015, http://www.mexica-movement.org

Moreno, Carolina. "9 Outrageous Things Donald Trump Has Said About Latinos." *Huffingtom Post*, July 20, 2016. http://www.huffingtonpost.com/entry/9-outrageous-things-donald-trump-has-said-about-latinos_us_55e483a1e4b0c818f618904b

Ngai, Mae. "The Architecture of Race in American Immigration Law: A Reexamination of the Immigration Act of 1924." *Journal of American History* 86, no. 1 (1999): 67–92.

Ngai, Mae. Hart–Celler Turns 50. *The Nation* 301, no. 18 (2015): 4.

Neal, Jo West. "The Policy of the United States toward Immigration from Mexico." Master's thesis, University of Texas at Austin, 1941.

"Nicaraguan Adjustment and Central American Relief Act (NACARA) 203: Eligibility to Apply with USCIS." U.S. Citizenship and Immigration Services. https://www.uscis.gov/humanitarian/refugees-asylum/asylum/nicaraguan-adjustment-and-central-american-relief-act-nacara-203-eligibility-apply-uscis. Accessed, June 30, 2015.

Nicodemus, Charles. "FBI Agents Get Training about Rights; Decree Ends 'Spying' Case Here." *Chicago Sun-Times*, December 15, 1997.

Padilla, Félix. "Salsa: Puerto Rican and Latino Music." *Journal of Popular Culture* 24, no. 1 (1990): 87–104.

Paterson, Tony. "Revealed: Tragic victims of the Berlin Wall." *Independent*, August 11, 2005. http://www.independent.co.uk/news/world/europe/revealed-tragic-victims-of-the-berlin-wall-411504.html

Pew Research Center. "Multiracial in America: Chapter 7. The Many Dimensions of Hispanic Racial Identity." June 11, 2015. http://www.pewsocialtrends.org/2015/06/11/chapter-7-the-many-dimensions-of-hispanic-racial-identity.

Pew Research Center. "Aging in the U.S. and Other Countries, 2010 to 2050: Chapter 2." January 30, 2014. http://www.pewglobal.org/2014/01/30/chapter-2-aging-in-the-u-s-and-other-countries-2010-to-2050/

"Pro-Immigrant Marches Surging Nationwide." *The Nation* (April 10, 2006). http://www.thenation.com/blog/pro-immigrant-marches-surging-nationwide

Pyle, Amy, and Beth Shuster. "10,000 Students Protest Prop. 187: Immigration: Walkouts around Los Angeles are largest yet showing campus opposition to initiative. The teen-agers are mostly peaceful, with only 12 arrests reported." *Los Angeles Times*, November 3, 1994. http://articles.latimes.com/1994-11-03/news/mn-58295_1_los-angeles

Ramos, George. "From the Archives: Bert Corona; Labor Activist Backed Rights for Undocumented Workers." *Los Angeles Times*, January 21, 2001. Background at http://www.latimes.com/local/obituaries/archives/la-me-bert-corona-20010117-story.html

Rodríguez, Clara E. *Changing Race: Latinos, the Census and the History of Ethnicity in the United States*. New York: NYU Press, 2000.

Santa Anna, Otto. *Brown Tide Rising: Metaphors of Latinos in Contemporary American Discourse*. Austin: University of Texas Press, 2002.

Skerry, Peter. *Counting on the Census? Race, Group Identity, and the Evasion of Politics*. Washington, DC: Brookings Institute Press, 2000.

Smith. James Morton. "The Enforcement of the Alien Friends Act of 1798." *The Mississippi Valley Historical Review* 41, no. 1 (1954): 85–104.

Stefancic, Jean, and Richard Delgado. *No Mercy: How Conservative Think Tanks and Foundations Changed America's Social Agenda*. Philadelphia: Temple University Press, 1996.

Sued-Badillo, Jalil. "Christopher Columbus and the Enslavement of the Amerindians in the Caribbean; Columbus and the New World Order 1492–1992." *Monthly Review* 44, no. 3 (July 1992): 77ff.

Sundaram, Anjalo, and George Gelber, eds., *A Decade of War: El Salvador Confronts the Future*. New York: Monthly Review Press, 1991.

Tutino, John. "From Involution to Revolution in Mexico: Liberal Development, Patriarchy, and Social Violence in the Central Highlands, 1870–1915." *History Compass* 6, no. 3 (2008): 796–842.

Vincent, Theodore G. *The Legacy of Vicente Guerrero, Mexico's First Black Indian President*. Gainesville: University Press of Florida, 2001.

Weems, Judge Sam. "This entire Armenian genocide claim is as bogus as a three-dollar bill and (they) know it!" *The Other Side of the Falsified Genocide*. http://www.tallarmeniantale.com/census.htm

Wolf, Eric. *Sons of the Shaking Earth: The People of Mexico and Guatemala—Their Land, History, and Culture*. Chicago: Phoenix Books, 1959.

Woodward, Ralph Lee, Jr. *Central America: A Nation Divided*, 2nd ed. New York: Oxford University Press, 1985.

Yardley, Jim. "Pope Francis Suggests Donald Trump Is 'Not Christian.'" *New York Times*, February 18, 2016.

SELECTED VIDEOS

Audiopedia. "Mestizo," YouTube video, 37:43, posted July 24, 2014. https://www.youtube.com/watch?v=Ry7yGbpET1I

"The Black Migration to the North 1910–1920," YouTube video, 7:51, posted by yaraz3, December 14, 2010. https://www.youtube.com/watch?v=sUKTT7Yd4eA

Burton, Ryan. "The Color of America: Debating Racial Classification in the U.S. Census," YouTube video, 9:59, posted by mdhumanites, August 4, 2011. https://www.youtube.com/watch?v=jaw-xgpmNug

Caballero, María. "El machismo invisible y los micromachismos," YouTube video, 12:48, posted May 31, 2015. https://www.youtube.com/watch?v=-oLWb0021P8

Delicezeytin, "Maquiladora women—spots from the film MAQUILAPOLIS," YouTube video, 4:03, posted January 20, 2010. https://www.youtube.com/watch?v=yK2KzIGb44I

"Ellis Island—History of Immigration to the United States (1890–1920), Award Winning Documentary,"YouTube video, 28:26, posted by The Best Film Archives, June 20, 2013. https://www.youtube.com/watch?v=8X4CypTaOQs

The Film Archives. "Chiapas and NAFTA Documentary," YouTube video, 16:40, posted August 9, 2012. https://www.youtube.com/watch?v=QfSH4kZ_y0g

Films, David. "Illegal cross border hopping from Canada to the United States," YouTube video, 5:59, posted November 4, 2011. https://www.youtube.com/watch?v=xKp9F3VdQAU

"'Forbidden Puerto Rico': America with Jorge Ramos (Part 1 of 3)," YouTube video, 11:26, posted by InYourFaceTv, September 17, 2014. https://www.youtube.com/watch?v=G1UrSXgrqDg

Freeston, Jesse. "Free trade and Mexico's drug war," YouTube video, 9:55, posted by TheRealNews, May 2, 2009. https://www.youtube.com/watch?v=1ctoiMYe5RM

Hughes, Keith. "History of Immigration in the US for Dummies," YouTube video, 10:01, posted August 4, 2010. https://www.youtube.com/watch?v=Iheb2HqZPiw

"The Immigration Act of 1924." YouTube video, 9:20, posted by adrianennett's channel, February 26, 2011. https://www.youtube.com/watch?v=iJUCPq7wJH4

"Immigration Act of 1921," YouTube video, 2:48, posted by AndrewZ28, October 30, 2014. https://www.youtube.com/watch?v=CufN4zPukTk

"The Impact of the Immigration and Nationality Act of 1965," YouTube video, 10:00, posted by the Center for Sacramento History, March 28, 2013. https://www.youtube.com/watch?v=FwraZQb2Ofk

Meettheprimates's channel. "The history of racial classification," YouTube video, 4:43, posted September 25, 2011. https://www.youtube.com/watch?v=21saXbRo0XY

MrNapper1. The Americas as "New World" (3), YouTube video, 1:49, posted June 29, 2016. https://www.youtube.com/watch?v=C3_WoRgNZrs

"MS-13—Root Of All Evil," SALViiD0RiAN's channel, YouTube video, 44:50, posted February 26, 2012. https://www.youtube.com/watch?v=ky3BT4BewFI

"On Patrol with Arizona's Minutemen," YouTube video, 22:15, posted by Journeyman Pictures, November 7, 2007. https://www.youtube.com/watch?v=NkXjMvUy5ak

"Operation Wetback 1954," YouTube video, 4:41, posted by kks02011, December 10, 2012. https://www.youtube.com/watch?v=zJ3u2Cc6kyE

Orshan, Michael. "US Mexican Border—Migration History," YouTube video, 9:22, posted May 19, 2007. https://www.youtube.com/watch?v=sFC4WeqIUNo

Pasodelsur. "Indignity on the border," YouTube video, 8:19, posted December 24, 2008. https://www.youtube.com/watch?v=3Nz-253RaQo

"Pat Buchanan brings up operation Wet Back with open border liberal," YouTube video, 8:18, posted by Irish Austrian American, April 29, 2010. https://www.youtube.com/watch?v=1yyPYYz-_Rc

"Peter Brimelow, Immigration Road to Hell," YouTube video, 28:48, posted by WarriorClass III, July 23, 2013. https://www.youtube.com/watch?v=_XEUxhObLBs

TheRealNews. "War on drugs and Mexico's demise," YouTube video, 12:42, posted May 8, 2009. https://www.youtube.com/watch?v=Yj7LKauVzro

The RealNews. "Free trade and Mexico's drug war," YouTube video, 9:55, posted May 2, 2009. https://www.youtube.com/watch?v=1ctoiMYe5RM

Rexpuestas. "Hombres que evitan educar a sus hijos, por machismo," YouTube video, 12:11, posted February 2016. https://www.youtube.com/watch?v=vS6pY5y0kwI

Rodenburg, Paul. "The Wonderful World of NAFTA (Part 1/2)," YouTube video, 7:07, posted October 9, 2007. https://www.youtube.com/watch?v=ZnVL0d9fwkYbe.com/watch?v=ZnVL0d9fwkY

The Skeptic Feminist. "George Carlin—On Patriarchy," YouTube video, 15:03, posted July 31, 2015. https://www.youtube.com/watch?v=dP5Pv4HthIk

Sweet, Frank W. "A Brief History of Census 'Race.'" YouTube video, 15:38, posted April 9, 2011. https://www.youtube.com/watch?v=KlEmR5cLVsk

Teamster Power. "NAFTA: Ten Years of Broken Promises," YouTube video, 9:23, posted September 12, 2006. https://www.youtube.com/watch?v=MNLnBnTuxvU

TV - 365 Day. "1,000s of immigrants try to cross the border at once," YouTube video, 2:56, posted July 11, 2015. https://www.youtube.com/watch?v=waHPeTcIucM

"Up South: African-American Migration in the Era of the Great War," YouTube video, 3:39, posted by ASHP CML, March 23, 2011. https://www.youtube.com/watch?v=—8N42vDDTM

"US: California: Proposition 187 Affects Illegal Immigrants," YouTube video, 2:40, posted by AP Archive, July 21, 2015. https://www.youtube.com/watch?v=twVyV9jcyYs

U.S. Customs and Border Protection. "CBP Border Patrol Graduates 1000th Class," YouTube video, 4:50, posted May 21, 2012. https://www.youtube.com/watch?v=XDtdoTQcQeg

"U.S. to deport Central American migrants," YouTube video, 3:36, PressTV News Videos, posted December 25, 2015. https://www.youtube.com/watch?v=DnG3MqnhbRo

VOCESMedia, "VOCES: Bracero Stories," YouTube video, 2:27, posted August 5, 2009. https://www.youtube.com/watch?v=BGeB7kG6Q88

Thewalldoc. "Does the Border Fence work?" YouTube video, 2:36, posted March 22, 2011. https://www.youtube.com/watch?v=AfVENwfeGHw

Weese, Patricia. "Race and Gender Discrimination in the United States Work Place." YouTube video, 3:17, posted April 18, 2012. https://www.youtube.com/watch?v=WASXswcX9bA

"Why Puerto Ricans are U.S. Citizen," YouTube video, 1:00, posted by Video Embelecos, January 25, 2009. https://www.youtube.com/watch?v=gaKCtv8vSWk

"Why Puerto Rico will never become a state," YouTube video, 5:31, posted by Christian Rodríguez, June 14, 2011. https://www.youtube.com/watch?v=PFlY7hFUEQA

The Wise Guy Killer of Ignorance—Anthropology TV. "The Racial History of Latin America (Since 1492)," YouTube video, 8:06, posted August 20, 2014. https://www.youtube.com/watch?v=O6eK7y1yqRg

6

Affirmative Action

BACKGROUND

Affirmative action is about equality and the role of government in bringing equal protection to everyone. President Lyndon Johnson, a Southerner, in 1965 said, "You do not take a person who, for years, has been hobbled by chains and liberate him, bring him up to the starting line of a race and then say you are free to compete with all the others, and still just believe that you have been completely fair" (Affirmative Action). Society has tried to level the playing field (The Leadership Conference, 2016). It has come to accept handicap parking and handicap access to public places as part of citizens' public lives. Some businesspeople have spent money to bring this access about. Movie theaters and restaurants give senior citizens' discounts, and civil service gives veterans 10 points on civil service examinations because they served in the armed forces. Federal, state, and local governments require some public organizations to give religious holidays to religious groups.

Are these examples of preferential treatment? How do they differ from affirmative action? Is white privilege preferential treatment? Do the sons and daughters of the rich get preferential treatment?

Historically, education has been the main highway to the middle class for immigrants, minorities, and the poor. In recent years, because of the transformation of the U.S. economy with factories that once paid union-scale salaries moving to third-world countries, this route has changed. Today, the main options for workers are low-paying service sector and low-paying factory jobs. This change has clogged the education highway. This transformation of the economy has had social consequences as well; today, it is getting harder to get into prestigious universities where students have better opportunities to get admitted to graduate programs and professional schools. Without this access, social mobility is cut to a snail's pace, which prolongs social inequality.

Does everyone get an equal education? Does family income play a role in the quality of your education?

Affirmative action has been misconceived to be a creature of the 1960s. In reality, it has been part of the civil rights tradition of this country as far back as World War II when African Americans and Latinos complained about not getting equal access to government employment. President Franklin Roosevelt issued Executive Order 8802, which forbade discrimination against workers in defense industries. He established the Federal Employment Practices Commission, which monitored compliance. But even though blacks and Latinas/os fought in the war, the policy was avoided, and employers discriminated against people of color (Vertreace, 2010).

Why would the question of equality become more of an issue during war time?

After the war, minorities experienced even worse discrimination as industries gave white males preference in jobs. Because of a lack of education, many minorities were ineligible to take advantage of the GI Bill to help them go to college, and housing developers denied Latinas/os GI loans for homes in integrated areas. Meanwhile, consciousness of their rights increased among blacks and Latinos. Decisions such as *Mendes v. Westminster School District* (1946) and *Brown v. the Board of Education* (1954) ended de jure segregation, yet unequal access persisted.

In 1961, President John F. Kennedy issued Executive Order 10925 in which he instructed federal contractors to take "affirmative action to ensure that applicants are treated equally without regard to race, color, religion, sex, or national origin." Simultaneously he also created the Committee on Equal Employment Opportunity (Americans for a Fair Chance). In 1965, President Lyndon Johnson signed the historic Civil Rights Act, which prohibited employment discrimination by owners who employed more than 15 workers and established the Equal Employment Opportunity Commission (EEOC). The next year, President Johnson issued Executive Order 11246 requiring all government contractors and subcontractors to expand job opportunities for minorities. Johnson created the Office of Federal Contract Compliance in the Department of Labor to monitor compliance. In 1967, he amended Executive Order 11246 to include women and required a good faith effort to give minorities and women equal opportunities (Americans for a Fair Chance, 2003).

Why was it important to include women in President Johnson's Executive Order?

President Richard Nixon in 1969 issued the Philadelphia Order authorizing flexible goals and timetables to correct "underutilization" of minorities by federal contractors. The next year, Order No. 4 expanded the plan to include nonconstruction federal contractors; this order was also revised to include women. That same year, Nixon issued Executive Order 11625, which ordered comprehensive plans and specific programs for a national Minority Business Enterprise Constructing program, and, just before he left office in 1973, he issued a "Memorandum—Permissible Goals and Timetables in State and Local Government Employment Practices" (Kotlowski, 1998).[1] Nixon did this because he was a pragmatist. The nation was being torn apart by riots; he had to act "not to have the goddamn country blow up" (Colby, 2014). Thus, Nixon took affirmative action.

The federal authorities included institutions of higher learning because universities were among the largest beneficiaries of government contracts; lawmakers considered colleges and universities as the key to equality.

Richard Nixon was one of the nation's most conservative presidents. Why did he support affirmative action?

A large sector of American society opposed affirmative action programs. The John Birch Society (JBS), which had been founded in 1958, fiercely opposed the Civil Rights Movement (Tabachnick, 2014). The JBS was the forefather of the Tea Party and the ongoing "Ron Paul Revolution," which have rebranded themselves as "libertarian." The JBS continues to be a significant force behind the nullification of federal laws. The JBS, the Tea Party, and other right-wing movements are heavily funded by a cabal of billionaires who don't want to pay taxes or be regulated by the government.

In 1971, Lewis Powell issued a political manifesto that was a call to action (Powell Memo, 1971). Over the next few years, Corporate America created the Heritage Foundation (1973), the Manhattan Institute (1978), the Cato Institute (founded as the Charles Koch Foundation in 1974), Citizens for a Sound Economy (1984), Accuracy in Academe, and other powerful organizations. Corporations moved to control communication and lead the charge against reformers. By the 1980s, many of these foundations played to the fears of an aging white population and waged war on trade unions and immigrants.[2] They changed the trajectory of Kennedy, Johnson, and Nixon in his 1973 Manifest, The1977 book *Time for the Truth*, by William E. Simon, set the rationale for conservatives to begin philanthropic foundations to oppose social, economic, and political reform and showed them how to get tax write-offs and promote their right-wing politics (McCarthy and Faber, 2005, p. 90).

According to Webster's Dictionary, a philanthropist is "a wealthy person who gives money and time to help make life better for other people." Does William E. Simon fit that definition?

The level of opposition to affirmative action depended on the economic cycle. The 1960s were a time of economic prosperity and low unemployment, so saying no to affirmative action was difficult while a war was going on and when minorities were dying disproportionately in that war. Racial discontent and urban rebellions also played a role in convincing many Americans that something had to be done about discrimination and inequality. Affirmative action was a part of the proposed solution.

The mood of the country quickly changed after the 1973 recession, and the job market and upward mobility tightened for white males. Previous generations always had faith that their children would own their homes and have it better than their parents. However, corporations were in the process of eliminating industrial jobs that had once been the stepping-stone of European ethnics into the middle class. Other changes occurred, such as a restructuring of the middle-class American family. During the 1950s, most households were supported by a single wage earner. By the 1970s, women no longer had the option of staying home; they had to work to maintain a middle-class lifestyle. In the crunch, fewer Americans could afford to own a home on a husband's salary alone. Thus, anti-affirmative action rhetoric became more heated and specific.

Hypocritically, Roger Cregg, the head of the Center for Equal Opportunity, a conservative think tank, said his Center was devoted to "colorblind public policy." Cregg added that affirmative action in higher education put the country on the path to grievous error because it promoted policy that "passes over better qualified students, and sets a disturbing legal, political, and moral precedent in allowing racial discrimination." According to Cregg "[affirmative action] stigmatizes the so-called beneficiaries," promoting separatism and diluting academic excellence (Chace, 2011).

How and why did the support for affirmative action change during and after the 1970s?

Simultaneously, institutions of higher learning, spurred by affirmative action, began actively to recruit minority students, notably avoiding balancing their faculties. At California State University, Northridge, the percentage of Mexican American professors was 3 percent in 1970 and is today 3 percent. Faculty members hire their own color. They are snow-blind (Acuña, 2005, 2012). The competition is even keener in graduate and professional schools and the more prestigious private and public institutions. This activity was threatening too many white families and it encouraged a backlash to the 1960s. Even Nixon, who saw the need for affirmative action, began to backtrack on enforcement, laying the groundwork for the policy's demise by his federal court nominees, who had a conservative view of affirmative action. The federal judges and the justices appointed by Gerald Ford, Ronald Reagan, and George H. W. Bush deconstructed the 1960s and the policy of educational equality through affirmative action.

Conservatives based their opposition to affirmative action on the fallacy of preferential treatment of minorities entering college. Unexpectedly, they were joined by Jewish American organizations, which had historically been at the vanguard of social change. They claimed they opposed affirmative action programs because they set quotas. In the past, quotas were used to limit the number of Jews admitted into prestigious universities and graduate and professional schools. These Jewish organizations said they did not oppose the admission of minorities but opposed quotas for achieving equality. In other cases, angry white men believed they were being discriminated against, calling affirmative action reverse discrimination.

Words have meaning. How does the use of the term "preferential treatment" change the image of "affirmative action"? Would a handicap parking permit be preferential or affirmative treatment?

Within less than a decade, the white backlash gained momentum to challenge special programs for integrating medical and other professions schools. Whites said there was a tension existing between equality and equity, and they argued that the special admission of Latinos and African Americans lowered the quality of education and subverted the American ideal of individualism. They argued that if individuals worked hard enough, they could achieve anything they wanted. After all, they said, this was America, and if Latinos and blacks were not doing as well, it was because they were not working hard enough. Why should deserving and better-prepared white students suffer because of past injustices?

By the second half of the 1970s, the courts increasingly sided with those challenging the constitutionality of special admissions programs. Nixon appointed Associate Justices Harry Blackmun, Lewis F. Powell, and William Rehnquist to the Supreme Court. As governor of California, Ronald Reagan (1967–1975) also stacked the appellate and Supreme Courts of the State with conservative judges. It is not surprising that the courts held that although these programs were serving compelling state interests, they denied due process to white males. The debate came to a head in 1976 when the California Supreme Court held that the University of California at Davis' special admissions program was unlawful and enjoined the university from considering the race of any applicant. The court ordered Allan Bakke's admission.

Bakke, 36, a white male, applied to the Davis Medical School in 1973 and 1974 and was denied admission in both instances. The medical school considered him under the general admission's program, and Bakke received an interview. Despite a strong benchmark score of 468 out of 500, the medical school rejected Bakke. His application had come late in the year, and no applicants with scores below 470 in the general admissions process were accepted. At the time, four special admissions slots were left unfilled for which Bakke was not considered. His faculty interviewer found Bakke "rather limited in his approach" to the problems of the medical profession and found disturbing Bakke's "very definite opinions which he based more on his personal viewpoints than upon a study of the total problem" (Liu, 2002).

How did Bakke set back civil rights?

The second time around, UC Davis again rejected Bakke's application. In both years, applicants were admitted under the special program with grade point averages, MCAT scores, and benchmark scores lower than Bakke's. After the second rejection, Bakke sued in the Superior Court of California, seeking mandatory, injunctive, and declaratory relief compelling his admission to the medical school, claiming UC Davis excluded him because of his race, violating his rights under the Equal Protection Clause of the Fourteenth Amendment, the California Constitution, and Title VI of the Civil Rights Act of 1964. The California Supreme Court agreed with the trial court (*Regents of the University of California v. Bakke*, 1977; Cooper, 2003). (Also pertinent at the time was that medical schools regularly rejected applicants in their thirties as being too old.)

Two years later, the U.S. Supreme Court in part affirmed the California Supreme Court. The high court held that Davis could use race as a variable but not as the sole criterion for admission. The justices used the now dictum that the courts had to work toward a color-blind society. Justice Thurgood Marshall, the only African American Supreme Court Justice, wrote a stinging rebuttal:

> I do not agree that petitioner's admissions program violates the Constitution. For it must be remembered that, during most of the past 200 years, the Constitution as interpreted by this Court did not prohibit the most ingenious and pervasive forms of discrimination against the Negro. Now, when a State acts to remedy the effects of that legacy of discrimination, I cannot believe that this same Constitution stands as a barrier. (Caplan, 2015)

Justice Marshall then historically dissected the history of discrimination against blacks:

> We consider the underlying fallacy of the plaintiff's argument to consist in the assumption that the enforced separation of the two races stamps the colored race with a badge of inferiority. If this be so, it is not by reason of anything found in the act, but solely because the colored race chooses to put that construction upon it. The relationship between those figures and the history of unequal treatment afforded to the Negro cannot be denied. At every point from birth to death the impact of the past is reflected in the still disfavored position of the Negro. . . . In light of the sorry history of discrimination and its devastating impact on the lives of Negroes, bringing the Negro into the mainstream of American life should be a state interest of the highest order. To fail to do so is to ensure that America will forever remain a divided society. (Cashin, 1978)

Justice Marshall continued his scathing attack on the majority opinion:

> I do not believe that the Fourteenth Amendment requires us to accept that fate. Neither its history nor our past cases lend any support to the conclusion that a university may not remedy the cumulative effects of society's discrimination by giving consideration to race in an effort to increase the number and percentage of Negro doctors . . . . While I applaud the judgment of the Court that a university may consider race in its admissions process, it is more than a little ironic that, after several hundred years of class-based discrimination against Negroes, the Court is unwilling to hold that a class-based remedy for that discrimination is permissible. In declining to so hold, today's judgment ignores the fact that for several hundred years Negroes have been discriminated against, not as individuals, but rather solely because of the color of their skins. It is unnecessary in 20th-century America to have individual Negroes demonstrate that they have been victims of racial discrimination; the racism of our society has been so pervasive that none, regardless of wealth or position, has managed to escape its impact . . . . The dream of America as the great melting pot has not been realized for the Negro; because of his skin color he never even made it into the pot. (Cashin, 1978)[3]

Why did the words of Thurgood Marshall matter?

Critics accused the court of judicial activism, which is when justices make laws not specifically based either on the Constitution, on laws passed by Congress, or on case precedent. The dissent saw the color-blind argument as pretextual. Justice Harry Blackmun wrote, "In order to get beyond racism, we must first take account of race. There is no other way. And in order to treat some persons equally, we must treat them differently." The dissent pointed out that although Congress passed the fourteenth Amendment to remedy the Constitution's legalization of racism, it was used historically to limit the integration of blacks and others. Instead of working toward a color-blind society, it helped create racial inequality, favoring the interests of whites (Acuña, 1998). The dissent accused the court of replacing a commitment to equality with a policy of denial and evasion and of manipulating the truth through the use of metaphors that distorted the reality of racism and inequality.

Is the term "color-blind" pretextual? Does it lead to what some people call a snow-blind society?

The court cases legitimized the political struggle of the right, which was part of the culture war in American society during the past two decades of the 20th century. As the Supreme Court and the mood of the country grew more conservative, a persistent whittling away of the principle of affirmative action occurred. Conservative think tanks and foundations actively participated in the reconstruction of the definition of race and equality.

Not satisfied with their victories, California's anti-affirmative action zealots succeeded in putting Proposition 209, opposing affirmative action, on the November 1996 ballot. John H. Bunzel—a past president of San Jose State University, a former member of the U.S. Commission on Civil Rights, and a senior research fellow at Stanford's ultraconservative Hoover Institution—argued that equality was the antithesis of merit. During the debate over Proposition 209, Bunzel said:

> It is precisely this kind of moral simplicity, however, what makes Proposition 209 so troublesome. The proposition's backers asserted the superiority of pure principle. They asked, "Doesn't everyone agree that we want a color-blind and equal-opportunity society?" (Bunzel, 1996)

The heat of the discourse spawned dozens of books and articles carrying the simple message that white males were being discriminated against. The anti-affirmative action voices portrayed themselves as the defenders of fairness and champions of a color-blind society, concluding that if the people want a color-blind society, society has to have color-blind policies. This sophistry angered minorities, who strongly objected to the portrayal of Latinas/os and blacks being unqualified. The hyperbole over affirmative action divided Americans.

Does affirmative action discriminate against white males?

Voters passed Proposition 209 by a 54 to 46 percent margin. Some 73 percent of African Americans and 70 percent of Latinos voted against Proposition 209. Asian Americans also voted against it, although only by 56 percent. White males voted for 209 by a 66 percent margin and white females by 58 percent. In California, three-fourths of the voters were white. This vote did not end a bitter debate over how to reach equality of opportunity in the United States. The attitude of voters had changed dramatically since the 1960s when middle-class Euroamericans defied their parents to protest for free speech, civil rights, and the end of the Vietnam War (Douglass, 1998).

A long string of cases followed the Bakke decision. In *Hopwood v. Texas* in 1996, the court ruled that "the University Of Texas School Of Law may not use race as a factor in deciding which applicants to admit in order to achieve a diverse student body . . . . The use of race, in and of itself, to choose students simply achieves a student body that looks different. Such a criterion is no more rational on its own terms than would be choices based upon the physical size or blood type of applicants." The court added ". . . that any consideration of race or ethnicity by the law school for the purpose of achieving a diverse student body is not a compelling interest under the Fourteenth Amendment" *(Hopwood v. Texas).*

The University of Texas admittedly had higher test score standards (199) for resident whites and nonpreferred minorities. Mexican Americans and blacks needed a score of 189. For denial, a score for nonminorities was 192; for denial the cutoff for blacks and Mexican Americans was 179. Resident white applicants had a mean GPA of 3.53 and an LSAT of 164. Mexican Americans scored 3.27 and 158 and blacks scored 3.25 and 157. The category of "other minority" achieved a GPA of 3.56 and an LSAT of 160. In 1992, the entering class included 41 blacks and 55 Mexican Americans, 8 percent and 10.7 percent of the class, respectively.

Questions: Do tests really gauge potential? Does a compelling societal interest trump scores? For example, does the education and income of a student's father affect test scores? Does what school the student attended play a factor? Finally, do LSAT review classes make a difference? Wealthy students often take numerous review classes, retaking the exam several times. Private tutoring for graduate school exams can cost upward of $6,000. Is this fair? Proponents of affirmative action also argue that the question of GPA is problematic. How much difference is there between a 3.27 and a 3.56? How does having to work 30 to 40 hours a week affect GPA? It could be argued that a 3.27 from Harvard would mean more than a 3.53 from a state university, that is, if one does not consider that at Harvard the student can drop a class on the day of the final examination, whereas a California state university does not permit a student to drop a class after the third week of instruction, which usually is before students have had the opportunity to take their midterms.

Does a compelling societal interest trump GPA? Is it discriminatory to have all nine Supreme Court Justices come from Ivy League schools?

Besides wanting to make society more equal by bringing Latinas/os, blacks, and women into the mainstream, another goal of affirmative action was to serve underserved areas better. For example, medical schools give applicants from rural areas preferential admissions because of the lack of doctors in isolated rural areas. In minority communities in California in 1975, one Euro-American lawyer practiced for every 530 Euroamericans and one Asian for 1,750 Asians; the ratio for blacks was 1 to 3,441; for Latinos, 1 to 9,482; and for Native Americans, 1 to 50,000. In primary care medicine, 1 white doctor practiced for every 990 whites; the ratio for blacks was 1 to 4,028; for Native Americans, 1 to 7,539; and for Latinos, 1 to 21,245 (Durant, 1978). Bakke supporters argued that an oversupply of professionals existed and that service did not depend on the professional's ethnic or racial background. Admittedly, there is little research in this area. However, no one can deny the need for doctors in black and Latino areas, and the probability is higher that black and Latino doctors (and other black and Latino professionals) will work with the poor and with clients of their color more readily "than middle-class practitioners." (Fernández, 2008).

Does the public subsidize the education of professionals for the public good or to make individuals rich? Who is more apt to practice in a minority neighborhood, a white doctor or a member of a minority group?

Prior to the fall of 1972, universities did not give gender, race, and ethnic integration at the college level much thought. In 1970, there were few white women at the leading law schools and medical schools. Affirmative action changed that with the admittance of more women into professional schools. The number of women radically changed the gender composition in the universities and the professions. For students of color, there was pushback largely because of their color and economic class. The presumption was that they came from inferior schools and were unqualified.

In most civilized societies the needs of the communities are taken into account. In the United States it was a statistical fact that few white doctors chose to practice in underrepresented communities. But for the nativists, this fact did not matter; ideology trumped needs. Few of them questioned the fact that foreign students were welcomed into medical school and state universities because they paid double the tuition of resident students. They allowed medical and professional schools to make huge profits, which they placed in discretionary funds. Religion was also a factor at many schools and veterans received extra points. Athletes and the sons and daughters of alumni were given legacy admissions.

Does the admittance of foreign students impact the access of minority students?

The anti-affirmative rulings were further confused when in 1994 an Appellate Court struck down the University of Maryland's Banneker scholarship practice of awarding this scholarship only to African American students. The Supreme Court was asked to overturn a U.S. Court of Appeals ruling that the University of Maryland scholarship program being restricted to black students was unconstitutional. The highest court refused to review that the Banneker Fund was unconstitutional because it was restricted to black students. According to the *Chicago Tribune*, "The Supreme Court made no legal ruling, but its refusal to disturb the decision of the U.S. Court of Appeals for the 4th Circuit disappointed university officials nationwide" (Greenburg and Hanna, 1995).

The Supreme Court ruled for the University of Michigan Law School in the *Grutter v. Bollinger* case (United States Supreme Court, 2003). The Court found: "The Law School's narrowly tailored use of race in admissions decisions to further a compelling interest in obtaining the educational benefits that flow from a diverse student body is not prohibited by the Equal Protection Clause, Title VI, or §1981. Pp. 9–32." Justice Sandra Day declared: "Today we endorse Justice Powell's view that student body diversity is a compelling state interest that can justify the use of race in university admissions" ("Supreme Court Upholds Use of Race in Admissions Decisions," 2003). Bakke had ruled that race-based affirmative action programs were constitutional if they were intended to promote diversity and there were no quotas or set-asides. Thus, the University of Michigan's Law School admissions fit all the criteria for a permissible program. It held that in the case of Michigan, race was considered a plus factor (not a deciding factor). Race was only one factor (*Grutter v. Bollinger* et al., 2003).

How did the Michigan case advance the discussion of affirmative action?

One of the negative fallouts in the argument over affirmative action was the assumption that minority admits were all affirmative action admits when many were in fact highly qualified. The other assumption in the Fisher case discussed below was that the plaintiff was qualified because she was white. *Fisher v. University of Texas* is informative on this score. Abigail Fisher, a white woman, was denied admission to the University. Fisher alleged that her denial was due to her race and thus a violation of the Equal Protection Clause of the Fourteenth Amendment. Texas' race-conscious admission policy was upheld in District Court. Fisher appealed to the Supreme Court in 2012, which sent the case back to the Fifth Circuit in 2014. Fisher again appealed (Nelson. 2015; Good, 2013; Angyal, 2016).

Fisher was being funded by the ultraconservation Free Enterprise Institute. The more one looked into the case, the more holes were obvious. Fisher had a 3.59 GPA and scored a not overwhelming 1180 out of 1600 on her SATs. She did not finish in the top 10 percent of her high school class, so, like everyone else, she had to compete for the 841 spots reserved for non-top-tier students that year. Because she wasn't a top 10-percent student, UT Austin evaluated Fisher using her grades, test scores, and what was called a "personal achievement index" (Hannah-Jones, 2013). Upon review the university rejected her as not being good enough and denied her admission. Only 5 of the 47 students admitted with lower grades and test scores than Abigail's were minority, while 42 were white. Never mind that 168 black and Latino/a students were minority; 42 were white with grades as good as or better than Fisher's were also denied entry into the university that year (Reilly, 2015).

One article castigated Fisher, writing, "Seven years ago, Abigail Fisher sued the University of Texas because she believed that she was denied acceptance, not because everyone in her graduating class was smarter than her, not because they busted their butts harder than her, but because she was white. Fisher claimed that she knew people who were accepted that were less qualified than her but were accepted just because they had different skin color." The article continued, "For just one second, let's forget that the University of Texas' admission rate is 40 percent and that it's on record only 5 people of color with grades worse than her were accepted and 42 white people with grades worse than her were accepted from her class that year. Let's forget that there were 168 Black and Latino students who got the same grades or even better grades than her but were denied admission." It went on, "Affirmative Action is not just for minorities but for women as well; there is a history of both of these disenfranchised groups of people being discriminated against by businesses and education institutions. Talent is universal, but opportunity is not." Concluding, "So to all the Abbys in the world, you can either continue to get mad, or stop being mediocre. Your choice" (Musoni, 2015).

Is it an injustice to assume that all white students are meritorious and minority students special admits?

Summing Up!

President Lyndon Johnson believed that we could not bring about social and political equality without achieving economic equality. Further, affirmative action has made a significant difference for Latinas/os and blacks. Even President Nixon supported affirmative action as a vehicle for ending inequality and discrimination and moving Latinas/os into the middle class. In the 1990s, 10.6 percent of Latinas/os had a bachelor's degree or higher compared with 28.1 percent of non-Hispanic whites. Before affirmative action programs, less than 4 percent of Latinas/os were professionals. Most reputable studies also show that affirmative action programs closed the gap between rich and poor, yet because many of these programs have been diluted, the gap has widened in recent years.

Conservatives have politicized the debate over affirmative action to take the focus away from the overall crisis in public education. As minority enrollment has increased, so has the per capita expenditures per student. California, which in the 1950s spent more per student than any other state except New York, ranks among the lowest today. Tuition at California state universities has risen from $50/100 annually in 1970 to nearly $2,000. Because of growth in population, competition for admission has increased, and higher education is no longer guaranteed. Also, elite schools have tightened their admission requirements. Even if no minorities were admitted to premier universities, the number of slots for white males would be negligible. Moreover, minorities who are being admitted are in the top 5 to 10 percent of their graduating classes.

Minorities should not be singled out for receiving preferential admissions. They make up only a small part of the admissions pool. Universities routinely lower admission standards for legacies to the children of alumni. For example, special admission was not an issue when George W. Bush was admitted to Yale, when former Vice President Dan Quayle received preferential admission into law school, or when Vice President Dick Cheney twice flunked out of Yale University. Indeed, George W. Bush was not admitted to the University of Texas Law School, but he was admitted to Harvard's School of Business as a special admit. Athletes are also admitted to prestigious institutions though they often fall well below admission standards. However, the assumption is that Latinos and blacks are not qualified and that the legacy admits are qualified.

The children of alumni at Harvard University in 1991 were three times more likely to be accepted than other students who applied. Harvard University admits about 20 percent of its entering class based on the criterion that the student is the son or daughter of an alumnus or donor (Liebman, 1998). Sixty-six percent of applicants accepted at the University of Pennsylvania were children of alumni. At Notre Dame, 25 percent of its first-year class was reserved for the children of alumni. In other words, the sons and daughters of the rich inherit privilege in the United States, but no one talks about this preferential treatment.

Preferential treatment is an unacceptable argument. Today, there are handicap ramps, and some people would call this preferential treatment. Yet, would it be fair not to have them? Criticism of affirmative action usually boils down to what in Spanish is called *chisme*, which means rumors or gossip. Affirmative action has not had a negative impact on white workers. Seniority systems protect white workers, and in times of recession, minority workers are the last hired—and the first fired. Older union members routinely get special favors for their sons to join the union.

Affirmative action has worked. The Labor Department reports that affirmative action has helped 5 million minority members and 6 million white and minority women move up in the workforce. People believe what they want to believe. Most of the public wants to believe that minorities are getting special help when in reality they are not. For example, union members widely accept that nonwhites get preferential treatment when it comes to education overall. But the reality is white schools have better facilities and better-qualified teachers and counselors. They have more advanced placement classes. More minority students are apt to hold jobs than white students while in high school and in college, which affects their school performance. Even with this glaring inequality, affirmative action is not about doing away with standards. It is not about selecting unqualified candidates. Whites' averages on test scores are higher, and that is why there is a push for better public schools in minority areas. But to set the record straight, many minority applicants have higher grades and scores than their white counterparts. Many who supposedly get preferential treatment have as high, equivalent, or higher scores than legacy admittees despite the privileged education of the latter. Also, many do not consider that most middle-class whites and Asians have, through the years, taken special Kumon-like tutorial math classes, which presently have an enrollment of more than 2.9 million children. Kumon Math and Reading Centers offer an after-school supplemental education program. Most Latinos cannot take these classes because of the cost.

Most minority students do not take SAT prep classes; most white middle-class and Asian students do. The Princeton Review advertises "better scores, better schools" and guarantees the outcome. Their advertising brochure brags, "Our SAT students improve an average of 140 points, and the top 25% improve by a whopping 256 points! When you take our SAT classroom course, we guarantee your SAT score will improve by at least 100 points, or we'll work with you again for up to a year, FREE." The tuition ranges from $99 to $699 for online courses; classroom classes cost more, and the student can take private tutoring classes that run into the thousands of dollars. These benefits add to the advantages of better high schools and counseling.

The work of Dr. Patricia Gándara of the University of California at Davis clearly shows the benefit of good schooling and documents that Latinos who attend integrated schools do much better than those in segregated environments. Indeed, peer group conversations influenced their decisions to pursue higher education more than their school counselors. Gándara noted the following:

> Many pegged their own performance against the standard set by particular white, Asian, or Jewish students. They believed that if they were

> competing favorably against these students, they were probably pretty capable. One subject talked at great length about this phenomenon. (Gándara, 1994)

The subjects of her study "all came from families in which neither parent completed high school or held a job higher than skilled labor; the average father finished grade four, and most were sons and daughters of farm workers and other unskilled laborers. Most began school with Spanish as their primary language, yet all completed doctoral-level educations from the country's most prestigious institutions" (Gándara, 1994). Gándara's studies show that the parents cared and the students achieved because of programs such as affirmative action. It was a form of encouragement and created a culture of learning. Affirmative action has had a tremendous impact on Latinos, creating a small but expanding middle class.

What Latinas/os want is a better-educated populace where people of all colors are participating in society. Latinos want equality with white America. Latinos can no longer rely on well-paying blue-collar jobs, so Latinos have to go to college if they are going to make it into the middle class. Since the 1960s, Latinos have made tremendous strides because affirmative action has given them opportunities to succeed and to fail occasionally. If society doesn't want preferential admissions, then they should be cut for everyone, rich and poor. Why should race be the only variable excluded from preferences? Eliminate the legacy admits. Eliminate the SAT, LSAT, and all testing where a student can pay to get a better score. Stop playing politics and start concentrating on educating more people in college instead of eliminating them.

ANOTHER POV (POINT OF VIEW)

Affirmative Action Is Reverse Discrimination and Violates the 14th Americans Equal Protection Clause

Dulcinea Lara, Associate Professor of Criminal Justice at New Mexico State University

The notion of "reverse discrimination" is one employed by opponents of Affirmative Action (AA) policies who feel that granting special opportunities to underrepresented groups violates to the fourteenth Amendment to the U.S. Constitution's Equal Protection Clause. Opponents of AA argue from multiple angles. Because the implementation of AA policies is aimed to improve opportunities (educational, employment, legal protections, etc.) for women and racialized minorities, opponents are often whites and male. Arguments from these groups include the following: AA policies are unfair because they unfairly remove opportunities from whites and men, and this approach is discriminatory by its very nature because it logically contradicts the aim of achieving equality. Prominent neoliberal conservative minorities such as Richard Rodríguez, Ward Connerly, and Shelby Steele have also argued contra AA, stating that the implementation of policies that seek to "aid" women and racial minorities is offensive and assumes that these groups cannot achieve success on their own. The white conservative movement, by its nature opposed to AA, has leaned heavily on these kinds of arguments by Latinos and blacks to emphasize its own agenda. While there are a few outspoken racial minorities and women who make these politically conservative claims, most people in these groups support policies and efforts to improve their livelihood.

Civil rights icon Dr. Martin Luther King Jr. witnessed his own notions of equality and the American Dream distorted by those who oppose AA. He was heralded by the conservative right as a leader who would oppose the kinds of measures proposed by AA for reasons mentioned above. King himself replied to these warped notions directly. He wrote in "Where do We Go From Here: Chaos or Community?" (King, 1967), "A society that has done something special against the Negro for hundreds of years must now do something special for the Negro." This statement supports AA most clearly by insisting that history matters when considering the social construction of racial categories for the purpose of uneven resource distribution. AA implements policies that work to distribute resources more equitably.

What is also at odds in this virulent debate is the question of equality versus equity. A true desire for equality has equity at its core. This is what Dr. King's emphasis on history demands—that until extra resources (proportional to the oppressions faced by underrepresented groups) are made available to create a level quality of life across social statuses, there can be no true equality. This is the crux of the debate, inherently, because people with more means and unearned privileges often feel threatened by the concept that in order to reach true equality, they will have to lose their privileges and benefits assigned to them because of socially constructed categories that include benefit.

The debate spans the spectrum of discourse from academic and legal spheres to the public sphere. While few people truly know the tenets and history of AA, most people have opinions and feelings about it; there is a polarizing nature to AA because it relates to social locations, access to resources, and, most notably, race. To illustrate the power and sensitive nature of AA and to teach about the contention to youth and college-aged students, I often refer to comedian Aamer Rahman. He critically discusses the concept "reverse discrimination" in his comedy tour, "Fear of a Brown Planet" (2013). In the sketch, he says that people call him a "reverse racist" because he talks disparagingly about whites. Rahman paints a theoretical scenario whereby Europeans are invaded by leaders of other nations and continents and forced into slavery, forced to assimilate to nonwhite standards of beauty, forced to believe in their own culture's inferiority, etc. Rahman says that if he got into a time machine and did this to Europeans then, yes, this would be "reverse discrimination." While this is a comedic approach to dismantling the concept of "reverse discrimination," it also demonstrates the historical legacy of dehumanization that people who occupy underrepresented groups endure. In getting the audience to laugh, albeit uncomfortably at times, Rahman is asking us to consider this notion absurd and ill-informed.

Quote Justice Sonia Sotomayor

"With my academic achievement in high school I was accepted rather readily at Princeton and equally as fast at Yale, but my test scores were not comparable to that of my classmates. And that's been shown by statistics, there are reasons for that—there are cultural biases built into testing, and that was one of the motivations for the concept of affirmative action to try to balance out those effects."

Source: Charlie Savage. "Videos Shed New Light on Sotomayor's Positions," *New York Times*, June 10, 2009. http://www.nytimes.com/2009/06/11/us/politics/11judge.html?_r=0

Affirmative Action

Luis H. Moreno, Instructor, Bowling Green State University School of Cultural and Critical Studies, Department of Ethnic Studies

As historian Rodolfo Acuña stated, "Affirmative action comes down to equality and the role the government has about bringing equal protection to everyone." Those policies have impacted the Latina/o community in many different ways. In addition, he raised President Lyndon Johnson's dicta that "In order to have political equality a nation must insure economic equality." Equality is interconnected with equity and affirmative action's mission is to provide everyone with access to be successful in this society. I do agree with his statement but the real question is how we define equality and what impact do politics and economics have on it.

Since the landmark affirmative action decision of *Regents of the University of California v. Bakke* (1978) to the passing of California's Proposition 209 (1996), Latina/os have faced decades of backlash due to affirmative action policies. In reality, affirmative action policies in education have given women, people of color, and especially Latina/os access to a higher education. A poll conducted in May 2013 by CBS News/*New York Times* "found that 53% of the public supported affirmative action programs in hiring, promoting and college admissions, while 38% opposed such programs" (Drake, 2014). If the majority of the population supports affirmative action policies, what is the real issue?!

In the debate over affirmative action, supporters and opponents believed in the idea of equality, which is aimed to promote fairness in society, but their perceptions are on the different side of the political sphere. Conservatives believe that people should be judged by their abilities, not their race or ethnicity, and any type of affirmative action is reverse discrimination. Liberals see affirmative action as a response to historic inequalities and discrimination toward women and people of color; it's not a discriminatory practice but a move toward being inclusive.

A survey conducted by the Pew Research Center showed that "while a majority (55%) of whites support affirmative action programs on campus, that compares with 84% of blacks who believe they are a good thing and 80% of Hispanics" (Drake, 2014). Clearly, this issue is divided by race and ethnicity. Furthermore, the report showed the differences between liberals and conservatives: ". . . nearly eight-in-ten (78%) Democrats back the programs as a good thing, as do 62% of independents; Republicans are mixed, with 50% seeing the racial preferences as a bad thing and 43% viewing them as a good thing."

The battle to end affirmative action in higher education is being led by many different conservative groups, especially by think tanks like The Heritage Foundation, which has focused on pushing a false perception of a color-blind society. As Acuña pointed out, "conservatives have politicized the debate over affirmative action to take the focus away from the overall crisis in public education." The demographics of the United States is changing, which has led to an increase of Latina/os in higher education. Those changes have led to many conservative groups demanding an end to affirmative action on campuses by supporting the following court cases: *Grutter v. Bollinger* and *Fisher v. University of Texas*. Furthermore, their battle against affirmative action is based on the idea that "race-based discrimination policies continue to undermine the American Dream, and the only way to end the vicious cycle of discrimination is to ensure that fair and equal treatment for everyone is a reality."

In closing, affirmative action is clearly impacted by policies (political equality) that influence the wages (economic equality) of women and people of color, especially Latina/os. And this can be clearly seen since 1996 as numerous states ended affirmative action programs.

NOTES

1. Nixon was not the first to implement affirmative action; however, he was the first to set quotas.

2. The Powell Memo (also known as the Powell Manifesto) was first published on August 23, 1971. "Confidential Memorandum: Attack of American Free Enterprise System, August 23, 1971" was addressed to Mr. Eugene B. Sydnor Jr., Chairman, Education Committee, U.S. Chamber of Commerce, from Lewis F. Powell Jr. In *Reclaim Democracy*, http://reclaimdemocracy.org/powell_memo_lewis/ Lewis was later appointed to the Supreme Court.

3. Although Congress passed the fourteenth Amendment to protect the due process of blacks from the state, courts during the 19th century rarely applied it in favor of blacks. Instead, they interpreted the word *citizen* to person and ruled that corporations were persons and that the states could not overly regulate them.

BIBLIOGRAPHY

Acuña, Rodolfo F. "The Illusion of Inclusion." *counterpunch*, June 1, 2012. http://www.counterpunch.org/2012/06/01/the-illusion-of-inclusion.

Acuña, Rodolfo F. "The Illusive Race Question & Class: A Bacteria That Constantly Mutates." East Lansing, Michigan. Occasional Paper No. 59, Latino Studies Series, November 2005.

Acuña, Rodolfo F. *Sometimes There Is No Other Side: Chicanos and the Myth of Equality*. Notre Dame, IN: Notre Dame University Press, 1998.

"Affirmative Action," Civil Rights 101. http://www.civilrights.org/resources/civilrights101/affirmaction.html

American Association for Access, Equality and Diversity. http://www.affirmativeaction.org/. Accessed July 24, 2003.

Americans for a Fair Chance. "The History of Affirmative Action Policies," Washington, DC, August 7, 2003, published in *In Motion Magazine*, October 12, 2003. http://www.inmotionmagazine.com/aahist.html

Angyal, Chloe. "Affirmative Action Is Great For White Women. So Why Do They Hate It?" *Huffington Post*, January 21, 2016. http://www.huffingtonpost.com/entry/affirmative-action-white-women_us_56a0ef6ae4b0d8cc1098d3a5

Background—*Mendez v. Westminster* Re-Enactment. United States Courts. http://www.uscourts.gov/educational-resources/educational-activities/background-mendez-v-westminster-re-enactment

Bell, Derrick. *And We Are Not Saved: The Elusive Quest for Racial Justice*. New York: Basic Books, 1987.

Bunzel, John H. *Affirmative Action in Higher Education: A Dilemma of Conflicting Principles (Essays in Public Policy).* Hoover Institution Press, 1998. http://www-hoover.stanford.edu/publications/epp/89/89a.html. Accessed August 2, 2003.

Bunzel, John H. "Affirmative action, race, and the pragmatic temper." *Academic Questions* 10, 2 (June 1997): 20–23.

Bunzel, John H. "The Nation: Post-Proposition 209: The Question Remains: What Role for Race?" *Los Angeles Times,* December 8, 1996. http://articles.latimes.com/1996-12-08/opinion/op-6968_1_affirmative-action-programs

Caplan, Lincoln. "Thurgood Marshall and the Need for Affirmative Action." *The New Yorker,* December 9, 2015. http://www.newyorker.com/news/news-desk/thurgood-marshall-and-the-need-for-affirmative-action

Cashin, Sheryll D. "Justice Thurgood Marshall: A Race Man's Race-Transcending Jurisprudence." *Howard Law Journal,* 52 How. L.J. 507, Spring, 2009.

Chace, William M. "Affirmative Inaction." *The American Scholar,* December 1, 2011. https://theamericanscholar.org/affirmative-inaction

Cohen, Carl. *Naked Racial Preference: The Case against Affirmative Action.* Boston: Madison Books, 1995.

Colby, Tanner. "The Massive Liberal Failure on Race: Part 2: Affirmative action doesn't work. It never did. It's time for a new solution." *Slate,* February 10, 2014. http://www.slate.com/articles/life/history/features/2014/the_liberal_failure_on_race/affirmative_action_it_s_time_for_liberals_to_admit_it_isn_t_working.html

Connolly, Ceci. "Report Says Minorities Get Lower-Quality Health Care: Moral Implications of Widespread Pattern Noted." *Washington Post,* March 21, 2002. http://www.healthpronet.org/prog_resources/news_041502a.html

Cooper, A. D. John. "The Bakke Decision 1978." *Academic Medicine* 78, no. 5 (2003): 482.

Darling-Hammond, Linda, and Ted Dintersmith, "A Basic Flaw in the Argument Against Affirmative Action." *Huffington Post,* July 22, 2014, http://www.huffingtonpost.com/linda-darlinghammond/a-basic-flaw-in-the-affirmative-action_b_5611188.html

Delgado, Richard. *The Rodrigo Chronicles: Conversations about America and Race.* New York: NYU Press, 1995.

Douglass, John Aubrey. "Anatomy of Conflict: The Making and Unmaking of Affirmative Action at the University of California." *American Behavioral Scientist* 41, no.7 (1998): 938–959.

Drake, Bruce. "Fact Tank—Our Lives in Numbers." Pew Research Center, April 22, 2014. http://www.pewresearch.org/fact-tank/2014/04/22/public-strongly-backs-affirmative-action-programs-on-campus/

Dreier, Peter. "How George W. Bush Benefited From Affirmative Action." *Huffington Post,* November 13, 2014. http://www.huffingtonpost.com/peter-dreier/how-george-w-bush-benefit_b_5814680.html

Durant, Celeste. "California Bar Exam—Pain and Trauma Twice a Year." *Los Angeles Times,* August 27, 1978.

Fernandez, Elizabeth. "Minority doctors in short supply in state. Latino, black physicians severely underrepresented, UCSF study says." *San Francisco Chronicle,* April 3, 2008. http://www.sfgate.com/bayarea/article/Minority-doctors-in-short-supply-in-state-3221270.php

Gándara, Patricia. "Choosing Higher Education: Educationally Ambitious Chicanos and the Path to Social Mobility." *Education Policy Analysis Archives* no. 8 (1994).

Good, Chris. "Abigail Fisher 'Confident That UT Won't Be Able to Use Race Again.'" *ABC News*, June 24, 2013. http://abcnews.go.com/blogs/politics/2013/06/abigail-fisher-confident-that-ut-wont-be-able-to-use-race-again

Greenburg, Jan Crawford, and Janan Hanna. "Race-based Scholarship Eliminated. Blacks-only Plan Denied An Appeal." *Chicago Tribune*, May 23, 1995. http://articles.chicagotribune.com/1995-05-23/news/9505230353_1_benjamin-banneker-scholarship-program-appeals-court-supreme-court

Greenhouse, Linda. "Government Tries to Restore Black Scholarship Program." *New York Times*, May 3, 1995. http://www.nytimes.com/1995/05/03/us/government-tries-to-restore-black-scholarship-program.html

Grutter v. Bollinger et al., Certiorari to the United States Court of Appeals for the Sixth Circuit, No. 02-241. Argued April 1, 2003—Decided June 23, 2003. http://diversity.umich.edu/admissions/legal/grutter/gru-ussc-op.html

Hannah-Jones, Nikole. "What Abigail Fisher's Affirmative Action Case Was Really About." *ProPublica*, March 18, 2013. http://www.propublica.org/article/a-colorblind-constitution-what-abigail-fishers-affirmative-action-case-is-r

Hawkins, Cong Gus. "Mr. Justice Marshall and the Allan Bakke Case." *Los Angeles Sentinel*, July 13, 1978.

Henry, William. *In Defense of Elitism*. New York: Anchor, 1994.

Hopwood v. Texas. 78 F.3d 932,962 (5th Cir. 1996). http://scholarlycommons.law.wlu.edu/cgi/viewcontent.cgi?article=1054&context=crsj

King Jr., Martin Luther. *Where Do We Go from Here: Chaos or Community?* New York: Harper & Row, 1967.

Kotlowski, Dean J. "Richard Nixon and Origins of Affirmative Action." *The Historian* (Spring 1998). https://www.highbeam.com/doc/1G1-20649393.html

Kull, Andrew. *The Color Blind Constitution*. Cambridge: Harvard University Press, 1992.

The Leadership Conference. "Civil Rights 101: Affirmative Action." 2016. http://www.civilrights.org/resources/civilrights101/affirmaction.html

Liebman, Alex. "How'd That Guy Get in, Anyway?" *Argos* 1, no. 2 (1998).

Liu, Goodwin. "The Myth and Math of Affirmative Action." *The University of Michigan Admissions Lawsuits*, April 14, 2002. http://diversity.umich.edu/admissions/statements/liu.html

Marín, Patricia, and Catherine L. Horn, eds., *Realizing Bakke's Legacy: Affirmative Action, Equal Opportunity, and Access to Higher Education*. Sterling, Virginia: Stylus Publishing, 2008.

McCarthy, Debora, and Daniel Faber, eds., *Foundations for Social Change: Critical Perspectives on Philanthropy and Popular Movements*. Boulder: Rowman & Littlefield, 2005.

Montoya, Robert. "Minority Health Professional Development: An Issue of Freedom of Choice for Young Anglo Health Professionals." Paper presented at the Annual Convention of the American Medical Student Association, Atlanta, GA, March 1978, p. 4.

Musoni, Malcolm-Aime. "Blame Your Own Mediocrity, Not People of Color, For Your College Admission Shortcomings." *Huffington* Post, December 14, 2015. http://www.huffingtonpost.com/malcolmaime-musoni/abigail-fisher-v-texas_b_8790810.html

National Park Service. "Civil Rights Act of 1964." http://www.nps.gov/subjects/civilrights/1964-civil-rights-act.htm

Nelson, Steve. "We're Not Racist . . . Are We? The Case for Affirmative Action in Fisher v. U of Texas." *The Huffington Post*, October 21, 2015. http://www.huffingtonpost.com/steve-nelson/were-not-racist—-are-we_b_8351980.html

Our Documents.gov. "Civil Rights Act (1964)." http://www.ourdocuments.gov/doc.php?flash=true&doc=97

Plous, S. "Ten Myths about Affirmative Action." Understanding Prejudice.org. http://www.understanding prejudice.org/readroom/articles/affirm.htm. Accessed 24 July 2003.

The Powell Memo (aka Powell Manifesto). "Confidential Memorandum: Attack of American Free Enterprise System," August 23, 1971. *Reclaim Democracy*. To: Mr. Eugene B. Sydnor Jr., Chairman, Education Committee, U.S. Chamber of Commerce. From: Lewis F. Powell Jr. http://reclaimdemocracy.org/powell_memo_lewis/

Regents of the University of California v. Bakke, 438 U.S. 265, *Regents of the University of California v. Bakke* (No. 7811). Argued: October 12, 1977. Decided: June 28, 1978.18 Cal.3d 34, 553 P.2d 1152, affirmed in part and reversed in part. Cornell University Law School. https://www.law.cornell.edu/supremecourt/text/438/265

Reilly, Molly. "5 Things To Know About The Woman Whose Case Could End Affirmative Action As We Know It." *Huffington Post*, December 16, 2015. http://www.huffingtonpost.com/entry/abigail-fisher-5-things-to-know_us_56719717e4b0dfd4bcc026a4

Rosenberg, Alec. "UC medical schools increase underrepresented minority students." University of California, January 31, 2011. http://www.universityofcalifornia.edu/news/uc-medical-schools-increase-underrepresented-minority-students

Stefanic, Jean, and Richard Delgado. *No Mercy: How Conservative Think Tanks and Foundations Changed America's Social Agenda*. Philadelphia: Temple University Press, 1996.

"Supreme Court Upholds Use of Race in Admissions Decisions." *Civil Rights Monitor*, Summer 2003. http://www.civilrights.org/monitor/summer_03/art7p1.html

Tabachnick, Rachel. "The John Birch Society's Anti-Civil Rights Campaign of the 1960s, and Its Relevance Today." *Political Research Associates*, January 21, 2014. http://www.politicalresearch.org/2014/01/21/the-john-birch-societys-anti-civil-rights-campaign-of-the-1960s-and-its-relevance-today

United States Department of Labor. "Chapter 7: Nixon and Ford Administrations 1969–1977." http://www.dol.gov/general/aboutdol/history/dolchp07

United States Supreme Court: *Grutter v. Bollinger* et al., (2003), No. 02-241. Argued: April 1, 2003. Decided: June 23, 2003. Find Law. http://caselaw.findlaw.com/us-supreme-court/539/306.html

University of California Regents v. Bakke, 438 Supreme Court of the United States, U.S. 265, 76–811 (1978). October 12, 1977, Argued, June 28,1978, Decided. http://caselaw.findlaw.com/us-supreme-court/438/265.html

Vertreace, Walter. "History of Employment Discrimination in America." *The Black Collegian - the Career and Self-Development Magazine for African Americans* 40, no. 2 (2010): 57, 58, 60.

West, Cornel. *Race Matters*. New York: Vintage, 1994.

SELECTED VIDEOS

College of the Holy Cross. "Jorge Gracia on 'Affirmative Action for Latinos,'" YouTube video, 40:24, posted July 14, 2015. https://www.youtube.com/watch?v=ONG6Wzh8c1A

CrashCourse. "Affirmative Action: Crash Course Government and Politics #32," YouTube video, 7:13, posted September 26, 2015. https://www.youtube.com/watch?v=gJgQR6xiZGs

ElectronicTricycle. "Hopwood v. Texas," YouTube video, 4:39, posted September 23, 2010. https://www.youtube.com/watch?v=KdFeXbV3AQg

emPower magazine. "The Great Debate, Episode 4: Affirmative Action," YouTube video, 28:26, posted November 14, 2012. https://www.youtube.com/watch?v=iuQvnqmfThM

Hughes, Keith. "Supreme Court Cases For Dummies: US History Review," YouTube video, 34:27, posted March 16, 2012. https://www.youtube.com/watch?v=HTVvZ1Sdkaw

i24News. "Women in politics: Should affirmative action be used to close the gap?" YouTube video, 16:00, posted January 6, 2015. https://www.youtube.com/watch?v=E7dFMJaqYXI

LatinoPoliticsNews. "Latino Politics Roundup: VP Debate, Arizona, DREAMers, Affirmative Action, Voter ID and more," YouTube video, 1:22, posted October 13, 2012. https://www.youtube.com/watch?v=k3zCjQJdlo4

NDTV. "Women and Affirmative Action," YouTube video, 4:20, posted June 15, 2009. https://www.youtube.com/watch?v=xMQhwZf0HZg

Oyez Today. "Fisher v. University of Texas—Background," YouTube video, 9:07, posted October 10, 2012. https://www.youtube.com/watch?v=cryI144dRm0

WhiteRoses8484. "Regents of the University of California vs Bakke," YouTube video, 5:22, posted December 17, 2012. https://www.youtube.com/watch?v=6rMT8nLaBFk

The Young Turks. "White Girl Blames Affirmative Action For Not Getting Into College," YouTube video, 6:43, posted June 30, 2015. https://www.youtube.com/watch?v=23VDkyygWSg

7

Interracial Dating and Marriage

BACKGROUND

In January 1896, authorities found the mutilated body of Aureliano Castellón in San Antonio, Texas. Aureliano made the mistake of courting Emma Stanfield, a white girl, over the objections of her brothers (Carrigan and Webb, 2013). He was shot eight times and his body was burned. Interracial friendships, let alone dating, have been taboo from the beginning of the country's history. It has only been until recently that it has become commonplace and then only in certain parts of the country.

Legal and social taboos also existed governing relationships between Anglo-Americans and Africans and Indians. Later, there was considerable tension with the Italians, Irish, and Jews. Immigrants often lived next to one other but did not date; when they did, there were problems. The reasons were varied: many Jewish immigrants did not want their daughters and sons to have relationships with Protestants or Catholics because they feared it would lead to intermarriage, lessening their children's ties to their religion. Catholics and Protestants often felt the same way about each other and about Jews.

Which is stronger: allegiance to religion or to one's national group?

Which would be a bigger obstacle in your parents' eyes?

INTERRACIAL MARRIAGE

During the 19th century, a minority of Mexicans intermarried with white Americans. However, intermarriage was more often limited to elites, with cohabiting rarer among the poor. As white women entered the Southwest, this fragile relationship ended, and white families frowned upon race intermixing with Mexicans. Generally, miscegenation, interracial marriages, was against the law. The exception was when the West was sparsely populated and there was a shortage of women.

The case of *In re: Rodriguez* (1897) set the precedent. Ricardo Rodríguez, a native of Mexico, lived in Texas for ten years. He petitioned to become a naturalized U.S. citizen but was denied. The catch-22 was that only white people could become citizens; Mexicans were not considered white, so they could not be citizens. The dilemma was resolved by classifying Mexicans as white, as inferred by the Treaty of Guadalupe Hidalgo. The treaty had made Mexicans white because only white people could be citizens. Time and time again the vicious circle was not resolved but short-circuited (LeMay and Barkan, 1999, pp. 79–80). Miscegenation was not legalized in the United States until 1967. Unfortunately, there is a history of legal opposition to interracial relationships that was arbitrarily applied to black intermarriage between Mexican women and Filipinos. For example, in 1947, Andrea Pérez (a Mexican American woman) and Sylvester Davis (an African American man) met while working in a defense plant in Burbank, California. The Los Angeles County Clerk denied them a marriage license because she had listed herself as white on the application and he had listed black. The clerk cited California Civil Code Section 60 that stated: "All marriages of white persons with Negroes, Mongolians, members of the Malay race, or mulattoes are illegal and void" ("California Civil Code") (Dodge, 2015). The California Supreme Court overturned this action and declared marriage a fundamental right that could not be denied on the basis of race. The couple married. Pérez later worked at Morningside Elementary School and lived in San Fernando until the late 1990s—she died in 2000. The case set the precedent for other cases—freedom to choose who you want to marry is protected by the Fourteenth Amendment's equal protection provision.

While legal barriers are surmounted, social taboos do not die easily. The younger generation, as with other social issues, appears to be more tolerant. Also, where you live plays a role: "As recently as 2010, a Louisiana justice of the peace in New Orleans refused to issue a marriage license to an interracial couple. He claimed he wasn't racist, but was concerned for their future children. In 2011 a Kentucky church even voted to ban interracial couples from their congregation" (Sánchez, 2012). In life there is also pressure from unknown bystanders. The data appear to suggest that as society becomes more integrated, there will be more intermarriage.

INTERRACIAL DATING

In the past, many Mexicans have reacted defensively and discouraged interracial dating; the wrongheaded logic was, "It's all right if my son goes out with a gringa (a white girl), but I wouldn't want him to marry her because gringas don't know our culture, and the first time they get mad at each other she is going to call him 'a dirty Mexican.'" In California and other western states, legislatures legally prohibited Asians from dating whites until World War II. The laws were directed at Filipinos, who often came to the States as bachelors (solos). They could be imprisoned for dating white women (Goodstein, 2012).[1]

Why did the newcomers marry into the families of Mexican elites?

Recently the Pew Research Center reported on the increasing popularity of intermarriage. In the United States in 2010, about 15 percent in California of all new marriages were between spouses of different races or ethnicities. Intermarriage has accelerated, and in that year 9 percent of whites, 17 percent of blacks, 26 percent of Latinas/os, and 28 percent of Asians married outside their race or ethnicity. Looking at all married couples in 2010, regardless of when they married, the share of intermarriages reached an all-time high of 8.4 percent. In 1980, that share had been just 3.2 percent (Wang, 2012). The report continued: "About 24% of all black male newlyweds in 2010 married outside their race, compared with just 9% of black female newlyweds. Among Asians, the gender pattern runs the other way. About 36% of Asian female newlyweds married outside their race in 2010, compared with just 17% of Asian male newlyweds. Intermarriage rates among white and Hispanic newlyweds do not vary by gender" (Goodstein, 2012). Most studies show that intermarriage is an excellent measurement of assimilation.

> **Do the results surprise you? Which do you believe would have an easier time in a mixed marriage, a male or a female?**

Another reason interracial dating between Latinas/os and whites was not common was because Latino neighborhoods (*colonias*) were usually segregated. The few Nicaraguans and Guatemalans who entered the country usually assimilated or integrated into a pre-existing Mexican or another Latina/o *colonia*. Among Latinas/os themselves, skin color often governed dating practices. Often, lighter-skinned Mexicans tended to date lighter-skinned people of their own nationality. Lighter-skinned Cubans and Puerto Ricans also discouraged dating darker-skinned people of the same nationality. The attitude was, "I don't want my daughter to go around with a dark Cuban. We're Cuban but we're more Spanish. That's the way life is. Dating leads to marriage and the children suffer." Dating was considered a prelude to marriage, so parents frowned upon dating outside the culture or race. Indeed, "Growing numbers have come with growing acceptance. In 1987, Pew found that only 13% of Americans completely agreed that interracial dating was acceptable; that share grew to 56% in 2009. Young people are even more open-minded: Roughly 9 in 10 millennials said they'd be OK with a family member marrying someone of another race or ethnicity" (Krupnick, 2014).

> **Why was there much resistance to race mixing in West Texas?**

INTERRACIAL DATING IN THE MOVIES

The musical *West Side Story* (1961) is the story of a Puerto Rican teenage girl and a white boy who fall in love. The film is an updated *Romeo and Juliet* story set in the streets of New York City in the 1960s. María and Tony are caught in the midst of a feud between two gangs, one Puerto Rican and the other Anglo. María's brother, Bernardo, is the head of the Sharks (the Puerto Rican gang) and Tony leads the Jets (the Anglo gang). Both gangs arrange the time, place, and weapons for a gang fight, or rumble as they called it. At a dance, María and Tony meet and fall in love at first sight, but one is Puerto Rican and the other white. The Jets and the Sharks symbolize the two races. At a crucial point in the story, Tony says to María, "We'll be all right. I know it." María responds, "It is not us. It is everything around us" (Woller, 2010).

Both the Puerto Rican and white Americans were poor, so why was there so much antagonism between them?

The fight is inevitable, and Tony kills María's brother. She is ready to forgive Tony and is even ready to elope with him. María sends Anita, her best friend, to give Tony a message, but Anita runs into the Jets, who hassle her. Frustrated, she says María is dead. In grief, Tony runs through the streets of New York, screaming for the killer to take his life, which happens. Latinas/os criticized the casting of Natalie Wood for the role of María. She was a white actress playing a Puerto Rican. Her voice was dubbed in the songs, and her Puerto Rican accent was not authentic. Most of the cast was also white. The most credible actor was Rita Moreno, a Puerto Rican, who played María's best friend, Anita.

Why would there have been resistance to Natalie Wood playing a Puerto Rican? Was there more resistance among males or females?

A second movie that deals with forbidden love is *Lone Star* (1996), which takes place in South Texas near the Mexican border. The sheriff, Sam Deeds, son of the late legendary lawman Buddy Deeds, investigates a murder. During the investigation, Sam's hostile relationship with his father unravels. The viewer learns that Sam has always loved Pilar (played by Elizabeth Peña), a Mexican single mother, but was kept from dating her. Sam always believed that the reason was racial. Pilar teaches high school history from a critical perspective, showing the negatives and positives of Texas society. Pilar wrestles with her feelings for Sam and copes with her teenage son. Pilar's mother, Mercedes (played by Miriam Colón), runs a Mexican restaurant. The film constantly shifts to the past, exploring the lives of Sam's father and Pilar's mother. Throughout the film, the theme is one of forbidden love. Sam discovers why so many people loved Buddy, and he also discovers that Buddy was also Pilar's father. Thus, "We should remember that history is not a prison. Even the truths of the past can be overcome by creating in the present a new and future-oriented reality" (Sandoval, 1996).

What was meant by "We should remember that history is not a prison. Even the truths of the past can be overcome by creating in the present a new and future-oriented reality"?

Antipathy to interracial dating was common even in the 1960s. During this time, the European ethnics began to lose their identities. The third and fourth generations prospered and often moved into the suburbs. Integration with other ethnic groups broke down resistance to interethnic dating. Also, as these groups became more mobile and moved west to other parts of the country, ethnic solidarity broke down, and being Irish or Italian did not have the same meaning. United States Latinas/os, who were mostly Mexicans in the Southwest and Puerto Ricans in the East, generally lived in their own barrios. Mixing, as they called it, was confined to those living in Anglo neighborhoods. Interracial dating with blacks was taboo. In 1963, 59 percent of whites told interviewers from the Survey Research Service of the National Opinion Research Center that there should be "laws against marriages between Negroes and whites." By 1970, whites were split down the middle. Since 1972, support for such laws among whites has lessened (Bowman, 2000).

Why would most immigrant groups begin assimilating in the third and fourth generation? What role is the media and popular culture playing in lessening taboos?

As mentioned, youth appear to be more open than their parents and grandparents to interracial dating and issues such as homosexuality, as suggested in a 1997 poll that found that 86 percent of black teens and 83 percent of Latina/o teens said they would date people of a different race. Their views clashed with those of their parents and surely those of their grandparents. The *Christian Science Monitor* wrote, "57 percent of U.S. teens who dated said they had gone out with a person from another race or ethnic group. That compares with 17 percent in 1980 (but that poll did not specifically include Hispanics)" (Tyson, 1997).

The pollsters cautioned that "teenage idealism did not always translate into adult behavior." The 1990s saw a sharp upswing in reported hate crimes as well as a continuation of racially motivated violence. Several widely publicized cases of black men being killed or beaten for associating with white women were reported (Tyson, 1997).[2] A 2000 poll conducted by Zogby America for Reuters asked more than 1,225 adults, "Would you approve of your son or daughter dating someone outside of your race?" Sixty-seven percent said they would approve of their child having an interracial relationship; more than 22 percent staunchly opposed it; 10 percent were not sure. More than 62 percent of the white respondents said they would approve of interracial dating by their son or daughter; 86.8 percent of Blacks supported interracial dating, as did 79.9 percent of Latinas/os. Slightly more than 52 percent of Asian Americans supported interracial dating; 35 percent of Asian Americans said they would not approve; 26 percent of whites said they would disapprove; and 9 percent of Latinas/os said no (Bowman, 2000).

Were the attitudes in 2000 much different from those today? Would you have expected them to have differed in 1960 and how? How would marrying someone of a different race make marriage more difficult?

DOES RACE MATTER?

Despite the optimism about interracial dating, color still plays a huge role; it is just more nuanced. David Harris, a University of Michigan sociologist, says, "Let's say you're white and you're involved in a relationship with a Latina, but she doesn't have many indigenous Indian characteristics . . . people may say she's white like you, or Mediterranean, or they won't know what's going on. They fly under the radar" (Fears and Deane, 2002). One woman told how her friends and family had no idea that her husband was Puerto Rican before they married. "A lot of people, when I say my husband is Hispanic, say they thought he was Italian . . . my parents love him dearly, but my father didn't know he was Puerto Rican until he liked him. I just didn't say anything. I think he assumed he was Italian" (Fears and Deane, 2002). Polls are often deceiving, and one could assume that the barriers to interracial dating and marriage have come tumbling down.

Would it have been more difficult to accept a dark-skinned or light-skinned Latina/o?

Anecdotal evidence contradicts, or at least questions, this optimism. As with the movies, land mines still exist in interracial relationships. The offspring of these unions are caught in limbo. Often the offspring must choose between what seem like two worlds. University of California at Davis Law Professor Kevin Johnson, an offspring of an interracial marriage, writes those mixed race individuals adjust to "the status of Whiteness" and expose "themselves to criticism from both Anglos and their own community." Johnson explains that the Latina/o's surname often plays a part in determining identity. Those with Spanish surnames have to either change their names or Anglicize them. In his case, the name Johnson partially hid his identity. As a child he never had to choose because his mother's family wanted to assimilate and perpetuated the myth of their having Spanish ancestry.

Ultimately, Johnson chose to pursue his Mexican American identity while his brother "with sandy blond hair and blue eyes, exercised his right to choose in a different way. He never identified as Mexican American." Johnson eventually married a Mexican American and chose to work with Latinas/os. "Many assume that I am White because of my surname and appearance and wonder how it is possible that a Latina/o could be named Johnson, how I could have children named Teresa, Tomás, and Elena, or why I am so interested in 'Latina/o' issues . . . mixed-race people have been marginalized when not ignored. The derogatory reference to 'half-breeds' exemplifies the marginalization. . . . Though animosity toward mixed-race people may be on the wane . . . [t]he rich diversity literally embodied by Multiracial people [has been] hidden from view, hidden from discourse, hidden from recognition and thus, invisible." Johnson concludes, "Mixed-background Latinas/os today may feel as if they fail to fit into either Anglo or Latina/o society and may be in a unique position to suffer subtle insults and other challenges to their identity" (Johnson, 1997).

Discuss Dr. Kevin Johnson's experience. How did it affect him?

Are young Americans color blind, and is the United States becoming a melting pot? The fact is that much of interracial dating is limited to the middle class.[3] For example, logically there would be limited contact between Latina/o and white students in many Los Angeles Unified Schools, where high schools such as Roosevelt and Garfield were upward of 96 percent Latina/o in the year 2000.[4] They are more segregated today. In 2014, UCLA's Civil Rights Project (Proyecto Derechos Civiles) called

Los Angeles the most segregated city for Latinos in the United States (Civil Rights Congress, 2014).

> **What are the consequences of Latinas/os going to highly segregated schools?**

The 2010 Census Report showed Los Angeles is the most segregated city in the United States. The UCLA Civil Rights Project found that residential segregation was at the root of residential isolation. The impact on the Latino population is dramatic, since 52.7 percent of public school enrollment in California is Latino (Orfield and Ee, 2014). In 2014, "the state has seen a dramatic increase in the segregation of Latinas/os, who on average attended schools that were 54 percent white in 1970 but now attend schools that are about 84 percent nonwhite. Latinas/os here also have fewer white classmates than Latinas/os in any other state; the typical Latina/o student here attends a school whose population is just 15.6 percent white, the study found. Statewide, the proportion of K–12 schools that are 'intensely segregated' has more than doubled from 15 percent in 1993–1994 to 31 percent in 2012–2013" (Gazzar, 2014). More than half of California Latina/o students in California attended schools that were "intensely segregated." Los Angeles high schools in the inner city were more than 90 percent Latina/o in 1999 and have remained that way. This same pattern is repeated in New York City and Chicago. The logical assumption is that students at highly segregated schools are not candidates for interracial dating since there is little contact in elementary through secondary schools (Orfield and Ee, 2014).

> **What is residential isolation? How does it impact group interaction?**
>
> **Why does more mixing occur at the college level?**

There will be greater interracial mixing in the future as more Latinas/os and people of color enter higher education. Consequently, there will be greater mixing since young people are generally more open to change. There is a strong correlation among Latinas/os between interracial marriages, economic success, and education. Latinas/os "with a college degree and a substantial income are more than five times as likely to out-marry than those who didn't finish high school or who live in poverty" (Suro, 1999). During the 1980s, the odds of interracial marriage increased by 9 percent for Latina/o men and 18 percent for Latina/o women.[5] An analysis of census data suggests that Latina/o intermarriage has been fairly stable and high, at about 14 percent (Lee and Edmonston, 2006, p. 1263). Moreover, almost two-thirds of children of these intermarriages identify as Latina/o.

WILL THERE BE MORE INTERRACIAL MIXING IN THE FUTURE?

> In the mid-20th century, Milton Gordon, a noted sociologist, presented the "straight-line" theory of racial and ethnic assimilation. He argued that levels of racial and ethnic intermarriage would increase steadily over generations as the social barriers between racial and ethnic groups diminished and preferences for in-group marriage faded (Stevens, McKillip, and Ishizawa, 2006).

The European immigrant has been the guidepost for most studies of Latina/o immigrants, and many social scientists once believed that Latinas/o would follow in the path of the European immigrant. This has not happened, with factors such as proximity to the mother country, retention of culture, and racism all playing a part. Sociologists have also found that demographic factors play a role in preferences. The number of Latinas/os is huge and they are less likely to intermarry because of that. It comes down to having more to choose from one's own group. Today racial and ethnic groups are more clustered and segregated than the European immigrant. Immigrant parents are more apt to play a role in the choice.

Finally, the size of each generation plays a role as to how many Latinas/os will intermarry. The first generation has more affinity to cultural distinctiveness. Segregation exists because income gaps persist into the second-generation adults. As mentioned, isolation and demographic constraints to choose limit the choices of Latinas/os. These factors break down in later generations only if economic choices and gaps improve. Thus, there are low levels of intermarriage in every generation when you are poor. The fact is that there is less opportunity today to enter the middle class or to buy a home than there was 50 years go.

Significantly, most interracial marriages are between whites and racial minorities rather than between the different racial minorities. The odds of Latinas/os intermarrying with whites are ten times higher than marrying African Americans or Asians. The same pattern is true for blacks and other minorities. They are more apt to marry a white person than they are to marry a Latina/o. As mentioned, where Latinas/os live plays a very important role in this process. Economics, education, language, and residential distance are all factors. The data suggest that native-born Latinas/os are more likely than immigrants to mix with whites. The fact that Latinas/os are more likely to intermarry with whites also infers that Latinas/os are assimilating much more rapidly into mainstream American society than either Asians or blacks. It also suggests that mobility is based on class. Nevertheless, assimilation among Latinas/os is much slower than among European immigrants who were white. The bottom line is that economic class, skin hue, generation, location, type of schooling, and culture all play a role in interracial dating.

Would it be easier for Asians, Latinas/os, or African Americans to mix? Why is intermarriage more common between whites and Latinas/os than between Latinas/os and other minorities?

ARE LATINAS/OS TURNING WHITE?

Will Latinos follow the patterns of Irish immigrants before them? A recent piece by Gabriel Arana in *Aljazeera America* stated, "Why Latinos won't become white: Assuming Latinos will join the white majority ignores the stark divisions in a racially diverse group." Studies have found that second- and third-generation Latinas/os identify as Latinas/os. Even in the third generation when Latinas/os have two Latina/o grandparents, 79 percent identify with the group. Arana concludes, "a simple but important factor in Latinas/os not identifying as white is the persistence of discrimination, which tends to strengthen existing racial categories" (Arana, 2014).

The discussion of the Latina/o race is confused by the media. The *Los Angeles Times* recently ran a story titled, "It's official: Latinos now outnumber whites in California" (Panzar, 2015). The U.S. Census has contributed to the charade of whiteness. The Obama Administration released a statement saying: " 'Hispanic' is an ethnicity, not a race. While the U.S. government first made this distinction in 1980, many Latinos continued to use the 'some other race' box to establish a Hispanic identity. So on the 2010 census forms we specifically instructed Latinos that Hispanic origins are not races and to select a recognized category such as white or black" (Lake, 2011). This ambiguity has confused the issue to the point that many Italians are rebelling and checking the black box because they are darker than Obama.

In a provocative article written by Sharon Chang in response to a question about the race of a mixed race couple, she answered, "Your child is neither white nor Asian. I once heard this description: When you have a glass of milk and add chocolate to it, you no longer have just a glass of milk and you no longer just have chocolate because you have created something completely different. A biracial or multiracial child is not either/or" (Chang, 2014). The truth is, it doesn't matter what you call yourself; it is how society perceives you. As long as white Americans have feelings of exceptionalism, the classification of "white" will mean that of superiority. Being "white" is what in the eyes of many people makes one truly an American. On the other hand, the Latina/o partner may have a colonial mentality that relegates nonwhite people to a lower caste. It is important to come to grips with not being white.

Do children of mixed races have a difficult time coping with the fact that they are not white?

Conclusion

Tina Turner's song, "What's Love Got to Do With It?" is the perfect question to ask in regard to interracial dating. Love has everything to do with it. A person should be able to choose whom she or he wants to date, and if marriage is the outcome, so be it. Would anyone want to go back to the times when it was against the law to marry or date a person of another color? Society has come a long way since the late 1960s when the courts held antimiscegenation laws to be unconstitutional.

Whether people like it or not, since 1960 interracial marriages have increased ten times over to 1.6 million. With the growth of the Latina/o middle class, it is natural that the number of Latina/o–white marriages will increase. Besides, most Latinos are no longer immigrants and thus have more in common with European Americans. Because of the 1960s and the media, ethnic stereotypes and taboos are not as bad as they were a generation ago. Race and ethnicity is not as important an issue as it was a hundred years ago. For example, Jews no longer marry just Jews, Irish no longer marry just Irish, and Italians no longer marry just Italians.

The argument goes that statistically, Latinas are moving up economically at a higher rate than Latinos and thus are apt to come into contact and date males of their same class. Thus, the issue becomes a matter of supply and demand. This situation is compounded by the fact that "U.S. Census Bureau data shows that females outpace males in college enrollment, especially among Hispanics and blacks" (Lopez and González-Barrera, 2014). In 1994, 52 percent of Latina high school graduates enrolled in college and a like number of Latino males enrolled. By 2012, these numbers were 76 percent Latinas versus 62 percent Latino males. This gap will become more apparent: In 2015, "Hispanic girls and women are one in five women in the U.S. and will comprise nearly one third of the country's female population by 2060" (Gándara, 2015).

The dating game among Latinas and black females is part of the adjustment to the fact that there are not enough men. Women have a harder time in same race dating than males. For instance, the U.S. Department of Labor says that the number of bachelors' and doctors' degrees awarded to Latinas more than doubled between 1977 and 1990. "Among Latinos enrolling in college, 61 percent are women and 39 percent are men. Latino males in 2009 received 37 percent of the Associate of Arts degrees [earned by Latinos] granted by community colleges nationwide" (Saenz, 2010). Educational achievement therefore plays a role in determining who one marries, and it is predictable that intermarriage will increase among Latinas with college degrees.

In sum, less intermarriage occurred before Latinas/os entered high school and then college. Racial isolation also meant that contact with other races was infrequent. This situation has changed and time marches on. Parents are also changing. Before 1970, Latino parents discouraged their daughters from leaving home and attending college. However, these taboos are rarer, and there has been a steady rise in the number of Latinas enrolled in colleges. Contact with other races is more common from high school through college (López and Fry, 2013). Increased contact breeds familiarity, which leads to other interactions and friendships.

ANOTHER POV (POINT OF VIEW)

Should There Be Interracial Dating?

Lydia Soto, National Board Certified Teacher, Social Studies, AMAE State President, 2012 (Association of Mexican American Educators), Political Activist

Over 500 years ago, a beautiful young slave was promised her freedom if she would translate from the Nahuatl and Mayan languages to Spanish for Hernan Cortes. Malinalli Tenepal, a controversial figure known as La Malinche, was one of the first Aztecs to adapt to a European culture. After the invasion, or the Conquest, depending on one's perspective, acculturation continued and has made Mexico what it is today: Spanish speaking, Catholic, democratic, and with an extraordinary gastronomy blending European and Mexican foods. So, we see that the merging of cultures is an integral part of history.

Culture is a way of life: our belief systems, traditions, customs, and heritage. They are alive and always changing. The "American" culture is a blending of the ethnic groups within specific regions. The Southwest is one of those unique regions which is continuously undergoing cultural change.

Starting from the 1500s, male European explorers, mostly Spaniards, came to this region and took native women as their wives. Mexicans, including mestizos (Spanish and Indian mix), also moved into the Southwest and intermarried with the local groups, again merging cultures. Later other Europeans and Anglo-Americans also migrated to this region and intermarried. The clash and eventual merging of cultures took place as these new societies learned to live side by side.

Miscegenation, the mixing of peoples from different cultures, had already taken place before the founding of the City of Los Angeles in 1781. It was founded by 44 settlers from Mexico. The adult founders, listed as the following in the 1781 Census, brought along their families, which added 22 others to this list:

1 Peninsular (Spaniard born in Spain)
1 Criollo (Spaniard born in New Spain)
1 Mestizo (mixed Spanish and Indian)
2 Negros (blacks of full African ancestry)
8 Mulattos (mixed Spanish and black)
9 Indios (American Indians)

Historically, we see that marriages between different cultures are a common occurrence when there is a movement of people. However, this was only the beginning of intermarriages in the Southwest. Anglo-Americans came to California and the Gold Rush of 1849 ensued. Thousands of people from around the globe moved to California and the merging of cultures continued.

Charles Darwin's theory of evolution, from where the phrase "survival of the fittest" was coined, has influenced perceptions regarding skin color. Many of European society's elite took the concept a step further and stated they were superior because European cultures had industrialized and accumulated enormous amounts of wealth. Those who had not industrialized and had no wealth were considered inferior; Africa fit the bill. The Europeans considered the Africans inferior and dark skin became associated with inferiority. This is evident today in

American and Mexican societies where lighter skin is preferred by the upper class. However, this notion did not stop miscegenation.

The State of California did try to put a stop to intermarriage in 1880 when it made miscegenation illegal by enacting California Civil Code Section 60, which states:

> "All marriages of white persons with Negroes, Mongolians, and members of the Malay race, or mulattoes are illegal and void."

This was only the beginning of discriminatory legislation. It continued into the 1940s and expanded to include Asians.

A young Mexican American woman was the first to legally confront this racist law. In 1948, Andrea Pérez and Sylvester Davis, an African American, applied for a marriage license in Los Angeles. The County Clerk refused to issue it, citing California Civil Code 60. The County Clerk also cited Section 69:

> "No license may be issued authorizing the marriage of a white person with a Negro, mulatto, Mongolian or member of the Malay race."

The U.S. Census Bureau classifies Mexicans, regardless of the color of their skin, as white. Of course, the classifications by the U.S. Census Bureau is another controversial topic on its own. However, the California State Supreme Court, in *Perez v. Sharp*, overturned California Civil Codes Sections 60 and 69, stating that they were in violation of the Fourteenth Amendment.

Miscegenation today is no longer a legal issue. The issues may be social mobility or peer pressure, though society has become more tolerant. If Latinas stay within their segregated communities, they are more likely to marry someone of a Latino culture. However, there is an increasing number of Latinas entering institutions of higher learning and becoming members of the workforce. Once in these multicultural environments, they meet non-Latino men and marry. Again we see couples from diverse cultures making a commitment realizing they face a variety of issues regarding daily life: foods, celebrations, values, upbringing, and finances, to name a few.

Skin color still influences society today. Many Latinas see marrying an Anglo or a Jew as a step up in society, and marrying an African American or someone of dark skin as a step down. Latinas who get an education and become independent tend to move out of neighborhoods like the Northeast San Fernando Valley, or East L.A. into predominantly Anglo neighborhoods where they raise their families. Many keep their Latino culture alive through foods and celebrations. They are either tolerated or become a part of American society. In essence, many Latinas are desegregating communities that were at one time exclusive.

History shows us that acculturation is inevitable in the Southwest. It shows us that the continual migration of Mexicans ensures that the Latino culture will continue to thrive. It also shows that the love between a man and a woman breaks through economic, cultural, and social barriers. It shows us that miscegenation has been taking place for centuries and will continue to do so.

Should Latinas acculturate? History shows us that you follow your heart.

Should Latinas/os Date Other Races?

Alice Herrera, MA Candidate, California State University, Northridge

Racism and segregation of the different groups and nationalities has and continues to segment society (Wells et al., 2005). Although I am inclined to agree with this poststructuralist assertion, the reality is that the segmentation of society is deeply rooted in the ideologies that have cemented different groups and nationalities. Segregation is evidenced in not only physical separations, but also in language, structure, and ideologies that produce, circulate, and enforce segregation. The initial statement implies that by not segregating the different groups and nationalities, then we move from segmenting society. This seems a basic and easily devisable approach to eliminating segregation, but realistically, the desegregation of society would require a more nuanced undertaking.

In his chapter, "Interracial Dating and Marriage," Rudy Acuña analyzes the history of interracial marriage and dating within the context of the United States, concluding that the younger generations are more open to it. In his analysis, Acuña suggests that degrees of assimilation can be measured in cases of intermarriage. Among Latinas/os specifically, Acuña asserts that dating practices are governed by skin color; dating "lighter" or white would be considered progressive. Acuña aims to highlight that the growing acceptability of interracial marriage and dating indicates ". . . that the barriers to interracial dating and marriage have come tumbling down." In emphasizing this, his analysis implies a positive trajectory in society.

Although this may be the case among the younger generations (at Acuña's suggestion), Acuña fails to address the historical reality of mate preference in relation to beauty ideals, socioeconomic status, and racism. Acuña does acknowledge the European construction of darkness as inferior, but does not thoroughly deconstruct the internalized racism that factors into why we are inclined to lighter partners. Writing on this topic requires an analysis of dating preferences in order to make evident how engrained racism is in us.

Acuña suggests class as a factor in the probability of interracial marriage. He argues that because of highly segregated schools, Latinas/os are limited in interracial contacts. Throughout the chapter, interracial dating refers to interactions between brown and white. Yes, dating between brown and black, brown and Asian, and so on, are less common, but still worth discussing further, especially since, as Acuña states, "Dating was considered a prelude to marriage, so [Latina/o] parents frowned upon dating outside the culture or race." Considering dating black as taboo, interracial dating often consisted of Latinas/os living in Anglo neighborhoods. Referring to the "mixing" of black and brown as taboo indicates black and brown tensions that beg discussion.

Further, according to Kevin R. Johnson, Latinas/os of mixed background often feel pressured to acclimate to either their Anglo or Latina/o backgrounds. Their ambiguous identities often make them prone to experiencing microaggressions and contestations of identity. This reality makes further discussion of race conflicts even more necessary as identity tension is riddled with historical tensions between races. Additionally, Acuña states, "A biracial or multiracial child is not either/or . . . it doesn't matter what you call yourself; it is how society perceives you." With this last point, desegregation would not necessarily diminish the desegregation of society. Rather, children produced by interracial marriage would still be separated and treated differently according to how they are perceived until further "mixing" diminishes any nonwhite characteristics.

Class is also indicated as a factor in the likelihood of interracial marriage. Acuña claims that ". . . much of interracial dating is limited to the middle class," a predominantly white population. He also finds a strong relationship among Latinas/os in terms of economic success, education, and interracial marriage. The more educated and financially successful someone is, the more likely they are to marry out. What is not articulated is that those who access higher education are doing so in predominantly white spaces, which further begs the question of assimilation. More importantly, simply stating a correlation between middle-class Latinas/os and interracial dating/marriage in terms of education requires a discussion of the pipeline and how working-class people of color are diverged from higher education.

Acuña defines culture as "... a way of life: our belief systems, traditions, customs, and heritage." Culture is dynamic and "'American culture is a blending of the ethnic groups within specific regions.'" Although increasing rates of interracial mixing is becoming more acceptable among the younger generations, it is still an indicator of the politics and ideologies that drive American culture. How then are these politics and ideologies that determine American culture (re)produced?

Overall, there's an underlying message in this chapter that intermarriage is an indicator of social improvement. Acuña asserts, "... [interracial marriage] improves the cultures because males are forced to compete and treat women better." If this is true, then why does domestic violence still consistently occur? It would be great if a true desegregation of society were possible just through the process of interracial marriage and dating. However, racism runs deep. Therefore, in order for desegregation to be truly plausible, a more nuanced critique and reflection about American culture would need to take place. Conclusively, interracial marriage and dating is a topic of discussion that requires far more inquiry.

NOTES

1. "The intermarriage rate, a bellwether statistic, has reached a high of 58 percent for all Jews, and 71 percent for non-Orthodox Jews—a huge change from before 1970 when only 17 percent of Jews married outside the faith. Two-thirds of Jews do not belong to a synagogue, one-fourth do not believe in God and one-third had a Christmas tree in their home last year" (Goodstein, 2012). Jewish identity has shifted from 93 percent from 1914 to 1927 to 78 percent from 1980 to 2013.

2. "Fifty-seven percent of teenagers who have been on dates have dated outside their race. Sixty percent of African American teenagers who date, 47 percent of whites who date and 90 percent of Hispanic teenagers who date have dated someone from another race" (Wang, 2015). Given the degree of segregation in places like Los Angeles, especially among Mexicans and Central Americans, these figures could be open to discussion.

3. Various authors argue that black America is becoming increasingly divided along class lines. The same thesis can be pursued with U.S. Latinos. Therefore, distinctions on where a U.S. Latino lives is important. Just like not all blacks are alike, neither are all Latinos.

4. Most of the articles take a black–white point of reference. This academic or scholarly article makes distinctions in the way scholars count ethnic groups other than blacks.

5. As early as 1910, interethnic marriage was relatively common among whites, but marriage across racial lines was extremely rare due in part to antimiscegenation laws forbidding marriage between persons of different races. This legal barrier was not abolished nationwide until 1967. Since then, interracial marriages have increased

dramatically, from 310,000 in 1970 to 651,000 in 1980 to 1,161,000 in 1992 (Suro and Passel, 2003). These marriages have increased from 0.7 percent of all marriages in 1970 to 2.2 percent in 1992. Roberto Suro and Jeffrey S. Passel, "The Rise of the Second Generation: Changing Patterns in Hispanic Population Growth." Pew Hispanic Center, October 14, 2003. http://www.pewhispanic.org/files/reports/22.pdf

BIBLIOGRAPHY

Acuña, Rodolfo F. "Latino Question." Rough draft, July 30, 2007. Arana, Gabriel. "Why Latinos won't become white: Assuming Latinos will join the white majority ignores the stark divisions in a racially diverse group." *Aljazeera America*, October 22, 2014. http://america.aljazeera.com/opinions/2014/10/why-latinos-won-tbecomewhiteraceethnicitygop.html

Bodnar, Susan. "Opinion: When being white doesn't help." *CNN*, February 4, 2012. http://inamerica.blogs.cnn.com/2012/02/04/opinion-when-being-white-doesnt-help

Bogira Steve. "Separate, Unequal, and Ignored: Racial segregation remains Chicago's most fundamental problem. Why isn't it an issue in the mayor's race?" *Chicago Reader*, February 10, 2011. http://www.chicagoreader.com/chicago/chicago-politics-segregation-african-american-black-white-hispanic-latino-population-census-community/Content?oid=3221712

Bowman, Karlyn. "Polls Shed Light on Future of Race Relations." American Enterprise Institute, Roll Call, July 9, 2003. http://www.aei.org/publication/polls-shed-light-on-future-of-race-relations/

Bowman, Karlyn. "Pollsters Examine Race Relations in the Nation." American Enterprise Institute, Roll Call, March 30, 2000. https://www.aei.org/publication/pollsters-examine-race-relations-in-the-nation/

"California civil code, section 60-1933 revision all." Course Hero, UCSB. https://www.coursehero.com/file/p1vejaq/California-Civil-Code-Section-60-1933-Revision-All-marriages-of-white-persons-w

Carrigan, William D., and Clive Webb. *Forgotten Dead: Mob Violence against Mexicans in the United States, 1848–1928*. Oxford: Oxford University Press, 2013.

Carrigan, William D., and Clive Webb. "The Lynching of Persons of Mexican Origin." *Journal of Social History* 37, no. 2 (Winter 2003): 411–438.

Chang, Sharon H. "Why Mixed with White Isn't White." *Hyphen: Asia America Unbridged* (blog). July 22, 2014. http://hyphenmagazine.com/blog/2014/7/22/why-mixed-white-isnt-white

The Civil Rights Project. "California The Most Segregated State for Latino Students." University of California at Los Angeles, May 14, 2014. https://civilrightsproject.ucla.edu/news/press-releases/2014-press-releases/ucla-report-finds-california-the-most-segregated-state-for-latino-students

Dodge, Robert V. *Andrea and Sylvester: Challenging Marriage Taboos and the Road to a Same-Sex Marriage*. New York: Algora Publishing, 2015.

Edmonston, Barry, and Sharon M. Lee. "Hispanic Intermarriage, Identification, and U.S. Latino Population Change." *Social Science Quarterly* 87, no. 1 (2006): 1263–1279.

Eschbach, Jenifer J. L. "'What About the Couple?' Interracial Marriage and Psychological Distress." *Social Science Research* 35, issue 4 (2006): 1025–1047.

Fears, Darryl, and Claudia Deane. "Biracial couples report greater tolerance. U.S. survey finds acceptance weakest among whites." *PG News*, July 8, 2002. http://old.post-gazette.com/headlines/20010708biracialnat2p2.asp

"Findings from University of Oregon Provides New Data About Social Science (The Whitening Hypothesis Challenged: Biculturalism in Latino and Non-Hispanic White Intermarriage)." *Sciences Letter*, 2014.

Fu, Vincent Kang, and Nicholas H. Wolfinger, "Broken Boundaries or Broken Marriages? Racial Intermarriage and Divorce in the United States." *Social Science Quarterly* 92, no. 4 (2011): 1096–1117.

Gándara, Patricia. "Fulfilling America's Future: Latinas in the U.S., 2015." White House Initiative on Educational Excellence for Hispanics. http://sites.ed.gov/hispanic-initiative/files/2015/09/Fulfilling-Americas-Future-Latinas-in-the-U.S.-2015-Final-Report.pdf

Gazzar, Brenda. "California's Latino students among the most segregated in the country, says UCLA report." *Los Angeles Daily News*, May 22, 2014. http://www.dailynews.com/social-affairs/20140522/californias-latino-students-among-the-most-segregated-in-the-country-says-ucla-report

Goodstein, Laurie. "Poll Shows Major Shift in Identity of U.S. Jews." *New York Times*, October 1, 2012. http://www.nytimes.com/2013/10/01/us/poll-shows-major-shift-in-identity-of-us-jews.html?_r=0.

Gurak, Douglas T., and Joseph P. Fitzpatrick. "Intermarriage Among Hispanic Ethnic Groups in New York City." *American Journal of Sociology* 87, no. 4 (January 1982): 921–934.

Harper, Casandra E., and Fanny P. Yeung. "College Student Characteristics and Experiences as Predictors of Interracial Dating." *College Student Journal* 49, no. 4 (2015): 599.

Hwang, Sean-Shong, Kevin M. Fitzpatrick, and David Helms. "Class Differences in Racial Attitudes: A Divided Black America?" *Sociological Perspectives* 41, no. 2 (1998).

Johnson, Kevin R. " 'Melting Pot' or 'Ring of Fire'? Assimilation and the Mexican American Experience." *LatCrit: Latinas/os and the Law: A Joint Symposium by California Law Review and La Raza Law Journal. California Law Review* 85, no. 5 (1997): 1259–1313.

Karthikeyan, Hrishi, and Gabriel J. Chin. "Preserving Racial Identity: Population Patterns and the Application of Anti-Miscegenation Statutes to Asian Americans, 1910–1950." *Asian Law Journal* 9 (2002).

Krupnick, Ellie. "Interracial Dating Is Fundamentally Changing America." Identities.Mic, November 20, 2014. http://mic.com/articles/104558/interracial-dating-is-making-america-more-beautiful-here-s-how#.i16oOQ9RO

Lake, Frank. "Hispanics are now Officially—'White.' " *Weekly World News*, October 1, 2011. http://weeklyworldnews.com/headlines/38964/hispanics-are-now-officially-white

Lee, Sharon M., and Barry Edmonston. "Hispanic Intermarriage, Identification, and U.S. Latino Population Change." *Social Science Quarterly* 87, no. 5 (2006): 1263–1279.

LeMay, Michael C., and Elliott Robert Barkan, eds,, *U.S. Immigration and Naturalization Laws and Issues: A Documentary History*. Westport, CT: Greenwood Press, 1999.

López, Mark Hugo, and Richard Fry. "Among recent high school grads, Hispanic college enrollment rate surpasses that of whites." Pew Research Center,

September 4, 2013. http://www.pewresearch.org/fact-tank/2013/09/04/hispanic-college-enrollment-rate-surpasses-whites-for-the-first-time

López, Mark Hugo, and Ana González-Barrera. "Women's college enrollment gains leave men behind." *Fact Tank—News in the Numbers*, Pew Research Center, March 6, 2014. http://www.pewresearch.org/fact-tank/2014/03/06/womens-college-enrollment-gains-leave-men-behind/

Mentzer, Marc S. "Minority Representation in Higher Education: The Impact of Population Heterogeneity." *Journal of Higher Education* 64, no. 4 (1993).

Miyawaki, Michael Hajime. *The racial identity of the offspring of Latino intermarriage: A case of racial identity and census categories*. New York: Fordham University, 2013

Morales, Erica. "Parental Messages Concerning Latino/Black Interracial Dating: An Exploratory Study Among Latina/o Young Adults." *Latino Studies* 10, no. 3 (2012): 314

O'Brien, Matt. "Couples look back on when interracial love defied laws." *Contra Costa Times*, May 17, 2009. http://www.eastbaytimes.com/news/ci_12391215

Orfield, Gary, and Jongyeon Ee, "Segregating California's Future: Inequality and Its Alternative 60 Years after *Brown v. Board of Education*." Civil Rights Project, May 2014.

Panzar, Javier. "It's official: Latinos now outnumber whites in California." *Los Angeles Times*, July 8, 2015. http://www.latimes.com/local/california/la-me-census-latinos-20150708-story.html

Pascoe, Peggy. *What Comes Naturally: Miscegenation Law and the Making of Race in America*. New York: Oxford University Press, 2009.

Saenz, Victor. "The Vanishing Latino Male in Higher Education." *Young Latino Males: An American Dilemma*. 2010. http://cronkitezine.asu.edu/latinomales/highered.html

Sánchez, Erika L. "Latina women chipping away at the stigma of interracial marriages." *NBC Latino*, September 13, 2012. http://nbclatino.com/2012/09/13/latina-women-chipping-away-the-stigma-of-interracial-marriages

Sándoval, Tomás. "The Burden Of History and John Sayles' Lone Star: We should remember that history is not a prison. Even the truths of the past can be overcome by creating in the present a new and future-oriented reality." *Bad Subjects*, Issue 28, October 1996. http://bad.eserver.org/issues/1996/28/sandoval.html

Stevens, Gillian, Mary E. M. McKillip, and Hiromi Ishizawa. "Intermarriage in the Second Generation: Choosing Between Newcomers and Natives." *Migration Information Source*, October 1, 2006. http://www.migrationpolicy.org/article/intermarriage-second-generation-choosing-between-newcomers-and-natives

Suro, Roberto. "Mixed doubles. Interethnic marriages and marketing strategy, statistical data included." *American Demographics* 21 (November 1999): 56–62.

Suro, Roberto, and Jeffrey S, Passel. "The Rise of the Second Generation: Changing Patterns in Hispanic Population Growth." Pew Hispanic Center, October 14, 2003. http://www.pewhispanic.org/files/reports/22.pdf

Tyson, Ann Scott. "Young Love Bridges Race Divide: It's A Date." *Christian Science Monitor*, December 3, 1997. http://www.csmonitor.com/1997/1203/120397.us.us.4.html

Vasquez, Jessica M. "The Whitening Hypothesis Challenged: Biculturalism in Latino and Non-Hispanic White Intermarriage." *Sociological Forum* 29, Issue 2 (June 2014): 386–407.

Wang, Wendy. "The Rise of Intermarriage." Pew Research Center, February 16, 2012. http://www.pewsocialtrends.org/2012/02/16/the-rise-of-intermarriage

Wang, Wendy, "Interracial marriage: Who is 'marrying out'?" *Fact Tank—News in the Numbers*, Pew Research Center, June 12, 2015. http://www.pewresearch.org/fact-tank/2015/06/12/interracial-marriage-who-is-marrying-out/

Watanabe, Teresa. "Gap in Census Leaves Need for Religious Data." *Los Angeles Times*, April 27, 2000. http://articles.latimes.com/2000/apr/17/news/mn-20490

Wells, Amy Stuart, Jennifer Jellison Holme, Anita Tijerina Revilla, and Awo Korantemaa Atanda. "How Desegregation Changed Us: The Effects of Racially Mixed Schools on Students and Society." A Study of Desegregated High Schools and Their Class of 1980, Graduates Teachers College, Columbia University, University of California at Los Angeles, 2004. http://cms.tc.columbia.edu/i/a/782_ASWells041504.pdf

"What do Hispanic women think of White women with Hispanic men?" Prisontalk.com. Forum. http://www.prisontalk.com/forums/showthread.php?t=394999

Woller, Megan B. "A place for West Side Story (1961): Gender, race, and tragedy in Hollywood's adaptation." Master's thesis. Urbana: University of Illinois at Urbana-Champaign, 2010. https://www.ideals.illinois.edu/handle/2142/18412

SELECTED VIDEOS

CCR MOM. "Mom, I am dating a Mexican," YouTube video, 2:50, posted May 14, 2013. https://www.youtube.com/watch?v=x1jdQWXBn10

Chindian Diaries. "Is It Better To Be Mixed Race?" YouTube video, 47:28, posted November 27, 2014. https://www.youtube.com/watch?v=lZZAckwJHsQ

Divorce Court. "Machismo Hurts This Relationship," YouTube video, 2:27, posted November 11, 2015. https://www.youtube.com/watch?v=BgvrAmRUaOw

Jews for Judaism. "INTERMARRIAGE—Why Marry Jewish?" YouTube video, 1:00:25, posted March 21, 2012. https://www.youtube.com/watch?v=AHxKvxqs9qs

Kiggers, Roger. "Interracial Dating In America!!" YouTube video, 1:11:04, posted February 11, 2014. https://www.youtube.com/watch?v=Ld3AUZ_bTyI

Martínez, Ana. "Latina's & Higher Education," YouTube video, 4:14, posted December 5, 2013. https://www.youtube.com/watch?v=QAwBAK4g0-M

NeverStopAmando. "G&C Video 1: Black Latino Multiracial Interracial Mixed Couple/Dating/Marriage . . . YEP !" YouTube video, 14:24, posted April 15, 2012. https://www.youtube.com/watch?v=Np0WVDqwrJQ

New York Times. "U.S.: Mixed Marriages in the South," YouTube video, 5:55, posted March 28, 2011. https://www.youtube.com/watch?v=uKkpEcrwV94

Oakland Latinosunited. "Interracial dating in the latino/a community," YouTube video, 9:08, posted September 15, 2008. https://www.youtube.com/watch?v=yxL9QbPjpKQ

Reed, Frances. "Generational Diversity 101," YouTube video, 5:15, posted October 1, 2012. https://www.youtube.com/watch?v=5iCg8h_9Lq8

ScalesNBalances2. "More Proof: Latinos & Mexicans Are 'White,'" YouTube video, 5:02, posted April 20, 2013. https://www.youtube.com/watch?v=tj0K65xL4UA

8

Latina/o Health Issues: Education and Health Care Are Basic Human Rights Issues

BACKGROUND

Education and health care are basic human rights that most modern nations take for granted. However, in the United States there is a debate as to whether this country can or should pay for healthcare services of unauthorized workers and their families or for the education of their children. Driving this debate are shifts in the costs of health care and education from corporate America to the middle class. A rationalization for this concern is the downturn of the economy in the 1980s and early 1990s, which is the product of the privatization and financial manipulation of the U.S. economy. A discussion of the issue is complicated by the rising cost of health care, especially the cost of hospitalization.

United States health care policies thus subvert the nation's goal of a healthy society. The medical establishment and the pharmaceutical industry have rejected solutions such as universal health—labeling them "socialistic" (Mier, 2002). In recent years, immigrants have disproportionately been underserved by free clinics. The reality is that American medicine is privatized and a cash cow for Health Maintenance Organizations (HMOs) and hospitals. Simultaneously, xenophobes have pressured the system to limit care to immigrants. Immigrant women have been especially impacted by the war against agencies such as Planned Parenthood. A report by Planned Parenthood states, "Because many immigrant women are unable [in many states] to access private or public health insurance coverage, they are less likely to access preventive health care, such as Pap tests, STD screenings, and birth control than U.S. women" ("Immigration Reform"). It goes on, "Asian and Pacific Islander immigrant women have high rates of cervical cancer, and more than half of all pregnancies among Latina women are unintended" ("Immigration Reform").

Does business have the duty to pay for the costs of social production that profit it? What is the privatization of health care?

Harry S. Truman was the first president to propose a prepaid health insurance plan to Congress. In November 1945, Truman suggested a comprehensive, prepaid medical insurance plan for all people through the Social Security system. Congress turned down the proposal. In the early 1960s, a national survey showed that only 56 percent of those 65 years of age or older had health insurance, which prompted President John F. Kennedy to push for health insurance for the aged. In 1965, President Lyndon B. Johnson signed a bill to provide health insurance for the elderly and the poor, establishing both Medicare and Medicaid. Medicare was placed under the Social Security Administration (SSA), and Medicaid assisted state Medicaid programs. Over the years, Congress has narrowed the eligibility of health insurance recipients largely to Social Security beneficiaries. As union jobs have dwindled, so has the opposition to low-cost medical care.

Germany has had a form of universal health care since the late 1800s. Why do you believe that the United States has a similar program?

Enter the HMOs

During the late 1980s, Congress advertised HMOs as a solution to the health care dilemma. It was modeled after Henry Kaiser's World War II program that was started to keep the shipyard workers healthy. The basic objective was to have employers or workers pay for these low-cost health plans. However, over the years the costs of insurance skyrocketed, and employers refused to pay for the cost of social production, leaving many people without health care. This problem was especially acute among the working poor.

HMOs were hyped as a solution to health care costs and the problem of health delivery. It pretended to give quality health care while keeping the costs down. However, medical expenses climbed steadily, and by 2014 approach $8,000 per person annually. Individuals also had to pay deductibles, copayments and coinsurance costs. The costs of medication constantly rose, as have the costs of items such as prescription glasses. Treatment is driven by the profit motive rather than by quality care. This is most evident in psychiatric care, physical therapy, and emergency services. Cost-cutting strategies such as early hospital discharge and control of referrals are regularly used. It is often difficult to get referrals to specialists and the quality of the HMOs varies.

Germany is also challenged by rising health care costs, which are 10.4 percent of the country's gross domestic product (GDP). However, Germany has acted more proactively in reigning in costs. Like the United States, Germany does not rely on single payers. Incentives are used to limit drug expenditures. In the United States, however, health care is much more political and the medical establishment has considerable clout. "Germany's public insurance is largely financed by a 14.9% payroll tax, 7.9% of which is paid by the employees. Germany sets reimbursement rates for hospitals and drug companies; patients pay the difference between drug prices and reimbursement rates. General Practitioners earn about half their counterparts in the U.S. Not all German doctors accept the low public reimbursement" (Haupt, 2009). As a consequence, German per capita spending on health insurance has risen to $191 annually versus $516 for Americans. United States doctors and many Americans rationalize the cost, saying "the cost may be unfortunate but the U.S. has 'the best health care in the world'" (Kane, 2012), a statement that is disputed. In the United States:

- There are fewer physicians per person than in most other OECD countries. In 2010, for instance, the United States had

2.4 practicing physicians per 1,000 people—well below the OECD average of 3.1.

- The number of hospital beds in the United States was 2.6 per 1,000 population in 2009, lower than the OECD average of 3.4 beds.
- Life expectancy at birth increased by almost nine years between 1960 and 2010, but that's less than the increase of over 15 years in Japan and over 11 years on average in OECD countries. The average American now lives 78.7 years in 2010, more than one year below the average of 79.8 years. (Kane, 2012)

By 2015, not much had changed since the Affordable Care Act was passed five years before. Even under the reforms of The Patient Protection and Affordable Care Act signed by President Barack Obama, which was designed to make health insurance more affordable for low-income Americans, the undocumented residents "did not have access to taxpayer-funded subsidies or credits to buy health insurance through exchanges" ("Are Illegal Immigrants Covered Under Obamacare?", 2014). According to an international survey, "The U.S. spends more money on health care compared with other industrialized countries, but Americans still get the least bang for their buck . . . according to . . . the Commonwealth Fund . . . access to health care services among 11 industrialized countries: Australia, Canada, France, Germany, the Netherlands, New Zealand, Norway, Sweden, Switzerland, the U.K. and the U.S.," the United States ranked the lowest (Firger, 2014). The prestigious *New England Journal of Medicine* wrote, "evidence that other countries perform better than the United States in ensuring the health of their populations is a sure prod to the reformist impulse. The World Health Report 2000, "Health Systems: Improving Performance," ranked the U.S. health care system 37th in the world—a result that has been discussed frequently during the current debate on U.S. health care reform." The Journal concluded that the high cost of health care cost thousands of lives (Murray and Frenk, 2010).

It is assumed that the United States has the best health care in the world; does it?

Out of an estimated 11.1 million undocumented immigrants residing in the United States as of 2011, some 81 percent were born in Latin America. The number of undocumented Latina/os was estimated at

9 million. Many noninsured students included children attending schools.

Unfortunately, Americans do not share the communitarian viewpoint of Europeans toward health insurance and other social services. Instead of talking about the duty of business to pay for the cost of social production, such as in the case of Germany, Americans joined in scapegoating immigrants. As more Americans became obsessed with the growing Latina/o population, the health care issue became embroiled with the question of undocumented workers. Nativist groups became more vocal and scapegoated the immigrant for the health crisis instead of the system. This rhetoric is driven by organizations such as the Federation of American Immigration Reform (FAIR), which blames Mexican and Central American immigrants. According to FAIR, these uninsured immigrants are a severe risk to the health and well being of people on both sides of the border. These organizations spent millions of dollars scapegoating the immigrant.

Are immigrants scapegoated for the lack of access and quality of the U.S. health system? What was to be done when those children became ill?

Human rights activists argue that all workers and all families have the right to good health care. They point out that the goal is to have healthy, productive, democratic citizens. According to the Immigration Policy Center, undocumented immigrants paid a combined $11.2 billion in state and local taxes in 2010. Undocumented immigrants pay income taxes as well, as evidenced by the Social Security Administration's "suspense file" (taxes that cannot be matched to workers' names and Social Security numbers), which grew by $20 billion between 1990 and 1998. It added that "Alan Greenspan pointed out, 70% of immigrants arrive in prime working age. That means we haven't spent a penny on their education, yet they are transplanted into our workforce and will contribute $500 billion toward our Social Security system over the next 20 years" (Anchondo, 2015). Undocumented workers are part of the working poor who cannot afford health insurance and receive public health-care assistance because the cost of health care is too high; business has the duty to pay for this cost of social production. Thus, the issue is not that the workers are undocumented, but that the cost of health insurance is too high, the workers receive low wages, and business does not want to pay taxes (Mukherjee, 2013).

Is health care a human right? Would you want to live or go to school and sit next to someone who does not have medical care? How do the American and European solutions differ?

Health-care services and schooling for undocumented immigrants set the context for California Proposition 187 (1994); the so-called Save our State initiative in November of 1994, denying publicly funded social services to undocumented California residents. Governor Wilson proposed to deny citizenship status and public education to the children of undocumented immigrants. Moreover, Proposition 187 was successfully pitched by the media as saving the state from illegal immigrants who were foreign invaders of the state (Mukherjee, 2013).

Whether for or against Proposition 187, was it correct for the media to pitch it as saving the state from illegal immigrants who were foreign invaders of the state?

The scapegoating of the undocumented has detracted from what the needs are. According to University of California Los Angeles Health sociologist David Hayes-Bautista, part of the solution is that academics should stop looking at Latinas/os as problems. "Hayes-Bautista began thumbing through fresh data from the Los Angeles County Health Department, and something caught his eye: Latinos had fewer heart attacks, less cancer, fewer strokes and a lower infant mortality rate than the overall population of L.A. County." Hayes-Bautista challenged the negative research and negative stereotypes of Latinas/os that ignored their strong family ties, strong work ethic, and good health (Cárdenas, 1999; Gutiérrez, 2008). The sociologist's research has inspired other scholars. For instance, in a coauthored article, Hayes-Bautista and others challenged whether acculturation is good for the Mexican American and other Latinas/os' health. The authors point out that the criteria are often faulty. "First, important indicators of population health vary among Latinos of Mexican, Puerto Rican, Cuban, and other Latino origin and others. For instance, mortality and prevalence rates of chronic illness vary among both Latino children and adults of these different subgroups. Second, wide ranges of factors have been explored to explain this heterogeneity. Factors such as socioeconomic status, educational level, and age, as well as language fluency and immigration status should be studied" (Brown, 2015). The authors hypothesized that "there was a possible relationship between acculturation and selected health and behavioral outcomes among U.S. Latinos" (Lara, Gamboa, Kahramanian, Morales, and Hayes-Bautista, 2005).

In Dr. Hayes-Bautista's view, is acculturation good or bad? Why?

Researchers are now looking at cultural elements in the dominant society such as language, food choice, dress, music, and sports that may be dangerous to the immigrants' health. The human capital brought by the immigrant is often ignored and forgotten. Some sociologists believe that acculturation negatively affects health behaviors overall, influencing substance abuse, diet, and birth outcomes (low birthweights and prematurity) of Latinas/os living in the United States.

Why are variables such as language, music, and exposure to the media important to take into account?

Most studies on the impact of acculturation on Latinas/os have been done on Mexicans (Lara et al., p. 377). However, it is important to compare Latinas/os, for instance, in comparing acculturation and its effects on Mexicans and Puerto Ricans, the UCLA team found a higher risk of childhood asthma and related factors among Mexicans and Puerto Ricans according to place of birth. Puerto Ricans born on the island who are thought to be less acculturated have a higher prevalence of asthma than do those born in the United States and the District of Columbia. Less acculturated (foreign-born) Mexican American children had a lower prevalence of asthma and related risk factors than did their more acculturated U.S.-born counterparts. More study has to be done on the outcomes of acculturation and the development of a culturally competent health care system.

What were the differences between Mexicans and Puerto Ricans and why are they important? What other variables could be taken into account?

Diabetes is an epidemic among the 55 million Latinas/os in the United States. However, it is an error to generalize the problem, since diabetes affects each Latina/o group differently (Alexandria, 2014).

Even within Latino groups there are inequities to access to and the quality of health care that are determined by economic status, which gives individuals fewer opportunities. In this regard, "to make healthy choices where people live, learn, work and play all contribute to the rates of obesity being higher for Latino adults and children compared to Whites" (Ogden, 2014). In general, however, 42 percent of Latina/o adults are obese compared with 32.6 percent of whites. Close to three-quarters of Latina/o adults are overweight or obese compared with 67.2 percent of whites; 22.4 percent of Latino children, from 2 to 19 years of age, are obese compared with 14.3 percent of white children. More than 38.9 percent of Latino children are overweight or obese compared with 28.5 percent of white children. Diabetes requires intensive health care and medications. This was accompanied by a rise in type 2 diabetes in old age (Obesity Prevention in Latino Communities, 2014).

In treating diabetes, why is it important to know what nation-origin group the patient is from? Why is having insurance important?

Obesity is associated with starchy and fast foods—the poor people's foods. Obesity continues into the second generation. According to the American Heart Association, "The first large-scale data on body mass index (BMI) and cardiovascular disease risk factors among U.S. Hispanic/Latino adult populations suggests that severe obesity may be associated with considerable excess risk for cardiovascular diseases" (American Heart Association, 2014). Research on 16,344 people of diverse Latina/o origins (from the Bronx, Chicago, Miami, and San Diego, with men averaging 40 years of age and women 41 years of age; Mexicans comprised 37 percent of subjects, Cubans 20 percent, and Puerto Ricans 16 percent) found that 8 percent of women and 12 percent of men had high levels of obesity. This finding also indicated that they had high cholesterol levels as well as high blood pressure ("Young Hispanics," 2014).

Why is diet important in controlling obesity? Are fast foods good for one's health?

Health specialists also found that Latinas/os are at higher risk of kidney failure. "According to the United States Renal Data System (USRDS), in 2005, there were 12,000 new cases of ESRD [End Stage Renal Disease] treated with dialysis or transplant in Hispanics, representing an increase of 63% since 1996. Hispanics have an incidence rate of ESRD which is 1.5 times greater than for non-Hispanics Whites." Compared to other Latina/o groups, Mexican Americans have a higher incidence of "serum cystatin C, a potentially more sensitive marker of early kidney dysfunction compared with other racial/ethnic groups studied" (Lora et al., 2009).

Associated with liver disease is heavy consumption of alcohol. According to a study by the National Institute on Alcohol Abuse and Alcoholism, statistics showed that 10.4 percent of Mexicans needed treatment for alcohol abuse; 10.1 percent of Puerto Ricans, 8.2 percent of South/Central America, and 9.1 percent of Cubans. "Among Hispanics who drink, Mexican American men and women and South/Central American men are most likely to receive a citation for driving under the influence of alcohol. Research shows that between 1992 and 2002, there was a decrease in the number of Hispanic men (ages 18–29) who received a DUI, but an increase in the number of Hispanic women (ages 18–29) who received this citation." The study concludes, "Limited research shows that treatment can help Hispanics who speak English and who are highly acculturated to American life. Nevertheless, Hispanics with severe alcohol problems are less likely than non-Hispanic Whites to seek the treatment they need. Hispanics also are less likely to join Alcoholics Anonymous (AA), even though AA groups are available for free and in Spanish" (National Institute of Health, 2015).

Why is it important to know the specific Latina/o culture in the treatment of alcoholism? Does economic class play a role?

This brief survey is not conclusive of the health issues of Latinas/os, many of which are associated with a particular group's economic circumstances. These diseases, in addition to mental health counseling, take time and professional intervention. Latinas/os are less apt to get quality care. Not all caregivers are the same. This also applies to other health issues such as drug abuse, pregnancies, anger management, and depression. The availability of these services depends on location.

When people do not have sufficient access to medical care, they will turn to folk remedies that have been shaped by their cultural background. Specific causes, preventions, and cures are based on theories of illness often handed down through family sources and cultural funds of knowledge. They often vary significantly from the diagnoses and treatments of modern medicine. Increasingly, Latinas/os, for instance, are receptive to acupuncture. Historically, traditional healers have existed in most cultures; they are—people who recognize, interpret, and treat illnesses using folk therapies and local plants. They are called *curanderas*; midwives are common among those who do not have the means to go to the so-called doctor. They are not too far removed from priests' confessionals, which functioned as a sort of psychological counseling.

What are curanderas? Have you ever encountered one? What is their psychological value? What is their medicinal value?

Folk remedies depend on factors such as ethnicity, national origin, region, and levels of acculturation. Among the common afflictions treated by folk healers is *empacho* (upset stomach), *susto* (fright sickness), *mal de ojo* (evil eye), and *mollera caida* ("pulling a baby away from the breast or bottle too quickly, having the baby fall to the ground or carrying the baby incorrectly" (Carteret, 2010). However, this care should not be trivialized such as when infants get colic. Not unlike modern medicine, the cure often comes via psychological comfort and often depends on the empowerment of the individual. As Erin Kennedy puts it, "In Mexican American communities, health care reaches beyond curing an illness and treating a patient. Mexican folk medicine dates back to the ancient Aztecs and is rooted within the Mexican culture as treatment practices are passed down through generations. Whereas Western medicine is primarily scientifically based and focuses on directly pinpointing a disease then treating it, Mexican folk medicine practices attempt to return the mind, body and spirit to balance when an illness arises" (Carteret, 2010).

It should also be remembered that, "Folk medicine has existed for as long as human beings have existed. In an effort to cope with an environment that was often dangerous, humans, and their ancestors, began to develop ways of lessening pain and treating physical and mental problems" ("Folk Medicine"). It is much older than modern medicine and has incorporated knowledge gained from thousands of years of practice—trial and error. Chinese folk medicine was derived from these practices and included acupuncture, which had a hard time being accepted by Western European practitioners. "These home healing practices are handed down by word of mouth and are used to treat a variety of illnesses, including anxiety and depression, coughs and colds, burns and sunburns, bladder and kidney infections, bedwetting, bites and stings, asthma, arthritis, birthing problems, bleeding, diarrhea, fever, infertility, insomnia, skin problems, and mouth and gum disorders." Folk medicine is part of every world culture (Huff, 2002).

Mesoamericans as well as other ancient civilizations' peoples developed advanced agriculture based on major crops, now distributed worldwide (i.e., maize, beans, squashes, peppers, etc.). They also paid attention to other little-known crops that they cultivated or gathered from their surroundings, which could be used for medicines.

Is medical care a human right? How does it protect the community?

MENTAL HEALTH AND LATINA/O HEALTH CARE

Anxiety and suicide are affected by the quality of mental health care because both can be ameliorated and, in the case of suicide, prevented with proper intervention. Studies show that Latina/o adolescents have an elevated risk for depression and suicide compared to other ethnic groups. They suggest that it may be necessary to develop hybrid approaches to reduce depression/suicide disparities for Latino youth such as educating community stakeholders. As in other population groups, the risk factor for suicide attempts is highest among lesbian, gay, and bisexual (LGB) ethnic minority youths. Race increases the risk factor for suicide attempts relative to white LGB youths. When studying suicide, it is dangerous to assume that suicides are drug related. Sexual relationships also greatly depend on their acceptance within the family and the anxiety of coming out.

Being a sexual minority in itself causes stress and may have negative consequences. The literature on sexuality tends to focus on individuals whose self-identifications reflect sexual minority categories such as gayness or bisexuality. The intersections with ethnicity and race are yet to be fully explored. The expectation of Latino masculinity causes considerable stress. Anxiety and suicide often follow.

Suicide is the 12th leading cause of death for Latinas/os of all ages. It is the third leading cause for males ages 15 to 24, placing them at a greater risk of suicide than other ethnic groups. It is understood that the research is limited and lacks specificity. Social scientists recommend that in doing research on Latinas/os, investigators move the focus away from generic labels such as Hispanic or Latino and be more group-specific—Mexican Americans, Puerto Ricans, and so on. There are genetic differences between the groups.

Moreover, more research is needed on the workplace environments. For example, farmworkers show that "one in four migrant farmworkers experienced an episode of one or more mental health disorders such as stress, depression, or anxiety in their lifetime" (Winkelman, Chaney, and Bethel, 2013). Anxiety is related to physical stress, which is related to working conditions. Moreover, low-wage workers experience mental stress related to family situations, work environment, immigration status, and lack of resources. They also experience depression because of their separation from family and their lack of resources. A lack of mental health services and the stigma of mental illness all contribute to anxiety.

ANXIETY IS TREATABLE, SUICIDE PREVENTABLE

Just as there are differences among Latina/o groups, there are also gender differences. Women are more concerned with health and medicine. In a survey, 52 percent of women said health and medicine are among the top three topics of interest to them compared to 22 percent of men (Kennedy and Funk, 2015). This interest cuts across generations and carries over to genetically modified foods (GMOs). In general, Latinas/os are more conscious of the safety of GMOs, with 65 percent considering them unsafe versus 32 percent generally safe. This perception contrasts to the opinion of 53 percent of whites who see them as unsafe to 41 percent who consider them generally safe. This difference can partially be explained through the culture where Latinas plant geraniums and other plants in coffee cans and observe the cycles of plants. They appear to have an openness to childhood vaccinations that is slightly higher than other groups. On climate change, 44 percent of whites believe that it is caused by human activity versus a 70 percent belief in human activity as its cause to 19 percent for Latinas/os (Rainie and Funk, 2015).

As a group, Latinas/os, although less educated than whites (by middle-class white standards), are more open to medicine and science. Overall they are a healthy people. They are important: about 1 in 6 people in the United States are Latinas/os (almost 57 million). It is estimated that by the year 2035, nearly 1 in 4 will be Latinas/os. The death rate among Latinas/os is 24 percent lower than whites. "Yet, about 50 percent more [Latinos are] likely to die from diabetes or liver disease than whites" (Centers for Disease Control and Prevention, 2015).

The Pew Research Center concludes, "When the Pew Research Center reported this month that almost half of adults in the United States are living with one or more chronic diseases (cancer, diabetes, obesity) it was more than a wake-up call—it was a fire alarm to say the least. In a country where the constitution guarantees free speech, and 'life, liberty and the pursuit of happiness' is contained in our Declaration of Independence, our health and wellness is not an inherent right" (Llopis, 2012). Some health experts predict that the numbers of Latinas/os will bring about a revamping of the American health system, which is part of the American illusion that excuses and condones enormous profits made by the American medical establishment. They live under the illusion that it has the greatest medicine establishment in the world.

American society is divided between the insured and those who are not—between servers who are good and bad. The well-off insured can get private policies. The HMO, the PPO, and the point-of-service (POS) plans are the most prevalent. HMOs are the least expensive; however, they are not inexpensive. They are the least flexible types of health insurance plans and a policyholder is required to go through a primary care physician for referrals that are generally within the plan. In PPOs, the policyholder skips referrals to specialists; the subscriber usually pays higher copayments and deductibles in PPOs. Like the HMO, PPOs have networks of doctors and it gets more expensive if you go out of network. Unlike the HMO, PPO health insurance plans generally will pick up some of the cost of out-of-network care. The POS plan is a combination of PPO and HMO insurance. The POS plan functions like an HMO but gives the patient the flexibility to more easily go out of network. As mentioned, the lack of universal coverage and the policyholder's carrying the costs of insurance, unlike the German plan, have not kept costs down. Because the plans operate for profit, they cut corners, which does not always translate into quality health care. For example, quality care is more than mere processing and, as mentioned, anxiety can be ameliorated and suicide prevented. Care involves crisis intervention. In 2015, Kaiser Permanente was criticized for a rash of suicides caused by a failure to intervene. In one case, Nicholas Acuña committed himself four times. He was detained for three days and then dumped onto the streets. He did not have a drug problem. He was referred to a Kaiser facility and had hopes. However, each time a psychiatrist prescribed medicine and assigned him to a nurse practitioner for group therapy. Acuña protested that he needed to see a psychiatrist, to talk to someone. Each time he complained that he wanted to commit suicide. He was denied one-on-one therapy and finally, in the summer of 2015, he jumped off a bridge in San Pedro, California, leaving a note that he could not stand the pain. THIS SUICIDE COULD HAVE BEEN PREVENTED.

This situation was not an aberration. Similar to Nicholas, Barbara Ragan, 83, wrote a note to her family saying she "couldn't stand the pain" (Espinoza, 2015). As with Nick, there was a history of delayed appointments. Patients are expected to go to group sessions, which does not end the pain. Rosemary Milbrath, a former executive director of the Sonoma County chapter of the National Alliance on Mental Illness, said many health plans are struggling: "All the health plans are facing the same challenges of how to provide effective mental health services in a cost-effective way under the new guidelines of health parity. . . . I hear the same frustration that people express from those individuals who are insured by BlueShield, by UnitedHealthcare—all of them" (Espinoza, 2015). There are hotspots that bring on anxiety, such as bullying and homosexuality, which make victims the irrational targets of sick people.

Americans must consider: "The U.S. spends more money on health care compared with other industrialized countries, but Americans still get the least bang for their buck—and many still don't have access to care—according to a report just published by the Commonwealth Fund. The report from the private health care research foundation examined data on expenditures, delivery and access to health care services among 11 industrialized countries: Australia, Canada, France, Germany, the Netherlands, New Zealand, Norway, Sweden, Switzerland, the U.K. and the U.S." (Firger, 2014).

ANOTHER POV (POINT OF VIEW)

There Should be Universal Health Care Coverage for All

Juan José Montes, Student, California State University, Northridge

Health care coverage should be universally available to all individuals regardless of their legal status. There are many people currently working who are being paid "under the table" and who contribute taxes, as mentioned. Today they pay billions of dollars in taxes that go into a "suspense file" and do not count as credit toward Social Security and other programs denied to undocumented workers and their families by the United States government. The most essential of these benefits is health care—something that most industrialized countries consider a social right.

The undocumented worker, like every other resident of this country, contributes to the betterment of society. The majority perform jobs that only immigrants are willing to do and that are often higher in risk than other jobs. These jobs put the individual who lacks citizenship in more dangerous situations than someone who has a "legal" status. The majority of companies are aware of these risk factors and yet they don't provide health coverage. This seems to be a money game. Acuña mentioned the contribution, or the lack of contribution, companies make to employees' health plans. It goes without saying that a majority of undocumented individuals don't have any access to health benefits. This situation can become deadly when individuals become injured at the job site. A couple of years ago, an accident occurred at a construction job site. A construction worker was digging a trench when a cement wall fell on him, almost killing him. It took an army of men to lift the wall up and get him out. As it turned out, the individual was a day laborer, working for $60 a day in hazardous conditions. He was undocumented. He was rushed to the hospital and was in the ICU for quite some time. Because of his status, he did not receive the total care he should have. He was kept there until he was labeled "stable" and then was discharged from the hospital. It's such experiences as this that can occur at any moment and that make universal health care for all so important.

There are also specific health problems that Latinas/os are more prone to than other people. Conditions such as alcoholism, abuse, mental health, cancer, and other health risks should get early treatment; they have been shown to affect Latinas/os and other poor people at a higher rate. Mental health is an area that is taken lightly by insurance companies and is out of reach for many individuals who need help. The lack of mental health care is a tragedy that is reaching epidemic levels. Anxiety and suicide are preventable.

Instead of universal health coverage, the United States lets the insurance companies reduce health care to a commodity. A variety of management plans are franchised and insure that the private sector controls and manages health care for profit. The most popular management approaches are the HMO, PPO, and the PMO plans. They all manage health but do not necessarily provide quality treatment. Services available to individuals are limited to access by primary physicians. This medical quagmire makes it difficult for even a person who has medical insurance to obtain the help he or she needs. The current method provides very limited care and does not provide it in a timely way. We should put quality health care above profit—it is everybody's right.

Alternative Health Medicine

Walter Acuña, Independent Scholar and Superior Court Clerk

The escalating cost of medical care and its privatization coupled with the elitism of the American medical health care establishment raise the question of whether our laws should be liberalized to allow the practice of alternative medicine. We are reaching the point where people are losing faith in their medical practitioners, much the same way as when many Europeans lost faith in the Roman Catholic Church during the black plague of the Middle Ages, preferring instead to rely on evidence-based treatments, which consequently gave rise to colleges and universities for training doctors. Today, again, there are a growing number of people demanding more empirical data as to whether the medical profession is working at cures or just making a profit.

As noted by the author's chapter, "Latino Health Issues," health care costs in this country "have skyrocketed." At the same time, there are fewer physicians per capita and fewer hospital beds. Life expectancy has not increased at the level of other countries. Free clinics and Planned Parenthood offices are also closing, further increasing costs because of a lack of preventative medicine. Based on Pew Research Center reports, the consequence is an explosion of chronic diseases such as cancer, diabetes, and obesity (Llopis, 2012).

Current medical practices and institutions are not serving the needs of the public. This is so because medicine is either being motivated or limited "by profit motive" and because the system itself is overburdened. It can therefore be reasonably assumed that the medical system we have in place is dysfunctional and seems to need more than a tweaking in order to meet our current needs.

European political values of "conservative" and "liberal" are different from those in the United States, and the reason why is rooted in history. A highlight in the European struggle for human rights began in the 13th century with the Magna Carta, which influenced the Glorious Revolution and Bill of Rights of 1688, the French Declaration of the Rights of Man, and finally, the Declaration of Independence and the American Revolution. The struggle for rights was led by groups who impressed upon the monarch that they were fighting for group rights. In general, Europeans developed communitarian societies whereas in the United States, the struggle has been for individual rights.

The arguments between "conservatives" and "liberals" as to whether "health care is an individual or human right" are largely unimportant; a right is a malleable and evolving thing that can be argued and rationalized from various perspectives. What is true is that a government does not exist without people. The people of this or any country give the government its legitimacy and can require that any policy be made, whether those policies are effective or not. So, it would be best to make good policy. One way to make good policy is to expand one's options when the current options are not working effectively, as in the case of our current healthcare system.

Indigenous medicine, like "alternative" medicine, has become a scapegoat. It is no longer a known quantity that people use to either scare others or use as a fad. Mention it and people think in terms of "witch doctors," "faith healing," "placebos," or "unscientific results." However, "Chinese herbal medicines, massage, and acupuncture" have been practiced for thousands of years (Qingfei et al., 2012). The Roman herbal tradition can be traced back to books written by Pliny the Elder in the year 23 CE and was continued by Christian monasteries well into the Renaissance, giving Western herbal and nutritive empirical tradition a history of nearly 2,000 years, as the findings contained in these books have built upon to this day. Mesoamerica was peopled by scientists capable of calculating the full procession of our galaxy through the universe. The Mayans discovered how to work rubber hundreds of years before Western empiricists, and they practiced extensive advanced herbal and medical procedures that exceeded Western abilities.

Yet, even the author of this book unwittingly minimizes indigenous medicine by relegating its importance to a purely "psychological value," saying that people seek it out when they ". . . do not have sufficient access to medical care." Allegedly, "Western medicine is primarily scientifically based and focuses on directly pinpointing a disease, then treating it" (Kennedy, Mexican Folk Medicine, n.d.). The author cannot be faulted because he is expressing the majority view of "indigenous medicine," which ignores the millennia of empirical data contained in each of these herbal traditions. "Indigenous medicine" has become a catch-all phrase that means nothing unless you have some context to evaluate it.

A growing body of evidence points to the need to challenge the medical establishment's monopoly. Monopolies are wrong, whether in business, religion, or medicine. As in chess, one should never surround oneself with oneself. So the question becomes, should universal health coverage laws be liberalized to allow for the findings of indigenous medicine?

Data show that when immigrants arrive in this country, they are generally in good health. Nonacculturated immigrant populations develop diseases when they become Americanized. They are generally healthier than the acculturated population, but subsequent generations begin to develop the diseases of the acculturated population. Many of them have been sustained by using the indigenous medical practices they have brought with them.

Aside from the medical establishment, agribusiness may be to blame for a great many of the health problems in this country: obesity may be caused by a person's need to overeat, choosing starchy food because his or her body is hungry. This food lacks nutritional value, which begins a chain reaction: the food he or she is eating leads to alcoholism and drug abuse in a similar fashion to the self-medication that masks mental health issues.

Failures in the food chain drain nutrients out of the soil, such as nitrogen. Hydrocarbon fertilizers cause depleted soil and hence bad nutrition; seed stock is bred for looks and handling instead of for nutrition. Pesticides and weed-controlling chemicals are finding their way into fruits and vegetables and may be causing rising rates of asthma, allergies, autism, ADHD, and other ailments such as cancer. The result is that there is an epidemic in this country which may be caused by current agribusiness practices.

I paint this doomsday scenario to point out that modern medical practices are not addressing these issues. It treats symptoms and not causes. In order to promote the public good, we must approach the topic with an open mind. An indigenous and practical form of health care does exist: diet. Food IS health care, while drugs and surgery are disease management. There are cultural elements that may cause disease in a dominant society, such as "language, food choice, dress, music, and sports," or "health care." We must ask how they influence our choices.

Of late, a great deal is being learned about the benefits of indigenous diets. "Chicken soup," "menudo," and "salty lemon" do have healing qualities. Mainstream medicine notes that diabetes and obesity rates among Native Americans have risen because of the processed foods they are allotted. A re-evaluation is taking place even by the normally conservative USDA. Food distribution services have begun reintroducing blue corn into food programs directed at Native Americans. Other foods, such as mesquite and cactus fruits (tunas), add sweetness but no sugar to foods, thus lowering glycemic levels and the risk of diabetes, which would benefit the general population as well.

Indigenous peoples had highly varied diets that supplied a wide range of nutrients which have been lost in today's modern diet. Medieval garden books list hundreds of foods in the form of fruits, vegetables, herbs, flowers, and fungi cultivated in Europe. The Hopi cultivated 200 plants and foraged a thousand more. This is true of almost all Native American tribal societies, and that is the "indigenous medicine" we need to get back to, featuring a wide and varied diet.

Our educational institutions receive a great deal of program and research funding from major agribusinesses and medical industries.

Much is made of the need for "meat protein" and "genetically modified" foods designed to meet the needs of our advanced scientific society, though, strangely, little is said about indigenous medicine. Much can be said about the need for organically fed and humanely treated animals producing unstressed foods, but the fact is that meat protein is broken down and metabolized as amino acids. A more complete and broader range of amino acids than those found in meat proteins are available in fruits and vegetables, except for those found in vitamin B12.

A rational scientifically based society should also fund studies in our educational institutions, comparing the health of people eating organically raised foods to those eating commercial agribusiness food. Anecdotal evidence informs us that people earning $5 million dollars a year or more eat more organically raised and fresh food; they are living demonstrably longer.

The first step in implementing an "indigenous medicine" program is to simply change tax policy to include tax breaks for those companies that produce food organically, composting the soil and using little or no pesticides or herbicides.

The second step would be to fund programs and research projects in our educational system comparing foods produced organically to those produced by traditional agribusiness methods to see if traditional agribusiness practices should even receive tax subsidies or be allowed to guide the direction of our educational practices.

The institutionalization of alternative indigenous medicine would be a giant step in solving the deteriorating health crisis and the explosion of long-term health problems. It may seem like putting the cart before the horse, implementing the program before the raw data are in, but it is never too late or too soon. Nutrition affects everyone. The alternative is to continue allowing people to suffer and possibly die.

BIBLIOGRAPHY

Alexandria, Virginia. "Diabetes Among Hispanics: All Are Not Equal." *American Diabetes Association*, July 24, 2014. http://www.diabetes.org/newsroom/press-releases/2014/diabetes-among-hispanics-all-are-not-equal.html

American Heart Association. "Young Hispanics often obese, at higher risk for heart diseases." *Science Daily*, July 9, 2014. https://www.sciencedaily.com/releases/2014/07/140709164433.htm

Anchondo, Leo. "Top 10 Myths About Immigration." American Immigration Council," 2015. http://www.immigrationpolicy.org/high-school/top-10-myths-about-immigration

Becerra, David, David Androff, Jill T Messing, Jason Castillo, and Andrea Cimino. "Linguistic Acculturation and Perceptions of Quality, Access, and Discrimination in Health Care Among Latinos in the United States." *Social Work in Health Care* 54, no. 2 (2015): 134–157.

Belén, Picó, and Fernando Nuez. "Minor Crops of Mesoamerica in Early Sources (I). Leafy Vegetables." *Genetic Resources and Crop Evolution* 47, no. 5 (2000): 527–540.

Brown, Troy. "Hispanic Subgroups Have Different Health Risks, CDC Says." *Medscape*, May 5, 2015. http://www.medscape.com/viewarticle/844246

"The California Ballot: Proposition 187 save our state." *UK Essays*, March 23, 2015. http://www.ukessays.com/essays/history/the-california-ballot-proposition-187-save-our-state-history-essay.php

Cárdenas, José. "The Myth Buster." *Los Angeles Times*, May 24, 1999. http://articles.latimes.com/1999/may/24/news/cl-40337

Carteret, Marcia. "Folk Illnesses and Remedies in Latino Communities." Dimensions of Culture, 2011. http://www.dimensionsofculture.com/2010/10/folk-illnesses-and-remedies-in-latino-communities

Centers for Disease Control and Prevention. "Hispanic Health." *Vital Signs*, May 2015. http://www.cdc.gov/vitalsigns/hispanic-health/index.html

Chowdhury, Pranesh P., Lina S. Balluz, Guixiang Zhao, and Machell Town. "Health Behaviors and Obesity Among Hispanics with Depression, United States 2006." *Ethnicity & Disease* 24, no. 1 (2014): 92–96.

Duarté-Vélez, Yovanska M., and Guillermo Bernal. "Suicide Behavior Among Latino and Latina Adolescents: Conceptual and Methodological Issues." *Death Studies* 31, no. 5 (2007): 435–455.

Espinoza, Martin. "Kaiser Permanente faces renewed criticism over mental health services after Santa Rosa suicide." *The Press Democrat*, August 1, 2015. http://www.pressdemocrat.com/news/4257827-181/kaiser-permanente-faces-renewed-criticism?artslide=0

Evans, Lynda C. "Impact of obesity among American Latino women." Thesis, California State University, Los Angeles, 2012.

Firger, Jessica. "U.S. health care system ranks lowest in international survey." *CBS News*, June 16, 2014. http://www.cbsnews.com/news/u-s-health-care-system-ranks-lowest-in-international-survey

"Folk Medicine." Encyclopedia.com. http://www.encyclopedia.com/topic/folk_medicine.aspx

Ford-Paz, Rebecca, Christine Reinhard, Andrea Kuebbeler, Richard Contreras, and Bernadette Sánchez. "Culturally Tailored Depression/Suicide Prevention in Latino Youth: Community Perspectives." *The Journal of Behavioral Health Services & Research* 42, no. 4 (2015): 519–533.

García, Carolyn, Carol Skay, Renee Sieving, Sandy Naughton, and Linda H. Bearinger. "Family and Racial Factors Associated with Suicide and Emotional Distress Among Latino Students." *Journal of School Health* 78, no. 9 (2008): 487–495.

Garro, Linda Carol. "Variation and Consistency in a Mexican Folk Illness Belief System (Medical, Cognitive, Mesoamerica)." Unpublished manuscript: ProQuest Dissertations Publishing, 1983.

Gómez, Judelysse, Regina Miranda, and Lillian Polanco. "Acculturative Stress, Perceived Discrimination, and Vulnerability to Suicide Attempts Among Emerging Adults." *Journal of Youth and Adolescence* 40, no. 11 (2011): 1465–1476.

Gutiérrez, Mariana. "Understanding Latino health: David Hayes-Bautista: director, Center for the Study of Latino Health and Culture UCLA School of Medicine."

High Beam Research, February 1, 2008. https://www.highbeam.com/doc/1G1-176369906.html

Haupt, Norbert. "Comparison of Health Care Services: Germany vs. U.S." *Norbert Haupt, Books, Movies, Art, Paintings and General Musings* (blog). November 10, 2009. http://norberthaupt.com/2009/11/10/comparison-of-health-care-services-germany-vs-u-s

Hayes-Bautista, David E. "Hispanic Health: How Healthy is the Fastest Growing Population of the United States?" *Ethnicity & Disease* 12, no. 4 (2002): 459.

Hayes-Bautista, David E., and Gregory Rodriguez. "A Rude Awakening for Latinos." *Los Angeles Times*, November 11, 1994.

Holloway, Ian, Mark Padilla, Lauren Willner, and Vincent Guilamo-Ramos. "Effects of Minority Stress Processes on the Mental Health of Latino Men Who Have Sex with Men and Women: A Qualitative Study." *Archives of Sexual Behavior* 44, no. 7 (2015): 2087–2097.

Huff, Robert. "Folk Medicine." *Encyclopedia.com*, 2002. http://www.encyclopedia.com/topic/folk_medicine.aspx

"Immigration Reform." Planned Parenthood, 2016. https://www.plannedparenthoodaction.org/issues/immigration-reform

"Insurance: Industry Profile: Summary, 2016." *Opensecrets.org*. https://www.opensecrets.org/lobby/indusclient.php?id=F09

JHI Staff. "Does Profit Really Ruin Health Care?" *John Hopkins Medicine*, December 23, 2013. http://international.blogs.hopkinsmedicine.org/2013/12/23/does-profit-really-ruin-health-care

Kane, Jason. "Health Costs: How the U.S. Compares With Other Countries." *The Rundown*, October 22, 2012. http://www.pbs.org/newshour/rundown/health-costs-how-the-us-compares-with-other-countries

Kennedy, Brian, and Cary Funk. "Public Interest in Science and Health Linked to Gender, Age and Personality." Pew Research Center, December 11, 2015. http://www.pewinternet.org/2015/12/11/public-interest-in-science-and-health-linked-to-gender-age-and-personality

Kennedy, Erin. "Mexican Folk Medicine: Balancing the Mind, Body and Spirit." Empower Herm n.d., http://www.empowher.com/holistic-health/content/mexican-folk-medicine-balancing-mind-body-and-spirit?page=0,1

Lara, Marielena, Cristina Gamboa, M. Iya Kahramanian, Leo S.Morales, and David E. Hayes-Bautista. "Acculturation and Latino Health in the United States: A Review of the Literature and its Sociopolitical Context." *Annual Review of Public Health* 26 (2005): 367–368.

LeBron, Alana, Melissa Valerio, Edith Kieffer, Brandy Sinco, Ann-Marie Rosland, Jaclynn Hawkins, Nicolaus Espitia, Gloria Palmisano, and Michael Spencer. "Everyday Discrimination, Diabetes-Related Distress, and Depressive Symptoms Among African Americans and Latinos with Diabetes." *Journal of Immigrant and Minority Health* 16, no. 6 (2014): 1208–1216.

Llopis, Glenn. "Hispanics Will Change the Business of Healthcare." *Huffington Post*, December 18, 2012. http://www.huffingtonpost.com/glenn-llopis/hispanics-will-change-the_b_4461726.html

Longley, Robert. "Illegal Immigrants Pay Taxes, Too, But Do These Estimates Reflect Reality?" *About News*, May 17, 2016. http://usgovinfo.about.com/od/incometaxandtheirs/a/Illegal-Immigrants-Pay-Taxes-Too.htm

López, Rebecca. "Use of Alternative Folk Medicine by Mexican American Women." *Journal of Immigrant Health* 7, no. 1 (2005): 23–31.

Lora, Claudia M., Martha L. Daviglus, John W. Kusek, Anna Porter, Ana C. Ricardo, Alan S. Go, and James P. Lash. "Chronic Kidney Disease in United States Hispanics: A Growing Public Health Problem." *PMC* 19 (4) (Autumn 2009): 466–472. http://www.ncbi.nlm.nih.gov/pmc/articles/PMC3587111

Mier, Conrad F. "Health Care: Reformed or Deformed?" *The Heartland Institute,* 2002. http://cfmresearch.tripod.com/healthcare

Mukherjee, Sy. "Why Undocumented Immigrants Should Have Access To Taxpayer-Funded Health Care." *ThinkProgress,* May 24, 2013. http://thinkprogress.org/health/2013/05/24/2060541/undocumented-immigrants-taxpayer-funded-health-care

Murray, Christopher J. L., and Julio Frenk. "Ranking 37th—Measuring the Performance of the U.S. Health Care System." *The New England Journal of Medicine,* January 14, 2010. http://www.nejm.org/doi/full/10.1056/NEJMp0910064

Murse, Tom. "Is Medical Help for Illegal Immigrants Covered Under Obamacare? How the Affordable Care Act Treats Undocumented Immigrants." *AboutNews,* April 17, 2016. http://uspolitics.about.com/od/healthcare/a/Are-Illegal-Immigrants-Covered-Under-Obamacare.htm

National Institute of Health. "Alcohol and the Hispanic Community." National Institute on Alcohol Abuse and Alcoholism, 2015. http://pubs.niaaa.nih.gov/publications/HispanicFact/HispanicFact.htm

"Obesity Prevention in Latino Communities." *Special Report: Racial and Ethnic Disparities in Obesity.* September 2014. http://stateofobesity.org/disparities/latinos

O'Donnell, Shannon, Ilan H Meyer, and Sharon Schwartz. "Increased Risk of Suicide Attempts Among Black and Latino Lesbians, Gay Men, and Bisexuals." *American Journal of Public Health* 101, no. 6 (2011): 1055–1059.

Odgen, C.L., Carroll, M.D., Kit, B.K., and Fiegal, K.M. "Prevalence of childhood and adult obesity in the United States, 2011–2012." *JAMA* 311, no 8 (2014): 806–814.

Packham, Amy. "Talking To Men About Depression: David Baddiel, Jake Mills And Matt Haig On Why We Need To Communicate." *Huffington Post,* November 30, 2015. http://www.huffingtonpost.co.uk/2015/11/30/talking-to-men-about-depression_n_8680594.html

Pérez-Escamilla, Rafael. "Health Care Access Among Latinos: Implications for Social and Health Care Reforms." *Journal of Hispanic Higher Education* 9, issue 1 (2010): 43–60.

Picó, Belén, and Fernando Nuez. "Minor Crops of Mesoamerica in Early Sources (II). Herbs Used as Condiments." *Genetic Resources and Crop Evolution* 47, no. 5 (2000): 541–552.

Planas, Roque. "No Politico, Not All Undocumented Immigrants Are Latino." *Huffington Post,* April 23, 2013. http://www.huffingtonpost.com/2013/04/23/politico-immigrants-latino_n_3142061.html

Portman, Tarrell A. A., and Michael T. Garrett. "Native American Healing Traditions." *International Journal of Disability, Development and Education* 53, no. 4 (2006): 453–469.

Qingfei, Liua, Walter Luytenc, Klaartje Pellensd, Yiming Wange, Wei Wangf, Karin Thevissend, Qionglin Liange, Bruno P.A. Cammued, Liliane Schoofsb, and

Guoan Luoe. "Anti-fungal Activity in Plants from Chinese Traditional and Folk Medicine." *Journal of Ethnopharmacology* 143, no. 3 (October 1, 2012): 772–778.

Rainie, Lee, and Cary Funk. "How Different Groups Think about Scientific Issues." Pew Research Center, February 12, 2015. http://www.pewinternet.org/2015/02/12/how-different-groups-think-about-scientific-issues

Richman, Josh, and David E. Early. "Twenty years after Prop. 187, attitudes toward illegal immigration have changed dramatically in California." *Mercury News*, November 22, 2014. http://www.mercurynews.com/census/ci_26994670/twenty-years-after-prop-187-attitudes-toward-illegal

Rodríguez, Michael A., and William A. Vega. "Confronting Inequities in Latino Health Care." *Journal of General Internal Medicine* 24, no. S3 (2009): 505–507.

Rosado, Javier I., Suzanne Bennett Johnson, Kelly A. McGinnity, and Jordan P. Cuevas. "Obesity Among Latino Children Within a Migrant Farmworker Community." *American Journal of Preventive Medicine* 44, no. S3 (2013): S274-S281.

Rotberg, Britt, Rachel Greene, Anyul M. Ferez-Pinzon, Robert Mejia, and Guillermo Umpierrez. "Improving Diabetes Care in the Latino Population: The Emory Latino Diabetes Education Program." *American Journal of Health Education* 47, no. 1 (2016): 1–7.

Salcedo, Alfredo I. "Dance as a Tool to Reduce Childhood Obesity in Hispanic Youth." Unpublished manuscript, 2012.

Salguero, Laura E. "The Influences of Acculturation on Obesity in Hispanic Adolescents." Unpublished manuscript, 2012.

Stefancic, Jean, and Richard Delgado. *No Mercy: How Conservative Think Tanks and Foundations Changed America's Social Agenda*. Philadelphia: Temple University Press, 1996.

Tung, W.-C., and J. X. McDonough. Home Health Care Management and Practice. (Home Health Care Management and Practice, 13 August 2015, 27(3): 162–165)

Winkelman, Sloane Burke, Elizabeth H. Chaney, and Jeffrey W. Bethel. "Stress, Depression and Coping Among Latino Migrant and Seasonal Farmworkers." *International Journal of Environmental Research and Public Health* 10, no. 5 (2013): 1815–1830.

"Young Hispanics often obese, at higher risk for heart diseases." American Heart Association Rapid Access Journal Report. July 09, 2014. http://newsroom.heart.org/news/young-hispanics-often-obese-at-higher-risk-for-heart-diseases

Zvolensky, Michael, Jafar Bakhshaie, Monica Garza, Jeannette Valdivieso, Mayra Ortiz, Daniel Bogiaizian, Zuzuky Robles, Norman Schmidt, and Anka Vujanovic. "The Role of Anxiety Sensitivity in the Relation Between Experiential Avoidance and Anxious Arousal, Depressive, and Suicidal Symptoms Among Latinos in Primary Care." *Cognitive Therapy and Research* 39, no. 5 (2015): 688–696.

SELECTED VIDEOS

Al Jazeera English. "Fast food, Fat profits: Obesity in America," YouTube video, 23:14, posted November 19, 2010. https://www.youtube.com/watch?v=slwgXXVXM3I

FOX New Mexico. "Mexican Folk Healing," YouTube video, 3:30, posted May 29, 2013. https://www.youtube.com/watch?v=weqrLyEMi8M

GlitterForever17. "We Need To Talk: Bullying, Suicide, Anxiety & Depression . . . How To Beat It ALL!" YouTube video, 11:31, posted December 5, 2014. https://www.youtube.com/watch?v=0m40h9VHcFk

Marcus-Willers, Ben. "Chinese Medicine—An Ancient Practice," YouTube video, 8:36, posted June 5, 2013. https://www.youtube.com/watch?v=mcSAD-Cqs5o

New Mexico State University. "Ancient Roots, Modern Medicine—Borderlands," YouTube video, 29:34, posted September 28, 2009. https://www.youtube.com/watch?v=bOIfCGf3VO8

PublicResourceOrg, "Ancient Roots, Modern Medicine—Borderlands: USA/Mexico," YouTube video, 33:07, posted September 22, 2010. https://www.youtube.com/watch?v=JbhCxvHvhpM

Sahar Consulting, LLC. "Latino Culture celebrations, Latino Folklore and folk medicine for healthcare," YouTube video, 18:22, posted June 27, 2013. https://www.youtube.com/watch?v=pvGSuiPi1g8

Sahar Consulting, LLC. "Latino/Hispanic Culture and influence of nature in Latino patients for healthcare," YouTube video, 5:21, posted June 26, 2013. https://www.youtube.com/watch?v=eIHLzUgP3bQ

Sahar Consulting, LLC. "Barriers to Healthcare for Latino/Hispanic patients," YouTube video, 7:44, posted June 27, 2013. https://www.youtube.com/watch?v=dP4CHL6yENQ

SaludToday. "Latino Childhood Obesity—Short Film," YouTube video, 5:56, posted November 4, 2009. https://www.youtube.com/watch?v=pnfZvxXlTIc

Stony Brook University. "Provost Lecture—Luis Zayas: Understanding Why Latinas Attempt Suicide," YouTube video, 1:06:51, posted October 31, 2011. https://www.youtube.com/watch?v=nI3BG_zRkrE

Suarez, Ray. "Documentary: Why Does U.S. Health Care Cost So Much?" YouTube video, 6:36, posted by PBS News Hour, September 24, 2012. https://www.youtube.com/watch?v=4ZRgVQALFUA

Taylor, Jason. "History and Development of the U.S. Health Care System," YouTube video, 10:00, posted July 29, 2014. https://www.youtube.com/watch?v=nRFKCXvy3-g

Time to Change. "Author Matt Haig talks about men and mental health," YouTube video, 2:51, posted June 16, 2015. https://www.youtube.com/watch?v=9TID2bIiAOU

ViralMedia24. "Researching Suicide Among Latino's," YouTube video, 13:16, posted July 21, 2013. https://www.youtube.com/watch?v=9DJAEV9J5_s

Vlogbrothers, "Why Are American Health Care Costs So High?" YouTube video, 7:52, posted August 20, 2013. https://www.youtube.com/watch?v=qSjGouBmo0M

Wahi, Monika. "Historical Overview of U.S. Health Care Delivery," See blog post and download slides here: http://www.dethwench.com/?p=1011. https://www.youtube.com/watch?v=w31xY0Y87dE

Woodruff, Judy. "Former health care CEO argues America's medical system rewards bad outcomes," YouTube video, 7:31, posted by PBS News Hour, January 17, 2014. https://www.youtube.com/watch?v=LImml5sLZLg

9

Immigration and Losing Fear: DACA-DAPA

BACKGROUND

Immigration was not always the priority among Mexican Americans that it is today. In the 1970s, it seemed as if Mexicans along with Puerto Ricans made up the entire Latina/o population. Because the Southwest once belonged to Mexico, it felt like home to many Mexicans. Puerto Ricans were not immigrants; they were citizens. Puerto Rico became a colony in 1898 and the Southwest part of Mexico as a result of the Treaty of Guadalupe Hidalgo (1848) that ended the war between the United States and Mexico. Many Mexicans believed that the Treaty gave them special rights. They felt like people living in a home that once belonged to the family:

ARTICLE VIII of the Treaty stated:

> Mexicans now established in territories previously belonging to Mexico, and which remain for the future within the limits of the United States, as defined by the present treaty, shall be free to continue where they now reside, or to remove at any time to the Mexican Republic, retaining the

> property which they possess in the said territories, or disposing thereof, and removing the proceeds wherever they please, without their being subjected, on this account, to any contribution, tax, or charge whatever.
>
> Those who shall prefer to remain in the said territories may either retain the title and rights of Mexican citizens, or acquire those of citizens of the United States. But they shall be under the obligation to make their election within one year from the date of the exchange of ratifications of this treaty; and those who shall remain in the said territories after the expiration of that year, without having declared their intention to retain the character of Mexicans, shall be considered to have elected to become citizens of the United States.
>
> In the said territories, property of every kind, now belonging to Mexicans not established there, shall be inviolably respected. The present owners, the heirs of these, and all Mexicans who may hereafter acquire said property by contract, shall enjoy with respect to it guarantees equally ample as if the same belonged to citizens of the United States. Treaty of Guadalupe Hidalgo, 1848

A Treaty is a bilateral agreement binding both parties. As every school child knows, it is the law of the land. Yet the Treaty of Guadalupe Hidalgo was one sided and arbitrarily applied; Article VIII, among other articles, was violated. Many Americans, including Abraham Lincoln, had opposed the war, and northern abolitionists opposed the annexation of Mexican territory. According to historian Richard Griswold del Castillo, "The treaty established a pattern of political and military inequality between the two countries, and this lopsided relationship has stalked Mexican–U.S. relations ever since . . . . Beyond territorial gains and losses, the treaty has been important in shaping the international and domestic histories of both Mexico and the United States. During the U.S.–Mexican War, U.S. leaders assumed an attitude of moral superiority in their negotiations of the treaty." According to Griswold del Castillo, "the treaty ensured that Mexico would remain an underdeveloped country well into the twentieth century" (Griswold del Castillo, 2006).

How would the Mexican American War and the Treaty of Guadalupe Hidalgo contribute to Mexican migration into their former territories?

During the 19th century, border control was almost nonexistent, with both parties traveling back and forth at will. Throughout the latter 19th and most of the 20th century, the United States sold Latin American nations and leaders on the notion of Pan Americanism—that the Americas enjoyed a common history, and that we shared a colonial past.[1] The idea of Pan Americanism was expanded with the growth of U.S. commercial ambitions. In 1889, the United States convened a Pan American Congress in Washington, D.C. Secretary of State James Blaine negotiated arbitration treaties with Latin American nations and entered into trade agreements that were supposed to be reciprocal but in actuality strengthened U.S. political and economic hegemony in the hemisphere (Sotomayor, 1996).

Pan Americanism was never reciprocal and initial feelings of goodwill dissipated rapidly with rising jingoism in the United States. The United States became known as the "Colossus of the North" as American military and dollar interventions became common. The liberalization of commercial intercourse was a one-way street, benefiting Euro-American businesses. It reinforced inequality between the nations north and south of the U.S. border. There were high hopes among many Latinas/os that a form of Pan Americanism was possible within the United States and that they would be treated like sisters and brothers—a concept that was criticized within the United States itself.

What was Pan Americanism and how did it contribute to the illusion that Latinas/os were part of the family?

It was not until May 28, 1924 that Congress established the Border Patrol as part of the Immigration Bureau of the Department of Labor through the Labor Appropriation Act of 1924. The border was a revolving door and Mexicans were allowed to come and go, especially during the planting and harvesting seasons. Armies of workers labored in the railroads and mines but were regularly repatriated when they were no longer needed.

What was the symbolism of border control? Was it bilateral?

The Immigration Acts of 1921 and 1924 excluded Mexicans from quotas supposedly because of Pan Americanism, but this stipulation was actually because of the pressure of the Western growers who demanded a free flow of Mexican workers. However, in the 1930s because of the economic crisis and the growth of American nativist jingoism, 600,000 to

1 million Mexicans were repatriated. Mexicans, however, were welcomed back as braceros and undocumented during World War II. When Mexico tried to regulate the flow of braceros into the United States, the border was arbitrarily opened by the United States to allow them to come in at will. In October 1948, the Immigration and Naturalization Service (INS) allowed Mexicans to pour across the bridge into the United States, with or without Mexico's approval. Farmers waited with trucks, and a Great Western Sugar Company representative had a special train ready for the braceros. The unilateral opening of the border effectively destroyed Mexico's negotiating position. From January 23 to February 5, 1954, the United States unilaterally opened the border. Short of shooting its own citizens, Mexico could not prevent the flood of workers that followed. Mexico had no other choice but to sign a contract favorable to the United States.[2]

How did the disrespect for Mexican authority contribute to border enforcement?

A minority of Mexican Americans during the 1950s joined protection of the foreign-born organizations—most assumed that the flow would continue. By the late 1960s, it became evident that American policy toward Mexican was changing. American and Mexican neoliberal policies accelerated the decline of the Mexican rural farms, intensifying the push to the cities and the United States. In the 1970s, the State of California and federal anti-Mexican legislation increased. The flow of immigrants increased as Central Americans, driven by wars largely sponsored by the United States, flowed into the United States.

In 1971, California passed the Dixon–Arnett Act, fining employers who hired undocumented workers. How was this seen as a call to arms by pro-protection of the foreign born activists? Why?

The organization leading the fight was CASA (*Centros de Acción Social Autónomo)—Hermandad General de Trabajadores* (or simply, CASA), the brainchild of Bert Corona and Chole Alatorre, who argued that undocumented workers should be organized rather than deported. These organizations grew and spawned others with the passage of IRCA (Immigration Reform and Control Act) in 1986. Immigration had become a priority within the Latina/o community, eclipsing other movements from within that sector. IRCA legalized 2.7 million undocumented persons. The success of Proposition 187 in 1994 awakened the Mexican American and Latina/o communities. They joined Central American organizations in the fight for the protection of the foreign-born and politicized the next generation of activists. That year saw massive walkouts of students from Los Angeles schools and the largest march and rally in Los Angeles history (100,000) (Markman, 1994).

How did the protests politicize immigrant and Latina/o youth?

Within this historical context, a larger and more defined movement was emerging. The student walkouts during the 1990s added to the moral outrage and gave birth to a generation that had lost fear—they came out as undocumented. Marches escalated from 100,000 in Los Angeles in 1994 to 1 million in a half dozen cities in 2006. Nationally, the Latina/o presence swelled: it increased by 57.9 percent, from 22.4 million in 1990 to 35.3 million in 2000 (Guzmán, 2001). Over the next decade it grew to 50.5 million—and in 2015 to 55 million. Among children ages 17 and younger, the census counted 17.1 million Latinas/os, 23.1 percent of youth in this age group. Latino children grew 39 percent since the 2000 Census when 12.3 million Latina/o children were 17.1 percent of the population under age 18 (Passel, Cohn, and López, 2011). Conditions worsened in the sending countries, so for many there was no going back home—for most home was in the United States anyway—many had never seen Mexico or Central America (Yang, 2009).

How did the immigrant lose fear?

In the 2012 presidential election, Latinas/os were, for the first time, major players. Latinas/os were critical of Obama's deportation policies and failure to put through a meaningful immigration reform act. In mid-June Obama issued an executive order giving temporary relief to young undocumented youth in danger of being deported "to a country they never knew, having been brought here by their parents." According to exit polls taken by the Pew Hispanic Center, "Latinos voted for President Barack Obama over Republican Mitt Romney by 71% to 27%" (Lopez and Taylor, 2012). This was the highest margin since the Bill Clinton–Bob Dole election in 1996. Latino youth voted for Obama over Romney, by a 74 percent versus 23 percent margin. "Among Latino voters whose total family income is below $50,000, 82% voted for Obama while 17% voted for Romney. Among Latino voters with family incomes of $50,000 or more, 59% voted for Obama while 39% voted for Romney" (López and Taylor, 2012). It is important to mention that even before President Obama's executive order, bipartisan versions had unsuccessfully made it through Congress, enjoying bipartisan support.

Before his re-election, President Barack Obama had issued an executive order on June 15, 2012 creating a new policy calling for deferred action for selected undocumented young people who came to the United States as children, known as Deferred Action for Childhood Arrivals (DACA). It began on August 15, 2012. DACA allowed undocumented immigrants who entered the country before their 16th birthday and before June 2007 to receive a renewable two-year work permit and exemption from deportation. The program was a no-brainer. The Pew Research Center estimated that up to 1.7 million people were eligible and, as of June 2014, about 581,000 individuals had been issued permits.

It was a no-brainer—the DACA students attended U.S. schools for a dozen years. The cost of their education to the state amounted to hundreds of thousands of dollars for each student. Deportations were like throwing this investment away. These immigrant students represented the best in American society. Studies showed that an aging population prevents the growth and prosperity of a nation, and the United States was getting a fully assimilated and acculturated population. Another plus was that the Democrats would benefit from this policy change because it was very popular in the huge Latino population.

In 2012, Obama received 71 percent of the Latino vote. Although many Latinos were still unregistered to vote, the Pew Center found that Latinos made up 10 percent of the electorate, and their voting numbers were growing. Not taking anything away from the Dreamers who had organized nationally since 2000 and had come out of the proverbial closet, it was this gigantic pool of voters that had moved Obama.[3]

How and why did the Latina/o become a major player in the election of 2012?

OUT OF THE PAST

There always exists a historical context. Even before IRCA in 1985, the crusade against undocumented students was under way. California undocumented students challenged an education code that precluded undocumented students from establishing residence, claiming that it was unconstitutional. They had the right to establish state residence for tuition purposes for both the University of California (UC) and California State University (CSU) systems. This was challenged by a UC employee in the registrar's office named Bradford in 1991, who sued UC saying he would not follow the Leticia A. order to admit undocumented students as California residents. Bradford won an injunction against UC, which UC began implementing in the fall of 1991.

"Neither UC nor CSU appealed this state district court decision, and both segments allowed undocumented students to be classified as state residents if they could show that they had lived in the state for at least a year and intended to make it their residence" (*Regents of University of California v. Superior Court of Los Angeles County*, 1990). The CSU attempted to adopt guidelines but the Bradford forces successfully appealed.

What was the Bradford decision?

Thus, the Leticia A. Network, named after the student who successfully brought the suit to the state district court, was formed. It continued its advocacy but the UC, the CSU, and the community colleges were cut off from admitting undocumented students as residents. Proposition 187 in 1994 cemented this situation. "While undocumented immigrant students were still allowed to attend California's colleges and universities, the Bradford case remained the legal rule—regardless of how long they lived in California, they were required to pay nonresident tuition, over three times the rate that their high school classmates paid. This usually meant they could not afford the opportunity of a higher education, a loss to them and the state, especially considering they were academically eligible" (*Regents of University of California*). This condemned many undocumented youth to a life of menial labor.

What was the legacy of Leticia A?

Throughout the decade, undocumented students hung on to the illusion that America cared and that Congress would pass the Development, Relief and Education for Alien Minors Act (the "Dream Act"). The Dream Act struggle formally began nationally on April 25, 2001 when Representative Luis Gutiérrez (D-Illinois) introduced the "Immigrant Children's Educational Advancement and Dropout Prevention Act of 2001." But it is much older, and has come a long way since that time. Ownership today belongs to the Dreamers, young undocumented immigrants. The first Senate Bill was introduced on August 1, 2001. It would have allowed undocumented students to graduate from U.S. high schools—provided they had arrived in the United States as children, were of good moral character, and had been in the country continuously for at least five years before the bill's enactment. They had the opportunity to earn conditional permanent residency. They would be given temporary residence while they earned their degree. Since 2001, the immigrant youth have fought for the bill, often traveling to state capitols and Washington, D.C. at their personal risk and cost.

Who were the Dreamers? How are they part of the history of the foreign-born?

During the height of the Iraq and Afghanistan wars, the admission of undocumented students was attractive to conservatives who wanted to enlist them into the armed forces. Some Dreamers asked for the right to join the armed forces. In every case, it was part of the American Dream—of being American—to try to prove one's Americanism. For many, it was baffling that these targets of discrimination believed in the American Dream when so many citizens were disillusioned with it.

Do you believe that the Dreamers had to join the armed forced as a requirement for immigration status? How about to become President?

As mentioned, the undocumented students fought back and joined their parents in street protests. Poor people have few options. The U.S drug market and policies destroyed Mexico's economy and civil society, so there was no question of returning to their home country. Although physically they were not born in what is today the United States, this is their home. In reality, President Barack Obama moved assertively although belatedly to normalize the status of the Dreamers, which was a no-brainer. At a time when we actively recruit educated college graduates from Eastern Europe and drain Latin American countries of their professionals, it seems logical to look for those resources at home. In the case of the Dreamers, they are Americans, they attended American schools, they earned good grades, and they made it despite the inequalities of American system.

What options did the Dreamers have?

Skeptics point out that while the Dream Act holds out promise, the contradictions are full of illusions that have yet to be negated. The Dream Act is going to have to be crafted and the military enticements eliminated and replaced by incentives for the Dreamers to go beyond their bachelor degrees. They must be treated as a valuable asset and, under the principles of the 1965 Immigration Act, family preferences have to be kept intact.

Republican rhetoric, aside from being opportunistic, has reached hysterical levels. There is talk that the new immigrants should be required to pay back taxes or fines without Social Security benefits, although many have already paid into the system. Latinas/os are being treated differently, receiving disparate treatment. Many immigrants from Eastern Europe and the Middle East who have immigrated to this country draw benefits without having worked a day here. I do not begrudge them since it is the right thing to do. But it is also the right thing to correct the exploitation that the undocumented workers have suffered—not perpetuate it.

Are all races and economic classes treated the same in the immigration process?

The newly documented immigrants need to receive full labor rights. ICE has to be controlled. The immigration raids and the deportations must stop now. Our Berlin Wall has to come down and the militarization of the border ended. If we want to end the drug trade, let's control our domestic market. If we want to control the flow of guns into Mexico, control the source of these guns. Lastly, the government must abandon the idea of a guest worker program. It is a sop to big business and a way to further exploit and control labor. There isn't anything Pan American about it.

The passage of a fair and comprehensive immigration reform act will be more difficult now, as will be the correction of other forms of injustices. Looking back, I appreciate the role of numbers in the temporary transformation of society. The Latina/o community has to be given time to settle. In 1970, the Mexican/Latino student population in the mammoth Los Angeles Unified School District was 22 percent; today it exceeds 80 percent. In the City of Los Angeles the Latino population has zoomed from about 15 percent to just over 50 percent.

In order for Americans to build a future, issues have to be resolved. For example, Mexican Americans, Latinas/os, and blacks were not building walls, but society was. There is something in American culture that builds walls around those who are different. Symbolic of our walled society is the Berlin Wall (*Berliner Mauer*), which was constructed in August of 1961. It was guarded by towers and armed men. Those who built the wall claimed that it was built to keep the people away from fascist elements in West Germany. However, it was built to stop the massive emigration and defections that caused a massive brain drain in East Germany.

We condemned the Berlin Wall and referred to it as the "Wall of Shame." It came over time to symbolize the "Iron Curtain" that separated Western and Eastern blocs. We are going to have to stop pointing fingers. The walls constructed to keep Mexicans out are going to have to be looked at through another prism, and we will need to realize the impact of the rhetoric of people such as Donald Trump, Ted Cruz, and Marco Rubio. Words contribute to walls.

Is the American Wall a Wall of Shame? Do Americans approve of it? What is the difference between the American Wall and the Berlin Wall?

The inhumane results of Operation Gatekeeper in California, Operation Hold-the-Line in Texas, and Operation Safeguard in Arizona need to be examined. The latter is the most insidious, with the migration of people and drugs purposely funneled through the Arizona corridor. The strategy is that if the wall does not get them, the desert, the heat, or a lynch mob of vigilantes will, with people insidiously calling it the Great Wall of Mexico. It is reinforced by the most modern detection devices. Most Americans are complicit. A Fox News/Opinion Dynamics poll indicates that the American people favor the building of the wall by a 51 to 37 percent margin (Acuña, 2012).

The causes of the migration are obvious. In 2005, the per-capita income differential between U.S. and Mexican workers was $30,000 to $4,000 annually. The Dreamers' perspective must be examined. The Dreamers are exiles through circumstances beyond their control. Too young to make a choice, they migrated with their parents. The American Dream is more intense for the Dreamer. The American Dream has different meaning for immigrants than for the ordinary American citizen. There were almost 3 million Dreamers in 2012.

If the status of the Dreamer is not normalized, he or she will not go back to the home country. They will remain in the margins of society, vulnerable to predators. They will not be able to get a license and thus unable to get car insurance. Therefore, other drivers will have to bear the cost of liability. Unable to get insurance, they will be unable to go to the doctor. Their criminalization forces undocumented persons to live the life of the hunted.

The Humanization of the Dreamer

It has been suggested that a problem in understanding the Dreamer is that they are faceless for most Americans. A good source of documentaries on Dreamers is YouTube. Often children with and without their parents flee violence to reach safety. Many students tell the story of being put in a truck tire while crossing the border in order to avoid detection. It is difficult for the average person to comprehend or appreciate that what these persons want are their right to dream for something that Americans believe belongs exclusively to Americans. As a movement, they feel that they are helpless but that they can help each other. The video, "We All Belong, Dreamers, Citizens, and Immigrants from Everywhere" (see Selected Videos, "Atlas DIY"), shows ten students from many nations dreaming for the same thing Americans take for granted. The Dream Network has helped many undocumented students to live out of the shadows. For them, fear has a cure: education. According to interviews in "Democracy Now!", Dream Act supporters have "braved the threat of deportation to fight for the rights of undocumented youth as human beings" (see Selected Videos, "Democracy Now!").

Why is important to put a face on the Dreamers?

Jessica Esparza, a Washington State student, wants to become a registered nurse but her life is overshadowed by politics (see Selected Videos, "KCTS9"). Tedora is a Brazilian student left behind to get a better education when her parents were deported. After six years she travels to the Arizona border to see her mother through a fence. She is emotionally bent in traveling to the rusty fence without being able to hug her mother. She is part of a group called United We Dream, which confronts Senator Marco Rubio. Members are spread out over 26 states. The video, "Undocumented and Unafraid," sums up the mood of the Dreamers and their growth in the past 15 years. The Dreamers had lost their fear; nine of them crossed into Mexico and sought to re-enter the United States at Nogales ("Los Dreamers"). Lizbeth Mateos, a recent graduate from California State University, Northridge, was in the group. Lizabeth had been accepted to the University of Santa Clara School of Law. They were detained in jail for over a week. The purpose was to call attention to the breaking up of immigrant families.

On July 11, 2012, Marco Saavedra purposely had himself detained by immigration authorities in Miami, Florida where he hoped to be sent to the Broward Detention Center. Saavedra wanted to organize the other undocumented detained migrants and collect their stories, exposing the reality behind closed doors (see Selected Videos, "Dream Activist"). The actions of the Dreamers called attention to millions of children brought to the United States illegally and without choice. Even though many of them integrate and become active members of their American communities, they face the hardship of not being able to go to college, drive, or get jobs, and they constantly fear deportation. The people eligible for DACA came here as children and have been here for a substantial amount of time, and they are of good character (see Selected Videos, "Barbara Astrini").

Hate has a cure: education. Which of the case studies did you mostly identify with, or not, and why?

Meanwhile, the immigration debate goes on. No one seems to like the word *amnesty*, although for different reasons. Pro foreign-born groups resent the meaning of the word and the implication that the undocumented committed a crime. As most immigration and human rights activists know, hunger knows no borders. The purpose of legalization is to decriminalize the undocumented immigrant. Another insinuation that is resented is that immigrants are cutting into the front of the line—as if the process was the same as cutting into the line to see a movie. Latina/o and undocumented immigrants are not asking for anything more than immigrants did in the 19th century. They are demanding the same benefits, rights, and privileges afforded to legal immigrants. It is a frivolous argument, since the government gives preferences to those who come with money, thus ignoring that labor is capital.

The United States was built by the labor of immigrants. History shows that immigration benefits America in at least two ways. First, increased immigration expands the American workforce and encourages more business start-ups. Second, immigrants increase economic efficiency by raising the supply of low- and high-skilled immigrants.

In many cases, immigrants' educational backgrounds complement, rather than displace, the skills of the native-born labor market. Some economists are concerned because recently there has been a reverse trend and more Mexicans are entering the country. Mexico is important because it is the second largest Latin American nation, with 140 million people. The reversal is due to the pull factors lessening due to the economic recession that began in 2008 and the adjustments that are taking place.

As one source put it, "Their history was also shaped by wars and depressions, by the Treaty of Guadalupe Hidalgo and the Gadsden Purchase, and by shifting attitudes toward immigration" (Immigration Equality, 2015). The current xenophobia is driven by assumptions rather than education. The fact is that the Dreamers are the best educated advocates for immigration reform that the immigrant community has had. They have taken full advantage of American education and are extremely proficient in the use of technology—much more so than the average xenophobe. Each new generation is better prepared, which is what disturbs the average nativist who is afraid of the competition. Most Americans also do not understand the communitarianism that the Dreamers seem to express.

Does fear have a cure?

For the normalization of immigration

Nativists so often repeat the notion that amnesty encourages disrespect for the law that many Americans believe this assertion without criticism. This notion is hypocritical since agribusiness interests break laws every day by violating the rights of undocumented workers, yet the public turns the other way. Every day, investigators from the California Occupational Safety and Health Administration (Cal-OHSA) find unsafe working conditions in U.S. factories. According to Cal-OSHA, industries such as apparel and agriculture are hard to regulate because so many workers are undocumented immigrants, and they are afraid to come forward.

Even the Supreme Court has contributed to this charade. On March 27, 2002, the Supreme Court ruled five to four that the federal government may not compel employers to award back pay to undocumented immigrants whom an employer illegally fired for trying to join a labor union. The Supreme Court held that the National Labor Relations Board (NLRB) had avoided the national immigration law's purpose of preventing the hiring of undocumented immigrants when the lower court ordered Hoffman Plastic Compounds Inc. to pay almost $67,000 to José Castro, a Mexican undocumented worker fired for joining a union. Here, the Supreme Court offered employers immunity in violating the rights of undocumented workers and in violating labor laws. Due to this ruling, undocumented workers cannot join unions for fear of being fired, although the law specifically gives workers the right to join unions. A new amnesty law would give protection to these workers and end union busting.

Amnesty is needed, and makeshift measures like the guest worker program for workers from Mexico or Latin America are no solution because they further exploit workers who do not gain equity in society. When the United States had a guest worker program during and after World War II, there were gross violations of worker rights. Europe had guest worker programs, and they spawned racism in European countries. Americans mainly respect power, and the only power poor people have is the ballot box. Because undocumented workers do not have a vote, politicians and nativists target them.

The present immigration policy of the United States is based on family reunification. Even conservatives such as Utah Republican Senator Orrin Hatch and the conservative Heritage Foundation have supported the principle of family reunification. Many of those to whom Congress would grant amnesty are longtime residents of this country, and most have children who were born here. Immigrants are hardworking people, and for the most part they are younger than white Americans, so they will be productive workers for many years. Most research proves that fewer of them will seek public assistance than is the norm in the general population and that many of them will become highly skilled professionals if given a chance.

University of Maryland economist Julian Simon says, "Immigration is the same good bargain for Americans that it was 100 years ago—and even more so today because we can provide them even more opportunities to make their dreams come true and enrich our nation as a result. . . . The evidence is clear: Immigrants don't come here to take welfare, they come here to make jobs" (Specht, 1996). Unfortunately, well-funded hate groups distort the facts and malign hardworking people. People forget that as a group, undocumented Latinos represent one of the largest groups of workers killed at the Twin Towers on September 11, 2001. They forget that more than 37,000 noncitizen immigrants, many of whom had parents without documents, fought in the recent war in Iraq; some died for this country.

Some white Americans cannot come to grips with the fact that most of those who will benefit from amnesty do not look like them. In

Chicago alone, "[m]ore than 130,000 Chicago residents, mostly from Mexico, could become new citizens by December, and that could translate into increased political power for Latinos." Immigrants are showing that they are assimilating politically, and hundreds of thousands have become citizens, and they are voting. This is going a long way in ending the historical discrimination that has marred this great nation (Oclander, 1994).

At one time the American Federation of Labor (AFL) was the greatest enemy of both unauthorized and authorized immigrants. The AFL has changed its stance and today supports amnesty. Undocumented workers are among the most faithful union members, and their presence creates jobs and expands the economy for higher-paying jobs. Still, most Americans have a less favorable view of Latin American immigrants, which is in part based on biases toward their home countries and their race. For instance, a September 6, 2001 Gallup Poll showed that Americans overwhelmingly opposed amnesty or citizenship to undocumented workers or their families. The data also suggest that much of the opposition is because the public believes Congress will grant amnesty or citizenship mainly to Mexicans. What is clear is that the public associates negative stereotypes of Mexico with immigration. Where does the public get these negative views of Mexicans?

In 2001, a Gallup Poll showed that just 17 percent of Americans in 2001 had a very favorable view of Mexico, ranking well below the 51 percent who had a very favorable view of Canada, 43 percent with a favorable view of Australia, and 41 percent with a favorable view of Great Britain. Mexico was on par with Israel, Egypt, and Brazil. Where do Americans get this view? The media has constructed much of the negative images of immigration, from the War on Drugs to negative discourse about unsafe trucks operating on U.S. highways (Saad, 2001).

Yet U.S. prosperity is tied to Latin America. Today, the United States exports much more to Latin America than the United States buys from it. In addition, at one time the United States did not have a quota on Latin American immigration because Americans claimed they had a common heritage with Latin Americans. Europe, after all, had colonized all of the Americas, and the United States took the lead in forming a Pan American union. The United States has also intervened in the affairs of Latin American countries by overthrowing constitutionally elected presidents.

Ironically, Americans want Latin Americans to be grateful to them. Americans resent when Latin American countries elect communist or even socialist leaders. So why not help those countries help themselves?

If every undocumented immigrant were to return home, they would bankrupt those countries. Remittances earned by the sweat of the undocumented workers keep their homelands afloat. A regularization of immigration would help those countries financially and contribute to the health of the region.

Finally, the argument that the immigration acts discriminate against the Irish and other Europeans is wrongheaded. For years, U.S. immigration laws excluded Asians altogether and no one complained. Today, there are literally hundreds of thousands, if not millions, of Irish, Poles, Canadians, and others who are in the United States on unauthorized status and are free to move about the country.

The United States has also granted a large number of visas to refugees from other countries because these refugees were supposedly fleeing tyranny. This country has been generous in admitting hundreds of thousands of Soviet Jews because of anti-Semitism in the former Soviet Union. All that the refugees had to show was "a well-founded fear of persecution." Soviet Jews in 1989 alone cost the U.S. government $350 million. Unlike Latino immigrants who are fleeing hunger, Soviet Jews, as refugees, are eligible for public assistance. The United States has granted hundreds of thousands of Armenians special status as well (Washburn and Hasemyer, 2001; Chapman, 1989; Ferriss, 1993). In 2000, there were more than 50,000 Armenians in Glendale, California alone, which is great because they add to the diversity of the region. The nativists are against the regularization of immigration because they believe that it will benefit darker-skinned people, changing the racial profile of the United States.

Much of the immigration debate is based on rumor. The truth is the debate is dumb. Take the case of the Dreamers. They have been totally acculturated. They know the language, the history of this country, and they indulge in its culture. They want to become citizens and even serve in the armed forces. Just to appease a fringe that does not understand the issues, the opposition wants to rescind Obama's 2012 order and ship them back. It doesn't make sense.

ANOTHER POV (POINT OF VIEW)

The Dreamers and Other Undocumented Immigrants Are Assets to American Society

Ana Miriam Barragan, Dreamers Coordinator, University of California, Irvine

Wake up. Undocumented immigrants are the backbone of this country—a country that uses them for labor, that exploits them for profit, and that deprives them of their human rights. Undocumented immigrants are major contributors to the stability of this nation's capitalist society. Politicians and corporations want to make sure it continues this way while the media fails to cover the true ways of how undocumented immigrants are valuable assets to American society.

History repeats itself. Undocumented immigrants are a monetary asset that benefits the government and corporations. Throughout the history of the United States, well thought out plans have been developed to target, control, and dehumanize vulnerable groups of immigrants. It is estimated that unauthorized workers pay close to $12 billion in state and local taxes every year. Congress will not issue these individuals a Social Security number but has created a way for these people to file their taxes, encouraging them to believe that this is the only way they can prove their "good moral character." Furthermore, the government does not accept the responsibility of these people because of their immigration status. This means the government does not allocate additional funding for programs to serve the undocumented community. In conclusion, even though undocumented immigrants greatly contribute to public services, they do not have access to federally funded programs and their most basic needs are not met.

The government is also the key player that lawfully encourages corporations to take advantage of undocumented people in order to make profit. For example, there are many undocumented immigrants working for the agricultural sector and the textile industry where they are overworked and deprived of fair wages and benefits. In other cases, they face dangerous or poor working conditions and they are not compensated for their work. Undocumented immigrants are discouraged from joining unions, asking for worker's compensation, or accessing health care. Most often, they do not have a means to voice this extortion because the law simply does not rule in favor of undocumented individuals. This situation allows for the exploitation of undocumented immigrants and for an increase in corporation profits.

The media strengthens the relationship that the government and corporations have regarding undocumented immigrants. They contribute to the criminalization of this population and allow corporations to get away with writing hateful, anti-immigrant laws, such as SB 1070 in Arizona. These types of laws are supported by the bed quota that the government established in 2009. Immigration Custom Enforcement is required by law to have an average of 34,000 people in detention every day (Robbins, 2013). This ultimately benefits the corporations who own private prisons and make $200 per person a day. This sums up to $5 billion in profit that private prisons make in one year (Díaz and Keen, 2015). Overall, undocumented immigrants are an asset to these corporations, which work hard to increase xenophobia among American citizens. These types of laws and quotas influence the maltreatment of these people, instilling fear among the community in order to keep them invisible and quiet.

The same way politicians create laws to support corporations, the media influences policies and laws. The media overall contributes to the intangible walls that exist within the undocumented community. For years, Americans have believed the ideology of the desirable, good immigrant versus the undesirable, bad immigrant. The desirable immigrants tend to be the youth who assimilate faster, know English, and have the potential to attend institutions of higher education. This is problematic because it creates a disconnect between people rather than addressing the real issues.

Take DACA and DAPA (Deferred Action for Parents of Americans and Lawful Permanent Residents), for example. They are social constructs of "worthiness" written for the so-called desirable immigrants who have more to contribute to American society because they are young adults with at least a high school diploma or who have children who have lawful status in the United States. Even though people who benefit from DACA have been able to contribute to society and the economy to a greater extent, this hurts the undocumented community as a whole. It damages the efforts that individuals and organizations have made toward comprehensive immigration reform for all, not just for the glorified youth. With DACA in place, life has become easier to navigate for a lot of undocumented young people. A lot of these young adults are inspired to do well academically and to develop professional skills. As a result, most of DACA recipients have changed their occupations to higher-paying jobs, which means they pay more state and federal taxes. Some of them have also started buying homes, purchasing cars, and getting loans, all of which contributes to the economy of this country.

Obama announced DAPA in November of 2014. It was an immigration policy to grant deferred action status to undocumented immigrants who have lived in the United States since 2010 and had children who were either American citizens or lawful permanent residents (Posner, 2015).

However, people need to be critical of the negative effect that programs such as DACA and DAPA have on the overall undocumented community. The new generation of individuals who are now protected under DACA and have a temporary work permit feel a disconnect to the undocumented. Most of them are not advocating for immigrants' rights and most of them do not feel comfortable disclosing their immigration status. It is true that more undocumented people have come out of the shadows in recent years; however, these people make up a very small percentage of the estimated 11 million undocumented immigrants in the nation.

"Undocumented, Unafraid, and Unapologetic" is a political strategy that gave undocumented people the courage to yell their existence. However, the community is driven by fear. People do not have any other option except to put their fear aside and to go to work with the hope that life will provide a better future for their children. Fear does not allow undocumented immigrants to voice injustices, ask for benefits, and demand their human rights. Many undocumented individuals continue to live hidden away and have internalized the misbelief that they do not deserve protection, rights, or benefits because they have engaged in criminal activities by crossing the border or by overstaying their visas. The fear of deportation and family separation does not allow undocumented immigrants to risk their stay in this country even though fear is used to oppress the undocumented community. Both politicians and corporations instill fear among undocumented individuals in order to use them as puppets, to take their power, and to divide them. Ultimately, fear is what drives the undocumented community. Fear is what keeps them moving. Fear is the backbone of their social justice. Undocumented individuals have not lost their fear; they have learned to control it.

Even though undocumented immigrants put food on our tables, clean our universities, cut our grass, do our hair and nails, make our clothes, and serve us every single day, most people fail to humanize their existence. In addition, immigration is not a Latinx issue but a multiracial and multiethnic problem that affects many people from different parts of the world. All undocumented immigrants are a valuable asset to the United States. Not only do undocumented immigrants enrich the diversity of this nation, but they also create revenue and profits that benefit all the people in this country. People of all ethnicities and cultures have to stop glorifying young, undocumented immigrants because they truly are just a product of their parent's hard work and sacrifices.

Undocumented Immigrants Should be Excluded: Key Arguments in a Political Debate

Ronald López, Professor, California State University, Sonoma

Caveat: *The author does not ascribe to these views, but was given the task of effectively presenting these ideas.*

The law and upholding legal standards of admission to the United States:

Arguments made by xenophobes to exclude undocumented immigrants.

Political Arguments

1. Undocumented immigrants have either entered illegally or have overstayed their visas. In a nation of laws like the United States, persons living here should be identified according to an established system that includes citizens, legal residents, and temporary or "guest" workers. To allow a permanent class of people who are undocumented or "illegal" to reside here is to accept the principle that U.S. laws do not apply equally to all people. To uphold the principle that we are a nation of law, determined by constitutional processes, a permanent class of "undocumented" people should NOT be allowed to reside here.
2. Allowing immigrants "amnesty" rewards illegal behavior. One solution that has been proposed, and has been attempted in the past has been to reward undocumented immigrants by awarding them amnesty or allowing the undocumented to apply for legal status, and to come out of the shadows. However, this effectively rewards those who have managed to enter the United States illegally (or to overstay their visas) and who have managed to evade deportation. This is counterproductive and indicates that the United States is not serious about enforcing its laws.
3. Undocumented immigrants are unregulated. This both allows criminals and repeat offenders to live freely in the United States and creates pockets of populations unfamiliar with American laws and institutions. In areas of the U.S.–Mexico border region and in concentrations of Mexican and other undocumented immigrants in the United States, crime and criminal enterprises thrive. Although most of the community is peaceful and law-abiding, they provide "cover" for international criminal "gangs" that traffic and control the street sale of drugs and also engage in human trafficking, both for immigration and for prostitution. This unregulated population also creates a potential threat of unregulated disease and cover for possible terrorists. Therefore, such populations should be disallowed and deported when possible.

Economic Arguments against Immigration

4. Undocumented immigrants swell the ranks of unskilled and low-paid workers. A surplus of labor supply keeps wages low. Undocumented immigrants also make unionization efforts difficult, if not impossible. This suppresses the aspirations of American workers, especially legal immigrants (legal residents and guest workers) and low-skilled American citizens, especially those from the same ethnic groups. Because many undocumented workers have a "dual frame of reference," they see themselves and the low wages they are willing to accept in terms of their earning potential back home. They may earn much more than they would in their home countries and be willing to accept comparatively low wages here in the United States. This allows them to compete effectively even with better-trained and more skilled U.S. workers. And they are likely to compete primarily with workers of similar backgrounds: Mexican undocumented workers will compete primarily with U.S. Latino workers. So while U.S. Latino workers may in some cases be sympathetic, they are the ones most likely to be hurt by undocumented workers from Latin America.
5. Millions in remittances represent a net loss of wealth to the United States. Undocumented immigrants, especially those from Mexico and Central America, send millions to family members in their countries of origin each year. These "remittances" are the second largest source of revenue for the Mexican economy, after oil production. This money, if held by U.S. citizens and legal resident aliens, would more likely be spent here in the United States.
6. Local community economic expenditures are greater than the economic contributions of undocumented immigrants because they do not pay taxes. The presence of undocumented workers puts a fiscal strain on local economies. Many argue that because many workers are paid in cash, and because undocumented workers often engage in a cash economy, their earnings in the United States are largely untaxed. And while their children may, in some cases, be U.S. citizens, undocumented immigrant families are not paying their fair share in taxes. The costs of police, hospital, and educational services, it is argued, are far greater than the sales taxes paid by the undocumented. It is true that undocumented immigrants can obtain a Taxpayer Identification Number from the IRS and pay income tax, but

not all do so. And because undocumented immigrants live in poor and run-down areas, the cost of police and emergency services to those areas is much higher than to middle-income areas. In short, even if the low wages of the undocumented stimulate local economies, as has been argued by proponents, that economic boon is not used to offset the higher costs incurred by undocumented immigrants for public services. In short, undocumented immigrants are a strain on local and regional economies.

Cultural arguments against undocumented immigration

7. Undocumented immigrants, especially Mexican undocumented immigrants, resist assimilation and are slow to learn English. The refusal to learn English creates problems in communicating with the police and other emergency services, thus incurring increased public expense. Their refusal to assimilate, even among many Mexican Americans, means that ethnic enclaves exist wherever Mexican Americans live, thus creating unneeded divisions in the United States. This reveals that although many Mexicans wish to live and work in the United States, they are actively refusing to truly become part of the United States. People who immigrate to the United States should make an effort to learn the culture and the English language. Ironically, many of their children, who are also undocumented and thus equally subject to removal, are highly assimilated and competitive with talented and skilled Americans, both in education and in employment, although some argue that their talents should be exploited
8. Mexican immigrants, by refusing to assimilate, are transforming the culture in areas of the United States, and large swaths of the United States are being "Mexicanized" or "Latinized." If American culture is to change, the American people should have something to say about this, but there has been no public debate on this issue. The United States should not adopt the culture of its economically inferior neighbor by a passive "reverse assimilation" process. Immigrants to the United States should adopt the culture of the United States: Americans should not be forced to learn Spanish and become "Latinized."

Education

Undocumented students should not have their education subsidized by American taxpayers. Undocumented immigrants, especially Mexicans, but also Central Americans and others, should be charged the same fees as "foreign students" or "out of state" students when attending American public universities and colleges. Today, many schools and states are not only charging undocumented alien students "in-state tuition," but are even allowing them to compete for grants intended for American or legal resident students! Some undocumented students have even been class valedictorians! This is unfair to students who are U.S. citizens and legal residents. It rewards illegal behavior, and even if these students were brought to the United States by their parents as children, these advantages must be maintained for U.S. citizens and legal resident students! Their parents and they themselves should apply to legalize their status, and students or their parents should be required to serve a minimum number of years in the U.S. armed services before they are allowed to apply to public colleges and universities.

Arguments have been made against each of these points in the preceding pages. How would you refute or agree with each point?

NOTES

1. It was severely criticized as a new form of the Monroe Doctrine.
2. According to David Gutiérrez, League of United Latin American Citizens (LULAC) was among the foremost opponents of the bracero program and the use of undocumented labor.
3. The "Dream Act" struggle formally began nationally on April 25, 2001 when Representative Luis Gutiérrez (D-Illinois) introduced the "Immigrant Children's Educational Advancement and Dropout Prevention Act of 2001." But it is much older and has come a long way since that time. Ownership today belongs to the Dreamers, young undocumented immigrants.

BIBLIOGRAPHY

Acuña, Rodolfo F. "Today's American Dream doesn't separate reality from the dream." *Latina Vista*, February 8, 2013. http://latinalista.com/columns/guestvoz/guest-voz-todays-american-dream-doesnt-separate-reality-from-the-dream

Acuña, Rodolfo F. "Acuña on the American Dream as Nightmare." *Mexmigration: History and Politics of Mexican Immigration*, February 4, 2013. http://mexmigration.blogspot.com/2013/02/acuna-on-american-dream-as-nightmare.html

Acuña, Rodolfo F. "The Wall." *counterpunch*, March 9, 2012. http://www.counterpunch.org/2012/03/09/the-wall

The American Committee for the Protection of the Foreign Born. "Our Badge of Infamy, A Petition to the United Nations on the Treatment of the Mexican Immigrant." April 1959, 24.

Anderson, Henry. *The Bracero Program in California*. Berkeley: School of Public Health, University of California, 1961.

Benavides, D., and R. Golten. "Righting the Record: A Response to the GAO's 2004 Report Treaty of Guadalupe Hidalgo: Findings and Possible Options Regarding Longstanding Community Land Grant Claims in New Mexico." *Natural Resources Journal* 48, no. 4 (2008): 857–926.

Berlin Wall Foundation. "Fatalities at the Berlin Wall, 1961–1989." http://www.berliner-mauer-gedenkstaette.de/en/todesopfer-240.html

Castle, William R. "The Monroe Doctrine and Pan-Americanism." *The Annals of the American Academy of Political and Social Science* 204, Democracy and the Americas (July, 1939): 111–118.

Center for Immigration Studies. "Poverty and Income." http://www.cis.org/articles/2001/mexico/poverty.html

Chapman, Stephen. "Which Refugees Deserve Our Help." *The Baton Rouge State Times*, September 16, 1989.

Chávez, Leo R. "The Power of the Imagined Community: The Settlement of Undocumented Mexicans and Central Americans in the United States." *American Anthropologist* 96, no 1 (1994): 52–73.

Coalson, George O. *The Development of the Migratory Farm Labor System in Texas: 1900–1954*. San Francisco: R&E Research Associates, 1977.

Craig, Richard B. *The Bracero Program*. Austin: University of Texas Press, 1971.

"DACA (Deferred Action for Childhood Arrivals)," *Immigration Equality*, 2015. http://www.immigrationequality.org/get-legal-help/our-legal-resources/path-to-status-in-the-u-s/daca-deferred-action-for-childhood-arrivals

de la Garza, Rodolfo, Louis DeSipio, F. Chris Garcia, John Garcia, and Angelo Falcon. *Latino Voices: Mexican, Puerto Rican, and Cuban Perspectives on American Politics*. Boulder: Westview, 1992.

Delgado, Hector L. *New Immigrants, Old Unions: Organizing Undocumented Workers in Los Angeles*. Philadelphia: Temple University Press, 1993.

Democracy Now, "After Years of Struggle, DREAM Act Activists Hail Monumental Victory for Immigrants Living in Fear," PBS, June 18, 2012. http://www.democracynow.org/2012/6/18/after_years_of_struggle_dream_act

Díaz, Melanie. and Timothy Keen, "How US Private Prisons Profit from Immigrant Detention," COHA, May 12, 2015. http://www.coha.org/how-us-private-prisons-profit-from-immigrant-detention/

"Dream Act: Summary." *National Immigration Law Center*, May 2011. https://www.nilc.org/issues/immigration-reform-and-executive-actions/dreamact/dream summary/

Epstein, Gil S., and Avi Weiss. "The Why, When, and How of Immigration Amnesties." *Journal of Population Economics* 24, no. 1 (2011): 285–316.

Equal Employment Opportunity Commission. "Immigration Reform and Control Act of 1986." 8 USC 1101 note. https://www.eeoc.gov/eeoc/history/35th/thelaw/irca.html

Ferriss, Susan. "Census Data Reveal Wide Immigrant Diversity: Ex-Soviets among the Poorest." *The San Francisco Chronicle*, September 23, 1993.

Furchtgott-Roth, Diana. "How Immigrants Boost U.S. Economic Growth." *The Fiscal Times*, December 2, 2014. http://www.thefiscaltimes.com/2014/12/02/How-Immigrants-Boost-US-Economic-Growth

Galarza, Ernesto. *Tragedy at Chualar: El Crucero de las Treinta y dos Cruces*. Santa Barbara, CA.: McNally & Loftin, 1977.

Galarza, Ernesto. *Merchants of Labor*. Santa Barbara, CA: McNally & Loftin, 1964.

Gonzales, Roberto, Veronica Terriquez, and Stephen Ruszczyk. "Becoming DACAmented: Assessing the Short-Term Benefits of Deferred Action for Childhood Arrivals (DACA)." *American Behavioral Scientist* 58, no. 14 (2014): 1852–1872.

Griswold del Castillo, Richard. "War's End: Treaty of Guadalupe Hidalgo," *PBS*, March 14, 2006. http://www.pbs.org/kera/usmexicanwar/war/wars_end_guadalupe.html

Guillen, Liz. "Undocumented Immigrant Students: A Very Brief Overview of Access to Higher Education In California," Policy Advocate for Public Advocates, Inc., ca. 1991. https://tcla.gseis.ucla.edu/reportcard/features/5-6/ab540/pdf/UndocImmigStud.pdf

Gutiérrez, D. *Walls and Mirrors: Mexican Americans, Mexican Immigrants, and the Politics of Ethnicity*. Oakland: University of California, 1995.

Guzmán, Betsy. "The Hispanic Population: Census 2000 Brief." U.S. Census Bureau, May 2001. http://www.census.gov/prod/2001pubs/c2kbr01-3.pdf

Hinojosa-Ojeda, Raúl. "The Economic Benefits of Comprehensive Immigration Reform." *The Cato Journal* 32, no. 1 (2012): 175.

Immigration Equality. "DACA: Deferred Action for Childhood Arrivals." 2015. http://www.immigrationequality.org/get-legal-help/our-legal-resources/path-to-status-in-the-u-s/daca-deferred-action-for-childhood-arrivals

"Immigration . . . Mexican." Library of Congress. http://loc.gov/teachers/classroommaterials/presentationsandactivities/presentations/immigration/mexican.html

Karlson, Stephen H., and Eliakim Katz. "Immigration Amnesties." *Applied Economics* 42, no. 18 (2010): 2299–2315.

Klein, Christine. "Treaties of Conquest: Property Rights, Indian Treaties, and the Treaty of Guadalupe Hidalgo." *New Mexico Law Review* 26 (1996): 201–655.

Krogstad, Jens Manuel, and Jeffrey S. Passel. "Those from Mexico will benefit most from Obama's executive action." Pew Research Center, November 20, 2014. Accessed November 21, 2014. http://www.pewresearch.org/fact-tank/2014/11/20/those-from-mexico-will-benefit-most-from-obamas-executive-action

Leticia A. v. Board of Regents. No. 588982-4 (Superior Court, County of Alameda, May 7, 1985). California Education Code § 68062(h).

Ling-Ling, Yeh. "United States Must Reject Mexico's Amnesty Demands." *The Union Leader*, August 13, 2001.

Longacre, Ryan D. "National Mythology, Private Histories, and Public Debates: A Critical Reading of Alma Lopez's '1848: Chicanos in the U.S. Landscape After the Treaty of Guadalupe Hidalgo.'" Master's thesis, California State University, Long Beach, 2010.

López, Mark Hugo, and Paul Taylor. "Latino Voters in the 2012 Election." Pew Research Center, November 7, 2012. http://www.pewhispanic.org/2012/11/07/latino-voters-in-the-2012-election

Markman, Jon D. "Prop. 187's Quiet Student Revolution: Activism: In Contrast to More Publicized Walkouts, Latino Youngsters Are Turning Opposition to Immigration Measure into a Real-Life Civics Lesson." *Los Angeles Times*, November 6, 1994.

Miles, Richard. "What Mexican immigration problem?" *USA Today*, January 5, 2015. http://www.usatoday.com/story/opinion/2015/01/03/mexican-immigration-richard-miles/21056155

Muller, Thomas. *California's Newest Immigrants: A Summary.* Washington, DC: Urban Institute Press, 1984.

Nakamura, David. "Obama's 7 State of the Union talking points. No. 4: Immigration: The president is expected to highlight the economic benefits of immigration reform, framing the debate in a light that might appeal to Capitol Hill conservatives." Weblog post. *Washington Post*, January 26, 2014.

National Coalition for Dignity and Amnesty for Undocumented Immigrants. "Experts: Illegal Workers Pay Dividend." *New York Times*, October 15, 2000.

Nicholls, Walter, and Tara Fiorito. "Dreamers Unbound: Immigrant Youth Mobilizing." *New Labor Forum* 24, no. 1 (2015): 86–92.

"No Visa-Free Travel to US for Central Europeans." *Migration News* 4, no. 9 (September 1997).

Oclander, Jorge. "New Citizens Could Power Latino Bloc." *Chicago Sun-Times*, July 17, 1994.

Passel, Jeffrey S., D'Vera Cohn, and Mark Hugo Lopez. "Hispanics Account for More than Half of Nation's Growth in Past Decade." Pew Research Center, March 24, 2011. http://www.pewhispanic.org/2011/03/24/hispanics-account-for-more-than-half-of-nations-growth-in-past-decade

Posner, Eric. "Faithfully Executed." *Slate*, February 19, 2015. http://www.slate.com/articles/news_and_politics/view_from_chicago/2015/02/obama_s_dapa_immigration_program_is_legal_judge_hanen_s_injunction_will.html

Regents of University of California v. Superior Court of Los Angeles County (Bradford) (1990) 225 Cal.App.3d 972, reh. den. (1991).

Reisler, Mark. *By the Sweat of Their Brow: Mexican Immigration to the United States, 1900–1940.* Westport, CT: Greenwood Press, 1976.

Robbins, Ted. "Little-Known Immigration Mandate Keeps Detention Beds Full." NPR, November 19, 2013. http://www.npr.org/2013/11/19/245968601/little-known-immigration-mandate-keeps-detention-beds-full

Saad, Lydia. "Americans Clearly Oppose Amnesty for Illegal Mexican Immigrants; Poll Analyses: Few Favor Increasing Immigration More Generally." *Gallup News Service*, September 6, 2001.

Sotomayor, Teresa Maya. "Estados Unidos Y El Panamericanismo: El Caso De La I Conferencia Internacional Americana (1889–1890)." *Historia Mexicana* 45, no. 4 (1996): 759–781.

Specht, Jim. "Welcome to America: Law barely slows rate of influx." *Esquire*, December 16, 1996. http://www.enquirer.com/editions/1996/12/16/loc_immigrantsnational.html

The Treaty of Guadalupe Hidalgo, February 2, 1848. http://www.militarymuseum.org/Hidalgo.html

U.S. Department of Homeland Security. "1924: Border Patrol Established." U.S. Customs and Border Protection. http://www.cbp.gov/about/history/1924-border-patrol-established

"US–Mexico Border Fence / Great Wall of Mexico Secure Fence." *GlobalSecurity.org.* http://www.globalsecurity.org/security/systems/mexico-wall.htm

Washburn, David, and David Hasemyer, "Exploited Visas Making 'a Sieve' of U.S. Border." *San Diego Union-Tribune*, October 28, 2001.

Yang, K. Wayne. "Organizing MySpace: Youth Walkouts, Pleasure, Politics, and New Media." *Educational Foundations* 21, no. 1–2 (2009): 9–28.

SELECTED VIDEOS

Atlas DIY. "We All Belong, Dreamers, Citizens, and Immigrants from Everywhere," YouTube video, 5:00, posted February 17, 2013. https://www.youtube.com/watch?v=8JMArfZQuaY

Barbara Astrini. "Undocumented Shadows—A Dream Act Infographic," YouTube video, 2:49, posted December 2, 2011. https://www.youtube.com/watch?v=MXnqhG2h9QA

BBC News. "I'm a trucker not an immigration officer," YouTube video, 12:39, posted June 10, 2015. https://www.youtube.com/watch?v=P5FIsmquQqA

CNN. "Grad student's illegal immigrant life," YouTube video, 3:02, posted September 25, 2012. https://www.youtube.com/watch?v=PCgFdCkmREE

Democracy Now! "DREAM Act Activists Hail Monumental Victory for Immigrants Living in Fear," YouTube video, 23:23, posted June 18, 2012. https://www.youtube.com/watch?v=7G6zP8KLTyA

DonahayAcademy. "Treaty of Guadalupe Hidalgo," YouTube video, 14:59, posted February 24, 2014. https://www.youtube.com/watch?v=6hfCC7uwoO8

DreamActivist. "DREAMers Infiltrate Immigration Detention Center," YouTube video, 4:00, posted August 2, 2012. https://www.youtube.com/watch?v=QPqEuTop41g

Florence3711. "Migration Case Study—Mexico to USA," YouTube video, 2:15, posted June 3, 2012. https://www.youtube.com/watch?v=Ubiq0tXjJ-M

Greenafghan. "Stephen Colbert on immigration," YouTube video, 5:28, posted September 24, 2010. https://www.youtube.com/watch?v=hl8G2rgkSIw

Herschelskywalker. "BEST VERSION: Reagan on Amnesty & Illegal Immigration," YouTube video, 2:07, posted July 18, 2014. https://www.youtube.com/watch?v=HjrBjLSz5aA

Historicas y noticias relevantes en Arizona. "Los Dreamers 9, son liberados del centro de detención y regresan a la garita de Nogales, AZ," You Tube video, 1:47, posted September 29, 2013. https://www.youtube.com/watch?v=7VQ4kF9GgB0

Hometheaterdoctor. "Reagan, Clinton, Ford, Bush I and Bush II Explain it all to Obama," YouTube video, 5:43, posted March 3, 2010. https://www.youtube.com/watch?v=79pvVpN7-9s

KCTS9. "I'm a Dreamer." YouTube video, 7:45, posted August 29, 2013. https://www.youtube.com/watch?v=1PWJFowO1u4

Kinetic Typography 101. "Case Study: Project Dreamer." YouTube video, 1:05, posted June 14, 2013. https://www.youtube.com/watch?v=lFUlKVokdyI

Kountouris, John. "The Truth Behind The Treaty of Hidalgo and the Illegal Immigration Issue in the USA," YouTube video, 8:39, posted May 9, 2010. https://www.youtube.com/watch?v=Gqyl-H5-KkY

Mawizaaable. "My Life As an Undocumented Student! #Dreamer," YouTube video, 6:58, posted September 1, 2015. https://www.youtube.com/watch?v=jcqDWrufuiE

Nuñez, Byron. "The Deletion of Article X from the Treaty of Guadalupe Hidalgo," YouTube video, 4:05, posted December 8, 2014. https://www.youtube.com/watch?v=QujrIz3J_uk

Shatteredverve. "Undocumented and Unafraid," YouTube video, 7:59, posted February 28, 2011. https://www.youtube.com/watch?v=xdOrxLLHo0U

TCCTV. "Stop Amnesty for Illegal Immigrants—Expert Reveals the True Cost of Amnesty," YouTube video, 9:57, posted March 22, 2007. https://www.youtube.com/watch?v=hrF9V2e4A1o

VOA News. "'Dreamers' Give Human Face to Immigration Reform." YouTube video, 2:48, posted July 11, 2013. https://www.youtube.com/watch?v=Oq5mhWUrqWQ

10

Changing Cuban Relations: U.S. Military and Political Presence in Cuba

BACKGROUND

Cuban independence predates the Spanish American War. In the 1880s, the Spanish crown forced Cuban revolutionaries into exile. Among them was the poet and political essayist José Martí. Many of these exiles spent time in the United States, returning to the island in 1895 to lead an armed rebellion. By 1898, relations between the United States and Spain worsened, largely due to American sugar growers in Cuba and a jingoistic American people who pressured the United States to intervene.

American intervention was not popular among the Cuban revolutionaries, who resented U.S. opportunism. It had for 30 years ignored their pleas for help. But now that the rebels were about to win, the United States hijacked their revolution. On the 18th of May in 1895, Martí wrote to Mexican revolutionist Manuel Mercado and bitterly complaining, "*Viví en el monstruo y le conozco las entrañas*" (I lived in the monster and know its entrains). Years of exile in the United States exposed Martí to

American racism, and he feared that the United States would appropriate its independence (Gambitos, "Carta inconclusa de Martí a su amigo Manuel Mercado").

Why was José Martí cautious about American involvement in the War for Independence? How did he represent the collective historical memory of Cuban exiles?

Cuba is just 90 miles off the Florida coast, and Americans have always considered it within America's sphere of influence and vital to the security of the region. After the Mexican American War (1848), slave interests pressured Washington D.C. to invade the island and financed and equipped filibustering expeditions in an attempt to claim the island. The ambition of most was to mimic the seizure of Texas in 1836. In 1854, the Ostend Manifesto claimed that the U.S. had a right to Cuba (to take it by force if Spain refused to sell it). Southern cotton growers and sugar planters wanted to extend slavery to Cuba. Fortunately, their ambitions were checked by U.S. abolitionists and Northerners.

Why would some Americans believe that Cuba belonged to them?

Martí and the other independistas knew this history and did not want to become a vassal of the United States. In the end, the peace treaty ending the Spanish American war was exclusively between Spain and the United States. Cubans and Puerto Ricans did not sit at the table. The Cuban revolutionaries had no say and were not a part of the negotiations. The Treaty of Paris gave the United States Guam and Puerto Rico and political control of the Philippines. Cuba was supposedly independent; however, it was forced to accept the Platt Amendment that restricted Cuba's right to make treaties with other nations and gave the United States the right to intervene in Cuban affairs. The Platt Amendment further gave the United States the right to lease Guantanamo Bay for the purpose of building a U.S. naval base. Cubans at first resisted the U.S.-approved constitution but was forced to sign it in return for American withdrawal from the island.

Why are many Cubans and Latinas/os resentful about the Platt Amendment?

American growers controlled Cuba's sugar economy amid widespread government corruption and a disregard for the poor. Cubans made progress building railroads and seaports. However, their work was plagued by yellow fever. The Cuban economy was shaped to meet the needs of American capitalists and was made dependent on the United States which protected American business interests through support for dictators favoring American interests. During the Great Depression of the 1930s, Cuban students led protests to reform the government at which time Sgt. Fulgencio Batista, leader of the noncommissioned officers, became the military commander of the Cuban armed forces and the de facto head of state.

U.S. President Franklin D. Roosevelt nulled the Platt Amendment in the 1930s but continued to rent Guantanamo Bay. In 1940, Batista was elected president of Cuba, and during World War II the sugar industry prospered. In 1944, Batista lost the presidential election and left for the United States. In 1952, Batista returned and led a coup d'état, beginning a repressive and notoriously corrupt era.

Why is Batista revered by many Cuban exiles? Why would poor Cubans have another point of view?

Enter Fidel Castro, a young student activist, who, on July 26, 1953, led an unsuccessful attack on the Moncada Army Barracks in Santiago de Cuba. After serving six months in jail, Castro went into exile in Mexico, organizing the 26th of July Movement. Joined by the Argentinean Ernesto "Che" Guevara in December of 1956, Castro, with fewer than 60 revolutionaries, landed in Oriente Province. Unsuccessful, the survivors fled to the Sierra Maestre Mountains, from where they waged a guerrilla war. After prolonged fighting, the revolutionaries entered Havana in January of 1959 and took control of the government.[1]

Fidel Castro's successful revolution brought back memories of what happened in 1895. The fears of Latin American reformers increased in 1954 when a CIA-backed coup overthrew Guatemalan President Jacob Arbenz. It sent the message that the United States would not permit political, economic, or social reform in Latin America. It began an era of CIA intervention and intervention via the Eisenhower Doctrine.

The events made Castro the standard-bearer of reform. Not only had he overthrown a dictator but he challenged U.S. hegemony in the hemisphere. Addressing the people of Santiago, Castro recalled a history of betrayal: on January 3, 1959, he promised the Cuban people, "The

Revolution Begins Now"—Castro pledged not to sell out the revolution as in the case of 1895:

> PEOPLE OF SANTIAGO, COMPATRIOTS OF ALL CUBA
> We have finally reached Santiago de Cuba. The road was long and difficult, but we finally arrived. . . . Our Revolution will go forward nonetheless and this time cannot be over the power. It will not be like 1895 when the Americans came and took over, intervening at the last moment, and afterwards did not even allow Calixto García to assume leadership, although he had fought at Santiago de Cuba for 30 years . . . (Castro, 1959)

What is the significance and importance of Castro's words that it was not 1895?

The new revolutionary government vowed to end corruption, promote Cuban nationalism, and improve the lives of the poorer classes. Foreigners and large landowners owned much of the island, which was dependent on a single crop—sugar. The new government promised a leveling of society; this policy alienated much of the Cuban middle and upper classes. Above all, Castro threatened U.S. corporations that monopolized the land. In another controversial act to lessen dependence on sugar and to diversify, Castro introduced industrialization programs. Unable to get aid from the United States, Castro signed a treaty with the Soviet Union in 1960. The Soviet Union would give Cuba massive amounts of industrial equipment and technical aid in return for sugar. Finally, the Cuban government nationalized American-owned properties, which included 36 large sugar mills, the national phone system, the national electrical system, oil refineries, and U.S.-owned banks. The United States retaliated with a trade embargo, placing sanctions on countries trading with Cuba.

In 1961, Castro announced that the revolution was a socialist revolution. He initiated a massive education and literacy campaign and poured resources into the health system. Meanwhile, the United States sponsored an ill-fated invasion of Cuba at the Bay of Pigs, using Cuban American volunteers. A year and a half later, the United States discovered Russian nuclear missiles on Cuban soil. Pressured by the United States, the nation members of the Organization of American States (OAS), with the exception of Mexico, broke diplomatic relations with Cuba.

Was the embargo justified? Why? Why would Cuba have Russian missiles on its soil?

Castro had to heal a history of racial divisions on the island. Cubans historically struggled with race. The Apostle of Cuban Independence, José Martí said:

> To insist on the divisions into race, on the differences of race . . . is to make difficult both public and individual enterprises, which depend for their success on a greater rapprochement between the groups that must live together. . . . Everything that divides men, everything that classifies, separates, or shuts off men is a sin against humanity. . . . Man is more than white, more than mulatto, more than Negro.
>
> —José Martí, "My Race" (April 16, 1893)

What did Martí say about race?

Racism on the island differed from the American slave tradition. However, after 1898 racism increased when American military personnel and businessmen brought their views to the island. After race relations deteriorated, as a consequence a "race war" broke out in 1912 which resulted in a brutal slaughter of blacks in Oriente by the Cuban army. In 1931, Philip G. Wright wrote: "It must be remembered that from a fourth to a third of the population of Cuba is negro or mulatto and while the social status of the blacks is relatively much better than in the United States, nevertheless the Spaniards and white Cubans, like business men in the United States, hesitated at the prospect of democracy with so large a proportion of the population persons of color" (Morales Domínguez, 2013; "Introduction to Race in Cuba").

How did American business heighten the tension between the races?

During the 1960s, an exodus of former Batista supporters and members of the disaffected middle class accelerated. This wave was in great part composed of criollos (descendants of Spaniards), who formed an exile colony in Miami. A second wave of emigrants left the island during the 1970s. This group included many who did not approve of socialism and/or the policies of the new government and its growing dependence on the Soviet Union. This wave also included middle-class Cubans who did not want to endure the poverty induced by the U.S. embargo, a general leveling of society, and reallocation of resources.

Why would the middle class feel more disenchanted with the reforms aimed at levelling society?

Cuban public policy promoted health care for every citizen, building free clinics throughout the country, even in rural areas. Life expectancy among Cuban men today is 74 years and 77 years among Cuban women. Infant mortality rates are about 12 per 1,000 births. Cuba has sent medical assistance to other third-world countries and has sent medical relief teams to countries struck by national disasters such as earthquakes. Critics allege that Castro squandered money by sending troops to Somalia and Angola to help revolutionaries, which further alienated the United States. On the other hand, many third-world and European countries applauded Cuba's support of revolutions.

What advances has Cuba made in medicine? Why would it appeal to the poor?

There is no doubt that the Cuban government made gains in the fields of education and health. Critics say Cuban education had always been better than in other Latin American republics. In 1931, the literacy rate reached 72 percent, but literacy never rose higher than that and was often limited to lighter-skinned Cubans. Before the 1960s, school enrollment rates did not rise above 60 percent. Castro's revolutionary government sent nearly 300,000 children and adults into the countryside to teach literacy. By 1979, the literacy rates in Cuba rose above 90 percent, comparable to the rates in the United States and other developed countries.

According to Senator Tom Harkin, D-Iowa, in 2014, the Cuban infant mortality rate was lower than in the United States: in Cuba there was "an estimated 4.76 deaths per 1,000 live births in 2013, compared to 5.90 for the United States . . . [it] has a better child mortality rate—that is, the likelihood of death under 5 years of age. According to the World Health Organization, Cuba had 6 deaths under age 5 per 1,000 live births between 2005 and 2010, compared to 8 deaths for the United States." Further, "life expectancy for both sexes in 2013 was 78.62 in the United States, compared to 78.05 years in Cuba" (Jacobson, 2014). In addition, Cuba, a poor country, found cures for certain types of cancer and exports medical doctors to other parts of Latin America and Africa.

Why would the sending of doctors to third world countries be more attractive than sending arms?

Without a doubt, the economic embargo hurt Cuba and isolated the island from the United States. Plots to overthrow Castro unsettled the Cuban government, which tightened security. In April 1980, a crisis resulted when six Cuban dissenters drove to the Peruvian Embassy in Havana seeking asylum. Peruvians refused to turn over the dissenters to Cuban authorities. Encouraged by this, thousands of Cubans descended on the embassy asking for asylum. Castro opened the Mariel port, west of Havana, letting anyone who wanted to emigrate leave the island. More than 120,000 undocumented Cubans arrived in Florida. But the arrival of so many Cubans unsettled Cuban Americans because so many of the *marielitos,* according to them, had criminal records and allegedly many were mentally disturbed. The *marielitos* also had darker skin, and this bothered many nativists. In 1984, Cuba and the United States came to an agreement and set a quota of 20,000 Cubans entering the United States. The agreement ended soon after when the United States in 1985 launched Radio Marti, which broadcasted anti-Castro propaganda to the island. Both countries reinstated the agreement in 1987, and by 1998 only six countries sent more authorized immigrants to the United States than Cuba. Mariel and later arrivals tended to be mostly working class immigrants, and a large number were black.

How did the Marielitos change the Miami Cuban community?

After 1991, because of a lack of aid from the Soviet Union and its bloc, the Cuban economy collapsed. The United States tightened the economic embargo and it forbade foreign subsidiaries of American companies to trade with Cuba, which further worsened economic conditions on the island. Throughout this period, Guantanamo periodically housed Cuban, Haitian, and Dominican refugees and remained a source of friction. In 2002, the United States housed Taliban and other suspected terrorists there.

Whether the United States violated the sovereignty of Cuba with its economic embargo of the island and its military presence in Guantanamo Bay is an important issue. These violations of Cuban sovereignty not only affected U.S. international relations but also created tension between Cuban Americans and other U.S. Latinos. For instance, they caused splits within the Hispanic Congressional Caucus between Cuban Americans and other representatives when the former insisted that members adopted an anti-Fidel Castro posture.

Why would Guatanamo become a symbol of colonialism?

Critics of the United States view the stationing of U.S. troops in Guantanamo Bay Naval Base and its economic embargo as flagrant violations of international law. Moreover, Guantanamo and the economic embargo deny the Cuban people's right to self-determination and sovereignty. Still others argue the United States should not pull its troops out of Cuba because the presence of U.S. forces on the island is vital to the interests of the United States and the region. According to them, the presence proves the United States' commitment to human rights. They argue obsessively that the embargo is important because it weakens the communist regime and sends a message to the world that the United States does not approve of dictatorships.

Did the embargo send the message that we will not tolerate tyrants?

Cuban Americans

Throughout this history there has been controversy over what the policy the United States should be. Cuban American exiles have actively pursued a policy that the United States framed in Cold War terminology: democracy versus communism—them and us. For them, Castro is the problem, the symbol of communist oppression on the island, and the reason they cannot return home. They ignore the history of oppression, racism, and inequality that brought about the revolution.

Cuban American conservative leaders could not be ignored because they were economically prosperous. Also, government entitlements freed them from having to deal with economic and social issues. Special interest organizations, such as the Cuban American National Foundation (CANF), headed by the late Jorge Mas Canosa, formed links with conservative Republicans. Cuban Americans were better educated than other U.S. Latinos and, although much smaller in number, they enjoyed an influence beyond their numbers. For example, only 5 percent of the U.S. Latino population lives in Miami, but Cuban

Americans own 40 of the largest Latino-owned businesses in the country. Cuban Americans own 30,000 total businesses, by far the highest rate of per capita ownership of U.S. businesses among Latinos (U.S. Government/CANF).

How did Cuban Americans become an economic power? Have other Latina/o groups had the same level of economic support as the Cuban Americans?

A 2012 article reported: "Cuban Americans are somewhat a special case. The vast majority, specifically, 85 percent, identify as white. This is a higher proportion than the number of self-identified whites in Cuba, and a function of the skewed nature of the migration out of Cuba socially and economically. By and large, the white elites of the island fled Castro's revolution to a far greater extent than the black lower classes" (Khan, 2012).

How were Cubans divided according to race?

Politically, Cuban Americans acted as a pressure group. In February 1996, Cuban Russian-made fighters shot down two civilian planes, killing four Cuban Americans who were members of Brothers to the Rescue, a militant Miami-based anti-Castro group. Brothers to the Rescue were dropping anti-Castro literature over Havana just before the Cuban planes attacked. Cuba defended shooting down the planes because the group violated Cuban airspace. The United States supported the Cuban Americans, alleging that the downing occurred in international airspace. Pro-Cuban American members of Congress immediately pushed for a tightening of the embargo. As a consequence, Congress passed the Helms–Burton Act, which denied visas to anyone who did business with anyone currently holding property that had been confiscated by the Castro government during the revolution. The act gave American citizens the right to file in domestic courts for financial compensation for the lost property.

Finally, the Helms–Burton Act restricted the movement of Cuban diplomats within the United States, closed off charter air routes to and from Cuba, and expanded Radio Martí. Thirty-two members of the Organization of American States—every Latin American nation, but not the United States—supported a resolution labeling Helms–Burton a violation of international law. Human rights activists argued that this was a blatant violation of Cuba's sovereignty: first because the airplanes had violated Cuban airspace, and second, because it was intervening in the internal affairs of a sovereign nation and violated U.S. citizens' right to travel.

What was the significance of Helms–Burton?

Guantanamo

Guantanamo's size is 45 square miles on Cuba's southeastern coast and houses both military and civilian personnel. The ocean surrounds the naval base on three sides, and on the fourth side, U.S. Marines guard the bay. The U.S. presence is a thorn in the side of the Cuban government since well before Castro took power in Cuba. Pentagon documents suggest that the United States has probably stored nuclear weapons at Guantanamo since the 1962 Cuban missile crisis.

The U.S. Marines set up base at Guantanamo on June 6, 1898, at the beginning of the Spanish–American War. In 1903, under pressure from the United States, Cuba leased Guantanamo for 2,000 gold coins a year, today about $4,085. The alleged reasons were to protect Cuba and provide defense for the United States. According to critics, the United States used the base to house military personnel to ensure that leaders friendly to the United States stayed in power. In 1934, the two countries renegotiated and stipulated that if the United States abandoned the fort or agreed through mutual consent, Guantanamo would revert to Cuba. Castro has said that the base is an affront to Cuban sovereignty and has refused to take payment for Guantanamo's rent. It is also reported that the United States uses Guantanamo to spy on Cuba and other islands. Guantanamo is strategically situated and is a base for anti-drug (or) smuggling operations.

Does the United States have a legal right to be there?

The Case of Elián González

In November 1999, six-year-old Elián González was found clinging to an inner tube in the Atlantic Ocean off the coast of Florida. His mother and 10 other people drowned when their boat capsized en route to the United States from Cuba. Elián was one of three survivors. For the next five months, Elian became a prize in a struggle between the Cuban exiles in Miami's Little Havana barrio and the people of Cuba. The Miami

Cubans showered Elian with toys and gifts, and he became a TV superstar. A great-uncle, Lazaro González, and his daughter, Marisleysis González, led a campaign to keep Elian in the United States against the wishes of his father, Juan Miguel González, who traveled to the United States to reclaim his six-year-old son. When Elián's father and his Miami relatives could not come to an agreement, immigration officials resorted to a dawn raid on April 22, 2000 on the Miami house, upon which government authorities reunited Elián with his father in Washington, D.C.

Why did the case of Elián González turn many people against Cuban Americans in Miami?

Lazaro González and his family were supported by the anti-Castro Cuban exile groups, including the Free Cuba Foundation, the Cuban American National Foundation (CANF), and the refugee support group called Brothers to the Rescue. Protesters threatened to burn Miami if the U.S. government returned the boy, who they called "a little miracle," to Cuba. Members of the Congressional Black Caucus supported Juan Miguel González as did the National Council of Churches and various other religious groups. They said a father had the right to his son and that the United States would be violating Cuban sovereignty if it did not give Elian back to his father.

The Latina/o community was split over the Elian case. For some time, Antonio González, president of the Willie C. Velásquez Institute of the Southwest Voter Registration Education Project, sent delegations to Cuba. At the time of the incident, the Mexican government had relations with Cuba, which caused tensions between Mexicans in the United States and Cubans over attacks on the Mexican government. When the former chair of the Hispanic Congressional Caucus, Rep. Xavier Becerra, visited the island, Cuban members of the caucus resigned. Most Latinos felt that parental rights were of utmost importance in the situation and that the boy belonged with his father. Coverage of the controversy dominated the front pages of Spanish-language newspapers, newscasts on Univision and Telemundo, and major mainstream news outlets across the country.

Did Elián belong with his father?

Meanwhile, Cuban Americans pressured Latino groups to support them. Their lobbying was largely unsuccessful, although national groups, such as the Congressional Hispanic Caucus, the National Council of La Raza, and the Mexican American Legal Defense and Educational Fund (MALDEF) remained silent. Latino politicos avoided the issue, with the exception of Rep. José E. Serrano (D-N.Y.), a Puerto Rican, who said, "I'm very bitter and angry about this." The general Latino sentiment was that the United States had routinely deported Mexicans, Dominicans, Colombians, Africans, and others, so why should Cubans receive special treatment ("Miami Divided over Elian," 2000)? "A Miami Herald poll . . . showed a sharp divide in South Florida over the Elian case, with more than 80 percent of Cuban Americans saying the child should remain in the United States along with a similarly large share of whites and blacks. Non-Cuban Miami Latinos were evenly split" ("A Chronology of the Elián González Saga," 2000). The drama ended when Elián was returned to his father.

What have been the consequences of the Elián González case?

The Wall Cracks: The End of the Embargo

By the second decade of the 21st century, a growing consensus among moderates felt that the embargo had lost moral standing; they either lost interest in it or came to the realization that it was hurting the people more than the so-called regime. While many conceded that there was a measure of political repression in Cuba, they also agreed that improvements had taken place. The Cuban government in the 1990s yielded to public pressure and allowed freedom of religion and increased freedom of speech.

The alleged aim of the embargo was to force Cuba to adopt a representative democracy. However, it had backfired. The government was able to blame many failures on the embargo. It did more harm denying poor people access to even aspirins. The embargo was seen as a war on people. After 50 years, it failed to bring down the government. Forgotten were the collective memories of the Cuban people, many of whom remembered Batista and the arrogance of the white elites. An MSNBC/Telemundo/Marist Poll from August 26 to September 9, 2015 showed that 62 percent of the American public approved of lifting the embargo, with 23 percent disapproving and 15 percent not sure. The approval rate on other national polls was higher.

President Barack Obama, in his 2015 State of the Union speech, called for Congress to end the embargo against Cuba. Cuban-American members of Congress such as Marco Rubio criticized Obama. However, many Latinas/os doubted that the embargo would promote democratic values. The Miami mafia, as it was called, lost its moral authority and there was a backlash among many Latina/o activists who resented their bullying tactics. The effect of many Latinas/os visiting Cuba with and without visas could also not be underestimated.

Why did the majority of Americans in favor of the boycott in the 1960s and oppose it in 2015?

THE EMBARGO HAS FAILED

Sanctions against Cuba failed because the global community did not support them. Instead of protecting the Cuban people, sanctions caused them to suffer more. Sanctions were successful against South Africa because the sanctions had moral authority. The Cuban embargo lacked moral authority. Even an appeal to religion failed and in November of 1996, Pope John Paul II and his successors asked for an end to the embargo. It was clear that sanctions failed to dislodge the military regime in Haiti, the poorest and most vulnerable country in Latin America. They had likewise failed in Cuba. Claiming that the United States, by preventing medicine and food from entering Cuba in the name of democracy, was ridiculous and hypocritical. Nations such as Saudi Arabia, Guatemala, China, Chile, and Indonesia have worse human rights records than Cuba but have received U.S. economic and political aid.

As Philip Peters, a member of the State Department during the Reagan and Bush administrations and a member of the ultraconservative CATO Institute, opined, "More than a decade after the fall of the Berlin Wall, Fidel Castro remains in charge in Havana, despising capitalism, taunting the Cuban-American community in Miami, theorizing about the evils of globalization, and keeping up with every imaginable statistic about Cuba. He has been in power for 41 years, outlasting U.S. strategies from the Bay of Pigs in the early 1960s to the tightened economic sanctions of the 1990s." According to Peters, Castro remained in power because of U.S. foreign policy that gave him an international forum and the sympathy of world opinion.

Peters concluded that it was in the U.S. interest to open relations with Cuba. "Economic reforms in Cuba are still incipient, but small enterprise, foreign investment, incentive-based agriculture, and other changes have had important impacts: They helped the economy survive its post-Soviet crisis, and Cubans working in those sectors have gained experience with markets and augmented their earnings" (Peters, 2000). In other words, the United States should open trade with Cuba, not isolate it.

Peters repeated that "Cuban Americans have increasingly joined this discussion, as a younger generation of exiles values contact with the island and some first-generation exiles begin to question the effectiveness of the trade embargo." The Elián González crisis heightened doubts about the embargo and weakened the pro-embargo hardline position in public and congressional opinion. It called into question "the rights of Americans to trade with, invest in, and travel to Cuba. . . ." Consequently, according to Peters, Americans should not make the mistake of assuming that all Cuban Americans are vehemently opposed to normalizing relations with Cuba. Many of the younger generation as well as the poorer Cubans arriving in the 1980s know that the policy hurts the poor.

In fact, the only reason that the United States holds on to Guantanamo is because of the Cuban lobby. It is a symbolic victory for a small and aging cabal. It is indisputable that it was obtained by undemocratic means and used to attempt to overthrow the Cuban government. Meanwhile, "Communist officials say there have been more than 600 documented attempts to kill Castro over the decades" (Snow, 2007). For many, the extremism of the Cuban American lobby was proven by the Elián González case when it sought to deny a father parental rights.

In order for the United States to be the moral leader of the free world, it must be consistent. The rest of the world does not look at Cuba in the same way the United States does. Cuba's unwavering support for decolonization during the 1970s and 1980s won it support in the third world. Today, Cuba has 2,000 physicians practicing humanitarian work in third-world countries. It has 300 volunteer physicians in South Africa alone. It has opened a Latin American university of medicine, the largest of its kind in Latin America. Many of its students are from less developed Latin American countries. Cuban medical teams also have provided much needed emergency aid to the cyclone-ravaged Central American countries of Nicaragua and Honduras.

Summary

Who did the embargo hurt? Did it free Cubans? Are the Castros causing all the present suffering in Cuba? Americans must look at the role of economic sanctions. Economic freedom is essential to sociopolitical freedom. Even if it is conceded that Castro is to blame, how do the sanctions hurt him? Did Castro himself have less access to medical supplies? Did Castro get less food? Was it rational to starve an entire nation because the United States did not agree with its leader? For 50 years, the United States tried this failed tactic, and it did not work. It is up to the Cuban people to overthrow the government from within, not for those outside Cuba.

Aaron Lukas, an analyst at the ultraconservative Cato Institute, says Cubans may not like Americans, but Cubans do not wish to harm Americans. About 80,000 U.S. citizens visit Cuba each year, and they are warmly received. In 2012, Cuban Americans sent $2.6 billion in remittances to relatives in Cuba, without which many Cubans would have starved. The bottom line is that the embargo lacked moral authority.

ANOTHER POV (POINT OF VIEW)

U.S. Military and Political Presence in Cuba

Victor M. Rodríguez, Chicano and Latino Studies, California State University, Long Beach

Since December 17, 2014 when President Obama announced a policy of rapprochement between Cuba and the United States, there has been widespread speculation as to what will this mean for the Cuban people. Unfortunately, because Cuba has been under an economic, political, and military blockade for more than 50 years, many developments within Cuba are not known except by Cuba specialists. The reality is that the process of "normalization" between the United States and Cuba has been mostly symbolic and has not yet led to any comprehensive changes in the economic relationship between the United States and Cuba.

Cuba is still unable to access U.S. markets, whether agricultural or financial, in any significant way. The only area that has benefitted Cuba is tourism, but this industry, while important, will not provide Cuba with the technology and capacity to develop its economy. In fact, the much vaunted development of *cuentapropistas*, or independent private businesses, began much earlier when the Cuban state began to expand the possibilities for Cubans to engage in small business. Again, the new policy was implemented long before the current process of "normalization" and is not the result of it. President Raul Castro, while considered to be a rigid leader, as chief of the Cuban armed forces had engaged in the development of many commercial enterprises: Cuban officers were sent to various nations (social democratic) to learn and study business practices. A significant part of the Cuban economy is in the control of the armed forces, (e.g., hotels and cigars).

The problem that Cuba faces is that the Republican congress is the only agent that can remove the laws that have closed Cuban access to the capital and resource markets of the United States. Its Internet expansion with public WiFi in more than 60 areas of Cuba has been limited because it has had to rely on Chinese technology. Google, which is not a company trusted in Cuba, has had some conversations about providing technology in this area, but the Cubans are being very careful not to open their systems to entities that could subvert the achievements Cuba has made in education, health, and so on. However, despite the care that the Cuban government has taken, it has experienced an increase in inequality because many entrepreneurs have expanded their businesses, hired personnel, and are able to acquire some market power.

Another unintended result of the opening of a private market in Cuba is that race relations in Cuba, which had been improved after the revolution, are experiencing a rise in racial animosity. Many of the *paladares, casas particulares* (B&B), or shops that repair cell phones or TVs have been financed in part by money sent by Cuban American relatives in the United States. Since a disproportionate segment of the exile community is light skinned, it has meant that their light-skinned relatives have benefitted from financial and other resources brought or sent to Cuba. This development has increased the social and economic gap between white and black Cubans.

Unless the Cuban government, through its civil society organizations, is able to limit the inequities caused by expanding small businesses and, in addition, if the opening of Cuba is taking place too fast, many of the social and economic advances made by Cuba could be lost and social conflict could increase, affecting the stability of Cuban society. Most Cubans want improvement in their social and economic standing but do not want a deterioration of their health care system and their educational system. For most, those and other advances made by Cuba are not negotiable.

Cuban Relations: First Impressions from a Westerner of Color

Francisco N. Tamayo, Assistant Professor, Chicana/o Studies Department, California State University, Northridge

This past July (summer 2016), I had the opportunity to travel to Havana, Cuba with colleagues from California State University, Northridge and Dominguez Hills campuses. We were invited to participate and present at the Latitudes de Latinidad Conference sponsored by Casa de las Americas. On our way to the hotel, the city's aesthetics (billboards and murals) fostered feelings of hope and optimism; we landed in Havana a week after the reopening of the U.S. Embassy.

After 54 years of lingering Cold War politics, the U.S. Embassy opened its doors in this sovereign nation. To officially bring these two countries to the democratic negotiating table, John Kerry, Secretary of State, in a flag-raising ceremony, proclaimed, "We remain convinced that the people of Cuba would be best served by a genuine democracy, where people are free to choose their leaders."[2] It is clear that the Obama Administration is recycling tropes of American Exceptionalism by promising Cubans that "Uncle Sam" is in town to restore order by promising to create better living conditions for all economically sanctioned Cubans.

Like any other profiteering nation–state whose doctrine is to defend the last stages of capitalism (the disposability of the nonconsumer), the assimilationist statehood language shaped and equated with American Exceptionalism is not only associated with wealth and power. This hegemonic discourse sets up a counter-hegemonic language for those longing to materialize their social realities, more like superficial positioning. This positioning is superficial because the Cuban embargo is still in effect despite numerous rhetorical efforts by world leaders like Pope John Paul II and his successors, and recently, President Obama. On the ground, Cubans are divided and skeptical of such humanitarian gestures and compassionate politics of integration and belonging.

Based on my interactions with colleagues from Casa de las Americas, they seem skeptical of the generosity of the leaders of the free world to emancipate the social and economic conditions of the Cuban people. They acknowledge the role of capitalism in the demise of the Russian economy, but they point to the human rights violations of the North American Free Trade Agreement (NAFTA) and the unregulated excesses of China's economic liberalism. I also spoke to cab drivers whose perspectives were hopeful. They long to reunite with extended family members and play catch-up with the modern world and its social and technological advancements. However, they are against the neoliberal standardization of Cuban society emphasizing that Cuba does not need a fast-food industry, "*No quieren* Taco Bell," and other cheap labor venture capitalist projects.[3]

Despite the limited resources brought about by America's imposed economic sanctions as well as those of its capitalist allies, except for Canada and Mexico, the Cuban government has managed to guarantee health care access to all Cuban nationals and provide free post-secondary education. Moreover, Cuba's health care system is world renowned as the leader in preventive medicine and its position in strong scientific research and development is well known. Despite José Martí's patriotic efforts to gain independence from Spanish colonialism and Fidel Castro's struggle for independence from American Imperialism, the island still experiences the effects of colonialism and what Latin American globalization theorist, Walter Mignolo, calls coloniality. Coloniality critically analyzes the impact colonialism has had in occupied Latin America—as it relates to the modern experience—where asymmetrical power relations are constructed and social and cultural projects are subjugated and subjectivized. There is no doubt Cuba is being challenged by the last stages of capitalism. Fidel Castro calls on "Brother Obama" not to sugarcoat his remarks in reviving diplomatic conversations, but to acknowledge what the Cuban government has done to fight against imperialist powers that value profit over the humanity of the peoples.

NOTES

1. A cultural/political organization founded by the Cuban government in 1959.
2. "Cubans welcome John Kerry's call for 'genuine democracy' in country." *The Guardian*, August 15, 2015. http://www.theguardian.com/world/2015/aug/15/cuba-havana-john-kerry-us-embassy-democracy
3. The phrase, "Yo Quiero Taco Bell," became a pop culture punch line (1997–2000) enunciated by a Chihuahua to advertise the food menu items of this fast-food corporation.

SOURCES

"Fidel Castro rails on 'Brother Obama' after US president's trip to Cuba." *The Guardian*, March 28, 2016. http://www.theguardian.com/world/2016/mar/28/fidel-castro-obama-cuba-trip

Mignolo, W. The Darker Side of the Renaissance: Literacy, Territoriality, and Colonization, 2nd ed. Ann Arbor: University of Michigan Press, 2003.

BIBLIOGRAPHY

Acuña, Rodolfo F. "Los Cubano Americanos de Miami." *La Opinion*, April 23, 2000.

Acuña, Rodolfo F. "The Miami Myth Machine." *La Prensa San Diego*, April 28, 2000. http://www.laprensa-sandiego.org/archieve/april28/myth.htm

"Arguments Made for a Return to Cuba." *New York Times*, June 28, 2000. http://www.nytimes.com/2000/06/28/us/arguments-made-for-a-return-to-cuba.html?rref=collection%2Ftimestopic%2FGonzalez%2C%20Elian&action=click&contentCollection=timestopics®ion=stream&module=stream_unit&version=latest&contentPlacement=7&pgtype=collection

Bardach, Ann Louise. "Marielitos and the changing of Miami: Finding Manana A Memoir of a Cuban Exodus." *Los Angeles Times*, April 24, 2005. http://articles.latimes.com/2005/apr/24/books/bk-bardach24

Bardach, Ann Louise, and Larry Rohter. "A Bombers Tale: Taking Aim at Castro; Key Cuba Foe Claims Exiles' Backing." *New York Times*, July 12, 1998. http://www.nytimes.com/1998/07/12/world/a-bombers-tale-taking-aim-at-castro-key-cuba-foe-claims-exiles-backing.html

Boswell, Thomas, and James Curtis. *The Cuban-American Experience. Culture, Images and Perspectives*. Totowa, NJ: Rowman & Allanheld, 1984

Castro, Fidel. "The Revolution Begins Now." Spoken: January 3, 1959 at the Cospedes Park in Santiago de Cuba. Publisher: Revolucion on 3, 4 and 5 of January, 1959. Translated: FBIS. Transcription/Markup: Castro Speech Database/Brian Baggins. Online Version: Castro Internet Archive (marxists.org) 2002. https://www.marxists.org/history/cuba/archive/castro/1959/01/03.htm

Castro, Max J. "Grumpy Old Men: The Aging Exile Leaders Who Are Trying to Keep Elian Gonzalez in the United States Have a Lot in Common with Their Anti-Democratic Nemesis, Fidel Castro." *Salon.com*, April 6, 2000.

Chapman, Lindsey. "On This Day: Castro Allows Cubans to Emigrate in Mariel Boatlift." Finding Dulcinea, April 20, 2011. http://www.findingdulcinea.com/news/on-this-day/April/On-This-Day—Thousands-Authorized-to-Leave-Cuba-in-Mariel-Boatlift.html

"A Chronology of the Elián Gonzáalez Saga." *Frontline PBS*. http://www.pbs.org/wgbh/pages/frontline/shows/elian/etc/eliancron.html

Drain, Paul K. "Implications of Repealing the Cuban Embargo for US Medicine and Public Health." *American Journal of Public Health* 105, 11 (2015): 2210–2211.

Eckstein, Susan, and Lorena Barberia. "Grounding Immigrant Generations in History: Cuban Americans and Their Transnational Ties." *International Migration Review* 36, no. 3 (Fall 2002): 799ff.

"Economic Embargo Timeline." Historyofcuba.com. http://www.historyofcuba.com/history/funfacts/embargo.htm

Ferrer, Ada. "Cuba, 1898: rethinking race, nation, and empire." *Radical History Review* 73 (1999): 22–46. doi:10.1215/01636545-1999-73-22.

Gambitos. "Carta inconclusa de Martí a su amigo Manuel Mercado." Campamento de Dos Ríos, 18 de mayo de 1895. http://www.gabitos.com/LACUBADELGRANPAPIYO/template.php?nm=1368555552

García-Chediak, Rosa. "Cuba: A History." *International Journal of Cuban Studies* 5, no. 1 (2013): 81–83.

González, M. "Cuba's Lost History." *Policy Review* 165 (2011): 55–67.

Guerra, Lillian. "Elian Gonzalez and the 'Real Cuba' of Miami: Visions of Identity, Exceptionality, and Divinity." *Cuban Studies* 38, no. 1 (2007): 1–25.

"Helms–Burton Act: Resurrecting the Iron Curtain." *Council on Hemispheric Affairs*, June 10, 2011. http://www.coha.org/helms-burton-act-resurrecting-the-iron-curtain

Hernández, José M. "Cuba in 1898." Library of Congress, June 22, 2011. http://www.loc.gov/rr/hispanic/1898/hernandez.html

Interview with Cuban Ambassador Olga Chamero Trias, "Cuba: Against the Odds." *Frontline* 16, no. 8 (April 10–23, 1999). http://www.frontline.in/static/html/fl1608/16081110.htm

"Introduction to Race in Cuba," historyofcuba,com. http://historyofcuba.com/history/race/RaceIntro.htm

Jacobson, Louis. "Sen. Tom Harkin says Cuba has lower child mortality, longer life expectancy than U.S." *PolitiFact*, January 31, 2014. http://www.politifact.com/truth-o-meter/statements/2014/jan/31/tom-harkin/sen-tom-harkin-says-cuba-has-lower-child-mortality

Jacoby, Jeff. "The Cuban Embargo's Moral Justification." *Boston Globe*, April 2, 1998.

Khan, Razib. "The case of the white Cubans." *Discover Magazine*, April 15, 2012. http://blogs.discovermagazine.com/gnxp/2012/04/the-case-of-the-white-cubans

Lindsay, James M. "Why Are Cuban Americans Singled Out as an Ethnic Lobby? Getting Uncle Sam's Ear/Will Ethnic Lobbies Cramp America's Foreign Policy Style." *Brookings Foreign Policy Studies* 20, no. 1 (2002): 37–40.

Lukas, Aaron P. "It's Time, Finally, to End the Cuban Embargo." *Cato Institute's Center for Trade Policy Studies*, December 14, 2001.

Martí, José. "My Race," Patria, April 16 1893 in http://www.historyofcuba.com/history/race/MyRace.htm

McPherson, Alan, William M. LeoGrande, and Peter Kornbluh. *Back Channel to Cuba: The Hidden History of Negotiations Between Washington and Havana*. Chapel Hill, NC: University of North Carolina Press, 2015.

"Miami divided over Elian." *BBC News*, April 9, 2000. http://news.bbc.co.uk/2/hi/americas/707626.stm

Morales, Emilio. "Cuba: $2.6 Billion in Remittances in 2012." *Havana Times*, June 11, 2013. http://www.havanatimes.org/?p=94444

Morales Domínguez, Esteban. "Race in Cuba: Essays on the Revolution and Racial Inequality." *New York: Monthly Review Press*, 2013.

Murphy, Sean D. "Return of Elian Gonzalez to Cuba." *The American Journal of International Law* 94, no. 3 (2000): 516.

"Notes on Guantánamo Bay." Historyofcuba.com. http://www.historyofcuba.com/history/funfacts/guantan.htm

Pan, Philip P., and Michael A. Fletcher. "Other Latinos More Divided Over Fate of Cuban Boy." *Washington Post*, April 10, 2000. http://www.latinamericanstudies.org/elian/other.htm

Peters, Philip. "A Policy toward Cuba That Serves U.S. Interests." *Cato Policy Analysis*, no. 384 (November 2000).

Rampersad, Indira. "The Anti-Cuban Embargo Movement in the United States." *Peace Review* 26, no. 3 (2014): 402–411.

Raphael, Daniel. "End the Cuban Embargo." *Huffington Post*, March 24, 2014. http://www.huffingtonpost.com/daniel-raphael/end-the-cuba-embargo_b_4633832.html

Roosevelt, Franklin D. "Address at Chautauqua, N.Y. August 14, 1936." American Presidency Project, UCSB. http://www.presidency.ucsb.edu/ws/?pid=15097

Safa, Helen. "The Cuba Reader: History, Culture, Politics." *Cuban Studies/Estudios Cubanos* 36 (2006): 168–171.

Santamarina, Juan C. "The Cuba Company and the Expansion of American Business in Cuba, 1898–1915." *Business History Review* 74, no. 1 (2000): 41–83.

Sharpe-Caballero, Felix. "Americans lack an understanding of Cuba." *Michigan Chronicle*, February 11, 2015, A.3.

Snow, Anita. "CIA Plot to Kill Castro Detailed." *Washington Post*, June 27, 2007. http://www.washingtonpost.com/wp-dyn/content/article/2007/06/27/AR2007062700190.html

Speech Given by William Walker in New Orleans, May 30, 1857. "Filibusterism." *New York Daily Times*, June 8, 1857, 2. http://www.latinamericanstudies.org/william-walker.htm

"The U.S. Government/CANF Propaganda Machine." Cuba Debate, October 10, 2003. http://www.cubadebate.cu/especiales/2003/10/10/the-us-governmentcanf-propaganda-machine

Weaver, Jay, Ana Acle, and Manka Lynch. "U.S turns up the pressure in Elian case." *Miami Herald*, April 10, 2000. http://www.cubanet.org/htdocs/CNews/y00/apr00/10e9.htm

Webster, Sidney. "Mr. Marcy, The Cuban Question and the Ostend Manifesto: I." *Political Science Quarterly* (1886–1905) VIII.1 (March 1893): 1–32.

Zamora, Enríque. "Impact of the Cuban Embargo on Inheritances by Cuban Nationals." *St. Thomas Law Review* 24, no. 3 (2012): 525.

SELECTED VIDEOS

Al Jazeera English. "Inside Story—Guantanamo Bay—08 Aug 07—Part 1." YouTube video, 11:33, posted August 9, 2007. https://www.youtube.com/watch?v=mUk0HHLZY9M

Bass, E. B. "APUSH 7.3 Imperialism." YouTube video, 1:03:43, posted December 10, 2012. https://www.youtube.com/watch?v=zKd8gZ5k7EE

Bladeboy05. "Black in Latin America E01, Cuba: The Next Revolution." YouTube video, 52:07, posted June 23, 2011. https://www.youtube.com/watch?v=k7p30a4auyA

ColdWarWarriors. "Cuba & Bay Of Pigs." YouTube video, 5:34, posted February 1, 2009. https://www.youtube.com/watch?v=8qXZp8bxpNY

Council of Foreign Relations. "Bay of Pigs Invasion: Lessons Learned." YouTube video, 6:05, posted April 17, 2012. https://www.youtube.com/watch?v=U6UkrevWYeY

Cuba Vive. "CUBA: Defending Socialism, Resisting Imperialism [2010]." YouTube video, 46:06, posted August 11, 2012. https://www.youtube.com/watch?v=xxFPZaurHZA

DigPhilosophy. "Fidel Castro Documentary Full—Fidel Castro Declassified—History Channel documentary." YouTube video, 44:15, posted September 28, 2015. https://www.youtube.com/watch?v=q-KfAJuVANY

Funk, John. "The 50s—David Halberstam—Guatemala—CIA Overthrow Jacobo Arbenz." YouTube video, 16:03, posted October 2, 2015. https://www.youtube.com/watch?v=nW2DPZW-_js

"Introduction to Race in Cuba." Historyofcuba,com. http://historyofcuba.com/history/race/RaceIntro.htm

Lu B. "The Story of Elian Gonzalez." YouTube video, 3:15, posted December 19, 2012. https://www.youtube.com/watch?v=v_r6Wtmc3lw

The National. "History of Guantanamo Bay." YouTube video, 4:57, posted May 13. 2015. https://www.youtube.com/watch?v=Y-_1-UcjB98

Notihabanacuba. "Fulgencio Batista El Golpe de Estato y la Llegada del Tirano." YouTube video, 7:20, posted September 28, 2008. https://www.youtube.com/watch?v=ID6iiOmiVQA

Our World—from EarBot.com. "Guantanamo Bay Cuba Controversy—VOA Story." YouTube video, 4:00, posted September 22, 2007. https://www.youtube.com/watch?v=nhAXFGdO2kc

Overlander.tv. "Life in Cuba; food shortages, low wages and exiled family members." YouTube video, 7:28, posted May 15, 2013. https://www.youtube.com/watch?v=xqEFDzq7TCg

Rothacker, George. "The History of Cuba." YouTube video, 7:25, posted October 8, 2012. https://www.youtube.com/watch?v=4-ySzgY5X4s

RT, "Embargo Ended: US lifts sanctions against Cuba." YouTube video, 3:53, posted December 17, 2014. https://www.youtube.com/watch?v=lwo6Ec6Dgkk

Seeker Daily. "The History Of America's Cuba Embargo." YouTube video, 2:51, posted April 20, 2015. https://www.youtube.com/watch?v=MUus0RinpbA

Sukhhayre, "A People's History of American Imperialism by Howard Zinn." YouTube video, 8:35, posted May 24, 2012. https://www.youtube.com/watch?v=s6E8fzKlK7w

TeleSUR English. "Interviews from Havana—Blacks in Cuba." YouTube video, 24:38, posted January 28, 2015. https://www.youtube.com/watch?v=m2bjYRdLoKw

Toliver, Sterling. "The Real Cuba." YouTube video, 7:25, posted May 4, 2014. https://www.youtube.com/watch?v=RpqN2u-7Aik

"USA: Washington: State Department Defends Helms—Burton Law." YouTube video, 1:47, posted July 21, 2015. https://www.youtube.com/watch?v=p3LOgDEJ660

X22Report. "Why Is The U.S. Reestablishing Ties With Cuba After 50 Years?—Episode 544." YouTube video, 39:11, posted December 17, 2014. https://www.youtube.com/watch?v=dNB938dFUCg

11

Puerto Rico's Status: Independence, Commonwealth, State, or Endependence

BACKGROUND

Puerto Rico is not a commonwealth; it is not a state; it is a colony of the United States. A commonwealth is a territory with independent powers to resolve its social and economic problems. As one writer puts it, "To call the island nation of Puerto Rico a 'commonwealth' is to condone U.S. imperialism's use of Puerto Rico," where its youth can be used as "cannon fodder for its wars of conquest and domination" (Soler, 2006). Canada is a commonwealth; Puerto Rico is a colony of the United States.

In 1969, the United Nations reprimanded the United States, finding that colonialism is a crime against humanity. On 33 occasions, the UN has asked the United States to comply with an international law prohibiting colonialism and to decolonize Puerto Rico. The United States has ignored the UN. In 1972, the United Nations Decolonization

Committee resolved that Puerto Rico had the right to "independence and self-determination." Yet Puerto Ricans are controlled overwhelming by a U.S. military and a congressional and judicial presence. United States corporate and financial institutions control the island.

Further, the United States controls and restricts external relations between Puerto Rico and other countries, preventing it from becoming economically independent. Since the 1940s, Puerto Rico had built a large public sector. It included "water, electrical power, shipping, telegraph and telephone, convention centers and several major hotels, radio and TV stations and a sizable network of public health facilities, ranging from diagnostic clinics to the largest medical center in the island" (Bernabe, 1997). This sector employed a large number of workers. However, since the late 1970s, the government has been selling off or subcontracting many of the services, causing massive unemployment. By the 1990s, the country was in crisis, with massive strikes.

An example of this privatization, but by far not the most heinous, took place in 2012 when Puerto Rico's governor approved turning over the operations of Puerto Rico's largest airport to a private company, Aerostar Airport Holdings. At least 20 years of privatization that ranged from utility services to water and land have wrecked the island's economy. The justification was the same: the Port Authority was nearly $1 billion in debt and new revenue would renovate the island's regional airports and its cruise ship piers. This is in the face of many Puerto Rican people struggling to preserve their language. As in the case of other Latinos, language preservation has become largely a class struggle, with "the children of upper middle class and middle class" families speaking among themselves in English, fighting against the death penalty and wiretapping (which is prohibited by the Puerto Rican Constitution). Eight million Puerto Ricans live on the mainland and the island of Puerto Rico. The latter has 3.55 million inhabitants. Mississippi has 2,992,333 residents.

Is Puerto Rico a colony? Does it matter? Why?

On November 6, 2012, Puerto Ricans held a plebiscite on the island's status. They were asked:

Do you agree that Puerto Rico should continue to have its present form of territorial status (commonwealth)?

Yes: 46 percent
No: 54 percent

Irrespective of your answer to the first question, indicate which of the following nonterritorial options you prefer:

Statehood: 61 percent
Independence: 5 percent
Sovereign Free Associated State: 33 percent

Many observers speculate that the failure to grant Puerto Rico statehood is racially motivated. Its people have never been treated as citizens but rather as subjects. There was considerable criticism of the plebiscite, which, according to many, was not accurate. The pro-statehood people controlled the process and did not allow the people to vote for the status quo, thus limiting the election to acceptable choices. Another critic pointed out, "The present pro-statehood governor, (Republican) Luis Fortuño, had been involved in major controversies almost since his first year, like corruption of party officials within his administration, massive layoffs of public service employees, raising tuition in the almost-free University of Puerto Rico and then unleashing a brutal police attack against the students who were protesting, to name a few" (Pabón, 2013).

How would it make a difference if Puerto Rico were a state?

History

Puerto Rico is an archipelago located between the Caribbean Sea and the Northern Atlantic Ocean. It is the smallest of the Greater Antilles Islands and is strategically located, historically a natural fort guarding the Caribbean and the Isthmus of Panama. The main island is Puerto Rico—smaller islands are Vieques, Culebra, and Mona, among others. Puerto Rico was heavily populated and in a small area, thus Puerto Ricans have an intense sense of place and identity.

Puerto Rico is 100 miles long and 35 miles wide and has 931 people per square mile, which makes it one of the most densely populated places on Earth. For example, Puerto Rico is 60 percent more densely populated than El Salvador, which is the most densely populated country on the Latin American mainland. In addition, because Puerto Rico's terrain is mountainous, only half the land can be used for farming. Puerto Ricans only have one-fourth acre of farmland per person, which is not much when compared with the United States, which has about four and one-half acres of farmland per person.

The first Indians reached the Caribbean around 2300 BC. Soon afterward another group arrived from the Orinoco Valley in South America—from as far north as the Guianas—and they introduced agriculture, hunted, and fished. The Taínos reached the Caribbean Islands in approximately 900 BC. They were from what is today Venezuela.

According to Spanish historians, the "discoverer" and conqueror of this island was Juan Ponce de León, who was under the command of the Admiral don Diego de Colón, the son of Christopher Columbus. The Taínos called the island Boriken or Borinquen. They lived in peace, much the same as the Hawaiians had before the arrival of the Americans. They showed the Spaniards gold nuggets in the river, and the rest is history.

Who were the Taínos?

There were as many as 50,000 Taíno or Arawak Indians on the island the Spaniards called San Juan Bautista, for St. John the Baptist. It became Spain's most important military outpost in the Caribbean. The Caribbean Indian population declined rapidly, and by 1501 Spain began to export African slaves to the Caribbean. By the end of the decade, the conquerors established the first *repartimiento* in Puerto Rico—a system of distributing fixed numbers of Indians for wage-free and forced labor to favored Spaniards. The Spanish Crown later established the *encomienda*.

In 1511, the Taínos unsuccessfully revolted against the Spaniards. The conquerors shot 6,000 Indians, driving the survivors to the mountains. Two years later, the Spanish introduced African slaves to Puerto Rico. By 1523, the first sugar cane processing plant was built. A 1530 census on the island showed that 327 white families owned 2,292 African slaves and 473 Indians. Until the end of the 18th century, Puerto Rico functioned as a presidio. The economy did not begin to improve until the 19th century. Administratively, Puerto Rico was part of the viceroyalty of New Spain, but for all intents and purposes, the governor was the head. Until the end of the 19th century Puerto Rico had no legislature.

By the last quarter of the 18th century, the population of Puerto Rico tripled. In 1802, it numbered 163,192 inhabitants: 78,281 were white, 55,164 mulattos, 16,414 free blacks, and 13,333 slaves. The population continued to grow throughout the century. As Puerto Rico grew in population, Spain lost its colonies with the exception of Cuba and Puerto Rico. It made concessions, but they came slowly. The islands were granted rights, such as a constitution with full voting representation in the Spanish Cortes. Constitutional changes broadened constitutional guarantees, and the island was assimilated into the Spanish political structure, becoming a province. These reforms gave Puerto Rico more autonomy under Spain than it has today under American rule. However, the reforms were too late.

El Grito de Lares was issued on September 23, 1868. It was written by Dr. Ramón Emetrio Betances and Segundo Ruiz Belvis, who assembled nearly 1,000 rebels on the outskirts of the town of Lares. Many of the rebels were escaped African slaves who were in hiding. They joined middle- and upper-class creoles who wanted to develop economic opportunities without the restrictions of a foreign power. The unsuccessful *grito* touched off a 30-year struggle for independence. "Betances authored several *proclamas*, or statements, attacking the exploitation of the Puerto Ricans by the Spanish colonial system and called for immediate insurrection. The *proclamas* soon circulated throughout the island as local dissident groups began organizing. Secret cells of the Revolutionary Committee were established involving members from all sectors of society, including landowners, merchants, professionals, peasants, and slaves" ("Puerto Rico at the Dawn of the Modern Age"). The Spanish American War came about in 1898 and lasted only four months. The evacuation of Cuba by Spanish forces led to its transfer to the United States. President William McKinley demanded Puerto Rico be handed over to the United States without compensation. By 1899, only 32,048 people lived on the island; its largest city, San Juan, had 9,000 people in 1800. The island had many assets, not least of which was its strategic location on the map as a point of entry to the Caribbean and Central and South America. This value to the United States increased at the end of the 19th century when commercial interests and military interests merged. Aside from being an outlet for excess manufactured goods, it became a strategic naval station in the Caribbean.

What happened to the Taínos?

According to the Smithsonian, "Some scholars estimate the Taíno population may have reached more than three million on Hispaniola alone as the 15th century drew to a close, with smaller settlements elsewhere in the Caribbean." The popular belief is that they died out or were wiped out. The Smithsonian wrote: "By 1514, barely two decades after first contact, an official survey showed that 40 percent of Spanish men had taken Indian wives. The unofficial number is undoubtedly higher" (Poole, 2011).

How were the Taínos absorbed?

By 1519, about a third of the Indian population had died from smallpox. The population continued to decline to the point where they were almost extinct by the 1530s—85 percent of the Taíno population vanished from the islands of the Caribbean, even in the heart of the islands in Hispaniola. In search of the Taíno, the Smithsonian found proof that they had in some form or other survived. "My ancestors were Indio," said Rosa Arredondo Vásquez. "My grandmother said we came from the Indians," said Gabriela Javier Alvárez.

University of Puerto Rico biologist Juan C. Martínez Cruzado performed an island-wide genetic study. He used 800 randomly selected subjects and found that 61.1 percent of those surveyed had mitochondrial DNA of indigenous origin, "indicating persistence in the maternal line that surprised him and his fellow scientists" (Poole, 2011). In addition, thousands of Puerto Ricans have discovered their Taíno identity. This discovery brought about a change in the 2010 census when 19,839 Puerto Ricans indicated that they were "American Indian or Alaskan Native."

Does the presence of Taíno DNA prove that the Taíno have survived as a people and culture?

Puerto Rico: An American Colony

In the 1890s, sentiment was divided on the island regarding independence, ranging from those who favored staying within the Spanish Empire where they were recognized as Spaniards, to those who wanted independence, to those who wanted annexation to the United States. The latter view was supported by the island's plantation owners, who welcomed the opportunity to annex Puerto Rico to the United States because of the passage of the Dingley Tariff (1897), which placed an import tax on sugar.

What role did class play in the opinion of Puerto Ricans toward U.S. annexation?

The Puerto Rican people had no say regarding the question of annexation to the United States. The Treaty of Paris signed by Spain and the

United States made Puerto Rico a U.S. possession. It was a time when the United States was expanding its markets and naval bases and was well on the road to becoming a world power. As mentioned, under Spanish rule, Puerto Ricans had been unconditionally Spaniards. Puerto Ricans had full representation in the Spanish legislature, all males could vote, and the island could pass its own tariffs. In contrast, under the Foraker Act of 1900, Puerto Ricans were not entitled to the protection of the U.S. Bill of Rights nor to American citizenship despite the fact that U.S. laws applied in Puerto Rico. The Foraker Act also opened Puerto Rico to American investors and encouraged Anglo-American monopolization of the island's resources.[1] As a consequence, American investors bought cane lands in Puerto Rico and formed corporations to process sugar. Eventually five of them cornered 40 percent of the sugar cane lands of the island. The production of coffee fell after 1898.

Did the status of Puerto Ricans change under U.S. rule? Was it for the better or for the worse?

The sugar boom killed the manufacturing of cigars in homes and small shops. Added regulations resulted in cigars being made almost exclusively in big workshops owned by the tobacco companies. The small family cigar makers and coffee farmers either went out of business or became wage laborers for large companies. The modernization of farming converted Puerto Rico into one large plantation, which was overly dependent on a single crop, making it vulnerable to natural disasters, such as storms, and to U.S. quotas on sugar. Ownership of land became more concentrated under U.S. rule: the rich got richer while the poor got poorer as the internal market gave way to imports.

What economic change did U.S. rule impose and how?

The demise of small farms and jobs in urban centers triggered an uprooting of Puerto Rican workers and their families. They were forced to migrate to the United States where large growers and industrialists recruited Puerto Ricans to fill labor shortages created by the 1917 Literacy Act and the 1921 and 1924 Immigration Acts, which cut European immigration to a trickle. This movement was facilitated in 1917 when Congress made Puerto Ricans U.S. citizens.

Worsening conditions led to widespread discontent which contributed to the growth of Puerto Rican nationalism and worker solidarity.

Under colonialism there was a greater consciousness of race. Ramón Romero Rosa in 1901 addressed a letter to black Puerto Ricans entitled "*La Miseria: A Los Negros Puertorriqueños.*" Romero Rosa was a Puerto Rican anarchist dedicated to organizing the working class. He was a printer, playwright, and agitator. He used the theater to teach workers to defend themselves against the power of the ruling class. For Romero Rosa, the recognition of African culture was essential. European traditions had been superimposed on Puerto Ricans, hiding their African essence. "*A Los Negros Puertorriqueños*" was a pamphlet circulated in 1899 and published in 1901.[2] Puerto Rican literature was especially rich during the first three decades of the 20th century.

Puerto Ricans were well aware of their colonial status and a minority of Americans recognized the colonial responsibility of the United States toward Puerto Ricans. Many journals acknowledged that the United States had destroyed the island's agrarian economy and compounded poverty on the island. However, the majority felt that Puerto Ricans should be grateful to be part of the United States. President Calvin Coolidge (1872–1933) said that Puerto Ricans should be grateful for the American occupation because it gave them the opportunity to trade with the United States as well as the blessing of American citizenship.

The United States had indeed destroyed Puerto Rico's subsistence economy, driving many people to the cities and forcing them to immigrate. Coolidge's letter raised the question of Borinquen sovereignty. President Coolidge declared that U.S. territorial possessions were not a help but a hindrance, and that the United States held them as a "duty."

In 1931, a number of academics and professionals formulated an economic strategy known as the Chardón Plan in 1934, named for the university chancellor who presided over the meetings. The plan called for the expropriation of corporate plantations of more than 500 acres, a limit established by the Foraker Act, which the United States never enforced. The intention was to distribute land among workers in order to diversify crop production and enhance traditional agriculture through methods and techniques recommended by agronomists.

In the years after World War I, the U.S. government, the medical community, and the local government of Puerto Rico had initiated a sterilization program as a form of birth control. During the Depression of the 1930s, discontent with American rule led to the rise of Luis Muñoz Marín and the Popular Democratic Party. In 1937, despite opposition from Puerto Ricans and the Catholic Church, a private organization allegedly supported by the U.S. government opened 23 birth control clinics. Sterilization, which the United States had banned for other than strictly medical purposes, became an alternative method of birth control along with contraceptives. Critics say that although the sterilization programs seemed voluntary, women were often unaware of the irreversibility of sterilization, and doctors and hospitals put subtle pressure on women to undergo the procedure. The targeted women were overwhelmingly from the lower classes. Moreover, there were no restrictions on the age, health, or number of children the women already had. By 1965, the programs would sterilize one-third of the female population of the island. Authorities also experimented with techniques developed in Puerto Rico in other Latin American countries such as Colombia and Bolivia, with the support of U.S. government agencies and private organizations.

Radical opposition was led by Pedro Albizu Campos, a key figure for the independence movement. It is important to distinguish him from the independence movement because although he believed in independence, there were two other segments to that movement. One believed in an armed revolution and the other believed in a constitutional amendment movement. Albizu Campos was a revolutionary and he and other champions of independence were under continual surveillance.

Albizu Campos received a law degree from Harvard Law School, served as a second lieutenant in the U.S. Army during World War I, and spent 25 years in and out of prisons for his belief in Puerto Rican independence. He became head of the Nationalist Party, which called for Puerto Rican independence. During the 1930s, he attracted a large following; he was a powerful speaker and would mesmerize crowds. Albizu Campos took part in an island-wide sugar cane strike and laid out the rationale for independence. While in jail, Albizu Campos, with other prisoners, was the subject of human radiation experiments. The FBI gathered 1.5 million to 1.8 million pages in its files on Albizu Campos. J. Edgar Hoover's 1961 memo refers to "our efforts to disrupt their activities and compromise their effectiveness" (Navarro, 2003). The *New York Times* wrote: "In 1965, the Federal Bureau of Investigation wanted to tap the home telephone of a dying Pedro Albizu Campos, then the titular head of Puerto Rico's Nationalist Party. But there was a problem: he did not have a phone" (Navarro, 2003).

In the 1940 elections, the Popular Democrats gained control of the Puerto Rican Senate and later the House of Representatives. In 1948, Muñoz Marin became the first elected governor of Puerto Rico. Previous governors had been appointed by the President of the United States. Muñoz Marin launched Operation Bootstrap, designed to industrialize the island by granting tax-exempt status to new factories. Operation Bootstrap created thousands of new jobs; however, more than

100,000 Puerto Ricans still moved to the U.S. mainland during the 1950s because of a lack of jobs.

By 1952, Puerto Rico became a self-governing commonwealth of the United States, and that same year Puerto Rico organized programs to preserve and promote traditional Puerto Rican cultural traditions. In the years that followed, the Institute of Puerto Rican Culture consolidated these cultural projects. Puerto Rico enjoyed relatively good prosperity until the 1970s when fuel crises economically depressed the island. There were some bright spots as the pharmaceutical industry developed beyond original expectations, but other industries, such as electronics, did not keep pace and the island's economy was not able to absorb the booming population.

Puerto Rico's agriculture worsened as it became even more commercialized. Unemployment reduced many Puerto Ricans to using food stamps and accelerated migration to the mainland. Increasingly, Puerto Rican entrepreneurship was limited to industries such as food processing, furniture manufacture, printing, publishing, construction materials, and producing farm products for local consumption.

The deindustrialization of the United States affected Puerto Ricans as U.S. manufacturers sent their products to Asia and then to Mexico to be assembled by cheap labor. As a consequence, Puerto Rico lost employment in the textile, apparel, footwear, and tobacco industries while gaining limited jobs in the pharmaceutical, computer, and electronics industries. The outcome was that during the 1970s, the number of Puerto Ricans living in the United States grew by some 600,000 people, or by 41 percent, to 2,014,000 (Odishelidze and Laffer, 2004). Puerto Ricans, both on the island and on the mainland, became disillusioned with the United States, which helped Europe with the Marshall Plan and the Middle East with large foreign aid packages, while Puerto Rico remained a stepchild to the United States.

Puerto Ricans have fought with distinction in every major U.S. war of the 20th century. They have lost 1,119 lives in American wars. Puerto Rico is a so-called commonwealth of the United States and elects its own governor. Puerto Ricans are citizens of the United States but cannot vote for president and do not have representation in the U.S. Congress—ironically rights that they would have had if still under Spain. Technically, Puerto Rico can pass its own laws, but its laws are subordinate to those of the United States. That is, Puerto Ricans cannot pass a law that conflicts with the U.S. Constitution or enter into a treaty with a foreign country.

Because of inequality and racism, Puerto Ricans have not fully assimilated into the United States. This segregation consequently contributes to a strong national identity. As one writer put it, "Puerto Rico's heart is not American. It is Puerto Rican. The national sentiment of Puerto Ricans is entirely devoted to our *patria*, as we call our homeland in Spanish, our language. We are Puerto Ricans in the same way that Mexicans are Mexicans and Japanese are Japanese. For us, "we the people" means "we the Puerto Ricans" (Martínez, 1997).

What has prevented Puerto Ricans from assimilating into the American mainstream? Did American racism play a role?

The Puerto Rican Independence Movement: "Interested in the cage, not the birds."

Pedro Albizu Campos, founder of Puerto Rico's modern independence movement, said in the 1930s that the United States was "interested in the cage, not the birds" (Martínez, 1997). Albizu Campos challenged American rule. Albizu Campos' Nationalist Party pressured the Liberal Party to declare independence as one of its priorities. In 1936, under the wartime Sedition Act of 1918, the United States indicted Albizu Campos and other Nationalist leaders, sentencing him to a federal penitentiary in Atlanta for almost a decade. In 1937, General Blanton Winship, the U.S.-appointed governor, ordered police to fire on a group of unarmed Nationalist Party members in the city of Ponce in Puerto Rico, killing 22 and wounding 97. This repression contributed to the end of the Nationalist Party and the purging of *independistas* (independents) from the ranks of other parties.

What does the independence movement tell you?

In 1950, after his release from prison, Albizu Campos organized armed attacks on Blair House in Washington, D.C., where President Harry Truman was living, and on the U.S. Congress in 1954. The Puerto Rican government labeled the Nationalist Party members and members of the Puerto Rican Independence Party (PIP) as subversives and imprisoned them on illegal arrest warrants. The police collaborated with U.S. intelligence agencies compiling a huge list of independence supporters.

In 1952, 81 percent of Puerto Rican voters backed the commonwealth in a yes-or-no referendum. By 1993, 49 percent of Puerto Ricans voted for a commonwealth and 46 percent for statehood. While only 4 percent voted for independence, many Puerto Ricans say that this vote was of historical significance. Although most Puerto Ricans do not favor independence, there has been an independence movement throughout the American period that is due to inequality and racism. As a consequence, Puerto Ricans have not fully assimilated into the United States. This segregation consequently has contributed to a strong national identity.

In 1954, Lolita Lebrón, a Puerto Rican nationalist and freedom fighter, led an attack on the U.S. Capitol. Lebrón bought a ticket from New York to Washington, D.C. on March 1, 1954. She and three fellow nationalists had lunch at Union Station and then walked to the Capitol. They made their way to the House gallery. A security guard asked whether they were carrying cameras; they were not; they had pistols. Lebrón envisioned the beginning of a war of independence. The four nationalists opened fire in the House chambers as more than 240 members of Congress debated an immigration bill. "*Víva Puerto Rico libre!*" Lebrón roared. Five congressmen and 35-year-old Alvin Bentley were struck by bullets. Lebrón was arrested, and, after serving 25 years in prison, she was released.

The Vieques Question: Disparate Treatment

The U.S. attitude toward Vieques was that it belonged to the United States even though it was clearly part of Puerto Rico. The people of Puerto Rico wanted the U.S. Navy to stop using Vieques for target practice. The Navy said that Vieques was irreplaceable, and the Navy needed it for purposes of national security. The United States also had military installations on the island of Puerto Rico, and U.S. military authorities said they need the installations for national security. In the end it all came down to respect and sovereignty. It was not a matter of gratitude, as Calvin Coolidge had claimed.

Vieques is six miles off Puerto Rico's east coast and is strategically in the center of the Antilles chain. It encompasses 33,000 acres of land, which is significant in a country as densely populated as Puerto Rico. The Taíno Indians inhabited Vieques before 1493. The Spaniards abandoned Vieques in 1843. In the second half of the 1800s, Vieques experienced a great sugar boom, with landowners importing black slaves from the neighboring British islands. Like the rest of Puerto Rico, Vieques became part of the United States in 1898.

By 1915, the population of Vieques reached about 12,000 people. When the U.S. Navy arrived in 1941, 10,362 people lived on the island and the island produced 8,000 tons of sugar annually. The Navy expropriated more than three-fourths of Vieques—26,000 of Vieques' 33,000 acres—including most of the land used for farming. The construction of the base killed the sugar industry and thousands of small farmers were uprooted, most of whose families had occupied the island for generations. The U.S. government paid large landowners a fixed price of $20 or $30 for their houses, forcing more than 800 worker-families to leave. The pretext for the low payments was that the workers could not prove legal title to their land. In many cases, the Navy gave the displaced families 24 to 48 hours to leave the island. Some workers stayed and took part in the construction of the Navy base. However, after the initial building boom, the jobs went away. After World War II, Puerto Rico tried to revive farming, but failed, and Vieques was a dying island.

Led by Puerto Rican intellectual Pedro Albizu Campos, Puerto Ricans vigorously protested the U.S. Navy's occupation of Vieques. In a series of articles, Albizu Campos accused the Navy of carrying out a policy of genocide against the Puerto Rican people on Vieques. The presence of thousands of Marines further heightened antagonism in the 1950s and 1960s. In 1953, Marines beat Pepe Christian, a 70-year-old storekeeper, to death and left his 73-year-old friend, Julio Bermudez, seriously injured. The old men had refused to sell the Marines more rum. Naval authorities acquitted the Marines. Two years later, 13-year-old Chuito Legrand stepped on a mortar shell while he and three friends were playing near a dairy farm. Cries of "Yanqi (Yankee) go home!" filled the island. According to critics, the Navy reacted arrogantly.

In 1961, the Department of the Navy unilaterally proposed abolishing the municipality of Vieques. In 1975, the Navy dropped a cruise missile next to a school, and in October 1993, the Navy dropped five 500-pound bombs that missed their targets and landed one mile from the Isabel Segunda village.

How did the presence of the U.S. military affect Puerto Ricans? Why were Puerto Ricans so passionate about the U.S. occupation of the island?

Tensions climaxed on April 19, 1999 when the Navy accidentally dropped two 500-pound bombs over the Observation Tower, killing a civilian guard and injuring four others. Puerto Ricans protested against the U.S. Navy. On May 26 of that year, the Navy admitted it accidentally fired 263 rounds of shells loaded with depleted uranium. They recovered only 57 of the shells. In protest, the Catholic Church of Vieques set up a campsite and chapel at Playa Yayi. Marches and arrests escalated, aimed at disrupting military operations.

On August 29, 2001, the people held a local nonbinding referendum. Sixty-eight percent voted to ask the Navy to stop the bombing immediately and leave the island (30 percent voted for the Navy to stay and continue the bombing). Under an arrangement with President Bill Clinton, the Navy was to cease all training on the Vieques naval training range by May 2003. Still, the Navy announced that not only would it continue the bombing until May 2003, but it also announced that the next maneuver would be full scale. Public opinion after 911 forced the Navy to moderate its position, and on May 1, 2003, the military commenced their moving out of Vieques.

Should the Navy have evacuated Vieques? Why did many Puerto Ricans consider it a symbol of American imperialism?

The bombing contaminated and destroyed the coral reefs, mangroves, and lagoons and seriously damaged the Vieques fishing industry, the livelihood of many islanders. The Navy has reduced the ability of the people of Vieques to farm, fish, or attract tourists, and in return it only provided 92 local jobs (custodial work, maintenance, and security). Because of this, unemployment worsened. Even if the military left, 14,000 acres of Vieques would go to the Department of the Interior, leaving almost nothing to the people. What would be left are unexploded bombs, trash, and contaminated beaches.

In the interim, United States did not agreed to clean up Vieques after six decades of intensive bombing. Nothing seems to deter the Navy. The Navy is planning to build giant fuel-storage tanks, floating piers, and troop barracks on the beaches and coastal areas of Vieques. Amidst all this, the Navy admitted to causing the death of a whale; it admitted to releasing tiny strands of silica glass, used to confuse radar, into the atmosphere. It is doubtful whether the United States would treat one of its 50 states in a similar manner.

Despite universal disapproval and a de-escalation of the tension during the Clinton administration, the Navy got the green light from George W. Bush to expand its activities. Congress did not check this activity and passed legislation stipulating that the navy would not vacate Vieques until a better site was found. In case of a national emergency, the Navy could keep its facilities. In April 2002, the Navy resumed its bombing exercises. Both the destroyer USS Mahan and the guided-missile frigate USS Barry conducted ship-to-shore training.

Within a week, protests resumed, and federal authorities arrested 14 people for trespassing. The total arrests grew to the hundreds. Military authorities used gas on the protesters; the pretext was that the protestors allegedly threw rocks, which eyewitnesses dispute. Police Colonel César García contradicted the Navy account: "I witnessed the incident, and there was no rock-throwing. Right now, my superiors are on the phone to complain to the Navy about the situation" (MIM Notes, 2002). Meanwhile, a news blackout about the Vieques crisis occurred in the United States. For the entire first week of April 2002, Lexis-Nexis, a news media reporting service, reported only 14 newspaper items, mostly short blurbs, on the resumption of the war exercises. The *Los Angeles Times* carried a 71-word item on April 2 and a 62-word item on April 7. The *New York Times* did no better.

The most difficult thing to accept was the indifference and arrogance of Americans. Congress refused to defend the rights of the Puerto Rican people and legislators had no intention of sticking out their necks. Since September 11, 2001, things have gotten worse, with dissidents portrayed as terrorists. The United Nations Special Committee on Decolonization, for the first time in 28 years, passed a resolution on the issue of Puerto Rican sovereignty on Vieques. Yet, U.S. authorities insisted that they have the right to endanger life on the island, although the world community, including the United Nations, has condemned the U.S. actions in Vieques.

In addition, the naval bombings there have had environmental consequences. The cancer rate in Vieques is much higher than elsewhere in Puerto Rico, and many rare diseases have appeared among the people. The Puerto Rican people have spoken with one voice, telling the American Congress to get out of both Vieques and Roosevelt Roads, the military base on the big island. Puerto Rico's 3.8 million U.S. citizens want equality, dignity, and full self-government as first-class citizens. Puerto Rico endured territorial status longer than any other American territory without becoming either independent, as with the Philippines, or a state, as in the case of Alaska and Hawaii. The American people must realize that the Cold War has ended in Europe; the Soviet threat is over. United States nuclear weapons and troops are no longer needed internationally for the defense of the United States.

In May 2003, the Navy withdrew from Vieques. The island was designated as a National Wildlife Refuge under the control of the United States Fish and Wildlife Service. Closure of 2,000 acres of land overlooking the Caribbean called Roosevelt Roads Naval Station followed in 2004. The colonizers left their footprints, however, and numerous beaches still retain names given by the navy (e.g., Red Beach, Blue Beach, and Green Beach). In fact, however, the foot dragging of the American government is insulting.

"Fiscal Year 2015 includes $17 million for the cleanup of Vieques and $1.4 million for the cleanup of Culebra" (Puerto Rico Report, 2015). The cleanup has been left to the Navy, who prioritized "funding to ensure that certain beaches and land areas are fully cleaned and made available for public access, including areas in western Vieques, the historic lighthouse and nearby beaches at Puerto Ferro, and the water and land areas around Playa La Chiva, often referred to as 'Blue Beach' " (Stanchich, 2013). Future funding will depend on the grace of the Republican Congress. Disrespect? The cleanup itself has been a disaster; several failing companies have been hired, used immigrant labor, underpaid the employees, and have done a very poor job, if anything, to actually clean the island. Also, all the activists involved in the protests are currently sick with cancer (Stanchich, 2013).

Puerto Rico Goes Bankrupt: Almost One Hundred Years after the Jones Act

According to the Wharton School of Business, Puerto Rico was "Facing $70 billion in debt and a 45% poverty rate, Puerto Rico's leaders are expected to meet with creditors soon in an effort to negotiate a debt restructuring deal. But experts caution that there is no quick fix to getting the island Commonwealth back on solid footing and allowing it to emerge from the crisis on a more sustainable path" ("Puerto Rico's Debt Crisis," 2016). Puerto Rico's population is projected to have 1 million less people by 2030. It has lost more than 250,000 jobs since 2006. Restructuring is almost impossible in the context of over one hundred years of mismanagement, neglect, and exploitation. The solution of neoliberal economists is to restructure the Puerto Rican legal system to allow it to pay the debt. Meanwhile, Puerto Ricans are pressuring U.S. Congress for relief from the Jones Act passed in the 1920s that protects the domestic shipping industry. Similarly, other American businesses have been protected. Consequently, the people of Alaska, Puerto Rico, Guam, and Hawaii have to pay a higher cost of living. Denied sovereignty, Puerto Rico cannot compete in the global economy.

Who is responsible for Puerto Rico's bankruptcy?

The "Greek Chorus" is chanting that Puerto Rico cannot be rewarded. This same press would ramp up the "Greek Chorus" if the United

States would not pay the debts of the 15 loser Red States at the bottom of the national economic scale. Sources such as Fox News criticize Puerto Rico, saying that "Under U.S. law, cities and towns can file for bankruptcy, but states and territories cannot" (Ferrara, 2016). The law changed by an amendment that was passed by Congress as recently as 1984 when "Congress defined the term 'State' to include 'the District of Columbia and Puerto Rico,' except for the purpose of defining who may be a debtor under Chapter 9 of this title" (Mihm, 2015). So the facts are these:

1. All Puerto Ricans are Americans, really.
2. Congress could easily address this situation, but hasn't.
3. Americans on the mainland hold Puerto Rico's debt.
4. Puerto Rico matters for 2016.
5. What's happening in Puerto Rico reflects the wider evisceration of the American middle class. (Planas and Usero, 2015)

Most Puerto Ricans acknowledge that jobs and the economy are what are most important to them. In the 1990s, more than 90 percent voted for statehood or continued commonwealth status. There were probably nuclear weapons at the military base at Roosevelt Roads. The excuse was that they were part of a war effort to combat communism and terrorism. Moreover, troops in Puerto Rico were vital because of the Cuban revolution of 1959. Puerto Rican bases are ideal for naval training and counterinsurgency training. They served as a springboard for U.S. invasions in the Dominican Republic, Panama, and Grenada. The best military minds say that Vieques is irreplaceable.

Defenders of American policy say that the Puerto Rican press is filled with exaggerated stories about the environmental disasters at Vieques and Roosevelt Roads. United States corporations such as General Electric, Johnson & Johnson, Abbott Laboratories, and many textile firms have made substantial investments there. Their contribution has brought one of the highest standards of living in the Caribbean, and indeed, in all of Latin America. Puerto Ricans have benefited from being U.S. citizens in that they have moved to the mainland at will, a freedom coveted by many other people. However, the question remains, have Puerto Ricans been treated as equals?

Postscript: The *New York Times* reported, "The money poured in by the millions, then by the hundreds of millions, and finally by the billions. Over weak coffee in a conference room in Midtown Manhattan last year [2014], a half-dozen Puerto Rican officials exhaled: Their cash-starved island had persuaded some of the country's biggest hedge funds to lend them more than $3 billion to keep the government afloat" (Mahler and Confessore, 2015). On the surface, the argument was whether Puerto Rico should be granted bankruptcy protections. The investors insisted that they would risk tens of billions of dollars without this protection to which the New York Times responded to do so would attest to "the power of an ascendant class of ultrarich Americans to steer the fate of a territory that is home to more than three million fellow citizens" (Mahler and Confessore, 2015). The super-rich have hedged their bets by contributing to the political campaigns of politicos on the island and the mainland. Thus the financial rescue for Puerto Rico resembled a poker game designed to starve out the Puerto Rican opposition to the "rescue" plan, which, from the beginning, was laden with interest rates. Hedge fund hustlers "began buying up the debt at a steep discount, confident that this was a bet they could not lose. Not only were the bonds guaranteed by the Puerto Rican Constitution, but under a wrinkle of federal law, the island's public corporations and municipalities—unlike those of the 50 states—do not have bankruptcy as a recourse" (Mahler and Confessore, 2015). In Washington, congressional committees were controlled by elected officials who, in turn, were controlled by lobbyists in the employment of the super-rich. There were no checks. Barack Obama appointed the foxes to guard the hen house, the Financial Oversight and Management Board for Puerto Rico: Andrew G. Biggs is a resident scholar at the ultraconservative American Enterprise Institute (AEI); José B. Carrión III is President and Principal Partner of HUB International CLC, LLC; investor Carlos M. García is the founder and Chief Executive Officer (CEO) of BayBoston Managers LLC as well as Managing Partner of BayBoston Capital L.P.; and José R. González is Chief Executive Officer and President of Federal Home Loan Bank of New York (FHLBNY). Obama could bail out the auto industry and the banks, but his proposal stopped short of a direct federal bailout of the people of Puerto Rico. (Siegel, 2016)

ANOTHER POV (POINT OF VIEW)

Neither Independence nor Statehood: Where Should We Go from Here?

Yarma Velázquez-Vargas, Professor of Chicana/o Studies, California State University, Northridge

In 1952, the island of Puerto Rico drafted its constitution and ratified its relationship with the United States by becoming a commonwealth of the United States. As a consequence of that move, Puerto Rico's colonial status was changed by the Special Committee on Decolonization at the United Nations. Following the establishment of its "commonwealth" relationship with the United States, scholars and politicians have reiterated Puerto Rico's right to self-determination as the key issue to study regarding the island. Moreover, the political partisan structure has been modeled around that same premises: independence, status quo, or statehood to the United States. However, the argument can be made that the world has changed and the three categories that ruled over the discourse and national identity of Puerto Ricans are obsolete. In the context of globalization and neocolonialism, Puerto Rico must reposition itself to reflect the new realities of the world.

Neocolonialism can be understood as the practice of using capitalism, globalization, and cultural imperialism to influence a country, meaning that powerful countries like the United States can use economic tools to control the government of another country. In the context of neocolonialism and globalization, the political situation of Puerto Rico and its political parties becomes obsolete because the United States has complete authority over the island's financial situation, controlling its debt and consequently its development. The idea of self-determination, which was at the core of Puerto Rico's commonwealth status, is now impossible given that external forces, and not a self-elected government, have economic control over the island. Currently, an entire generation of Puerto Ricans has been exiled from the island, and every day, the unbearable relationship with the United States seems more exploitative and unilateral. However, in the context of global international relationships, the fate of the island is not much different from other countries whose fates are now also determined by the creditors of their national debt.

Puerto Ricans have been exploited economically for decades in exchange for social services and benefits. Although Puerto Rico qualifies for federal services, much like the ones servicing all 50 states, the conditions of those services are quite different. In 2016, and in the context of the economic collapse of the island's economy, it has been made evident that (a) Puerto Ricans must and do in fact pay for those services through the contributions of their workforce at a higher percentage than any other state (e.g., the contributions to Medicare and Social Security are the same but the benefits received by taxpayers are calculated at lower rates than those in other states); and (b) the costs of such contributions far exceed the benefits that the island gets from the United States. The costs include: higher prices on all items imported to the island, the loss of land for agriculture, the loss of natural rights to water, the use of the land for military purposes, and the loss of a generation who were educated by the people of Puerto Rico and now have moved to the United States to provide bilingual services to U.S. Latinos.

Politically, the people of Puerto Rico have been taught to believe that they have a voice. Self-determination (the illusion of inclusion), or the belief that the people of Puerto Rico can decide their political destiny, is a lie. Local and U.S. politicians used local referendums to blame the political fate of the island on the people of Puerto Rico, stating that the residents of Puerto Rico must send an electoral message to change its political situation from its status quo to independence or statehood. Many referendums have been held and Puerto Ricans over and over again choose to be a commonwealth regardless of how it's framed. However, it is the U.S. Congress that can decide the fate of the island and has the ability to disregard the will of the people of Puerto Rico in their decision. In practical matters, what that means is that the future of Puerto Rico is in the hands of those who control the economic interests and debt of the island (which is neocolonialism).

In recent years, American billionaires found in Puerto Rico a taxing heaven; they can declare residency on the island, earn their money on the mainland, and avoid all taxes (a triple tax exception—local, federal, and state). The fate of the Puerto Rican political establishment still carries in the colors of the political parties' red (commonwealth), blue (statehood), and green (independence) a view from an unsustainable past that must be reconceived to adjust for the current global political environment. Even if the decolonial movement is successful and the independence of Puerto Rico is achieved through a social revolution, the island would still have to finance its massive debt through a financial institution such as the World Bank, and it still would be accountable to external forces for political determination. At this particular juncture in time, the only thing that is clear is that the island must go through a difficult process to understand its place in the world and reimagine its identity.

The Question of Puerto Rican Independence

Gisely Colón López, Board Member, Alliance for Puerto Rican Education and Empowerment (APREE)

As the Puerto Rican diaspora within the United States continues to grow and outnumber Puerto Ricans currently residing on the island, a new form of political activism and awareness becomes both possible and a reality. Coupled with the current internal economic catastrophe, riddled with corruption, greed, and imperialistic oppression, an awakening of the masses is finally bringing the conversation of self-determination, sovereignty, and autonomy to a platform that began to be constructed decades ago. With the efforts of those who fought in *El Grito de Lares*, and the advocacy of Dr. Pedro Albizu Campos as the foundation, the second half of the 21st century promises to be a new chapter for the Puerto Rican Independence Movement.

Because of the colonial reality of Puerto Rico and the continued exploitation of military bases, labor, and the ramifications of neocolonialism, a new moment in the history of the island manifests itself. Never has the moment for independence, self-liberation, and self-determination been such a possibility. For years, advocates, leaders, and historical literature have cried about the injustices and oppression of both the Puerto Rican people and the land, which has been occurring since the so-called encounter centuries ago. The imposition of foreign rulers, foreign law, and even foreign languages have led us to what we face today, the ground zero of colonialism and the outcome many *independistas* offered their lives trying to prevent. Many of these *independistas* have given the movement their lives through imprisonment, exile, forced migration, and death.

Much of the history of Puerto Rico is hidden behind Eurocentric narratives often told by the oppressing forces, such as the United States of America. The long struggle and desire for independence seems like a faint memory, one which dominant and hegemonic mainstream narratives would have you believe doesn't exist. Rather, it is a new tactic being used to pacify and discourage those still living with the light of hope inside. These warriors, such as the prominent Oscar Lopez Rivera and those Puerto Ricans refusing to leave the island amidst pleas from family members, remind us that Puerto Rico still has not only the resiliency to free itself from colonial ruling but also a strong commitment to ensuring Puerto Rico becomes the self-sustaining body it was destined to be.

Conversations with Puerto Ricans residing on the island reveal an enormous distrust and consciousness of the high levels of corruption and disconnect between the government and the Puerto Rican people being squeezed under it. The system of education, the infrastructures, and local businesses are all suffering because of the colonial and economic relationship imposed by the United States. It is at this moment in the story of Puerto Rico that the United States needs to finally set the nation of Puerto Rico free. Years of internal movements have been silenced or quickly dissolved by the United States, creating the illusion that an independent movement either doesn't exist, isn't strong, or isn't possible. On the contrary, the spirit and yearning for independence lives on.

Current dominant headlines would have us believe that Puerto Ricans are fleeing the island in a presumed fantasy of following an "American Dream." The reality being faced by Puerto Ricans (im)migrating to the United States is that of seeking refuge from the effects of U.S. imperialism plaguing them. Although Puerto Ricans are currently born U.S. citizens, the extended reality is that they are not treated as such once on U.S. soil. Many arrive with basic to no English language skills, which affects their employment and educational opportunities and leaves them in the same economically depressed situation they (im)migrated from in the first place. Misconceptions and stereotypes place them under the dominant criminalized Latino ethnic "minority" label, further marginalizing them from any privileges associated with U.S. citizenship.

Missing from the dominant headlines are the narratives and figures and statistics about Puerto Ricans, now identifying as DiaspoRicans, returning to the island ready to take up the *lucha* from home base. This renewed awakening and return home are the seeds being planted for the next chapter in the Puerto Rican Independence movement. The current catastrophe being endured by Puerto Rico will fuel a new legacy for Puerto Rico, one filled with new forms of thought, which will lead to anticolonial solutions coupled with sustainable ideologies that will begin to repair decades of colonial exploitation by imperial forces.

NOTES

1. Foraker Act (Organic Act of 1900). U.S. President McKinley signed a civil law that established a civilian government in Puerto Rico. The new government had a governor and an executive council appointed by the President, a House of Representatives with 35 elected members, a judicial system with a Supreme Court, and a nonvoting Resident Commissioner in Congress. Puerto Rico became the United States' first unincorporated territory.

2. Sources for the Study of Puerto Rican Migration, 1879–1930: *History Task Force,* Centro de Estudios Puertorriqueños Research Foundation of the City University of New York, 1982, pp. 30–33; in Rodolfo F. Acuña and Guadalupe Compean, eds., *Voices of the U.S. Latino Experience* (3 volumes), translated and edited by Guadalupe Compean, Westport, CT: Greenwood Press, 2008, vol. 1, pp. 317–319.

BIBLIOGRAPHY

Akiboh, Alvita. "Puerto Rico's Relationship with the United States?" *U.S. History Scene*, 2013. http://ushistoryscene.com/article/puerto-rico

Barreto, Amilcar Antonio. *Vieques, the Navy and Puerto Rican Politics*. Gainesville, FL: Florida University Press, 2002.

Bergad, Laird W. "Toward Puerto Rico's Grito de Lares: Coffee, Social Stratification, and Class Conflicts, 1828–1868." *The Hispanic American Historical Review* 60, no. 4 (November 1980): 617–642.

Bermúdez, Wanda. "Brief History of Vieques." 1998. http://www.vieques-island.com/history.shtml. Accessed July 25, 2003.

Bernabe, Rafael. "Puerto Rico's Strike Against Privatization." *Solidarity*, December 1997. https://www.solidarity-us.org/node/829

Brás, Marisabel. "The Changing of the Guard: Puerto Rico in 1898." Library of Congress. http://www.loc.gov/rr/hispanic/1898/bras.html

Brown, Emma. "Lolita Lebron, jailed for gun attack at U.S. Capitol in 1954, dies at 90." *Washington Post*, August 2, 2010. http://www.washingtonpost.com/wp-dyn/content/article/2010/08/01/AR2010080103400.html

Collazo, Frank J. "Part I—Puerto Ricans Contributions to All Wars." CNN iReport, August 26, 2010. http://ireport.cnn.com/docs/DOC-485498

Colón, Sonia, and Javier Vilariño. Puerto Rico's Extraordinary Case. *American Bankruptcy Institute Journal* 33, no. 10 (2014): 38.

Coto, Danica. "Puerto Rico OKs airport privatization amid protests." *USA Today*, March 1, 2013. http://www.usatoday.com/story/todayinthesky/2013/03/01/puerto-rico-airport-privatization-deal-lifts-off/1956407

Ferrara, Peter. "Puerto Rico's Debt Crisis: We can't reward fiscal failure with a bailout, bankruptcy." FoxNews.com, January 18, 2016. http://www.foxnews.com/opinion/2016/01/18/puerto-ricos-debt-crisis-cant-reward-fiscal-failure-with-bailout-bankruptcy.html

Figueroa, Ivonne. "Taínos." *El Boricua*, July 1996. http://www.elboricua.com/history.html

Glasser, Ruth. "Puerto Rican Farm Workers in Connecticut." *Hog River Journal*. http://www.hogriver.org/issues/v01n01/tobacco_valley.htm

Hoerlein, Sara. "Female Sterilization in Puerto Rico." *Patria_y_LaPava*, August 7, 2001. http://www.puertorico.com/forums/29852-post1.html

Kern, Frank D. "Dr. Carlos E. Chardon (1897–1965)," *Mycologia* 57, no. 6 (Nov–Dec, 1965): 839–844

Levy, Teresita A. *Puerto Ricans in the Empire: Tobacco Growers and U.S. Colonialism*. New Brunswick: Rutgers University Press, 2014.

López José. "Obama With The Same Lie About Puerto Rico Colonialism." *Modern Ghana*, April 15, 2015. http://www.modernghana.com/news/611408/1/obama-with-the-same-lie-about-puerto-rico-colonial.html

Mahler, Jonathan, and Nicholas Confessore. "Inside the Billion-Dollar Battle for Puerto Rico's Future." *New York Times*, December 19, 2015. http://www.nytimes.com/2015/12/20/us/politics/puerto-rico-money-debt.html

Martin, Gary. "Puerto Rico's Economy: History and Prospects." *Business America* 8, 25 (November 1985): 7(3).

Martínez, Rubén Berríos. "Puerto Rico's Decolonization: The Time Is Now." *Foreign Affairs* 76, no. 6 (1997).

Mihm, Stephen. "Congress Goofed. Puerto Rico Pays." *Bloomberg*, December 3, 2015. https://www.bloomberg.com/view/articles/2015-12-03/bankruptcy-was-option-for-puerto-rico-before-congress-goof

MIM Notes,"U.$ Navy resumes bombing Vieques in Puerto Rico." *MIM Notes*, May 1, 2002, p. 3. https://www.prisoncensorship.info/archive/etext/mn/html/mn257.html

Monge, José Trias. *Puerto Rico: The Trials of the Oldest Colony in the World.* New Haven: Yale University Press, 1997. http://www.nytimes.com/books/first/m/monge-puertorico.html

Navarro, Mireya. "New Light on Old F.B.I. Fight; Decades of Surveillance of Puerto Rican Groups." *New York Times*, November 28, 2003. http://www.nytimes.com/2003/11/28/nyregion/new-light-on-old-fbi-fight-decades-of-surveillance-of-puerto-rican-groups.html

Nieves, Efrain. "En Lares, Un Grito De Valor." *Pa'lante Latino*, September 23, 2011. http://palantelatino.com/2011/09/23/en-lares-un-grito-de-valor

Odishelidze, Alexander, and Arthur Laffer. *Pay to the Order of Puerto Rico*. Fairfax, VA: Fairfax Press, 2004.

Pabon, Julio. "Statehood Vote in Puerto Rico?" *Huffington Post*, January 9, 2013. http://www.huffingtonpost.com/julio-pabon/statehood-vote-in-puerto-_b_2094586.html

Pico, Fernando. "Let Puerto Rico Decide. (Chronology of Puerto Rico's History Since Before 1898 and the Need to Let the Country Decide on its Future Economic and Social Policies) (Editorial)." *America* 178, no. 19 (1998): 3ff.

Pierluisi, Pedro R. "A Lifeline for Puerto Rico." *American Bankruptcy Institute Journal* 34, no. 8 (August 2015): 8–9, 77.

Planas, Roque, and Adriana Usero. "5 Things Every American Should Know About Puerto Rico's Financial Crisis." *Huffington Post*, July 7, 2015. http://www.huffingtonpost.com/2015/06/29/puerto-rico-financial-crisis_n_7689994.html

Poole, Robert M. "What Became of the Taíno?" *Smithsonian Magazine*, October 2011. http://www.smithsonianmag.com/people-places/what-became-of-the-taino-73824867/?no-ist

"Porto Rico: A Colonial Responsibility." *The New Republic*, February 6, 1929, pp. 311–312. In Rodolfo F. Acuña and Guadalupe Compean, *Voices of the U.S. Latino Experience* (3 volumes), translated and edited by Guadalupe Compean, Westport, CT: Greenwood Press, 2008, vol. 2, pp. 461–463.

"Puerto Rican Emigration: Why the 1950s?" Lehman College. http://lcw.lehman.edu/lehman/depts/latinampuertorican/latinoweb/PuertoRico/1950s.htm

"Puerto Rico at the Dawn of the Modern Age: Nineteenth- and Early-Twentieth-Century Perspectives, The Grito de Lares: The Rebellion of 1868." https://www.loc.gov/collections/puerto-rico-books-and-pamphlets/articles-and-essays/nineteenth-century-puerto-rico/rebellion-of-1868/

Puerto Rico Report. "Vieques and Culebra Cleanup Efforts Receive Funding in Federal Law," June 5, 2015. http://www.puertoricoreport.com/vieques-culebra-cleanup-efforts-receive-funding-federal-law/

"Puerto Rico Population." Pew Research Center, August 11, 2014. http://www.pewhispanic.org/2014/08/11/puerto-rico-population

"Puerto Rico Upset by Chardon Plan; What Little Is Known of the Rehabilitation Scheme Leads to Disputes." *New York Times*, August 12, 1934. http://query.nytimes.com/gst/abstract.html?res=9A02E6DB1339E33ABC4A52DFBE66838F629EDE

"Puerto Rico's Debt Crisis: Why There's No Quick Fix." Wharton School, January 28, 2016. http://knowledge.wharton.upenn.edu/article/puerto-ricos-debt-crisis-why-theres-no-quick-fix

Rabin, Robert "Vieques: Five Centuries of Struggle and Resistance." Historia de Vieques. http://www.vieques-island.com/navy/rabin.html

Reilly, Philip R. *The Surgical Solution: A History of Involuntary Sterilization in the United States*. Baltimore and London: The John Hopkins University Press, 1991.

Rodríguez, Clara E. *Puerto Ricans: Born in the U.S.A.* Boulder, CO: Westview Press, 1991.

Roy-Fequiere, Magali. "Contested Territory: Puerto Rican Women, Creole Identity, and Intellectual Life in the Early Twentieth Century (Special Issue: Puerto Rican Women Writers)." *Callaloo* 17, no. 3 (Summer 1994): 916ff.

Siegel, Josh. "Is Obama Administration Plan for Puerto Rico a 'Bailout'? Congress Debates Action on Debt Crisis." *The Daily Signal*, February 25, 2016. http://dailysignal.com/2016/02/25/is-obama-administration-plan-for-puerto-rico-a-bailout-congress-debates-action-on-debt-crisis/

Soler, José A. "Puerto Rico is a colony, not a commonwealth." *People's World*, July 28 2006. http://www.peoplesworld.org/puerto-rico-is-a-colony-not-a-commonwealth

Somocurcio, Monica. "Millions cheer Vieques & Albizu." *Workers World News Service*, June 22, 2000. http://www.workers.org/ww/2000/prparade0622.php

Stanchich, Maritza. "Ten Years After Ousting US Navy, Vieques Confronts Contamination." *Huffington Post*, July 14, 2013. http://www.huffingtonpost.com/maritza-stanchich-phd/ten-years-after-ousting-u_b_3243449.html

"The Strategic Value of Puerto Rico." *The Struggle for Puerto Rican Autonomy*. http://aguil079.omeka.net/exhibits/show/american-imperialism-and-puert/why-puerto-rico-/the-strategic-value-of-puerto-

Suro, Roberto. *Strangers Among Us: Latinos' Lives in a Changing America*. New York: Vintage Books, 1999.

Varela, Julio Ricardo. "In New Supreme Court Amicus Brief, Obama Administration Questions Puerto Rico's Commonwealth Status." *Latino USA*, December 28, 2015. http://latinousa.org/2015/12/28/in-new-supreme-court-amicus-brief-us-confirms-that-congress-determines-fate-of-puerto-rico

VetFriends.com. "Puerto Rico Military Casualties—All War." 2016. https://www.vetfriends.com/memorial/mem_alphab.cfm?War_ID=0&page_id=1&states_id=55

SELECTED VIDEOS

AP Archive. "Puerto Rico: Vieques US Navy Base: Protest," YouTube video, 3:35, posted July 21, 2015. https://www.youtube.com/watch?v=PYhBEXCl_xQ

Boriken Tv. "1898 año que cambio la historia de Puerto Rico—Parte 1," YouTube video, 14:17, posted June 3, 2013. https://www.youtube.com/watch?v=UemnDTGxYg0

Bradley, Cailyn. "Puerto Rico: An Unsettled Dominican Dream," YouTube video, 26:20, posted March 13, 2014. https://www.youtube.com/watch?v=FKBDEhBHgF8

Center for Puerto Rican Studies–Centro. "La Operacion—Background." YouTube video, 4:54, posted June 7, 2013. https://www.youtube.com/watch?v=r6XEuu_auR8

Clifford, Paul F. "Origins of Salsa the Puerto Rican Influence." http://www.geocities.com/sd_au/articles/sdhsalsapr.htm. Accessed July 26, 2003.

Historia—Bel99TV. "Puerto Rico—Sights, Culture, Agriculture, Hat Making, Crafts—1940s Rural Life," YouTube video, 19:09, posted November 10, 2014. https://www.youtube.com/watch?v=8wkEpcXeNDo

InYourFaceTv. "'Forbidden Puerto Rico': America with Jorge Ramos (Part 1 OF 3)," YouTube video, 13:24, posted September 17, 2014. https://www.youtube.com/watch?v=G1UrSXgrqDg

Islas de Borinken TV. "Puerto Rico—Invasión de Estados Unidos y Albizu Campos," YouTube video, 27:50, posted June 14, 2014. https://www.youtube.com/watch?v=-a4tv8jHUPo

Manuelcrespo65. "Primer Lugar, World Salsa Open, Puerto Rico 2013," YouTube video, 2:23, posted July 27, 2013. https://www.youtube.com/watch?v=Tiy6xhcBU4k

Molyneux, Stefan. "The Fall of Puerto Rico. Prepare Yourself Accordingly," YouTube video, 43:56, posted July 3, 2015. https://www.youtube.com/watch?v=k4iuD7xQDxE

Náter, Jorge Emmanuelli. "Mi Puerto Rico (La Verdadera Historia)," YouTube video, 1:26:49, posted January 3, 2013. https://www.youtube.com/watch?v=E3OOwPjVg3g

Nephtali1981. "The TRUE Story Of Puerto Rico: Population Control, Genocide, Columbus & More," YouTube video, 1:12:56, posted August 9, 2015. https://www.youtube.com/watch?v=HKrt5u9g3_4

Salsa Clásico. "Soneros de Puerto Rico—'Yo Soy Boricua,'" YouTube video, 6:18, posted August 2, 2014. https://www.youtube.com/watch?v=S5ERpFSgV4M

Seeker Daily. "Should Puerto Rico Become A State?" YouTube video, 2:49, posted May 17, 2015. https://www.youtube.com/watch?v=1FQ8kmKSsqk

12

Central America

PLACE

Thomas Gage, an early European traveler to Central America, wrote *Travels in the New World, 1648.* A Dominican, he described Central America as an isthmus located at the southernmost end of North America abutting South America. Gage recognized its importance as the shortest landmass between the Atlantic and Pacific Oceans. This later made the region strategically important for American political, military, and economic interests. Panama was a center of commerce for Spain's colonies in America, which shipped trade items and slaves via Panama to Peru (Thompson, 1958).

Central America is roughly divided into a less populous Caribbean half and a slightly more congested Pacific coastal slope. Geography contributes to its being separated by relatively densely settled highland regions. Central America population density is one of the highest in the world. Although Spanish is the official language in most of the countries, many Indian languages are also spoken throughout the region.

Por que estamos com estamos

Southern Mexico and Central America are similar, but unalike. In both areas, there are indigenous people, *pueblos indígenas*, and also mestizos. The Spanish incorporation of indigenous peoples into the colonial system differed in this region from the central and northern plains of New Spain where massive mining strikes drove the conquest. Water had allowed for the development of early large urban centers and civilizations.

The native communities endured the devastation of the invasion and colonization of Mesoamerica, but not before Spaniards dramatically changed them. In order to control them, colonial authorities grouped native communities into *municipios*, townships. The largest town of the *municipios* was the *cabecera*, or head community. This structure allowed the survival of the indigenous community and the strengthening colonial control of the native village. Its purpose was to isolate natives in order for them to identify with the local village rather than forming class or ethnic identities. This division made it difficult for the different communities to unite against Spanish rule, destroying intercommunity regional networks and the preinvasion world system. This concentrated power in the hands of Indian *caciques*, chiefs, who ran the local system and were loyal to the Spaniards.

Colonial structures such as the *encomienda* controlled the native people. The conquistadors were given large tracts of land with natives whose labor paid tribute. This system began the first plantations. Independence brought the rule of the criollo, which gave way to the rise of the cult of the mestizo and the avarice of foreign investors. The 19th century liberal ideology meant a free market, secularization, and the cult of la Raza Cósmica (Vasconcelos, 1997). The indigene lands were no longer presumed to be public—privatization was essential. This new view brought a new assault on the native peoples, whom the "New People" believed were unproductive and wasteful. The process and subordination of *pueblos indigenas* continue to this day.

The Maya

The Mayan civilization covered southern Mexico through Belize, Guatemala, El Salvador, Honduras, Nicaragua, and northern Costa Rica. Guatemala is the heartland. The indigenous people arrived in the region approximately 8000 BC ("The Pre-Columbian Civilizations of Central America," n.d.). They flourished until the Spanish colonization of the Americas. They built numerous cities throughout Central America and Southern Mexico that housed between 5 and 10 million people.

Farmers supported these city–state populations; they were industrious and employed jungle farming and raised field methods, clearing large tracts of jungle.

In Central America, the Mayan civilization settled the northwestern part of the isthmus, from Chiapas and Yucatán in today's southern Mexico. The Mayans lived in Guatemala, Honduras, Belize, El Salvador, and Nicaragua. Present-day research suggests that the Maya area may have been larger. Although culturally the most advanced pre-Columbian civilization, it was never unified like the Aztec and Inca empires. Culture rather than political structures united the Maya (Amador, 2012).[1] The Mayan world differed from African and Eurasian civilizations. Native Americans lived in warm and humid regions and did not emerge in river valleys. They learned to plant corn, which became the basic food crop in most of the northern hemisphere. Corn supported the development of large cities. The Maya left footprints that included Tikal in Guatemala's northern El Péten region—one of the most impressive sites in Mayan civilization. The city–state housed 60,000 people in the city and up to a half million in the surrounding lands.

The Quiriguá ruins are located in the Izabal region of Guatemala. Quiriguá has a number of massive stelae—including one that's 35 feet tall! Numerous boulders are carved in detailed animal shapes called zoomorphs. The Xunantunich ruins are in western Belize's Cayo district. The Altun Ha ruins are among the best preserved archaeological sites in Belize. To the south in the Toledo District is the Lubaantun ruins. Caracol is the largest Maya site in Belize. It once occupied an area much larger than Belize City, with double the population. The Copan ruins in western Honduras are smaller in comparison to other Central America Mayan sites. In el Salvador, the Tazumal ruins are the best preserved (Hubbard, n.d.).

Why is Guatemala called the heart of the region?

Although there were no massive buildings in the areas of Costa Rica and Panama, there is evidence of early agriculture and the cultivation of corn. This area suffered disproportionately from droughts, making the building of large cities more difficult (Taylor, Horn, and Finkelstein, 2013). Nevertheless, there is evidence of advanced civilizations in Honduras, Nicaragua and Costa Rica, where new discoveries are being uncovered (Joyce et al., 1993).

The view of this society is expanding and becoming more nuanced. For example, as early as the Late Preclassic period (300 BC–100 AD), evidence has been found that the turkey existed at the archaeological site of El Mirador (Petén, Guatemala). This turkey was a distinct breed from the one found in central Mexico. In addition, a variety of domesticated animals were exchanged. Interestingly, the Mayan turkey was domesticated before the time of Christ. The El Mirador findings represent "previously unrecorded Preclassic exchange of animals from northern Mesoamerica to the Maya cultural region" (Thornton et al., 2012).

How and why is our view of Mayan civilization expanding?

CIVILIZATION INTERRUPTED

The Spanish colonial period occurred from the early 1500s to about 1821. At the time the Spaniards invaded the New World in 1494, at least 100 million people lived in the Americas—25 million in what is today Mexico (McCaa, 1997). There were more than 350 major tribal groups, 15 distinct cultural centers, and more than 160 linguistic stocks. No borders existed as we know them.

What is meant by a "Civilization Interrupted"?

Guatemala

It is said that the name Guatemala, meaning *Quauhtlemallan*, "land of forests," comes from a Maya "spoken by the indigenous people at the time of the Spanish conquest in 1523. It is used today by outsiders, as well as by most citizens, although for many purposes the descendants of the original inhabitants still prefer to identify themselves by the names of their specific language, which reflect political divisions from the sixteenth century" ("Guatemala, Countries and Their Cultures"). Others attributed the word to a Nahuatl root.

In 1609, the area became a captaincy general and the governor was also granted the title of captain general. The Captaincy General of Guatemala covered most of Central America, with the exception of present-day Belize and Panama. The Captaincy General of Guatemala lasted for more than two centuries, but began to fall apart after a rebellion in 1811. The underlying reasons were nationalism and the struggle between liberals and conservatives (Minster, 2015).

On September 15, 1821, colonies comprising the Captaincy General of Guatemala declared their independence from Spain. For two years,

Central America was ruled by Agustín de Iturbide—a self-designated Emperor. Municipalities from Chiapas to Costa Rica declared independence not only from Spain, but from Mexico and Guatemala. On July 1, 1823, a Central American convention declared Central America independent and formed the United Provinces of Central America, a federation that included Guatemala, El Salvador, Honduras, Costa Rica, and Nicaragua. From the beginning, there was resentment toward Guatemala's perceived economic and political dominance. Honduran General Francisco Morazán and other liberals (the Latin American definition of the times varied) advocated capitalism and republican government. They wanted to limit the power of the clergy. Conservatives supported a strong church, traditional landowners, and highly autonomous states. Finally, in 1824, Chiapas, which belonged to Guatemala, was annexed by Mexico (Burguete, 1994).

Los Indigenas de Guatemala

Despite efforts to erase the various languages and identities of Guatemalans, "The majority of Guatemala's population is indigenous (representing 60 percent of the total population), a fact that becomes particularly important when the principle of proportional representation is applied to categories of state employees" (Cojit Cuxil, 2007). The three distinct indigenous nations exist within Guatemala are not tribes but civilizations that have lived under colonialism since 1492.

The Maya are the most numerous. "Maya from different regions of Guatemala speak different" languages, such as Quiché and Chuj, and receive proportional representation within the various categories of state employees (Brown and Odem, 2011). *The Xinca* were invisible for almost 200 years and were thought to be on the verge of extinction. They are one of the non-Mayan pueblos that today are struggling to save their culture, identity, and language. To that end, they formed the Consejo del Pueblo Xinca to study the grammar of their language. The Xinca were among the pueblos that led the resistance against the Spaniards. Apart from the indigenous population, the state is dominated by a hierarchy of criollos and mestizo who want to homogenize their identity. "Identity and culture of public institutions is creole or ladino" (Morales, n.d.). Despite their resistance, only minor concessions have been given to the Xinca and other indigenous peoples.

The Garifuna people are a group of mixed racial ancestry concentrated in Central America, especially in Belize, Honduras, Guatemala, and Nicaragua. Around half a million people are considered members of this cultural group, with some Central American governments offering special protection to the Garifuna people who desire to preserve their culture and heritage. Like many minority ethnic groups, the Garifuna struggle with social and racial prejudice.

The Garifuna originated in the Caribbean, particularly on the island of Saint Vincent. In the 1700s, they were removed from Saint Vincent because they were considered a political threat. They were literally dumped onto the mainland where they established small communities. This began their diaspora to Central America and to U.S. cities such as Los Angeles. They are descended from African slaves who intermarried with native Carib and Arawak Indians, leading some people to refer to them as "Black Caribs." The African heritage of the Garifuna comes from escaped slaves who intermarried with native people to protect themselves from being recaptured and sold. The Garifuna are also of French and Spanish ancestry; racial miscegenation was common in the region during the colonial era (Aguedo, 2013).

In Guatemala, the Garífunas have been recognized as part of its multilingual and pluralistic society. This awareness encouraged efforts to save their language, culture, and identity. "On the Honduran North Coast, the Afro-indigenous Garifuna struggle to maintain access to and control of their ancestral lands" (Mollett, 2014). Today, Honduran Garifunas number roughly 100,000. They live mostly in towns and villages along the Honduran northern coast. The Garifuna in Nicaragua, Guatemala, and Belize form the Black Caribe. There has always been a trickle of migration from this community to the United States–especially the Bronx, where the largest Garifuna community outside of Central America lives. Thousands have walked through Central America and Mexico to the U.S. border. Mothers with small children have shown up in places like the Bronx, "seeking refuge with family members, wearing GPS ankle monitors placed on them by U.S. immigration officers who detained them" ("Who are the Garifuna people?" 2016). They fled urban violence, racial discrimination, and a lack of opportunity. They were refugees of the American-made War on Drugs, bad government, business interests, and drug traffickers (Bishop, 2016).

Recently in Honduras, Berta Isabel Cáceres Flores was assassinated by a government-backed death squad. "She spoke too much truth to power—for indigenous rights, for women's and LGBTQ rights, for authentic democracy, for the well-being of the earth, and for an end to tyranny by transnational capital and U.S. Empire" (Bell, 2016). In 1993, Berta cofounded the Civic Council of Popular and Indigenous Organizations of Honduras, or COPINH. She successfully reclaimed ancestral lands, winning communal land titles. This disturbed the oligarchy, who charged her with sedition.

Aside from the Garifuna, Honduras Has Mayas, Lencas, Miskito, Sumo, Ch'orti', Pech, and Tolupan

"The Lenca are an indigenous people of southwestern Honduras and eastern El Salvador. They once spoke the Lenca language, which is now considered extinct. In Honduras, the Lenca are the largest indigenous group with an estimated population of 100,000. El Salvador's Lenca population is estimated at about 37,000" ("Lenca," accessed 2015). Most of the Lenca have acculturated into the Ladino culture. Nicaragua is comprised of creoles, mestizos, and to a lesser extent, Miskitos, Ramas, and Sumos (Ryser, 2012).

Costa Rica has a wide range of small societies: the Bribri, Boruca, Cabecar, Guaymi, Maleku, Matambu, and Terrabas. Their numbers are small, roughly 64,000—about 1.7 percent of the population. They remained isolated because they moved to the mountains to avoid forced labor. "The decimation of the indigenous of Costa Rica was due mostly to diseases, rather than targeted genocide, as happened in other Latin American countries, most prominently Guatemala and El Salvador" (Gimlette, 2013).

El Salvador

The Maya migrated to El Salvador along with the Pipil—migrants from the Toltec civilization—in the 9th century. They were made up of different Toltec societies. Refugees from the Nawat-speaking[2] Pipil went to El Salvador. Some of the Toltec followed the refugees to El Salvador where they ruled for about 130 years until their centers were burned. A splintering of Toltec groups occurred. They brought their agriculture and their civilization to the region. According to the *CIA World Factbook*, Salvadorans speak Spanish, with a small minority speaking native languages. In 2007, "the population was estimated at mestizo 86.3%, white 12.7%, Amerindian 0.2% (includes Lenca, Kakawira, Nahua-Pipil), black 0.1%, other 0.6%" (USAID, 2016).

Panama

In 2007, the *CIA World Factbook* listed Panama's population as "mestizo (mixed Amerindian and white) 65%, Native American 12.3% (Ngabe 7.6%, Kuna 2.4%, Embera .9%, Bugle .8%, other .4%, unspecified .2%), the African descent 9.2%, mulatto 6.8%, white 6.7% (2010 estimate)." It had smaller numbers of Teribe, Wounaan, and Talamanca. Some sources estimate that the indigenous peoples make up between 5 and 8 percent of the population. The relations with natives have often been explosive, especially with exploitive mining companies.

Mining in indigenous peoples' territories has often resulted in explosive conflict. News accounts have rarely report on this topic. An example is the conflict surrounding decision making at Tiomin Resources' Cerro Colorado copper mine on Ngabe–Bugle land in western Panama, which, like so many other conflicts in Panama, is about environment justice (Whiteman, 2002). Much of the conflict is about water, the rain forests, and the preservation of the indigenous peoples' way of life. The Ngabe–Bugle land is home to about 300 members of a small community of indigenous people who moved from their traditional territory in the north to this region many years ago. For income, the community relies on the gold that's in the riverbanks, but they search for it the same way their ancestors did centuries ago using large wooden pans, shifting mounds of dirt round and round, sifting, sifting, until a speck of shiny mineral is left at the end (Fung, 2012).

How has geography formed attitudes of races in Central America?

THE YANKEE PERIL

The Second European Invasion: America for Americans

Even before the Texas filibuster (1836) and the American War with Mexico (1845–1848), southern slave owners and American business interests eyed the Caribbean and Central America for expansion. Stephen Austin and Sam Houston were the models for American filibusters. Filibustering was freebooting; many Americans wanted to be Sam Adams (a leader of the American Revolution of 1776). They staked out foreign territories for U.S. expansion.

In the 1850s, William Walker invaded Lower California, Sonora, and Nicaragua (Soodalter, 2010). The Tennessean led expeditions into Baja, California and temporarily seized control of Nicaragua in 1857. Throughout this period, U.S. newspapers and journals discussed the Cuban question and how democracy should be exported to Cuba and Central America (Harrison, 2004).

In a New Orleans speech, William Walker said that the United States should fix the problem permanently, not only in Cuba, but in Central America, which was in worse shape than under Spanish rule. Walker blamed mongrels for the waning fortunes of the region. "What was to be done?" According to Walker, it was the duty of Americans to Americanize

Central America and to regenerate the amalgamated race. Walker called the audience to arms: "I feel that my duty calls upon me to return." He continued, "Aye, fellow-citizens, I call upon you all, by the glorious recollections of the past, and the bright anticipations for the future, to assist in carrying out and perfecting the Americanization of Central America" ("Speech Given by William Walker in New Orleans, May 30, 1857").

How is William Walker symbolic of the American attitude toward Central America? Of American exceptionalism?

Walker, like Donald Trump, caught the imagination of Euro-Americans. However, there were other contenders, such as Commander Cornelius Vanderbilt, a wealthy banker who built a route through Nicaragua and then a railroad through Panama that joined the Atlantic and Pacific Oceans. Vanderbilt saw Walker as a fly in the ointment. Meanwhile, Costa Rica declared war on Walker and, in May 1857, he surrendered and was forced to leave Nicaragua. Next, Walker led an invasion of Honduras where he was captured and executed in 1860. Walker had wanted to save the "abominable bastard democracies of Central and South America" ("Speech Given by William Walker in New Orleans, May 30, 1857").

Tensions between Latin America and the United States did not abate with the Spanish American War of 1898 fanning Latin American fears of American designs. The war followed American interventions in the Caribbean and Middle America. The Colossus of the North and its encroachments in Cuba, Puerto Rico and repeated military interventions increased fears increased when Panama at the instigation of the United States broke away from Colombia in 1903. The U.S. almost immediately recognized Panama's independence and made plans to build a canal.

Most Central and Latin Americans were angered by the United States hijacking of Panama and the building of the Panama Canal. Rubén Dario, Nicaragua's foremost poet, expresses these sentiments in a letter to Theodore Roosevelt:

It is with the voice of the Bible, or the verse of Walt Whitman,
that I should come to you, Hunter,
primitive and modern, simple and complicated,
with something of Washington and more of Nimrod.

You are the United States,
you are the future invader
of the naive America that has Indian blood,
that still prays to Jesus Christ and still speaks Spanish.

You are the proud and strong exemplar of your race;
you are cultured, you are skillful; you oppose Tolstoy.
And breaking horses, or murdering tigers,
you are an Alexander-Nebuchadnezzar.
(You are a professor of Energy
as today's madmen say.)

You think that life is fire,
that progress is eruption,
that wherever you shoot
you hit the future.

No. (Darío, 1905)

Why did Latin Americans fear the United States?

The 1890s saw numerous interventions throughout Latin America and Central America caused by popular revolts in an effort to change the world order (Table 12.1). The United States assumed the role of the policeman of the world, intent on maintaining the world order. The United States introduced a neo-Monroe Doctrine era where America was for America (Dario, 1905).

Table 12.1 Armed Interventions into Central America

Nicaragua	1894	Troops	Month-long occupation of Bluefields
Panama	1895	Naval, troops	Marines land in Colombian province
Nicaragua	1896	Troops	Marines land in port of Corinto
Nicaragua	1898	Troops	Marines land at port of San Juan del Sur
Nicaragua	1899	Troops	Marines land at port of Bluefields
Honduras	1903	Troops	Marines intervene in revolution
Nicaragua	1907	Troops	"Dollar Diplomacy" protectorate set up
Honduras	1907	Troops	Marines land during war with Nicaragua
Panama	1908	Troops	Marines intervene in election contest
Nicaragua	1910	Troops	Marines land in Bluefields and Corinto
Honduras	1911	Troops	U.S. interests protected in civil war
Panama	1912	Troops	Marines land during heated election
Honduras	1912	Troops	Marines protect U.S. economic interests

(*continued*)

Table 12.1 Armed Interventions into Central America (*continued*)

Nicaragua	1912–1933	Troops, bombing	20-year occupation, fought guerrillas
Cuba	1917–1933	Troops	Military occupation, economic protectorate
Panama	1918–1920	Troops	"Police duty" during unrest after elections
Honduras	1919	Troops	Marines land during election campaign
Guatemala	1920	Troops	2-week intervention against unionists
Costa Rica	1921	Troops	
Panama	1921	Troops	
Honduras	1924–1925	Troops	Landed twice during election strife
Panama	1925	Troops	Marines suppress general strike
El Salvador	1932	Naval	Warships sent during Faribundo Marti revolt
Guatemala	1954–?	Command operation, bombing, nuclear threat	CIA directs exile invasion and coup d'etat after newly elected government nationalizes unused U.S.'s United Fruit Company lands; bombers based in Nicaragua; long-term result: 200,000 murdered
Panama	1958	Troops	Flag protests erupt into confrontation
Panama	1964	Troops	Panamanians shot for urging canal's return
Guatemala	1966–1967	Command operation	Green Berets intervene against rebels
El Salvador	1981–1992	Command operation, troops	Advisors, overflights aid anti-rebel war, soldiers briefly involved in hostage clash; long-term result: 75,000 murdered and destruction of popular movement
Nicaragua	1981–1990	Command operation, naval	CIA directs exile (Contra) invasions, plants harbor mines against revolution; result: 50,000 murdered
Honduras	1982–1990	Troops	Maneuvers help build bases near borders
Panama	1989	Troops, bombing	Nationalist government ousted by 27,000 soldiers, leaders arrested, 2000+ killed
Honduras	2009	Command operation	Support for coup that removed president Manuel Zelaya

Source: Adapted from William Blum, *Killing Hope: U.S. Military and CIA Interventionism Since World War II.* Monroe, ME: Common Courage Press, 1995.

Marc Becker's Home Page, "History of U.S. Interventions in Latin America." http://www.yachana.org/teaching/resources/interventions.html

The cycle of intervention was worsened by multinationals such as United Fruit Company, the symbol of American imperialism in Central America. United Fruit controlled governments, including that of the United States. It had enormous privileges in Central America where dictators dealt harshly with labor. Multinationals supplied dictators with money and fueled the economy (Bucheli, 2008; Ferreira, 2008).

What gave the United States the right to intervene? How have U.S. interventions worsened conditions in Central America?

In 1954, Jacobo Árbenz's overthrow in Guatemala sent shock waves throughout Latin America. According to new research, the U.S. decision to overthrow Árbenz was based on ideological grounds, although the influence of the banana monopoly, the United Fruit Company, played a part in persuading Secretary of State John Foster Dulles to intervene. His brother was the attorney for the United Fruit Company (United Fruit owned 42 percent of the nation and had been exempted from all taxes and duties on both imports and exports) (Ferreira, 2008). The documents of the U.S. Central Intelligence Agency prove that it ordered the assassination of ten people in a conference room (Schrider, 1997). Fifty-seven years later, Guatemalan President Álvaro Colom apologized to Arbenz's son for what he called a "great crime" (Malkin, 2011). It awakened Latin Americans, brought back memories of the Colossus of the North, and stiffened their resolve to change their societies.

Meanwhile, the intrusion in Guatemala intensified American cold war politics. President Harry S Truman had sought to contain communism whereas President Dwight Eisenhower took an aggressive course of action in Latin America. His policies went from containment to defending American interests abroad. The overthrow of Árbenz and the imposition of a dictator was intended to send a clear warning to Russia that America would not tolerate the spread of communism in the Western Hemisphere. The leader of the military coup, Carlos Castillo Armas, headed Guatemala—his job was to promote American interests in Guatemala (Guatemala, 1954; Holland, 2004). He launched a reign of terror in Guatemala and Central America and set the stage for U.S. intervention in Central America and for covert operations (Isenberg, 1989; Siengkhene, 2012). At the same time, the overthrow of Árbenz (1954) and Salvador Allende in 1973 radicalized Latin Americans (Hove, 2007).

How were U.S. intrusions in Central America part of American Cold War politics?

Belize was once part of Guatemala; it was occupied by the British and was known as British Honduras. Boundary disputes delayed the independence of Belize until 1981. The *World Factbook* lists the population as "mestizo 52.9%, Creole 25.9%, Maya 11.3%, Garifuna 6.1%, East Indian 3.9%, Mennonite 3.6%, white 1.2%, Asian 1%, other 1.2%, and unknown 0.3%" (Belize, *CIA World Factbook*). It is the smallest of the Central American nations, with a population of 347,369 people (Bridgewater, 2014).

El Salvador has a population that is "mestizo 86.3%, white 12.7%, Amerindian 0.2% (includes Lenca, Kakawira, Nahua-Pipil), black 0.1%, other 0.6% (2007 estimate)." It numbers 6,141,350. In size, El Salvador is the smallest and most densely populated country in Central America. The country is experiencing "slower population growth, a decline in its number of youths, and the gradual aging of its population" ("El Salvador," n.d.). Its fertility rate has declined from approximately 6 children per woman in the 1970s to replacement level today. Fertility differences between rich and poor and urban and rural women are narrowing. Today, El Salvador, as is most of Central America, is suffering from the devastation brought on by the civil wars of the 1980s (Silber, 2010).

Honduras, according to the *CIA Factbook*, after two and a half decades of mostly military rule, elected a civilian government in 1982. However, such an assertion is in doubt. Honduras has a population of 8,746,673. "Ethnic groups: mestizo (mixed Amerindian and European) 90%, Amerindian 7%, black 2%, white 1%." It has a high birthrate that averages approximately three children per woman—which is higher among rural, indigenous, and poor women. Because of population growth and limited job prospects outside of agriculture, emigration will increase. Today, remittances are about one fifth of Honduran GDP. Over half the population lives in poverty—poverty is higher among rural and indigenous people. Critics accuse Honduras of being a stooge of the United States. During the CIA's covert operations in the 1980s, Honduras was a base for Sandinista Contras supposedly fighting the Marxist Nicaraguan government. It was an ally of the Salvadoran government fighting the FMLN and a vassal of the United States (Rodríguez, 2015).

Why were the United States policies against the Nicaraguan government so damaging to Honduras?

Costa Rica in 1949 dissolved its armed forces. Its standard of living is relatively high. It is "83.6% white or mestizo, mulatto 6.7%, indigenous 2.4%, black of African descent 1.1%, other 1.1%, none 2.9%, unspecified 2.2% (2011 estimate)" (Central Intelligence Agency). The government spends almost 20 percent of its GDP annually on social programs. "The average number of children born per woman has fallen from about 7 in the 1960s to 3.5 in the early 1980s to below replacement level today. Its poverty rate is lower than in most in the hemisphere. Less than 3% of Costa Rica's population lives abroad." The overwhelming majority of expatriates have settled in the United States after completing a university degree or in order to work in a highly skilled field. Its population was estimated in 2015 at 4,814,144 (Sohn, 2013). Nicaragua, according to the *World Factbook,* has an estimated population of 5,907,881. Its racial composition is "mestizo (mixed Amerindian and white) 69%, white 17%, black 9%, Amerindian 5%" (Central Intelligence Agency, "Nicaragua"). It is one of the poorest countries in Latin America. However, it has improved its access to potable water and sanitation, ameliorated life expectancy and infant and child mortality, and improved its immunization rates. Its fertility rate has fallen from about 6 children per woman in 1980 to just over two (Morris, 2010).

Panama was originally part of Colombia. In a not very covert action, Panama seceded from Colombia in 1903. It promptly signed a treaty with the United States, allowing the construction of a canal and U.S. sovereignty over a strip of land on either side of the Panama Canal. The Panama Canal was built by the U.S. Army Corps of Engineers between 1904 and 1914. The population today is "mestizo (mixed Amerindian and white) 65%, Native American 12.3% (Ngabe 7.6%, Kuna 2.4%, Embera 0.9%, Bugle 0.8%, other 0.4%, unspecified 0.2%), black or African descent 9.2%, mulatto 6.8%, white 6.7% (2010 estimate)." Unlike many Central American countries, it has a low fertility rate. It has a population of 3,657,024 people (July 2015 estimate) (*CIA Factbook,* "Panama").

Unrest in Central America

The 1960s began a period of economic growth that lasted through the 1970s. The economic cycle ran its course and a period of national indebtedness and low economic growth rates followed in the 1980s. In 1979, the overthrow of the Somoza family in Nicaragua touched off civil wars. Accompanied by high inflation and a widening gap between rich and poor, most Central American countries had to seek foreign aid from the World Bank or the International Monetary Fund, which imposed more hardship through austerity measures squeezing the poor even more. Civil unrest displaced an estimated million people, about half of them Salvadorans. As a result of American influence, the region entered an epoch of neoliberalism, accelerating the privatization of companies, utilities, and free trade which displaced small operators. Free-trade zones brought *maquiladoras* (foreign-owned factories where goods are assembled by low-paid workers for export to the United States) (Fernã¡Ndez-Kelly, 2012).

Nicaragua was ruled by U.S. puppets continuously since the 1930s. Anastasio "Tacho" Somoza García was officially the President of Nicaragua from January 1, 1937 to May 1, 1947 and from May 21, 1950 to September 29, 1956. However, in effect he ruled the country from 1936 until his assassination in 1956. Opposition to the Nicaraguan government crystallized in 1978, and his son, Anastasio "Tachito" Somoza DeBayle, was overthrown by Sandinista guerrillas in 1979. His ouster sent rays of hope throughout the region.

Adhering to the Eisenhower doctrine of not tolerating communism, the United States used the pretext that Nicaragua had aided leftist rebels in El Salvador to intervene in Nicaragua. The U.S. sponsored anti-Sandinista Contra guerrillas through much of the 1980s. After economic sanctions and a worsening of the economy, President Daniel Ortega was voted out of office, only to be re-elected in 2006 and in 2011 (Solaún, 2005).

Did God bless the Eisenhower Doctrine? Is it still applied? Does the United States have the right to intervene in Latin America?

In El Salvador, the United States funded a 12-year civil war that cost about 75,000 lives. It ended in 1992 with the ARENA government signing a treaty with the FMLN that promised military and political reforms. During the civil war, Salvadorans fled mainly to the United States (Martín Alvárez, 2011). A high level of emigration continued after the civil war as a result of deteriorating economic conditions, natural disasters, and the U.S.-sponsored War on Drugs that saw deportation of gang members to El Salvador. Remittances to relatives from the United States account for close to 20 percent of its GDP (Wiltberger, 2014).

In 1980, the Guatemalan army launched "Operation Sophia"—it was to end guerrilla warfare by destroying the civilian base. The Mayan population was suspected of supporting the guerilla movement. In the next three years, the army levelled 626 villages, killing or "disappearing" more than 200,000 people. About 1.5 million were uprooted and over 150,000 sought refuge in Mexico. Political violence in the 1970s and 1980s was among the worst in the world, taking on genocidal proportions (Levy, 2006).

The Guatemalan government intensified military operations in areas settled by several distinct Maya groups. While some Maya and non-Maya were involved in the civil war, most suffered the brutalities of war. The government intensified forced conscription, attacked villages, and the military occupied and tortured and assassinated civilians. The cause of the persecution often was because they expressed Maya identity by wearing traditional clothes. "These terrible events spurred massive migration from the Maya areas to destinations inside and away from Guatemala" (Duvall, 2002).

Meanwhile, in Nicaragua, the rebels under the leadership of the Sandinista National Liberation Front (Frente Sandinista de Liberación Nacional, or FSLN) successfully set up a revolutionary government. The United States, fearing that a Marxist or left-of-center government would threaten its economic and political interests, backed counter-revolutionaries with the purpose of overthrowing the FSLN. (Nicaragua numbered 5 million people. The United States had a population of 226.6 million in 1980.) The United States intensified the war in Nicaragua under the pretext that Nicaragua was a threat to the security of the United States and that it was supplying arms to El Salvador's insurgents. Ronald Reagan's 1980 election escalated the war against the Sandinistas. Reagan stationed 2,000 troops in Honduras, where the CIA—with the Contras (the ultraright opposition)—led military operations against the Nicaraguan government. Thus, the CIA openly violated the Boland Amendment, which prohibited the use of U.S. funds to overthrow a foreign government (Scharfen, 1985). Reagan insisted that Soviet and Cuban influence in Nicaragua threatened U.S. security. But just as it did in 1954 in Guatemala, the Dominican Republic in 1963–1965, and in Chile on September 11, 1973, the United States moved to overthrow the Nicaraguan government. Reagan dubbed the Sandinistas undemocratic. In 1984, the Sandinistas held elections. While Western European and Latin American nations praised the elections for being open, Reagan labeled them a sham. Reagan and then George H. W. Bush isolated Nicaragua, and in 1990, the Nicaraguan people, weary of war, voted for the United Nicaraguan Opposition. The Sandinistas peacefully relinquished power. This ended the dirty little war, which led to Ronald Reagan's former Defense Secretary Caspar W. Weinberger being indicted on charges that he lied to Congress about his knowledge of the arms sales to Iran and efforts by other countries to help underwrite the Nicaraguan war. It was also charged that the CIA allowed illegal drugs to be imported into the United States by the

Contras, which were then sold and used by Contra leaders to buy arms. President George H. W. Bush pardoned Weinberger and five others, thus preventing an airing of evidence that Bush himself was involved in the conspiracy. The media called this unconstitutional operation Iran Contra (Walsh, 1993).

Central Americans in the United States

Each of the Central American nations is unique. They are constantly changing. The importance of El Salvador goes beyond its size. It takes only a few hours to get from the capital of El Salvador to another part of the country by car or bus. In modern times, there has been a rise of Salvadoran indigenous identity politics, which has brought about a new consciousness to the condition of Indians in El Salvador.

According to Brandt Gustav Peterson, aside from size, Salvadoran unity has been forged by a mestizo national "imagina." "They have chronicled the transformation of Indians into Salvadorans through the magic of *mestizaje*, the fantasy of blending and coupling that proclaims the birth of the new, hybrid but unique Latin American modern subject." This imaginary or mystification of *mestizaje* resembles that of José Vasconcelos' Mexico. It is the "promise of *mestizaje* to eradicate racial distinctions within the nation." Peterson underscores La Matanza of 1932 as part of the construction of the imaginary describing the alleged disappearance of Indians from the Salvadoran national scene and the return of the Indian in contemporary political movements (Peterson, 2005; Issacs-Martin, 2010; Peterson, 2007).

Guatemala is one of the poorest countries in Latin America; it is also one that has suffered most from a highly unequal distribution caused by a history of multinational dictators and the actions of the United States. It is a large country with a population of over 13 million people. Following the signing of the 1996 Guatemala Peace Treaties, there were high hopes for peace. However, everything returned to the normal state of violence once the international observers and media left. There was a surge of criminal violence. Collective memories were intact and cried to be remembered. There was an effort to understand post-civil war violence in Guatemala (Girón, 2007). The Guatemalans survived the negative impact of the civil war, the disruption of their education, and deaths that fell disproportionately on Mayan rural families (Chamarbagwala, 2011).

The Mayan diaspora took them to different parts of Guatemala, to Mexico City, to refugee camps in southern Mexico, to Belize, Arizona, Florida, North Carolina, Houston, Canada, and to Los Angeles.

Throughout this diaspora, the Maya never ceased being Maya; they were not Latino and resisted attempts to erase them, forming "Comunidades Mayas Indigenas" where they voted, among other things, on questions of identity. In one instance, they refused to mark "Latino" on the census, marking instead Native American, although some insist "we are not Native American, we are Maya" (LeBaron, 2012, pp. 186, 189).

An example of the Maya's diasporic creativity is the Los Angeles-based Maya radio show "Contacto Ancestral," created in 2003 by Maya immigrants, which "challenges the processes of Americanization carried by local and national state entities and reinforced through mainstream Spanish and English-language media" (Estrada, 2013). Maya identities are explored on radio station KPFK, and the community is informed on indigenous cultural, political, and economic rights. The show is becoming a "community archive." This archival memory includes indigenous and nonindigenous diasporic communities in the United States and a recalling of the transnational nature of their identities. A long-time value of the "community archive" is the creation and maintenance of community through "a shared history" (Estrada, 2013; Estrada, 2006; Estrada, 2011). It helps break the cycle of neoprocesses interconnecting shared experiences of marginalization, but more importantly, it confronts Spanish-language media's construction of a homogeneous Latino culture. With the Maya, it begins and ends with the question of identity.

In 1996, the government signed a peace accord with the Guatemalan National Revolutionary Unity (URNG). The UN organized a Commission of Historical Clarification (CEH) so not to forget dictators such as Rafael Carrera and José Efraín Ríos. "On February 25, 1999, the Guatemalan Commission for Historical Clarification presented its final report before a packed audience in Guatemala's National Theater. Most who attended the ceremony were surprised by the forcefulness of the report's conclusions, not because the content was unfamiliar, but because few had held high expectations for a commission whose mandate was circumscribed by the limits of Guatemala's dubious political transition" (Oglesby, 2007).

Salvadoran and Guatemalan immigrants are among the top ten foreign-born groups in the United States in 2009 (Terrazas, 2011). Because they were from countries that were not controlled by U.S.-friendly dictators, it was more difficult for them to obtain legal status even though they were clearly refugees (Menjívar, 2006; Manjivar, 2008; Conroy, 2006). El Salvador (39.4 percent) and Guatemala (27.4 percent) accounted for more than two thirds (66.8 percent) of all Central

American immigrants. The remaining one third of Central American immigrants came from Honduras (16.1 percent), Nicaragua (8.7 percent), Panama (3.6 percent), Costa Rica (3.0 percent), and Belize (1.7 percent).

Between 2000 and 2009, over 606,000 Central Americans gained permanent residency in the United States. "In 2009, California had the largest number of resident Central American immigrants with a total of 846,734, or 29.0 percent of the overall Central American-born population, followed by Texas (357,516, or 12.3 percent), and Florida (342,181, or 11.7 percent)" (Conroy, 2006). Almost one-fifth of Central American immigrants lived in the Los Angeles Metropolitan Area. More than a third of the foreign-born Central Americans arrived after January 2000 (Davy, 2006).

In 2014, a crisis developed as Central American children flooded the U.S.–Mexican border. The following tale of the refugees was overwhelming:

Cristián Omar Reyes, 11, was from Honduras. His father was robbed and murdered by gangs, His mother hired a smuggler to take her to Florida and, although she promised to send for Cristian, she has not. He told of murders en route to the United States. He was hoping to reunite with his mother.

Gangs arrived in force in Honduras and other Central American countries in the 1990s; once there they joined homegrown groups like Los Puchos. After a failed policy where the United States and Colombia spent billions of dollars to slow down the movement of drugs up the Caribbean corridor, the War on Drugs rerouted the movement inland through Honduras and other Central American states and Mexico. The *New York Times* reports that "79 percent of cocaine-smuggling flights bound for the United States now pass through there" (Nazario, 2014). Thousands of other children from El Salvador and Guatemala told similar stories. Many of these children were refused entrance and shipped back to their home countries (Norton, 2016).

The crisis at the border was not of the making of the children or their parents. The wars during the 1980s had disrupted the economies and lives of the people. Many point out that the crisis was created first by the American drug market. There would be no crime and lawlessness without that market. According to the UN in 1998, "With estimates of $100 billion to $110 billion for heroin, $110 billion to $130 billion for cocaine, $75 billion for cannabis and $60 billion for synthetic drugs, the probable global figure for the total illicit drug industry would be approximately $360 billion. Given the conservative bias in some of the estimates for individual substances, a turnover of around $400 billion per annum is considered realistic" (Gallahue, 2015). The drug market has produced at least one billionaire, mostly as a result of the War on Drugs. Meanwhile, the costs of public higher education in the United States has climbed beyond the ability of the taxpayer to pay for it. "Federal spending in the United States alone totals about $15 billion annually and according to one estimate, state and local drug-related criminal justice expenditures amount to $25.7 billion" (Gallahue, 2013). In fact, the War on Drugs is part and parcel of Eisenhower's overt actions, the "get tough on Marxists" so-called agenda. The most current chapter is that of President Bill Clinton and George W. Bush who, between 1999 and 2002, gave Colombia $2.04 billion in aid, 81 percent of which was for military purposes. This amount put Colombia just below Israel and Egypt among the largest recipients of U.S. military assistance, giving legitimacy to yet another client state under the guise of fighting the insurgents and drug cartels (Paul, Clarke, and Serena, 2014).

This situation was worsened by the United States emptying its prisons and dumping U.S.-made gang members on the Central American nation's fragile infrastructure. "With soaring revenues from transporting and selling cocaine and crack, the intergang violence and bloody territorial disputes have spread and grown more brutal. The gangs are not only fighting each other, but muscling in on territories of the well-entrenched drug trafficking transport networks tied to Mexico's Sinaloa cartel" (Farah, 2016; see Selected Videos, Tinker Salas, 2009). Let there be no doubt: there can be no solution to the immigration crisis as long as wrongheaded policies continue. Dumping gangs with tens of thousands of members into Central America was no solution to the immigration crisis.

Forgotten History

What prevents an awareness of the plight of Central Americans is the lack of coverage in the media. If we do not know about injustices, we don't have the collective memory to prevent their consequences. Thus, we are denied a historical context and an awareness of how the past contributed to a present crisis. For example, in 1994, NAFTA (North American Free Trade Agreement) went into effect, triggering an armed Mexican rebellion. According to the Pew Hispanic Research Center, "Since NAFTA was signed into law, illegal immigrants in the U.S. have increased to 12 million today from 3.9 million in 1993, accounting for an overall increase of over 300 percent" (Ensinger, 2011). About 50,000 rural people annually migrate each year from Chiapas to the United States.

Why is having a collective memory so important?

Just a decade later, the United States pressed Central American countries to adopt the Central American Free Trade Agreement (CAFTA). It bound five Central American countries (Costa Rica, El Salvador, Guatemala, Honduras, and Nicaragua) and the Dominican Republic. Like NAFTA, CAFTA does more than eliminate tariffs and trade barriers between those countries (Harrison, 2005). The treaty was opposed by trade unions. There was mass social mobilization against CAFTA in Costa Rica between 2002 and 2007. Popular opposition delayed the treaty until 2005 when President George W. Bush signed it into law (Armstrong, 2005).

In the context of history, do you believe that CAFTA will solve the region's economic problems?

Given U.S. policies such as the wars to maintain U.S. hegemony in Central America, the War on Drugs, the dumping of gang members on the fragile infrastructures of countries recently at war, and the imposition of CAFTA, is it any wonder that the children are at the gates of the United States? ("Surge of Central American Children Roils U.S. Immigration Debate," 2014).

ANOTHER POV (POINT OF VIEW)

"We Should Help Stabilize Central America and End the War on Drugs,"

Oriel María Siu, Latino Studies Director and Assistant Professor of Hispanic Studies, University of Puget Sound

Outside active war zones, the so-called Northern Triangle of Central America, consisting of Honduras, Guatemala, and El Salvador, is, in 2016, the deadliest region in the world. So normalized have dying and killing become in daily life in this area that death rates have surpassed those of the region's own civil wars, when from 1960 to 1996 over 400,000 people were killed and thousands more disappeared, caused mostly by U.S.-supported state security forces fighting organized social movements in the area. More people die today in the streets of San Pedro Sula, Guatemala City, and San Salvador than during those days of declared wars. Consequently, more people flee Central America today than during the wars' worst years of violence in the 1980s, when Ronald Reagan held the U.S. presidency. Since the end of the Central American civil wars in the 1990s, violence has steeply risen in the Central American region.

The unprecedented violence plaguing Central America today is directly linked to the heavily militarized drug war that the United States has been waging in the region for over a decade, particularly since the 2008 implementation of the Central American Regional Security Initiative (CARSI). In attempting to interdict illegal drugs en route to the United States from South America, the United States has since then poured more than 1.2 billion dollars into remilitarizing Central America and further strengthening the region's security forces. These security forces are the same law enforcement groups that the United States funded during the civil wars only two decades prior for the purposes of torturing, massacring, and disappearing thousands of people who opposed the U.S.-backed Central American governments. Trained in the art of killing, large sectors of the Central American security apparatuses receiving U.S. military aid to fight the drug war today are thus no strangers to effecting violence and instilling terror on civil society.

Numerous international human rights groups have noted a direct correlation between the heightened U.S. War on Drugs in the region and remilitarization, and the area's escalating death rates, human rights abuses, massive migrations of Central Americans to the north, and government repression of new and solidified social movements. Women, journalists, union and indigenous leaders, human rights defenders, lawyers, LGBTQ activists, and political opposition members have specifically become targets of rising extrajudicial killings in the area. Honduras alone today holds the title of the world's deadliest place for environmental activists, with at least 110 defenders of land rights having been murdered since 2010. Not coincidently, U.S. military aid to this country has exceptionally increased since 2009, the year that the U.S.-supported coup in that country ousted democratically elected President Manuel Zelaya. Led by sectors of the Honduran elite, the coup leaders were upset that President Zelaya had raised the poverty-inducing national minimum wage by 62 percent, to roughly $275 a month.

A region already plagued by massive inequality, weakened economies left by more than two decades of war, free-trade agreements, ruptured family structures, the gang phenomenon, impunity, and government corruption, military aid sent by the United States to the Central American region has done nothing but exacerbate Central America's postwar social problems. Equally problematic is the fact that U.S. remilitarization of Central America has done nothing to address the actual roots of the drug problem: the lack of social mobility opportunities for the majority of Central Americans and the ever-rising consumption of drugs in the United States.

If the objective of the War on Drugs has been to stop drugs from entering the United States, this war has proven a complete failure. Despite more than 40 years of the War on Drugs and after at least $1.5 trillion spent, the United States' drug usage rates have remained entirely unaffected. Worldwide, the United States continues to rank highest among drug-addicted countries. In the American continent, it has continuously and since the beginning of the War on Drugs ranked number one. Thus, while militaristically addressing the symptoms of the drug problem (drug trafficking), the U.S. government has conveniently forgotten to address its origins (U.S. drug addiction). Feeding a multibillion-dollar business of privatized prisons and military technology manufacturing, the War on Drugs' real profiteers are being kept away from public media discourse and away from the public eye. Drug cartels too have become ever more powerful, bloodthirsty, and rich due to the War on Drugs.

Moreover, the War on Drugs is a racialized war, with people of color constituting its greatest casualties, not just south of the border but also within the United States itself. Despite the fact that drug use and selling are comparable across racial lines in the United States, people of color are systematically incarcerated, arrested, prosecuted, stopped, and convicted at higher rates than whites. South of the U.S. borderlands, in regions like Central America, people of color also are the most affected by this war's violence. The ever-escalating migration of undocumented Central Americans to the United States, coming from the most marginalized communities of the area, including thousands of unaccompanied children, is enough proof of this reality.

It is time to end the War on Drugs and help stabilize Central America. As a historical producer of violence in the region, the United States has a moral and ethical responsibility to the region and its people. We must end the War on Drugs by halting all military aid to Central America's repressive security apparatuses and help stabilize the region by channeling money into economic and social infrastructures that will assist Central American societies, particularly those of the Northern Triangle, toward self-sufficiency. For the thousands of people, including children, who have been able to escape today's violence and arrive in the United States, the United States must offer asylum and not inhumane detention and deportation, as it currently does.

Noting a direct correlation between drugs and violence, various countries around the world have begun decriminalizing drugs, focusing their efforts instead on rehabilitation. Various Central American heads of states themselves have called for a legalization of this market. There are alternatives to the War on Drugs. The question is who benefits from halting it? And who for sustaining it?

"The Central American Nations Are in the State They Are In Because of Corruption, But Who Got Them There?"

Alicía Ivonne Estrada, Associate Professor of Chicana/o Studies at California State University, Northridge

While corruption is often reported in media outlets as more frequently occurring in "developing" nations, like those in Central America, political corruption is also pervasive in developed countries as, for instance, the United States, Spain, and the United Kingdom. Economists Andrei Shleifer and Robert W. Vishny define corruption as "the sale by government officials of government property for personal gain" (Shleifer and Vishny, 1993). This is often reflected in bribes taken by high-level officials when "providing permits and licenses, giving passage through customs, or prohibiting the entry of competitors" (Shleifer and Vishny, 1993). Though these high-level corruption cases often go undetected, there are also lower-level cases that take place openly and daily in countries where there is significant political instability. This is because the political corruption produced and maintained by higher-level state officials creates unstable state institutions and weak economies. This situation allows for lower-ranking state officials, including police officers, to solicit bribes mainly from the working poor as they access basic services and rights. In Central America, political corruption has created states that continuously protect the interests of the powerful national oligarchies as well as U.S, foreign policies and companies.

Since the 1800s, United States interventions in the isthmus have brought political instability, corruption, and violence. For instance, the U.S. hand-selected and backed Somoza family in Nicaragua ruled from 1927 to 1979. The Somozas, along with a few elite families, reaped most of the nation's wealth until 1979, when the leftist Sandinistas deposed them. The impact of the Somozas' corruption became evident to the world in the aftermath of the devastating earthquake that ravaged the country. On December 23, 1972, a 6.2 magnitude earthquake hit Nicaragua. The lack of adequate infrastructure and emergency resources as a result of decades of the Somozas' corrupt regime left over 250,000 homeless, 20,000 injured, and 6,000 killed. Countries all over the world sent much-needed relief aid, but it was never distributed to the thousands of victims. After weeks of aid not reaching victims of the earthquake, it was revealed that most of the aid was kept by the Somozas. When the dictator Anastasio Somoza Debayle was overthrown in 1979, the family's net worth was estimated at $1.5 billion. The Somozas left Nicaragua for the United States, where they were granted asylum. As the Sandinista revolutionary government attempted to rebuild a nation literally left in pieces due to decades of corruption and repression, the United States formed, trained, and financed an opposition group called the Contras to help overthrow the newly established revolutionary government. In these efforts, former Panamanian president Manuel Noriega (1983–1989), who, like many other Central American dictators, was trained in the U.S. School of the Americas, aided the U.S. government in providing the Contras with weapons and planes. With U.S. economic aid and on the Central Intelligence Agency (CIA) payroll, Noriega contributed to the U.S.-sponsored Contra War in Nicaragua by providing the military equipment needed for the war against the Sandinista revolutionary government. In Panama, Noriega trafficked drugs and laundered money, all with the knowledge of the CIA and U.S. government. This maintained Panama under varied forms of corruption stemming from legal and illicit trades that included drugs.

United States interventions in the isthmus have also been visible in the form of regional political and economic agreements such as the Dominican Republic–Central American Free Trade Agreement (CAFTA–DR), which was ratified in 2005 and implemented in most countries in 2006. In the decade since the implementation of CAFTA–DR, Central Americans have experienced vast economic disparities as a result of the neoliberal policies stipulated in the agreement. These provisions have mainly benefited U.S. companies, since they include the elimination of tariffs as well as the reduction of environmental and labor laws. The neoliberal policies have also increased the wealth of national politicians and elites as they illegally sell permits and licenses for national resources like water and land to U.S. and Canadian companies.

Historically, Central Americans have actively attempted to change the corrupt systems that have been shaped by U.S. foreign policies and interests. In the spring of 2015, massive anticorruption protests in Guatemala and Honduras made international news as daily demonstrations engulfed the capital cities of these nations. In Guatemala, these protests led to the ousting of President Otto Pérez Molina and Vice President Roxana Baldetti, who were arrested on a customs evasion scheme. In El Salvador, former president Francisco Flores of the conservative Nationalist Republican Alliance (ARENA) party was held under house arrest from 2014 until his death in January of 2016. He was pending trial on the misuse of $15 million donated by the Taiwanese government. Yet, efforts by Central Americans to eradicate corruption have often been met by U.S.-backed retaliation. In 2009, a conservative opposition that stood to lose vast profits and power ousted Honduran president Manuel "Mel" Zelaya (2006–2009). The coup that overthrew Zelaya was in response to his administration's moderate social reforms that aimed at addressing the vast economic disparities in the nation. This included uncovering and ending corruption of state-owned resources like Hondutel, which directly implicated the U.S.-owned company Latin Node. Honduran historian Suyapa Portillo notes that in 2011 the release of information by WikiLeaks demonstrated the role of the United States in the coup and "the culpability of [former] Secretary [of state Hillary] Clinton who expeditiously moved to ignore the illegality of the coup" (Portillo, 2016). Likewise, labor historian Dana Frank highlights that the post-coup government "rewarded coup loyalists with top ministries," which furthered the "violence and anarchy" in the nation (Frank, 2013). In her memoir, *Hard Choices*, Hillary Clinton recognizes she used her power to ensure Manuel Zelaya would not return to his presidential position. In doing so, Clinton's actions helped install a conservative, violent, and corrupt government to a country trying to fight corruption and inequality.

Thus, political corruption must be understood as occurring in both developed and developing nations. Additionally, we must recognize that corruption in "developing" Central American nations has historically been linked to U.S. foreign interests and interventions.

NOTES

1. Five million people in Mexico and Central America speak some 70 Maya languages. They are for the most part bilingual in Spanish.
2. Nawat is the language of the Nonualcos, Cuscatlecos, Mazahuas, and Izalcos and is differentiated from Nahuatl.

BIBLIOGRAPHY

Acuña, Rodolfo F., and Guadalupe Compeán, eds., *Voices of the U.S. Latino Experience*, 3 vols. Westport, CT: Greenwood, 2008.

Agudelo, Carlos. Movilidades y Resistencias de los Caribes Negros: Pasado y Presente de los Garífuna. *Revista CS* 12 (2013): 189–225.

Amador, Fabio Esteban. "Move Over, Mexico: The Maya in Central America." *National Geographic*, November 5, 2012. http://intelligenttravel.nationalgeographic.com/2012/11/05/move-over-mexico-the-maya-in-central-america

Armstrong, David. "Bush hails trade pact after tough fight in Congress." *SF Gate*, August 3, 2005. http://www.sfgate.com/business/article/CAFTA-signed-into-law-Bush-hails-trade-pact-2650745.php

"Belize." *CIA World Factbook*. https://www.cia.gov/library/publications/the-world-factbook/geos/bh.html

Bell, Beverly. "Berta Cáceres, Presente!" *Foreign Policy In Focus*, March 10, 2016. http://fpif.org/berta-caceres-presente/?utm_source=feedburner&utm_medium=feed&utm_campaign=Feed%3A+FPIF%2FLatinAmericaCaribbean+%28FPIF+Regions%3A+Latin+America+&+Caribbean%29

Bishop, Marlon. "Garifuna: A US–Honduran Story.' *Latino USA*, March 4, 2016. http://latinousa.org/2016/03/04/garifuna-a-us-honduran-story

Bridgewater, Samuel. *Natural History of Belize: Inside the Maya Forest*. E-book, 2014.

Brown, William, and Mary Odem. "Living Across Borders: Guatemala Maya Immigrants in the US South." *Southern Spaces*, February 16, 2011. http://southernspaces.org/2011/living-across-borders-guatemala-maya-immigrants-us-south

Bucheli, Marcelo. "Multinational Corporations, Totalitarian Regimes and Economic Nationalism: United Fruit Company in Central America, 1899–1975." *Business History* 50, no. 4 (2008): 433.

Burguete Cal y Mayor, Araceli. "Chiapas: Maya Identity and the Zapatista Uprising." *Abya Yala News* 8, 2 (June 30, 1994): 6. http://www.abyayalanews.org/document/1608

Central Intelligence Agency. "Costa Rica." *World Factbook* (2015). https://www.cia.gov/library/publications/the-world-factbook/geos/cs.html

Central Intelligence Agency. "Nicaragua." *World Factbook* (2015). https://www.cia.gov/library/publications/the-world-factbook/geos/nu.html

Central Intelligence Agency. "Panama." *World Factbook* (2015). https://www.cia.gov/library/publications/the-world-factbook/geos/pm.html

Chamarbagwala, Rubiana, and Hilcías E Morán. "The Human Capital Consequences of Civil War: Evidence from Guatemala." *Journal of Development Economics* 94, no. 1 (2011): 41–61.

Clayton-Bulwer Treaty, 1850. http://avalon.law.yale.edu/19th_century/br1850.asp. Accessed 2015.

Cojtí Cuxil, D. "Indigenous Nations in Guatemalan Democracy and the State: A Tentative Assessment. Social Analysis." *International Journal of Social and Cultural Practice* 51 (2007): 124–147.

Compromise of 1850, January 29, 1850. http://www.loc.gov/rr/program/bib/ourdocs/Compromise1850.html

Conroy, Kevin. "Resilient Guatemalan Immigrants Experience of Torture, Violence, and War: Speaking in Their Own Voice." Master's thesis, Cleveland State University, 2006.

Darío, Rubén. "To Roosevelt" (1905). http://inside.sfuhs.org/dept/history/Mexicoreader/Chapter4/dario.htm

Davy, Megan. "The Central American Foreign Born In The United States." Originally published on the Migration Information Source (www.migrationinformation.org) as a project of the Migration Policy Institute. http://www.fosterglobal.com/policy_papers/CentralAmericanForeignBornInUS.pdf

Duvall, Tracy. Review, *The Maya Diaspora: Guatemalan Roots, New American Lives*. James Loucky and Marilyn M. Moors, eds. Philadelphia: Temple University Press, 2000. *American Anthropologist* 104, no. 2 (June 2002): 685–686.

"El Salvador." https://www.cia.gov/library/publications/the-world-factbook/geos/es.html. Accessed 2015.

Ensinger, Dustin. "Illegal Immigration and NAFTA," February 05, 2011. http://economyincrisis.org/content/illegal-immigration-and-nafta

Estrada, Alicía Ivonne. "Cultural Transgressions in Omar S. Castaneda's Remembering to Say 'Mouth' or 'Face.'" *Studies in Twentieth and Twenty-First Century Literature* 37, no. 2 (2013): 131–148.

Estrada, Alicía Ivonne. "The (Dis)Articulation of Colonial Legacies in Calixta Gabriel Xiquín's Tejiendo Los Sucesos En El Tiempo/Weaving Events in Time." *Romance Notes* 51, no. 1 (2011): 137–147.

Estrada, Alicía Ivonne. "Ka Tzij: The Maya diasporic voices from Contacto Ancestral." *Latino Studies* 11, no. 2 (2013): 208–227.

Estrada, Alicía Ivonne. "Textual Transversals: Activisms and Decolonization in Guatemalan Mayan and Ladina Women's Texts of the Civil War and Postwar Periods." PhD diss., University of California Santa Cruz, 2006.

Farah, Douglas. "Central America's Gangs Are All Grown Up: And more dangerous than ever." *FP (Foreign Policy)*, January 19, 2016. http://foreignpolicy.com/2016/01/19/central-americas-gangs-are-all-grown-up

Fernández-Kelly, Patricia. *Encyclopedia of Global Studies*, 2012, "Maquiladoras," 1109–1111.

Ferreira, Roberto García. The CIA and Jacob Arbenz: History of a Disinformation Campaign. *Journal of Third World Studies* 25, no. 2 (2008): 59.

Frank, Dana. "Hopeless in Honduras? The Election and the Future of Tegucigalpa." *Foreign Affairs*, November 22, 2013. https://www.foreignaffairs.com/articles/honduras/2013-11-22/hopeless-honduras

Fulbright, J. William. *The Arrogance of Power*. New York: Random House, 1966.

Fung, Mellissa. "The New Conquistadors: Canadians mining in Panama." *Global Post*, December 5, 2012. http://www.globalpost.com/dispatches/globalpost-blogs/rights/the-new-conquistadors-canadians-mining-panama

Gallahue, Patrick. "How Much of Your Money Is Wasted in the War on Drugs." *Open Society Foundations*, February 13, 2013. https://www.opensocietyfoundations.org/voices/how-much-your-money-wasted-war-drugs

Gallahue, Patrick. "Spending on illegal drugs this year." http://www.worldometers.info/drugs. Accessed 2015.

García, Roberto. "The CIA and Jacob Arbenz: History of a Disinformation Campaign." *Journal of Third World Studies* 25, no. 2 (2008): 59.

"General Walker's Speech at New Orleans, New Orleans Delta, May 31, 1857." http://enriquebolanos.org/data/media/file/ABG-ING-T5-Truxillo%20-%20P8.pdf

Gimlette, John. "Lore of the jungle: life with Costa Rica's indigenous peoples." *The Guardian*, February 15, 2013. https://www.theguardian.com/travel/2013/feb/16/costa-rica-family-holiday-caribbean

Girón, Anna Belinda Sándoval. "Taking Matters into One's Hands: Lynching and Violence in Post-Civil War Guatemala." *Urban Anthropology and Studies of Cultural Systems and World Economic Development* 36, no. 4 (2007): 357–379.

"Guatemala 1954." The Cold War Museum, 1954. http://www.coldwar.org/articles/50s/guatemala.asp

"Guatemala, Countries and Their Cultures." 2001. http://www.encyclopedia.com/topic/Guatemala.aspx

Harrison, Brady. *Agent of Empire: William Walker and the Imperial Self in American Literature*. Athens, GA: University of Georgia Press, 2004.

Harrison, Nick. "CAFTA Fears." *Appropriate Technology* 32, no. 2 (2005): 43.

"History of U.S. Interventions in Latin American." http://www.yachana.org/teaching/resources/interventions.html. Accessed 2016.

Holland, Max. "Operation PBHISTORY: The Aftermath of SUCCESS." *International Journal of Intelligence and Counterintelligence* 17, issue 2 (2004): 300–332. http://www.tandfonline.com/doi/full/10.1080/08850600490274935

Hove, Mark T. "The Arbenz Factor: Salvador Allende, U.S.–Chilean Relations, and the 1954 U.S. Intervention in Guatemala." *Diplomatic History* 31, issue 4 (September 2007): 623–663.

Hubbard, Kirsten. "Mayan Ruins in Central America: Central America's Ancient Mayan Ruins, From Copan to Tikal." *About Travel.* http://gocentralamerica.about.com/od/mayaruinsinca/tp/Mayan_Ruins_Central_America.htm. Accessed 2016.

"Indigenous Peoples in Costa Rica." *Imagenes Tropicales.* http://www.travelcostarica.nu/indigenous-costa-rica. Accessed 2016.

Isaacs-Martin, Wendy. "The Politics of Violence: Gender, Conflict and Community in El Salvador by Mo Hume." *Nations and Nationalism* 16, no. 4 (2010): 779.

Isenberg, David. "Policy Analysis: The Pitfalls of U.S. Covert Operations." *Cato Policy Analysis* no. 118, April 7, 1989. http://www.cato.org/pubs/pas/PA118.HTM

Joyce, Rosemary A., Whitney Davis, Alice B. Kehoe, Edward M. Schortman, Patricia Urban, and Ellen Bell. "Women's Work: Images of Production and Reproduction in Pre-Hispanic Southern Central America [And Comments and Reply]." *Current Anthropology* 34, no. 3 (1993): 255–274.

LeBaron, Alan. "When Latinos are not Latinos: The case of Guatemalan Maya in the United States, the Southeast and Georgia." *Latino Studies* 10, no. 1–2 (2012): 179–195.

"Lenca." *IC Magazine.* https://intercontinentalcry.org/indigenous-peoples/lenca. Accessed 2015.

Letter from U.S. Secretary of State James Buchanan to R. M. Saunders, June 17, 1848, 193–204.

Levy, Guillermo. "Considerations on the connections between race, politics, economics, and genocide1." *Journal of Genocide Research* 8, no. 2 (2006): 137–148.

Malkin, Elisabeth. "An Apology for a Guatemalan Coup, 57 Years Later." *New York Times* (October 20, 2011). http://www.nytimes.com/2011/10/21/world/americas/an-apology-for-a-guatemalan-coup-57-years-later.html?_r=0

Martín Alvárez, Alberto. "De Guerrilla a Partido Político: El Frente Farabundo Martí Para la Liberación Nacional (FMLN)." *Historia y Política: Ideas, Procesos y Movimientos Sociales*, 2011, 207–233.

May, Robert E. *Manifest Destiny's Underworld: Filibustering in Antebellum America.* Chapel Hill, NC: University of North Carolina Press, 2004.

McCaa, Robert. "The Peopling of Mexico from Origins to Revolution." In Richard Steckel and Michael Haines, eds., *The Population History of North America.* Cambridge: Cambridge University Press, 2000. http://users.pop.umn.edu/~rmccaa/mxpoprev/cambridg3.htm

Menjívar, Cecilia. "Educational Hopes, Documented Dreams: Guatemalan and Salvadoran Immigrants' Legality and Educational Prospects." *The Annals of the American Academy of Political and Social Science* 620, no. 1 (2008): 177–193.

Menjívar, Cecilia. "Liminal Legality: Salvadoran and Guatemalan Immigrants' Lives in the United States." *American Journal of Sociology* 111, no. 4 (2006): 999–1037.

Minster, Christopher. "The Federal Republic of Central America (1823-1840): Five Nations Unify, Then Fall Apart." *About Education*, November 13, 2015. http://latinamericanhistory.about.com/od/historyofcentralamerica/a/09republicofCA.htm

Mollett, Sharlene. "A Modern Paradise: Garifuna Land, Labor, and Displacement-in-Place." *Latin American Perspectives* 41, no. 6 (2014): 27–45.

Morales, Amílcar. "Guatemala." *Caribe.net* (2006). http://www.caribenet.info/conoscere_06_morales_xincas.asp

Morris, Kenneth E.. Unfinished Revolution: Daniel Ortega and Nicaragua's Struggle for Liberation (Chicago: Chicago Review Press, 2010).

Nazario, Sonia. "The Children of the Drug Wars: A Refugee Crisis, Not an Immigration Crisis." *New York Times*, July 11, 2014. http://www.nytimes.com/2014/07/13/opinion/sunday/a-refugee-crisis-not-an-immigration-crisis.html?_r=0

"Nicaraguan Sandinistas." Latin American Studies, 2009. http://www.latinamericanstudies.org/sandinistas.htm

Norton, Ben. "'They are refugees': U.S. government deporting Central American migrants who fled 'extreme' violence." *Salon*, March 4, 2016. http://www.salon.com/2016/03/04/they_are_refugees_u_s_government_deporting_central_american_migrants_who_fled_extreme_violence/

Oglesby, Elizabeth. "Educating Citizens in Postwar Guatemala: Historical Memory, Genocide, and the Culture of Peace." *Radical History Review* 97 (Winter 2007): 77.

O'Neill, Kevin Lewis. "Writing Guatemala's genocide: truth and reconciliation commission reports and Christianity." *Journal of Genocide Research* 7, no. 3 (September, 2005): 331–349.

Ostend Manifesto, October 18, 1854. http://xroads.virginia.edu/~HYPER/HNS/OSTEND/ostend.html

Paul, Christopher, Colin P. Clarke, and Chad C. Serena. "Mexico Is Not Colombia." *RAND National Security Research*, 2014. http://www.rand.org/content/dam/rand/pubs/research_reports/RR500/RR548z1/RAND_RR548z1.pdf

Peterson, Brandt. "Remains out of Place: Race, Trauma and Nationalism in El Salvador." *Anthropological Theory* 7, no. 1 (2007): 59–77.

Peterson, Brandt Gustav. *Unsettled Remains: Race, Trauma, and Nationalism in Millennial El Salvador*. Austin, TX: The University of Texas at Austin, 2005.

Portillo. Suyapa. "Berta Cáceres: An Indomitable Feminist," *Huffington Post*, March 9, 2016. http://www.huffingtonpost.com/suyapa-portillo/berta-caceres-an-indomitable-feminist_b_9388850.html

"The Pre Columbian Civilizations of Central America—The Mesoamericans." https://sites.google.com/site/medievalwarmperiod/Home/drought-floods-famine-and-central-and-south-america/the-pre-columbian-civilizations-of-central-america. Accessed 2016.

Rodríguez, George. "Special U.S. Military Task Force Prepares to Land in Honduras, Critics Say to Secure U.S. Interests." *NotiCen: Central American & Caribbean Affairs*, May 28, 2015. https://www.highbeam.com/doc/1G1-417310965.html

Ryser, Rudolph C. *Indigenous Nations and Modern States: The Political Emergence of Nations*. New York: Routledge, 2012.

Scharfen, Jonathan. "The 1984 Boland Amendment." Digital National Security Archive - DNSA: Document Records (unstructured), 1985.

Shleifer, Andrei, and Robert W. Vishny. "Corruption." *Quarterly Journal of Economics* 108, no. 3 (August 1993): 599–617. http://projects.iq.harvard.edu/gov2126/files/shleifer_and_vishy.pdf

Schrider, Jim. "CIA coup files include assassination manual." *National Catholic Reporter* 33, issue 34 (July 18, 1997): 10.

Silber, Irina Carlota. *Everyday Revolutionaries: Gender, Violence and Disillusionment in Postwar El Salvador*. New Brunswick, NJ: Rutgers University Press, 2010, pp. 1–9.

Sohn, Ira. "Economic and Financial Reform in Costa Rica: Challenges and Opportunities to 2025." *Journal of Applied Business and Economics* 15, no. 1 (2013): 77–93.

Solaún, Mauricio. *U.S. Intervention and Regime Change in Nicaragua*. Lincoln, NE: University of Nebraska Press, 2005.

Soodalter, Ron. "Man of Destiny: Filibuster William Walker Aimed for the Stars but Got a Firing Squad." *Military History* 27, no. 1 (2010): 42.

Speech Given by William Walker in New Orleans, May 30, 1857. "Filibusterism." *New York Daily Times*, June 8, 1857, 2.

"Surge of Central American Children Roils U.S. Immigration Debate." Pew Research Center, July 16, 2014. http://www.people-press.org/2014/07/16/surge-of-central-american-children-roils-u-s-immigration-debate/

Taylor, Zachary P., Sally P. Horn, and David B. Finkelstein. "Pre-Hispanic Agricultural Decline Prior to the Spanish Conquest in Southern Central America." *Quaternary Science Reviews* 73 (2013): 196–200.

Terrazas, Aaron. "Central American Immigrants in the United States." *Migration Policy Institute*, January 10, 2011. http://www.migrationpolicy.org/article/central-american-immigrants-united-states-0

Thompson, J. Eric S., ed., *Thomas Gage's Travels in the New World*. Norman, OK: University of Oklahoma Press, 1958.

Thornton, Erin Kennedy, Kitty F. Emery, David W. Steadman, Camilla Speller, Ray Matheny, and Dongya Yang. "Earliest Mexican Turkeys (Meleagris Gallopavo) in the Maya Region: Implications for Pre-Hispanic Animal Trade and the Timing of Turkey Domestication: E42630." *PLoS One* 7, no. 8 (2012).

USAID. "Country Profile: El Salvador." Economic Analysis and Data Services (EADS), May 2016. https://idea.usaid.gov/prepared/FactSheets/el_salvador.pdf

Vasconcelos, José. *The Cosmic Race/La raza cosmic* 2nd ed. Baltimore, MD: Johns Hopkins University Press, 1997.

Walsh, Lawrence E., Independent Counsel. "Final Report of the Independent Counsel for Iran/Contra Matters." In Vol. I: *Investigations and Prosecutions*, August 4, 1993. Washington, DC, United States Court of Appeals for the District of Columbia Circuit Division for the Purpose of Appointing Independent Counsel, Division No. 86–6. http://www.fas.org/irp/offdocs/walsh

Whiteman, Gail, and Katy Mamen. "Examining Justice and Conflict Between Mining Companies and Indigenous Peoples: Cerro Colorado and the Ngabe-Bugle in Panama." *Journal of Business and Management* 8, no. 3 (Summer 2002): 293–329.

"Who are the Garifuna people?" *WiseGeek*, August 16, 2016. http://www.wisegeek.com/who-are-the-garifuna-people.htm

Wiltberger, Joseph. "Beyond Remittances: Contesting El Salvador's Developmentalist Migration Politics." *Journal of Latin American and Caribbean Anthropology* 19, no. 1 (2014): 41–62.

SELECTED VIDEOS

"An American Genocide—Guatemala," YouTube video, posted October 10, 2013. https://www.youtube.com/watch?v=viA5-K-KuIY
"Behind The Iran Contra Affair," YouTube video, 20:43, posted January 15, 2013. https://www.youtube.com/watch?v=feAUs9LqK6s
"Central American refugees flee violence," YouTube video, posted July 30, 2014. https://www.youtube.com/watch?v=v_sa0-6uEiU
"Children Crossing Border into U.S. to Escape Violence," YouTube video, posted June 17, 2014. https://www.youtube.com/watch?v=O3H_sR-Jfjc
"CIA, Guns, Drugs, Fraud, Iran Contra," YouTube video, posted November 10, 2006. http://www.youtube.com/watch?v=bbt9PsaSUiI
"El Salvador War Documentaries," YouTube video, posted July 1, 2012. https://www.youtube.com/watch?v=qvOFa-AWdJg
"Ending the Silence—Guatemala," YouTube video, posted March 26, 2008. https://www.youtube.com/watch?v=9O-_98zzw4I
"Fault Lines—The US and Honduras," YouTube video, posted August 13, 2012. https://www.youtube.com/watch?v=RWU1d_tTMEs
"Guatemalan Genocide," YouTube video, posted January 22, 2016. https://www.youtube.com/watch?v=-lKjPn-5uSI
"In the Name of the People: El Salvador's Civil War 1985 Documentary." YouTube video, posted November 10, 2011. https://www.youtube.com/watch?v=lHO-WiiZba0 ttps://www.youtube.com/watch?v=-lKjPn-5uSI
"Iran Contra Coverup: Part 1" (of eight parts on YouTube). YouTube video, posted Decemeber 7, 2008. http://www.youtube.com/watch?v=35KcYgMPiIM
Jazzgreek's channel. "Minefield Nicaragua," 1988 documentary on U.S.-sponsored contra war. YouTube video, posted February 18, 2011. https://www.youtube.com/watch?v=VHkD-CjwNe0
LanXang Siengkhene. "Central America: The Burden of Time," YouTube video, posted August 23, 2012. https://www.youtube.com/watch?v=pWdNq8lHdMA
"Murder and Migration in Honduras: Immigrant America." YouTube video, posted September 8, 2014. https://www.youtube.com/watch?v=1vINx0ajcVw
"Secret Wars of the CIA, John Stockwell." YouTube video, 2:48:49, posted January 27, 2013. https://www.youtube.com/watch?v=bmYZ_kWHk3Q
Tinker Salas, Miguel. "Free trade and Mexico's drug war," YouTube video, 9:55, posted May 2, 2009. https://www.youtube.com/watch?v=1ctoiMYe5RM
Vice News, "Undocumented and Underage: The Crisis of Migrant Children," YouTube video, posted August 13, 2014. https://www.youtube.com/watch?v=HVHqV0ibCWI

About the Author and the Contributors

AUTHOR

RODOLFO F. ACUÑA is the founding chair of the Chicana/o Studies Department at San Fernando Valley State College (now California State University at Northridge)—the largest Chicana/o studies department in the United States, with 27 tenured and 42 adjunct professors. He has authored twenty-two books, three of which received the Gustavus Myers Award for Outstanding Book on Race Relations in North America. Acuña has received the National Hispanic Institute Lifetime Achievement Award, Austin, Texas, 2008; the Lifetime Achievement Award from the Mexican American Legal Defense and Education Fund, 2010; the Distinguished Scholar Award from the National Association for Chicano Studies, 1969; the Emil Freed Award for Community Service; and the Founder's Award for Community Service from the Liberty Hill Foundation, among others. *Black Issues in Higher Education* selected Acuña as one of the 100 Most Influential Educators of the 20th Century, and in March 2016 he received the John Hope Franklin Award from *Diversity in Higher Education*. Among his best known books are *Voices of the U.S. Latino Experience* (Three Edited Volumes) (Greenwood Press,

2008); *Corridors of Migration: Odyssey of Mexican Laborers, 1600–1933* (2007) (winner of a CHOICE award [American Library Association] for Outstanding Academic Title); *Occupied America: A History of Chicanos*, 8th edition (2015); *Sometimes There is No Other Side: The Myth of Equality* (1998); *Anything But Mexican: Chicanos in Contemporary Los Angeles* (1996); *US Latinos: An Inquiry* (Greenwood Press, 2003), *Community Under Siege* (1984); *The Sonoran Strongman* (1974); and *The Making of Chicana/o Studies: In the Trenches of Academe* (2011). Acuña has also published *Guide to Chicana/o Studies* (2013). He has published three children's books and more than 200 academic and public articles in addition to over 200 book reviews in academic journals. Presently he is a professor emeritus.

CONTRIBUTORS

Walter Acuña
Independent Scholar and Superior Court Clerk, Los Angeles Superior Courts

Sean Arce
High School Teacher in Chicana/o-Latina/o Studies, Azusa Unified School District; Educational Consultant, Xican@ Institute for Teaching and Organizing; former Director, La Raza Studies, Tucson Unified School District, Tucson, AZ

Ana Miriam Barragan
Dreamers Coordinator, University of California, Irvine

José De Paz
Community Organizer, Los Angeles Unified School District, Los Angeles, CA

Alicía Ivonne Estrada
Associate Professor of Chicana/o Studies, California State University, Northridge

Celina Fernández-Ayala
Chicanx-Boricua, Undergraduate Student, California State University, Northridge

Jorge García
Professor Emeritus, Chicana/o Studies, California State University, Northridge

José Juan Gómez
Doctoral Student, Arizona State University, Tempe, AZ

Eliot Lee Grossman
Attorney-at-Law. Academic Member, Permanent Seminar for Chicano and Border Studies, Department of Ethnology and Social Anthropology, National Institute of Anthropology and History, Mexico City

Alice Herrera
MA Candidate in Chicana/o Studies, California State University, Northridge

Dulcinea Lara
Associate Professor of Criminal Justice at New Mexico State University, Las Cruces, NM

Gisely Colón López
Board Member, Alliance for Puerto Rican Education and Empowerment, APREE

Ronald López
Professor, California State University, Sonoma

Marta López-Garza
Professor of Chicana/o Studies and Gender & Women's Studies at California State University, Northridge

Juan José Montes
Student, California State University, Northridge

Luis H. Moreno
Instructor, School of Cultural and Critical Studies, Department of Ethnic Studies, Bowling Green State University, Bowling Green, OH

Mary Pardo
Professor of Chicana/o Studies, California State University, Northridge

Victor M. Rodríguez
Professor of Chicano and Latino Studies, California State University, Long Beach

Dennis Romero
LA Weekly, reporter

Elías Serna
Doctoral Student, University of California, Riverside and Founding Member, The Chicano Secret Service

Oriel María Siu
Latino Studies Director and Assistant Professor of Hispanic Studies, University of Puget Sound, Tacoma, WA

Lydia Soto
National Board Certified Teacher, Social Studies, Association of Mexican American Educators (AMAE) State President, 2012; Political Activist

Francisco N. Tamayo
Assistant Professor, Chicana/o Studies Department, California State University, Northridge

Benjamin Torres
President and CEO of CDTech, South Los Angeles, CA

Yarma Velázquez-Vargas
Associate Professor of Chicana/o Studies, California State University, Northridge

Ernesto Vigil
Author, Denver, Colorado

Index